Essential
Atlas
of the
WORLD

BARNES
&NOBLE
BOOKS
NEW YORK

Contents

Key Map and Legend

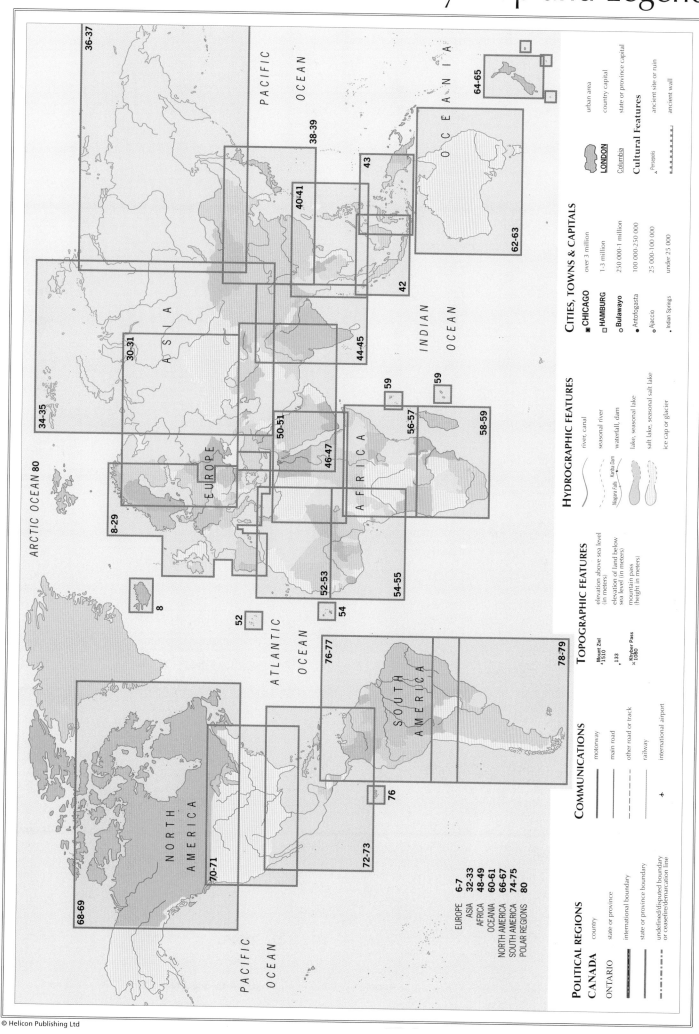

POLITICAL REGIONS

CANADA	country
ONTARIO	state or province
▬▬▬▬▬	international boundary
▬▬▬▬▬	state or province boundary
▬·▬·▬·▬	undefined/disputed boundary or ceasefire/demarcation line

COMMUNICATIONS

▬▬▬▬	motorway
▬▬▬▬	main road
-------	other road or track
▬▬▬▬	railway
✈	international airport

TOPOGRAPHIC FEATURES

Mount Ziel ▴1510	elevation above sea level (in meters)
,133	elevation of land below sea level (in meters)
⋊ Khyber Pass 1080	mountain pass (height in meters)

HYDROGRAPHIC FEATURES

	river, canal
	seasonal river
Niagara Falls — Kariba Dam	waterfall, dam
	lake, seasonal lake
	salt lake, seasonal salt lake
	ice cap or glacier

CITIES, TOWNS & CAPITALS

■ **CHICAGO**	over 3 million
□ **HAMBURG**	1-3 million
◦ **Bulawayo**	250 000–1 million
• Antofogasta	100 000–250 000
▴ Ajaccio	25 000–100 000
• Indian Springs	under 25 000

	urban area
LONDON	country capital
Columbia	state or province capital

Cultural Features

▴ Persepolis	ancient site or ruin
┈┈┈┈	ancient wall

EUROPE 6-7
ASIA 32-33
AFRICA 48-49
OCEANIA 60-61
NORTH AMERICA 66-67
SOUTH AMERICA 74-75
POLAR REGIONS 80

3

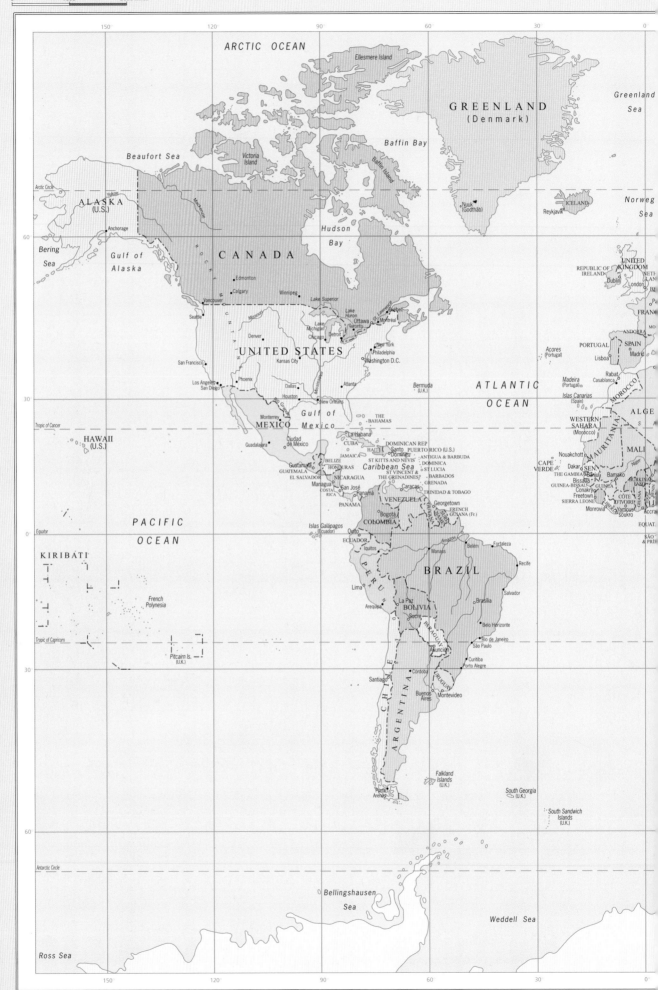

Equatorial Scale 1 : 112 000 000

0   1000   2000   3000   4000 km
0   1000   2000 miles

ARCTIC OCEAN

Ellesmere Island

GREENLAND
(Denmark)

Greenland
Sea

Baffin Bay

Beaufort Sea

Victoria
Island

Baffin Island

Norweg
Sea

Arctic Circle

Yukon

Nuuk
(Godthåb)

ICELAND

Reykjavík

ALASKA
(U.S.)

Anchorage

Mackenzie

Hudson
Bay

Bering
Sea

Gulf of
Alaska

CANADA

Edmonton

UNITED
KINGDOM

REPUBLIC OF
IRELAND

Dublin

London

Calgary

Winnipeg

Lake Superior

ROCKY

Vancouver

Seattle

Missouri

Lake
Huron

Québec

St Lawrence

Montréal

FRAN

Lake
Michigan

Ottawa
Toronto

Denver

Detroit

ANDORRA

MO

San Francisco

UNITED STATES

Chicago

New York

Philadelphia

Washington D.C.

PORTUGAL

Açores
(Portugal)

SPAIN

Lisboa

Madrid

Kansas City

Atlanta

Bermuda
(U.K.)

ATLANTIC

Madeira
(Portugal)

Rabat

Casablanca

Los Angeles
San Diego

Phoenix

Dallas

OCEAN

Islas Canarias
(Spain)

MOROCCO

Houston

Mississippi

New Orleans

Tropic of Cancer

HAWAII
(U.S.)

Monterrey

MEXICO

Rio Grande

Gulf of
Mexico

THE
BAHAMAS

WESTERN
SAHARA
(Morocco)

ALGE
S

Guadalajara

Ciudad
de Mexico

CUBA

La Habana

MAURITANIA

MALI

Nouakchott

Guatemala

BELIZE

Niger

CAPE
VERDE

Dakar

SEN

JAMAICA

DOMINICAN REP
Santo
Domingo

PUERTO RICO (U.S.)

HAITI

ANTIGUA & BARBUDA

THE GAMBIA

Banjul

Bamako

BURKINA

ST KITTS AND NEVIS

DOMINICA

GUINEA-BISSAU

Bissau

FASO

GUATEMALA
EL SALVADOR

HONDURAS

ST LUCIA

Conakry

GUINEA

CÔTE
D'IVOIRE

GHANA

Managua

NICARAGUA

Caribbean Sea

ST VINCENT &
THE GRENADINES

BARBADOS

SIERRA LEONE

Freetown

Yamou
ssoukro

Monrovia

San José

GRENADA

COSTA
RICA

Panamá

Caracas

TRINIDAD & TOBAGO

EQUAT

SÃO
& PRÍ

PANAMA

VENEZUELA

Georgetown

FRENCH
GUIANA (Fr.)

PACIFIC

Islas Galápagos
(Ecuador)

Bogotá

COLOMBIA

GUYANA

Quito

OCEAN

ECUADOR

Amazon

Belém

Fortaleza

KIRIBATI

Iquitos

Manaus

Recife

Lima

PERU

BRAZIL

French
Polynesia

Arequipa

La Paz

BOLIVIA

Sucre

Brasília

Belo Horizonte

Salvador

Tropic of Capricorn

PARAGUAY

Rio de Janeiro

São Paulo

Asunción

Curitiba

Pitcairn Is.
(U.K.)

Porto Alegre

URUGUAY

Santiago

Córdoba

CHILE

ARGENTINA

Buenos
Aires

Montevideo

Falkland
Islands
(U.K.)

South Georgia
(U.K.)

Punta
Arenas

South Sandwich
Islands
(U.K.)

Antarctic Circle

Bellingshausen
Sea

Weddell Sea

Ross Sea

ARCTIC OCEAN

Svalbard (Norway)

Zemlya Frantsa-Iosifa

Severnaya Zemlya

Barents Sea

Novaya Zemlya

SWEDEN

FINLAND

Helsinki

Stockholm

Tallinn EST.

Sankt-Peterburg

Arkhangel'sk

Yenisey

Lena

Arctic Circle

Anadyr'

RUSSIA

Yakutsk

60

Riga LAT.

LITH.

Vilnius

Minsk

RUS.

Moskva

Nizhny Novgorod

Yekaterinburg

Omsk

Irkutsk

Bering Sea

benhavn

POLAND

BELARUS

Warszawa

UKRAINE

Kharkiv

Kyyiv

Samara

Volgograd

Astana

Irtysh

KAZAKHSTAN

Petropavlovsk-Kamchatskiy

SLOVAK.

Budapest

MOLDOVA

HUNG.

CRO.

Beograd

Bucuresti

ROMANIA

YUG.

BOS.

Sofia

BUL.

Black Sea

GREECE

Istanbul

Ankara

TURKEY

Aral Sea

Almaty

UZBEKISTAN

Bishkek

Tashkent

KYRGYZSTAN

Ürümqi

MONGOLIA

Ulaanbaatar

GOBI DESERT

Harbin

Vladivostok

Sapporo

Sea of Okhotsk

MALTA

Athina

Tirane

ALB.

ARMENIA

GEORGIA

AZER.

Baki

TURKMENISTAN

Ashgabat

Düshanbe

TAJIKISTAN

Beijing

Shenyang

NORTH KOREA

P'yongyang

Sea of Japan

JAPAN

Mediterranean Sea

CYPRUS

LEB.

SYRIA

Dimashq

Baghdad

ISRAEL

JORDAN

IRAQ

Tehran

AFGHANISTAN

Kabul

PAKISTAN

Islamabad

Lanzhou

CHINA

Huang He

Qingdao

SOUTH KOREA

Tokyo

Osaka

Soul

LIBYA

Banghazi

EGYPT

El Qahira

SAUDI ARABIA

KUWAIT

BAHRAIN

Ar Riyad

QATAR

Abu Zabi

Masqat

U.A.E.

OMAN

Delhi

New Delhi

NEPAL

Kathmandu

Karachi

Ganges

HIMALAYA

BHT.

Dhaka

Chang Jiang

Wuhan

Chongqing

Shanghai

East China Sea

Taipei

Tropic of Cancer

CHAD

El Khartum

SUDAN

Makkah

YEMEN

San'a

Asmara

ERITREA

Adan

DJIBOUTI

Arabian Sea

Mumbai

INDIA

Hyderabad

Chennai

Bay of Bengal

Kolkata (Calcutta)

BANG.

MYANMAR (BURMA)

Yangon

LAOS

Vientiane

THAILAND

Krung Thep

Hanoi

VIETNAM

Hong Kong

TAIWAN

South China Sea

Manila

PHILIPPINES

Cebu

Northern Mariana Islands (U.S.)

MARSHALL ISLANDS

Ndjamena

CENTRAL AFRICAN REP.

Bangui

ETHIOPIA

Adis Abeba

SOMALIA

Muqdisho

SRI LANKA

Colombo

MALDIVES

CAMB.

Phnom Penh

Davao

PALAU

BRUNEI

Bandar Seri Begawan

FEDERATED STATES OF MICRONESIA

Equator

Kisangani

DEMOCRATIC REPUBLIC OF CONGO

Brazzaville

Kinshasa

UGANDA

KENYA

Nairobi

Lake Victoria

RW.

BUR.

TANZANIA

Dodoma

Kananga

Dar es Salaam

SEYCHELLES

MALAYSIA

Kuala Lumpur

SINGAPORE

Singapore

Banjarmasin

INDONESIA

Jakarta

Surabaya

NAURU

PAPUA NEW GUINEA

Port Moresby

SOLOMON ISLANDS

Honiara

KIRIBATI

TUVALU

ngola

ANGOLA

ZAMBIA

Lilongwe

Lusaka

Harare

MOZAMBIQUE

COMOROS

Moroni

INDIAN OCEAN

MADAGASCAR

Antananarivo

Réunion (France)

Port Louis

MAURITIUS

VANUATU

FIJI

Suva

NAMIBIA

ZIMB.

BOTSWANA

Gaborone

Pretoria

Maputo

SWAZILAND

LESOTHO

Durban

SOUTH AFRICA

AUSTRALIA

Brisbane

Tropic of Capricorn

Perth

Adelaide

Sydney

Canberra

Melbourne

NEW ZEALAND

Auckland

Wellington

Christchurch

Tasman Sea

Tasmania

Chatham Island (N.Z.)

Îles Kerguélen (France)

SOUTHERN OCEAN

Antarctic Circle

ANTARCTICA

London — Selected capital cities

Brisbane — Other cities

Country Abbreviations

ALB.	ALBANIA	LITH.	LITHUANIA
AZER.	AZERBAIJAN	LUX.	LUXEMBOURG
BANG.	BANGLADESH	MAC.	MACEDONIA
BEL.	BELGIUM	MAL.	MALAWI
BHT.	BHUTAN	RUS.	RUSSIA
BOS.	BOSNIA-HERZEGOVINA	RW.	RWANDA
BUR.	BURUNDI	SEN.	SENEGAL
CAMB.	CAMBODIA	SL.	SLOVENIA
CRO.	CROATIA	SLOVAK.	SLOVAK REPUBLIC
EST.	ESTONIA	SWITZ.	SWITZERLAND
HUNG.	HUNGARY	U.A.E.	UNITED ARAB EMIRATES
LAT.	LATVIA	YUG.	YUGOSLAVIA
LEB.	LEBANON	ZIMB.	ZIMBABWE

30   60   90   120   150   180

Scale 1 : 20 200 000

60° N · A · 1 · 30° W · B · 20° · C · 70°10° · D · 0° · E · 10° · F · 20°

ICELAND
Reykjavík

Arctic Circle

Norwegian
Sea

Faeroes
(Denmark)

Tromsø

Rockall

Shetland Is.
(U.K.)

Trondheim

Sundsvall

N·O·R·W·A·Y

Kir

Outer
Hebrides

Orkney Is.

Bergen

Stavanger

Oslo

Göteborg

Stockholm

Vänern

Gotland

Tampe

Gulf of Both

SWEDEN

SCOTLAND

Glasgow

Edinburgh

North
Sea

DENMARK

Århus

København
(Copenhagen)

Baltic Sea

Ta

LIT
Ka

ATLANTIC

OCEAN

NORTHERN
IRELAND

Belfast

REP. OF
IRELAND

DUBLIN
(BAILE ÁTHA CLIATH)

UNITED

KINGDOM

WALES

Cardiff

BIRMINGHAM

ENGLAND

Plymouth

LONDON

English Channel

Channel
Islands

s-Gravenhage
(The Hague)
Bruxelles
(Brussels)

Amsterdam

NETHER-
LANDS

BELGIUM

Luxembourg

LUXEMBOURG

PARIS

Bonn

Frankfurt

HAMBURG

Hannover

Ems

Elbe

Rhine

BERLIN

Bornholm

Gdańsk

RUSSIA

Kalinin

Hrod

Wisła

WARSZAWA
(WARSAW)

Odra (Oder)

POLAND

PRAHA
(PRAGUE)

Nistula

Hro

Loire

Seine

FRANCE

Strasbourg

MÜNCHEN
(MUNICH)

CZECH REP.

Danube

L

Cabo Fisterra

Bay
of
Biscay

Bordeaux

Lyon

Massif
Central

Rhône

Bern

4808
Mt.
Blanc

Vaduz

SWITZERLAND

LIECHTENSTEIN

Alps

WIEN
(VIENNA)

AUSTRIA

SLOVAK REP.

Bratislava

BUDAPEST

HUNGARY

Cluj
Napoc

PORTUGAL

Lisboa
(Lisbon)

Ebro

Tagus

MADRID

Pyrenees

Andorra
la Vella

ANDORRA

Marseille

MONACO

Genova
(Genoa)

MILANO
(MILAN)

SAN
MARINO

SLOVENIA

Ljubljana

Zagreb

CROATIA

Apennines

Adriatic Sea

BOSNIA-
HERZEGOVINA

Sarajevo

RO

BEOGRA
(BELGRA

Cabo de
São Vicente

SPAIN

Valencia

Islas Baleares
(Balearic Islands)

Menorca

Corse
(Corsica)
(France)

Ajaccio

VATICAN
CITY

ROMA
(ROME)

ITALY

YUGOSLAVIA

SOFIYA
(SOFIA)

Strait of Gibraltar

Gibraltar (U.K.)

Ceuta
(Spain)

BARCELONA

Eivissa

Mallorca

Sardegna
(Sardinia)
(Italy)

Mediterra

Cagliari

NAPOLI
(NAPLES)

Taranto

Tiranë
(Tirana)

ALBANIA

Skopje

MACEDON

RABAT

Melilla
(Spain)

Tyrrhenian
Sea

Kerkyra
(Corfu)

GREE

ALGER
(ALGIERS)

Palermo

Sicilia
(Sicily)

Mte. Etna
3340

Ionian
Sea

Ath
(Ath

Tunis

Valletta

MALTA

nean   Sea

A F R I C A

Tarābulus
(Tripoli)

Banghāzī

© Helicon Publishing Ltd

metres / feet
4000 / 13120
2000 / 6560
1000 / 3280
500 / 1640
200 / 656
0 / 0
200 / 656
1000 / 3280
2000 / 6560
4000 / 13120
6000 / 19690
8000 / 26250
metres / feet

D · 0° · E · 10° · F · 20°

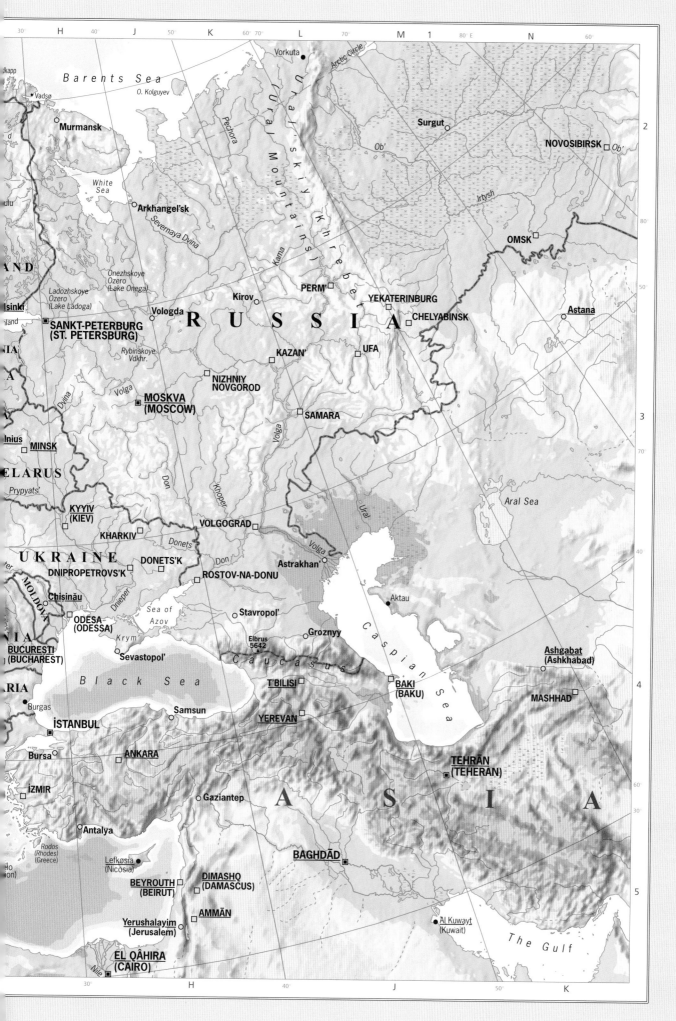

Barents Sea

Vadsø

Murmansk

O. Kolguyev

White Sea

Arkhangel'sk

Severnaya Dvina

Vorkuta

Surgut

NOVOSIBIRSK

Ob'

Arctic Circle

Irtysh

OMSK

Pechora

Ural'skiy Khrebet (Ural Mountains)

Onezhskoye Ozero (Lake Onega)

Ladozhskoye Ozero (Lake Ladoga)

Kirov

PERM'

YEKATERINBURG

CHELYABINSK

Astana

Vologda

R U S S I A

Kama

SANKT-PETERBURG (ST. PETERSBURG)

Rybinskoye Vdkhr.

KAZAN'

UFA

NIZHNIY NOVGOROD

Volga

MOSKVA (MOSCOW)

SAMARA

Volga

MINSK

Dvina

BELARUS

Prypyats'

Don

Khoper

Aral Sea

KYYIV (KIEV)

KHARKIV

VOLGOGRAD

Donets

Ural

Volga

U K R A I N E

DONETS'K

Don

Astrakhan'

DNIPROPETROVS'K

Dnieper

MOLDOVA

Chișinău

Sea of Azov

Stavropol'

Aktau

ODESA (ODESSA)

Krym

Groznyy

C a s p i a n   S e a

BUCUREȘTI (BUCHAREST)

Sevastopol'

Elbrus 5642

C a u c a s u s

Ashgabat (Ashkhabad)

Burgas

B l a c k   S e a

T'BILISI

BAKI (BAKU)

İSTANBUL

Samsun

YEREVAN

MASHHAD

Bursa

ANKARA

TĒHRĀN (TEHERAN)

İZMIR

Gaziantep

A **S** **I** **A**

Antalya

Rodos (Rhodes) (Greece)

Lefkøsia (Nicosia)

BAGHDĀD

BEYROUTH (BEIRUT)

DIMASHQ (DAMASCUS)

AMMĀN

Yerushalayim (Jerusalem)

Al Kuwayt (Kuwait)

T h e   G u l f

EL QĀHIRA (CAIRO)

Nile

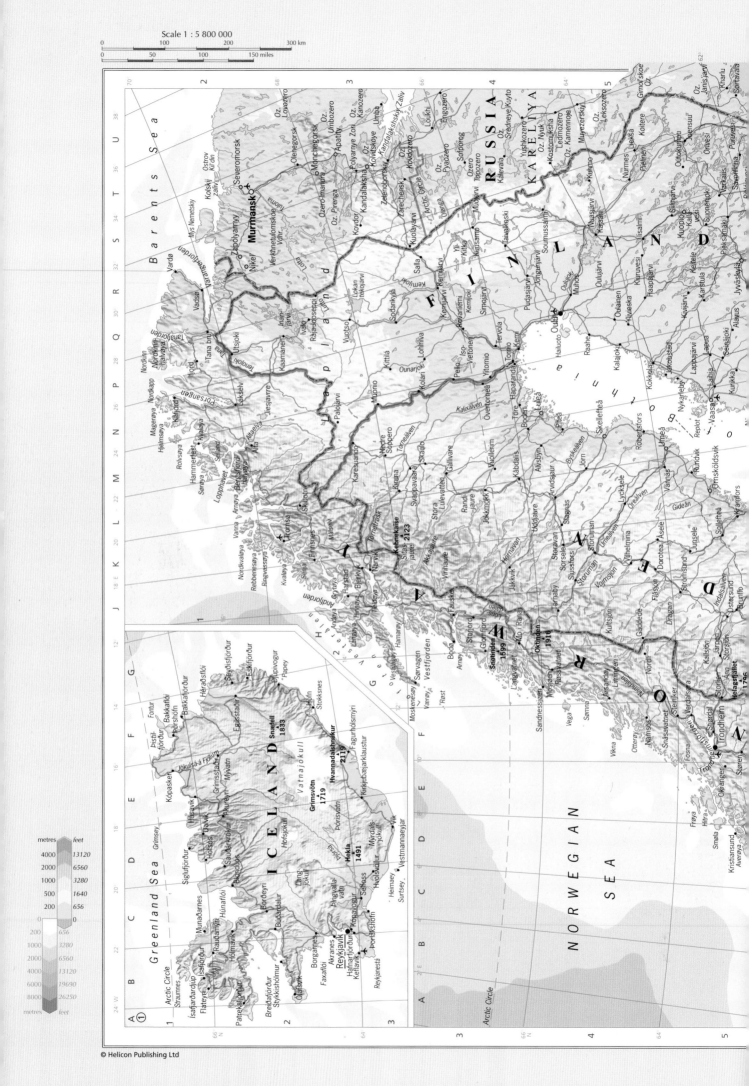

Scale 1 : 5 800 000

© Helicon Publishing Ltd

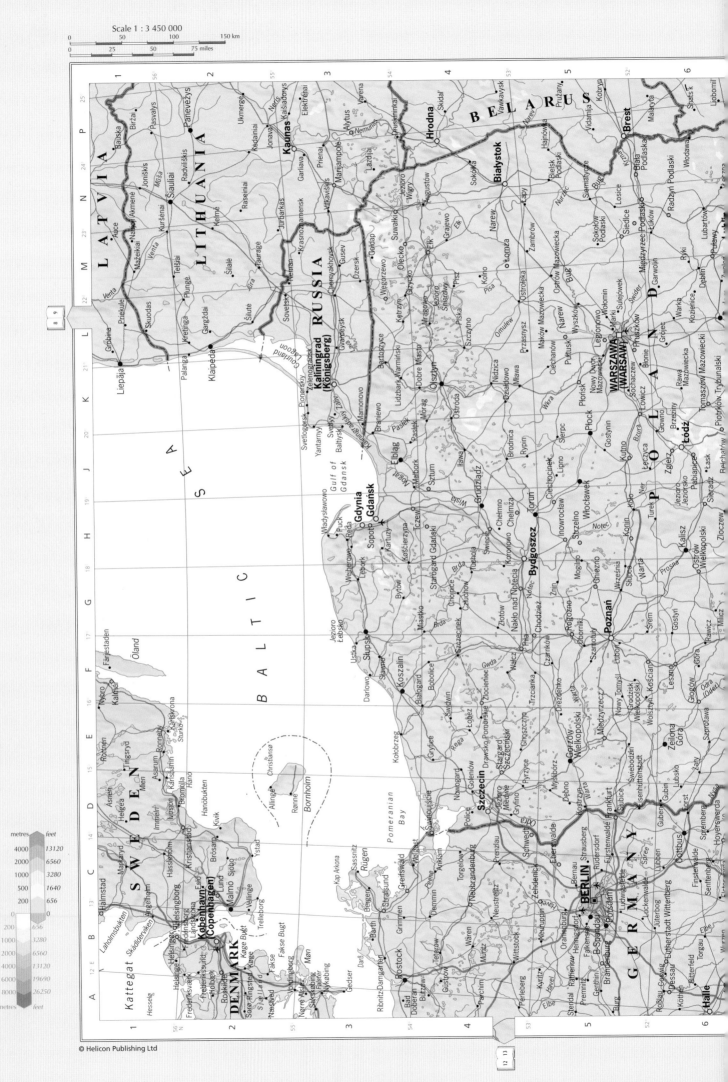

Scale 1 : 3 450 000

© Helicon Publishing Ltd

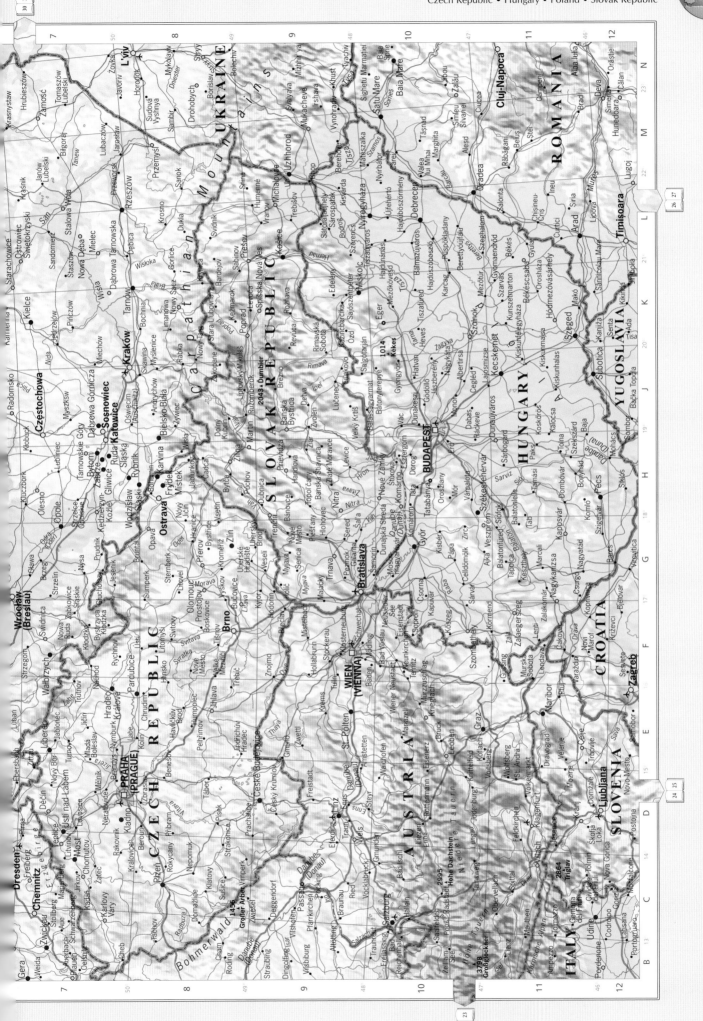

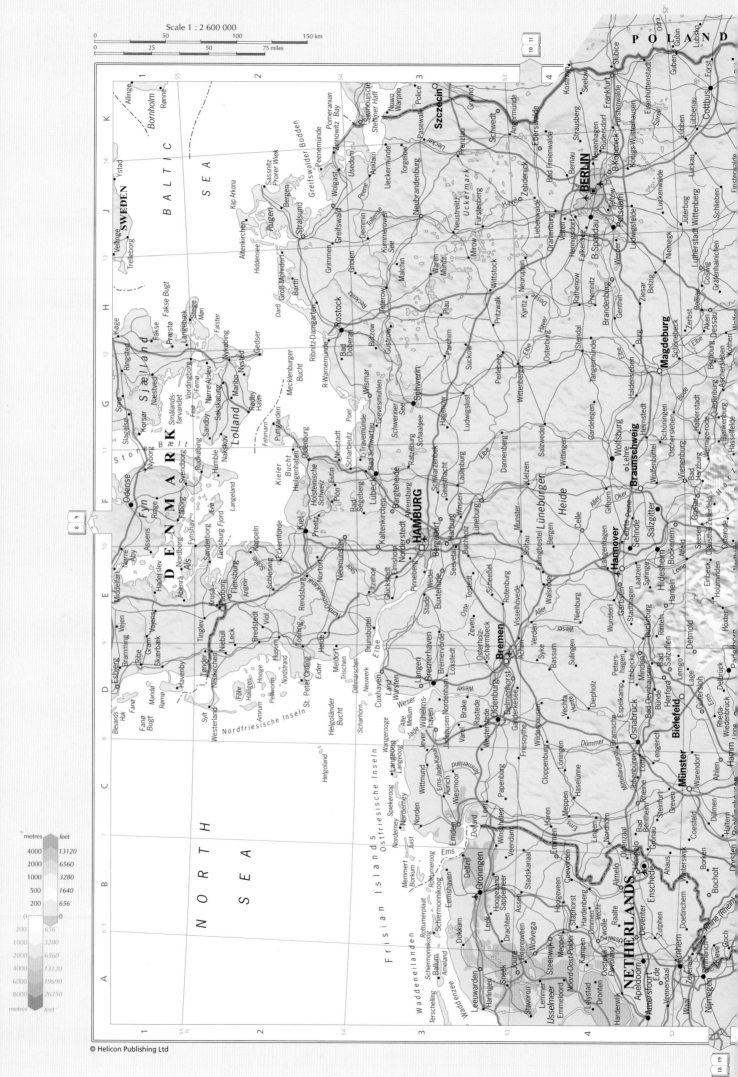

Scale 1 : 2 600 000

© Helicon Publishing Ltd

Scale 1 : 2 300 000

UNITED

KINGDOM

NORTH

SEA

ENGLAND

Buxton
Worksop
Chesterfield
East Retford
Louth
Mablethorpe
Matlock
Bolsover
Lincoln
Horncastle
Leek
Mansfield
Alfreton
Newark-on-Trent
Skegness
Sleaford
Derby
Nottingham
Grantham
Boston
The Wash
Hunstanton
Cromer
Long Eaton
Burton-upon-Trent
Cannock
Loughborough
Melton Mowbray
Spalding
King's Lynn
East Dereham
The Broads
Norwich
Great Yarmouth
Walsall
Tamworth
Leicester
Oakham
Stamford
Wisbech
Lowestoft
BIRMINGHAM
Nuneaton
Bedworth
Market Harborough
Peterborough
March
Ely
The Fens
Great Ouse
Yare
Coventry
Rugby
Kettering
Corby
Huntingdon
Thetford
Little Ouse
Diss
Southwold
Warwick
Redditch
Royal Leamington Spa
Wellingborough
Newmarket
Bury St. Edmunds
Stowmarket
Aldeburgh
Stratford-upon-Avon
Evesham
Daventry
Northampton
Cambridge
Bedford
Sudbury
Woodbridge
Orford Ness
Banbury
Towcester
Letchworth
Royston
Stour
Ipswich
Felixstowe
Chipping Norton
Milton Keynes
Bicester
Leighton Buzzard
Stevenage
Bishop's Stortford
Braintree
Colchester
Harwich
The Naze
Woodstock
Aylesbury
Luton
Welwyn Garden City
Harlow
Chelmsford
Clacton-on-Sea
Witney
Oxford
High Wycombe
Hemel Hempstead
St. Albans
Cheshunt
Thames
Abingdon
Didcot
Maidenhead
Slough
Watford
Enfield
Brentwood
Foulness
Swindon
Reading
Windsor
LONDON
Basildon
Southend-on-Sea
Hungerford
Newbury
Bracknell
Camberley
Staines
Kingston upon Thames
Grays
Gravesend
Rochester
Thames
Wallet
Basingstoke
Farnborough
Woking
Epsom
Gillingham
Whitstable
Herne Bay
Margate
North Foreland
Andover
Aldershot
Guildford
Sevenoaks
Faversham
Ramsgate
Salisbury
Alton
Reigate
Maidstone
Canterbury
Deal
Winchester
Haslemere
Crawley
East Grinstead
Royal Tunbridge Wells
Ashford
Dover
Romsey
Eastleigh
Petersfield
Horsham
The Weald
Folkestone
Strait of Dover
Southampton
Fareham
Havant
Uckfield
Rye
Dungeness
Portsmouth
Worthing
Brighton
Lewes
Bexhill
Hastings
Cap Gris-Nez
Gosport
Chichester
South Downs
Newhaven
Eastbourne
Lymington
Cowes
The Solent
Bognor Regis
Shoreham-by-Sea
Beachy Head
Newport
Ryde
Isle of Wight

English Channel

Zeebrugge
Knokke-Heist
Blankenberge
Oostende
Middelkerke
De Panne
Nieuwpoort
Veurne
Dunkerque
Gravelines
Calais
Diksmuide
Tielt
Roeselare
Poperinge
Ieper
Menen
Kortrijk
St-Omer
Bailleul
Tourcoing
Boulogne-sur-Mer
Desvres
Hazebrouck
Armentières
Lille
Roubaix
Étaples
Fruges
Béthune
Lys
Berck
Montreuil
Hesdin
Hénin-Beaumont
Lens
Avion
Douai
Baie de la Somme
Le Crotoy
St-Valéry-sur-Somme
Rue
St-Pol-sur-Ternoise
Arras
Abbeville
Doullens
Bapaume
Cap d'Antifer
Fécamp
Étretat
Le Tréport
Dieppe
Blangy-sur-Bresle
Somme
Amiens
Albert
Péronne
Fauville-en-Caux
Neufchâtel-en-Bray
Forges-les-Eaux
Breteuil
Montdidier
Roye
Tergnier
Cherbourg
Valognes
Bolbec
Yvetot
Barentin
Marseille-en-Beauvaisis
Noyon
Cap d'Antifer
Baie de la Seine
Le Havre
Gonfreville-l'Orcher
Lillebonne
Gournay-en-Bray
Beauvais
Compiègne
Carentan
La Haye-du-Puits
Isigny-sur-Mer
Bayeux
Oustreham
Honfleur
Seine
Rouen
St-Étienne-du-Rouvray
Clermont
Creil
Senlis
Crépy-en-Valois
Périers
Hérouville-St-Clair
Elbeuf
Louviers
Les Andelys
Méru
Chantilly
St-Lô
Caen
Lisieux
Vernon
Pontoise
Coutances
Villers-Bocage
Bernay
Évreux
Mantes-la-Jolie
Hertlay
St-Denis
Bobigny
Meaux
Granville
Falaise
Orbec
Vimoutiers
Conches-en-Ouche
Eure
St-Germain-en-Laye
PARIS
Marne-la-Vallée
Jullouville
Vire
Gacé
Houdan
Versailles
Créteil
Pontorson
Villedieu-les-Poëles
Condé-sur-Noireau
Flers
L'Aigle
Verneuil
Dreux
Trappes
Orsay
Orly
Courtacon
Avranches
Tinchebray
Argentan
Rânes
Mortain

Baie de la Seine

France

metres / feet
4000 / 13120
2000 / 6560
1000 / 3280
500 / 1640
200 / 656
0 / 0
200 / 656
1000 / 3280
2000 / 6560
4000 / 13120
6000 / 19690
8000 / 26250
metres / feet

16 17

18 19

© Helicon Publishing Ltd

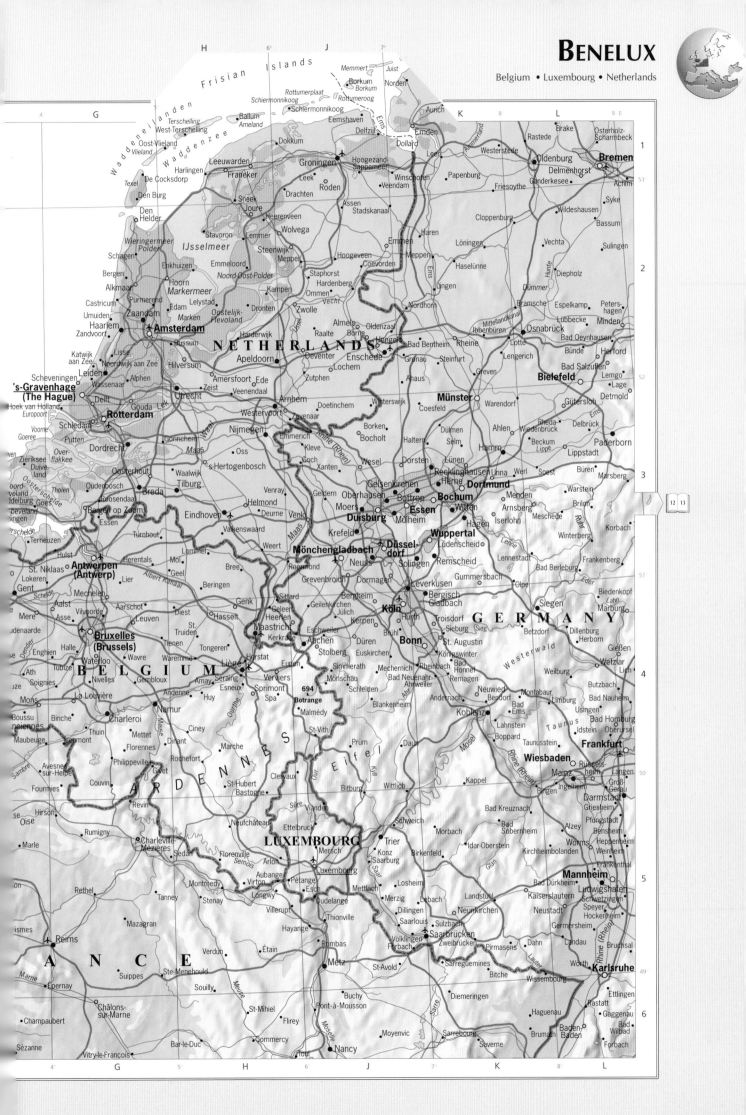

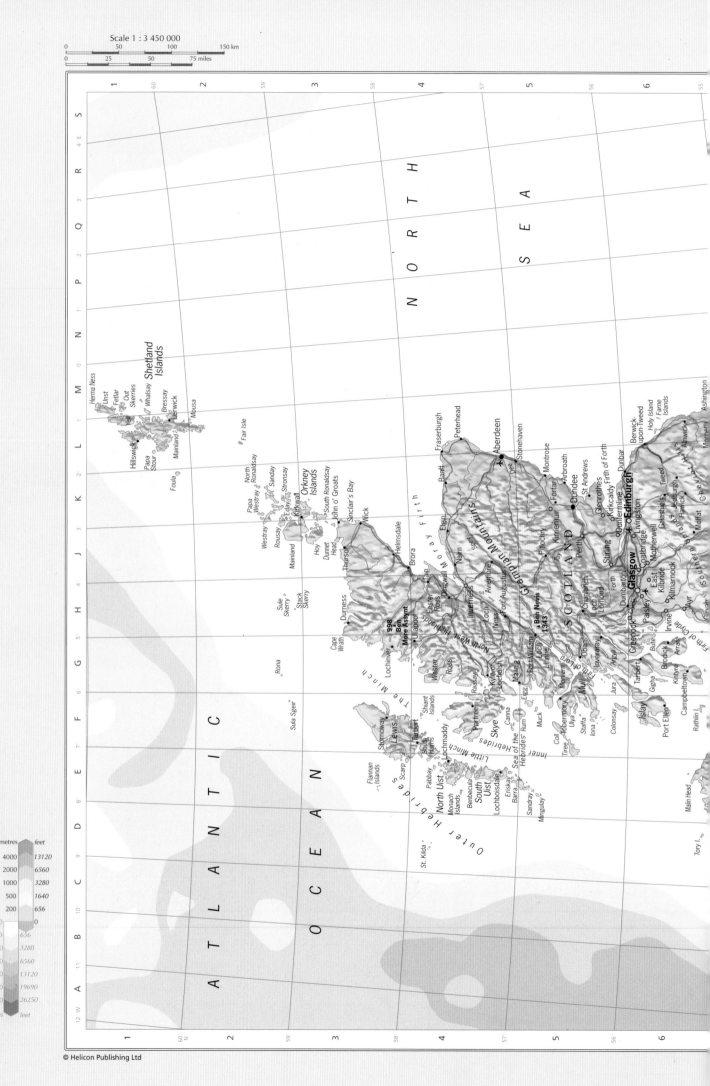

Scale 1 : 3 450 000

metres	feet
4000	13120
2000	6560
1000	3280
500	1640
200	656
0	0
200	656
1000	3280
2000	6560
4000	13120
6000	19690
8000	26250
metres	feet

© Helicon Publishing Ltd

ATLANTIC OCEAN

NORTH SEA

Shetland Islands

Herma Ness
Unst
Fetlar
Yell
Out Skerries
Whalsay
Bressay
Lerwick
Hillswick
Papa Stour
Mainland
Mousa
Foula

Fair Isle

Orkney Islands
North Ronaldsay
Sanday
Stronsay
Papa Westray
Westray
Eday
Rousay
Mainland
Kirkwall
South Ronaldsay
John o' Groats
Hoy
Sinclair's Bay
Wick
Dunnet Head
Thurso

Sule Skerry
Stack Skerry
Durness
Cape Wrath
Lochinver
Ben More Assynt 998
Ullapool
Wester Ross
Easter Ross
Dingwall
Helmsdale
Brora
Moray Firth
Nairn
Elgin
Banff
Fraserburgh
Peterhead

Rona
Sula Sgeir

The Minch

Shiant Islands
Raasay
Portree
Skye
Canna
Rum
Eigg
Muck
Coll
Tiree
Staffa
Ulva
Iona
Mull
Colonsay

Flannan Islands
Lewis
Stornoway
Scarp
Tarbert
North Harris
South Harris
Little Minch
Sea of the Hebrides
Inner Hebrides
Pabbay
Lochmaddy
Benbecula
North Uist
Monach Islands
South Uist
Lochboisdale
Eriskay
Sandray
Barra
Mingulay

Outer Hebrides

St Kilda

Kyle of Lochalsh
Mallaig
Fort William
Ben Nevis 1343
Loch Linnhe
Morvern
Firth of Lorn
Oban
Inveraray
Loch Awe
Jura
Islay
Port Ellen
Rathlin I.
Gigha
Kintyre
Campbeltown

North West Highlands
Inverness
Loch Ness
Fort Augustus
Aviemore
Grampian Mountains
Pitlochry
Kirriemuir
Forfar
SCOTLAND
Crianlarich
Loch Lomond
Stirling
Perth
Dunfermline
Kirkcaldy
Glenrothes
St Andrews
Arbroath
Montrose
Dundee
Firth of Forth
Dunbar
Edinburgh
Livingston
Coatbridge
Motherwell
East Kilbride
Kilmarnock
Galashiels
Hawick
Jedburgh
Moffat
Southern Uplands
Cheviot Hills

Aberdeen
Stonehaven
Dee

Glasgow
Paisley
Greenock
Dumbarton
Bute
Brodick
Arran
Kilbirnie
Ayr
Firth of Clyde

Berwick-upon-Tweed
Holy Island
Farne Islands
Alnwick
Morpeth
Ashington
Tweed

Malin Head
Main Head

Tory I.

14 15
18 19

Grid references (top): 7 54 8 53 9 52 10 51 11 50 12 49

Column letters (right margin): P N M L K J H G F E D C B

Seas and regions: ATLANTIC OCEAN · IRISH SEA · North Channel · St. George's Channel · Celtic Sea · English Channel · Strait of Dover · Bristol Channel · Cardigan Bay

Countries: REPUBLIC OF IRELAND · ENGLAND · WALES · FRANCE · ISLE OF MAN (U.K.)

England (selected places)
Hartlepool, Middlesbrough, Stockton-on-Tees, Darlington, Bishop Auckland, Northallerton, Thirsk, Ripon, Harrogate, York, Leeds, Bradford, Blackburn, Huddersfield, Wakefield, Barnsley, MANCHESTER, Stockport, Oldham, Bolton, Wigan, Warrington, Preston, Lancaster, Morecambe, Blackpool, Southport, St. Helens, Liverpool, Chester, Crewe, Stoke-on-Trent, Macclesfield, Chesterfield, Sheffield, Mansfield, Nottingham, Derby, Burton-upon-Trent, Stafford, Telford, Shrewsbury, Newcastle-under-Lyme, Wolverhampton, Walsall, Dudley, BIRMINGHAM, Coventry, Kidderminster, Bromsgrove, Worcester, Hereford, Great Malvern, Leominster, Warwick, Rugby, Nuneaton, Leicester, Loughborough, Kettering, Northampton, Milton Keynes, Bedford, Luton, Banbury, Stratford-upon-Avon, Cheltenham, Gloucester, Oxford, Aylesbury, Hemel Hempstead, High Wycombe, Reading, Newbury, Swindon, Cirencester, Stroud, Bristol, Bath, Weston-super-Mare, Bridgwater, Yeovil, Warminster, Salisbury, Frome, Taunton, Tiverton, Exeter, Exmouth, Teignmouth, Torquay, Brixham, Dorchester, Bournemouth, Poole, Weymouth, Bridport, Barnstaple, Bideford, Bude, Launceston, Bodmin, Newquay, St. Austell, Truro, Falmouth, Helston, Penzance, St. Ives, Land's End, Lizard Point, Isles of Scilly
Kingston upon Hull, Beverley, Bridlington, Scarborough, Whitby, Grimsby, Scunthorpe, Doncaster, Lincoln, Louth, Skegness, Boston, Spalding, Grantham, Peterborough, King's Lynn, Ely, Cambridge, Newmarket, Bury St. Edmunds, Thetford, Norwich, Great Yarmouth, Lowestoft, Cromer, Ipswich, Felixstowe, Harwich, Colchester, Chelmsford, Southend-on-Sea, LONDON, Basildon, Gravesend, Margate, Ramsgate, Herne Bay, Canterbury, Deal, Dover, Folkestone, Ashford, Maidstone, Gillingham, Sevenoaks, Royal Tunbridge Wells, Hastings, Rye, Eastbourne, Bexhill, Beachy Head, Newhaven, Brighton, Worthing, Chichester, Portsmouth, Southampton, Winchester, Havant, Eastleigh, Basingstoke, Alton, Guildford, Woking, Camberley, Bracknell, Slough, Staines, Watford, St. Albans, Hertford, Harlow, Letchworth, Stevenage, Crawley, Horsham, East Grinstead, Redhill, Newport, Isle of Wight

Wales
Cardiff, Swansea, Newport, Port Talbot, Bridgend, Llanelli, Merthyr Tydfil, Rhondda, Pontypridd, Ebbw Vale, Cwmbran, Abergavenny, Brecon, Builth Wells, Llandovery, Carmarthen, Haverfordwest, Milford Haven, Pembroke, Fishguard, St David's, Cardigan, Aberystwyth, Aberaeron, Barmouth, Dolgellau, Pwllheli, Caernarfon, Bangor, Holyhead, Holy Island, Anglesey, Menai Str., Snowdon 1085, Llandudno, Rhyl, Conwy, Wrexham, Mold, Cambrian Mountains

Ireland
DUBLIN (Baile Átha Cliath), Belfast, Cork, Limerick, Galway, Waterford, Kilkenny, Drogheda, Dundalk, Newry, Armagh, Lisburn, Lurgan, Portadown, Omagh, Enniskillen, Monaghan, Cavan, Longford, Mullingar, Athlone, Roscommon, Ballinasloe, Tuam, Castlebar, Westport, Ballina, Sligo, Donegal, Letterkenny, Coleraine, Carrickfergus, Bangor, Newtownards, Downpatrick, Kells, Navan, Naas, Dún Laoghaire, Bray, Wicklow, Arklow, Athy, Portlaoise, Tullamore, Carlow, Enniscorthy, Wexford, Rosslare, Carnsore Point, New Ross, Clonmel, Carrick-on-Suir, Cashel, Thurles, Tipperary, Nenagh, Ennis, Kilrush, Listowel, Tralee, Killarney, Kenmare, Bantry, Clonakilty, Schull, Kinsale, Mallow, Youghal, Dungarvan, Macroom, Skibbereen

Water features (Ireland): Lough Neagh, Lough Erne, Lower Lough Erne, Upper Lough Erne, Lough Allen, Lough Ree, Lough Derg, Lough Corrib, Lough Mask, Lough Conn, River Shannon, Suck, Boyle, Slaney, Barrow, Nore, Suir, Blackwater, Lee, Galway Bay, Clew Bay, Donegal Bay, Sligo Bay, Dundalk Bay, Dublin Bay, Wexford Harbour, Dingle Bay, Bantry Bay, Cork Harbour, Youghal Bay, Aran Islands, Achill I., Clare I., Inishmore, Lambay I., Saltee Islands, C. Clear, Mizen Head, Loop Head, Mouth of the Shannon, Connemara

France (selected)
Calais, Gravelines, Dunkerque, Boulogne-sur-Mer, Berck, Le Crotoy, Hesdin, St-Omer, Hazebrouck, Étaples, St-Valéry-sur-Somme, Abbeville, Amiens, Somme, Blangy-sur-Bresle, Le Tréport, Dieppe, Neufchâtel-en-Bray, Gournay-en-Bray, Beauvais, Pontoise, Versailles, St-Germain-en-Laye, Seine, Rouen, Louviers, Évreux, Vernon, Yvetot, Fécamp, Bolbec, Le Havre, Honfleur, Lisieux, Bernay, Bayeux, Caen, Falaise, Cap d'Antifer, Baie de la Seine, Cherbourg, Valognes, Carentan, Isigny-sur-Mer, Coutances, Périers, St-Lô, Cap de la Hague

Channel Islands (U.K.): Guernsey, St. Peter Port, Jersey, St. Helier, Sark, Alderney, Start Point, Bill of Portland, Lyme Bay, Poole Bay, Lundy, Hartland Point

Isle of Man (U.K.): Douglas, Point of Ayre, Calf of Man, Luce Bay

Lake District (England): Scafell Pike 978, Penrith, Keswick, Workington, Whitehaven, Kendal, Ulverston, Barrow-in-Furness, Carlisle

Rivers (England): Trent, Ouse, Great Ouse, Little Ouse, Nene, Wye, Severn, Avon, Thames, Exe, Tamar, Aire, Wharfe, Swale, Tees

The Wash

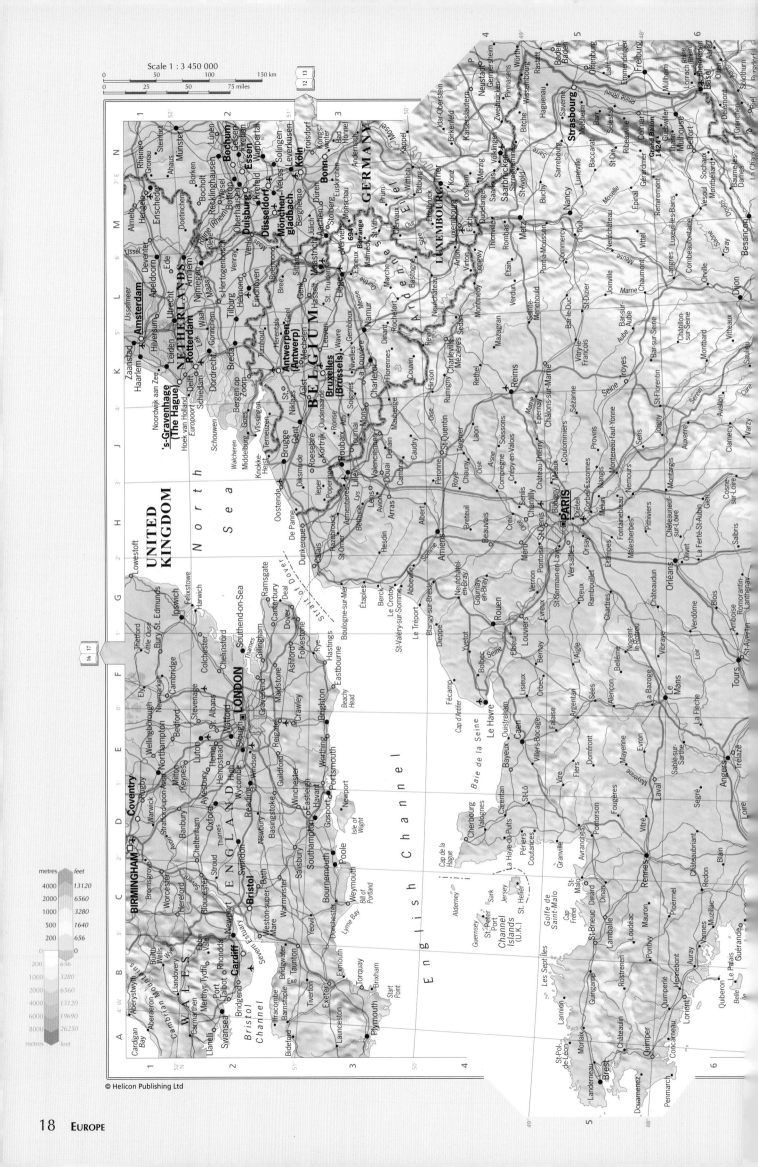

© Helicon Publishing Ltd

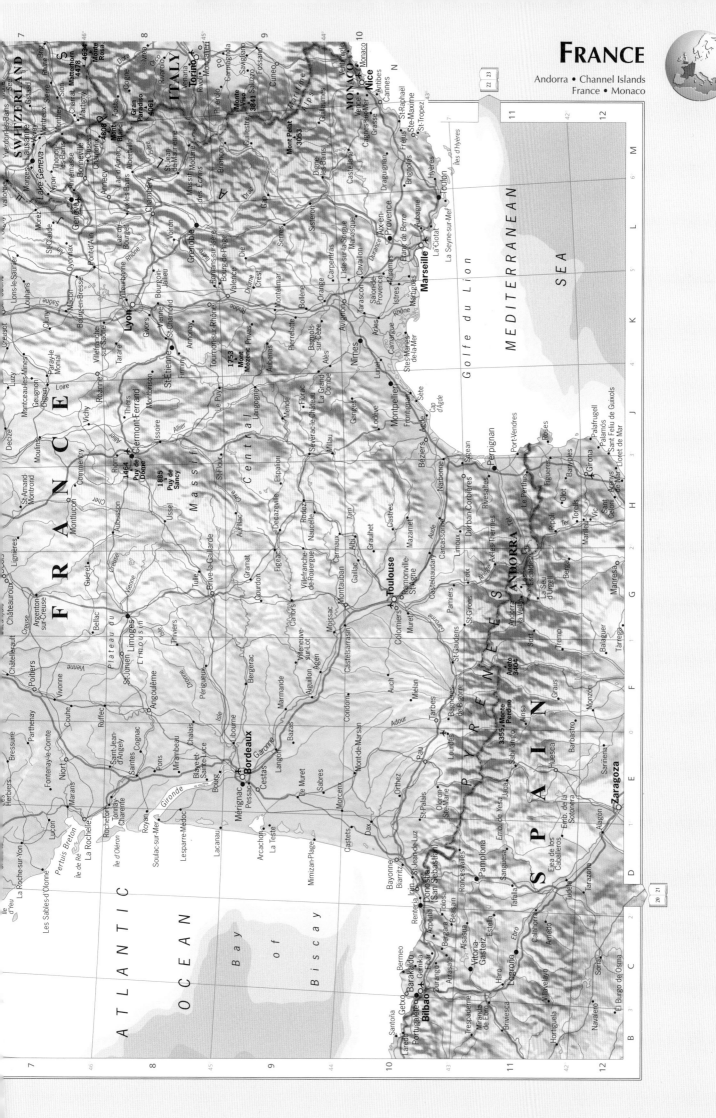

FRANCE

Andorra • Channel Islands
France • Monaco

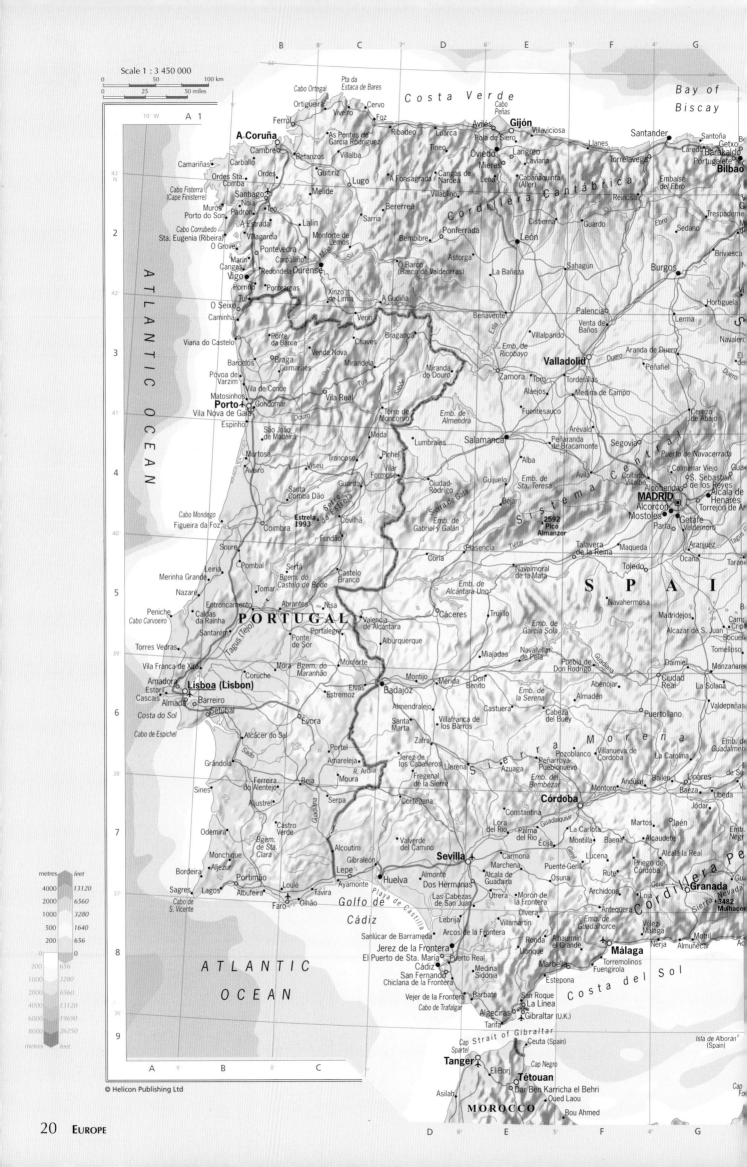

Scale 1 : 3 450 000

ATLANTIC OCEAN

Costa Verde

Bay of Biscay

Cordillera Cantábrica

PORTUGAL

SPAIN

Sistema Central

MADRID

Lisboa (Lisbon)

Sierra Morena

Córdoba

Sevilla

Huelva

Golfo de Cádiz

Cádiz

Málaga

Costa del Sol

Cordillera Penibética

Granada

ATLANTIC OCEAN

Strait of Gibraltar

Tanger

Tétouan

MOROCCO

© Helicon Publishing Ltd

FRANCE

Bayonne
Biarritz
Orthez
Muret
Béziers
Agde
Sète
Cap d'Agde

Irún
St-Jean-de-Luz
St-Palais
Castelnaudary
Aude
Carcassonne
Narbonne
Golfe du Lion

Azpeitia
Donostia
(San Sebastián)
Oloron-Ste-Marie
Pau
Tarbes
Lourdes
Pamiers
Limoux
Foix
Sigean

Bergara
Beasain
Roncesvalles
Bagnères-
de-Bigorre
St-Gaudens
St-Girons
Ax-les-Thermes
Rivesaltes
Perpignan
Port-Vendres

Alsasua
Pamplona
PYRENEES
ANDORRA
Le Perthus
Roses
Costa Brava

Estella
Sangüesa
Jaca
3355 Monte
Perdino
Aneto
3404
Andorra
la Vella
Les Escaldes
Figueres

Logroño
Tafalla
Sabiñánigo
Ainsa
Sort
La Seu
d'Urgell
Ripoll
Olot
Banyoles

Calahorra
Ejea de los
Caballeros
Huesca
Graus
Tremp
Berga
Torelló
Manlleu
Girona
Palafrugell

Arnedo
Tudela
Emb. de la
Sotonera
Barbástro
Balaguer
Vic
Sant Celoni
Palamós

Tarazona
Alagón
Sariñena
Monzón
Manresa
Terrassa
Granollers
Arenys de Mar
Lloret de Mar
Sant Feliu
de Guixols

Soria
Torrelapaja
Zaragoza
Lleida
Tàrrega
Igualada
Sabadell
Mataró
Badalona

mazán
El Burgo
de Ebro
Fraga
Montblanc
Vilafranca
del Penedès
Sant
Boi
BARCELONA

Aziza
Calatayud
Azaila
Caspe
Reus
Valls
Vilanova y
la Geltrú
Sitges
El Prat de Llobregat
Gava

Medinaceli
Daroca
Alcañiz
Gandesa
Tarragona
Cambrils

Alcolea
del Pinar
Molina
de Aragón
Calamocha
Montalbán
Tortosa
Cabo Tortosa
Costa Dorada

Cañaveras
Monreal
del Campo
Sierra
de Gúdar
Morella
Amposta
Sant Carlos
de la Rápita

Cuenca
Teruel
Vinaròs
Benicarló
Islas Baleares
(Balearic Islands)
Ciutadella
Menorca
Mahón

Torreblanca
Pollença
Cap de Formentor

Emb. de
Contreras
Barracas
Castelló de la Plana
Onda
Vila-real
Borriana
La Vall d'Uixo
Islas Columbretes
Soller
Sa Pobla
Inca
Arta

Motilla
del Palancar
Utiel
Sagunt
Golfo de
Palma
de Mallorca
Manacor

Requena
Paterna
Burjassot
VALENCIA
Valencia
Sa Dragonera
Llucmajor
Mallorca

Torrent
Carlet
Algemesí
Cullera
Eivissa
(Ibiza)
Santanyí
Cap de ses
Salines

Cofrents
Júcar
Alzira
Xàtiva
Gandia
San Juan
Bautista
Cabrera

La Roda
Munera
Albacete
Almansa
Oliva
Dénia
Xàbia
San Antonia
Abad
Eivissa (Ibiza)

Chinchilla
de Monte-Aragón
Ontinyent
Cabo de la Nao
Formentera

Yecla
Villena
Alcoi

Hellín
Elda
Benidorm
La Vila
Joiosa

Jumilla
Novelda
Aspe
Alicante
Santa Pola
Costa Blanca

Cieza
Crevillent
Elch

Caravaca
de la Cruz
Molina
de Segura
Orihuela

Alcantarilla
Murcia
Torrevieja

Zarzadilla
de Totana
Alhama
de Murcia
Torre-Pacheco
La Unión
Cabo de Palos

Lorca
Huércal
Overa
Golfo de
Mazarrón
Cartagena

Águilas
Albox
Vera
Mediterranean Sea

Nijar
Carboneras
Dellys
Tizi
Ouzou

Almería
Cabo
de Gata
ALGER
(ALGIERS)
Ain
Taya
Thepia
Roulba
Lakhdaria
Boghni

Bou
Ismail
Bonfarik
Bouira

Cherchell
Gouraya
Hadjout
Blida
Beni
Bessem
Sour el
Ghozlane

Ténès
Miliana
Médéa
Berrouaghia

Bouzghaia
Khemis
Miliana

Ain-Tédéles
Chélif
Bou
Kadir
Ech Chélif
ALGERIA

Mostaganem
Arzew
Relizane
Theniet
el Had
Bordj
Bounaam
Ksar el
Boukhari
Ain el
Hadjel

Mers el
Kébir
Oran
Gdyel
Mohammadia
Bougzoul

Cap Figalo
El Amria
Oued Tiélat
Sig

Hammam
Bou Hadjar
Mascara

Beni Saf
Aïn Témouchent

52 | 53

0   50   100   150 km
0   25   50   75 miles

| | A | 6° E | B | 7° | C | 8° | D | 9° | E | 10° | F | 11° |

St-Mihiel · Pont-à-Mousson · Buchy · Bitche · Lauter · Wörth · Bruchsal · Heilbronn · Schwäbisch-Hall · Crailsheim · Dinkelsbühl · Gunzenhausen
Bar-le-Duc · Flirey · Commercy · Wissembourg · **Karlsruhe** · Bietigheim-Bissingen · Bretten · Gaildorf · Ellwangen · Weißenburg
Nancy · Sarrebourg · Haguenau · Ettlingen · Pforzheim · Ludwigsburg · Backnang · Aalen · Treuchtlingen · Nördlingen · Eichstä
Houdelaincourt · St-Nicolas-de-Port · Lunéville · Saverne · Brumath · Gaggenau · Leonberg · **Stuttgart** · Schwäbisch-Gmünd · Göppingen · Donauwörth · Neub
Toul · **Strasbourg** · Molsheim · Kehl · Baden-Baden · Bad Wildbad · Calw · Esslingen · Kirchheim · Geislingen · Heidenheim · Dillingen · Ingolstad
Neufchâteau · Baccarat · St-Dié · Offenburg · Oberkirch · Freudenstadt · Herrenberg · Nürtingen · Metzingen · Langenau · Günzburg · Aichach · **Augsburg** · Friedberg · Dacha
Chátenois · Épinal · Ribeauvillé · Lahr · Nagold · Tübingen · Neckar · Reutlingen · Bad · Neu-Ulm · Ulm · Vöhringen · Bobingen · Olching
Vittel · Gérardmer · Colmar · Emmendingen · St. · Hechingen · Balingen · Ehingen · Blaubeuren · Laupheim · Krumbach · Fürstenfeldbruck · Germering
Val-de-Meuse · Remiremont · Munster · Freiburg · Villingen · Rottweil · Albstadt · Sigmaringen · Biberach · Illertissen · Mindelheim · Landsberg · Ammer-see · Gilchin
Langres · Fresnes-sur-Apances · Guebwiller · Thann · Müllheim · Donaueschingen · Schwenningen · Tuttlingen · Stockach · Bad Waldsee · Memmingen · Kaufbeuren · Starnberger See · Weilhem · Geret
Champlitte · Luxeuil-les-Bains · Mulhouse · Wutach · Schaffhausen · Singen · Überlingen · Bad Wurzach · Leutkirch · Schongau · Peißenber
Combeaufontaine · Vesoul · Lure · Belfort · Altkirch · Lörrach · Waldshut-Tiengen · Konstanz · Ravensburg · Wangen · Immenstadt · Marktoberdorf · Mur
Gray · Montbéliard · Sochaux · Basel · Rheinfelden · Bad · Rhine (Rhein) · L. Constance · Friedrichshafen · Kempten · Füssen
Besançon · Baume-les-Dames · Delémont · Olten · Säckingen · Aarau · Bülach · Frauenfeld · Arbon · Bregenz · Dornbirn · Sonthofen · Pflach · Garmisch-Partenki
Ornans · Grenchen · Solothurn · Aare · Wohlen · **Zürich** · Winterthur · Wil · Gossau · St. Gallen · Oberstdorf
Dole · Mouchard · Biel · Huttwil · Emmen · Zuger see · Zug · Schwyz · Herisau · Bludenz · Landeck · Innsbruck
Poligny · La Chaux-de-Fonds · Neuchâtel · Burgdorf · Luzern · Zug · Walen see · **LIECHTENSTEIN** · Vaduz · Feldkirch · Kappl · Steinach am Brenn
Lons-le-Saunier · Champagnole · Lac de Neuchâtel · Payerne · **Bern** · Köniz · Thun · Altdorf · Klosters · Pfunds · Sölden · Brenner · Vipiteno
St-Laurent-en-Grandvaux · Yverdon-les-Bains · Fribourg · Thuner See · Brienzer See · Meiringen · Vorderrhein · Chur · Davos · Nauders
Morez · Vallorbe · Bulle · Spiez · Interlaken · Andermatt · Thusis · Pfunds
Morges · Lausanne · Gstaad · **Jungfrau 4158** · Arolo · Vorderrhein · St Moritz · **Ortles 3905** · Silandro · Merar
St-Claude · Nyon · Vevey · Montreux · Sierre · Visp · Acquarossa · Biasca · Poschiavo · Bormio · Malé · Cles · Bolza
Oyonnax · **Genève** · Thonon-les-Bains · Monthey · Sion · Brig · Formazza · Ticino · Chiavenna · Sondrio · Edolo · Cavales
Annemasse · Bonneville · Cluses · Martigny · Zermatt · Locarno · Bellinzona · Colico · Morbegno · Darfo · Trento
Rhône · Chamonix · **4478 Matterhorn** · **4634 Monte Rosa** · Domodossola · Lago Maggiore · Lugano · Lago di Como · Lecco · Breno · Riva del Garda · Arco
4808 Mont Blanc · Aosta · Omegna · Verbania · Lago di Lugano · San Pellegrino Terme · Boario Terme · Rovereto
Annecy · Lac d'Annecy · Cogne · Varallo · Varese · Como · Albino · Gardone
Aix-les-Bains · **Gran Paradiso 4061** · Borgosesia · Borgomanero · Seregno · Bergamo · Val Trompia · Salò · Lago di Garda · Schio
Lac du Bourget · Seez · Moutiers · Cuorgné · Ivrea · Cossato · Biella · Busto Arsizio · Saronno · Monza · Rho · Treviglio · Rovato · Brescia · Valdagno · Arzignano
Chambéry · Isère · Rivarolo Canavese · Chivasso · Vercelli · Novara · Magenta · Rozzano · **MILANO (MILAN)** · Crema · Lodi · Cremona · **Verona**
St-Jean-de-Maurienne · Modane · Venaria · Trino · Garlasco · Pavia · Codogno · Villafranca di Verona
Grenoble · Massif des Écrins · Susa · Rivoli · **Torino (Turin)** · Moncalieri · Chieri · Casale Monferrato · Vigevano · Po · Stradella · Broni · Piacenza · Casalmaggiore · Mantova
Bardonecchia · Oulx · Pinerolo · Carmagnola · Asti · Alessandria · Voghera · Tortona · Piadena · Cerea
Valbonnais · Briançon · **Monte Viso 3841** · Saluzzo · Bra · Alba · Nizza Monferrato · Novi Ligure · Salsomaggiore Terme · Fidenza · Carpi · Ostiglia
Chauffayer · Guillestre · Savigliano · Fossano · Acqui Terme · Ovada · Bobbio · Fornovo di Taro · Collecchio · **Parma** · Guastalla
Gap · St-Paul · Argentera · Cuneo · Mondovì · Cairo Montenotte · Voltri · **Genova (Genoa)** · Borgo Val di Taro · Reggio nell'Emilia · **Modena** · Cer
Serres · St-Vincent-les-Forts · Borgo San Dalmazzo · Varazze · Savona · Rapallo · Chiavari · Pontremoli · Appennino Tosco-Emiliano · Sassuolo · Sasso Marconi · **Bo**
Sisteron · Digne-les-Bains · Guillaumes · Mondovì · Finale Ligure · Vado Ligure · Sta. Margherita Ligure · Sestri Levante · Aulla · **ITA**
Maritime Alps · Loano · Albenga · **Golfo di Genova** · La Spezia · Lerici · Sarzana · Carrara · Massa · Borgo
Manosque · Lac de Ste-Croix · Entrevaux · Alassio · Imperia · Pietrasanta · Forte dei Marmi · Camaiore · Pescia · Pistoia · Prato
Castellane · Vence · Monaco · Ventimiglia · San Remo · Gorgona · Viareggio · Lucca · Pontassie
Draguignan · Grasse · Cagnes-sur-Mer · **Nice** · **MONACO** · Pisa · Empoli · **Firenz**
Brignoles · Antibes · Cannes · **Ligurian Sea** · Arno · S. Miniato (Florence) · Figline
St-Raphaël · Livorno · Greve in Chianti
Toulon · Hyères · Fréjus · Ste-Maxime · St-Tropez · Certaldo · Poggibonsi · S. G
Rosignano Marittimo · Volterra · San
Gorgona Is. · Cecina

| | A | 6° | B | 7° | C | 8° | D | 9° | E | 10° | F | 11° |

G E R M A N
F R A N C E
SWITZERLAND
Glarner Alpen
Pennine Alps
Lepontine Alps
Lombardy Alps

feet
3000 · 13120
2000 · 6560
1000 · 3280
500 · 1640
200 · 656
0 · 0
200 · 656
1000 · 3280
2000 · 6560
4000 · 13120
6000 · 19690
8000 · 26250
metres · feet

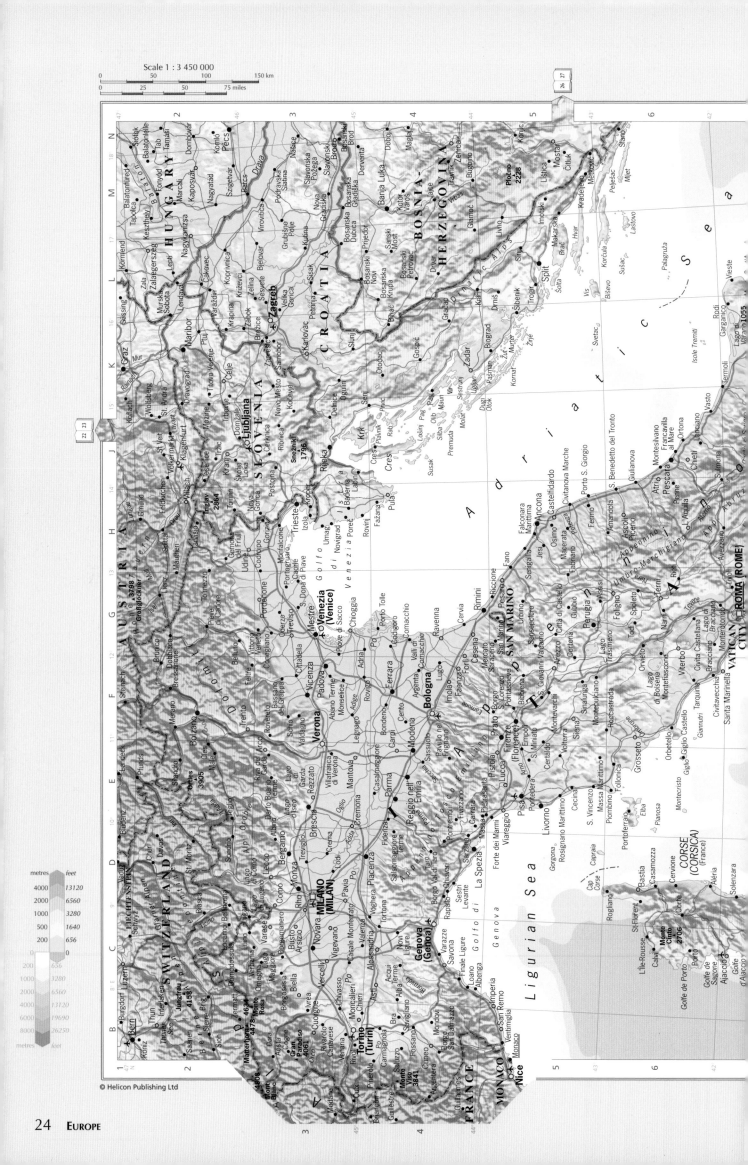

Scale 1 : 3 450 000

© Helicon Publishing Ltd

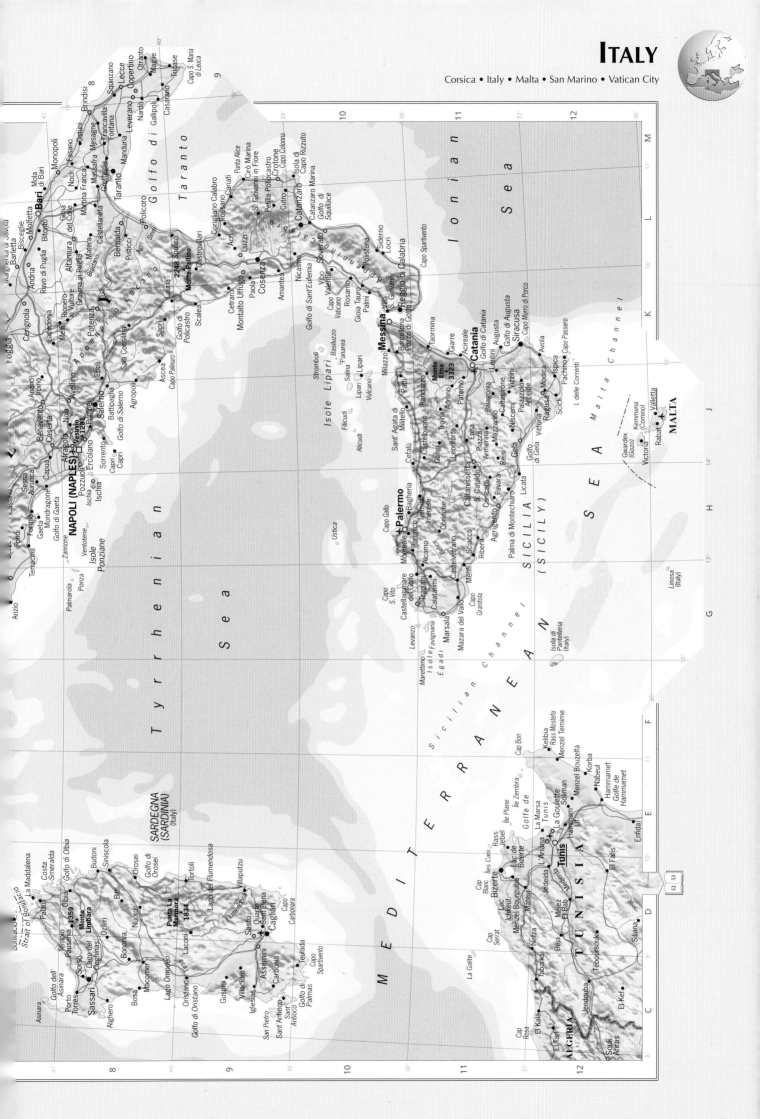

Scale 1 : 3 450 000

© Helicon Publishing Ltd

Scale 1 : 3 450 000

© Helicon Publishing Ltd

BLACK SEA

İSTANBUL

Marmara Denizi
(Sea of Marmara)

Bursa

ANKARA

Eskişehir

T U R K E Y

A N A T O L I A

İZMIR

Konya

Antalya

M E D I T E R R A N E A N   S E A

CYPRUS

Lefkosia
(Nicosia)

Olympus
1952

Varna

Burgas

Zonguldak

Kırıkkale

**İcel
(Mersin)**

Scale 1 : 10 400 000

0   200   400   600 km
0   100   200   300 miles

Norwegian Sea

NORWAY

Kristiansund
Molde
Verdalsøra
Namsos
Trondheim
Dømbas
2470 Galdhøpiggen
Røros
1796 Helagsfjället
Fagernes
Lillehammer
Mjøsa
Hamar
Hønefoss
Oslo
Moss
Arvika
Säffle
Karlstad
Skövde
Borås
Vänern
Örebro
Motala
Jönköping
Värnamo
Växjö
Kalmar
Karlskrona
Öland
Gotland

SWEDEN

Gäddede
Storuman
Vilhelmina
Åsele
Lycksele
Strömsund
Östersund
Ange
Särna
Mora
Ludvika
Falun
Gävle
Söderhamn
Hudiksvall
Sundsvall
Härnösand
Ljusdal
Örnsköldsvik
Umeå
Skellefteå
Luleå
Piteå
Boden
Arvidsjaur

BALTIC SEA

Gulf of Bothnia

Tärnaby
Jokkmokk
Arctic Circle
Pello
Övertorneå
Tornio
Kemi
Kemijärvi
Salla
Rovaniemi
Sodankylä

FINLAND

Oulu
Kokkola
Jakobstad
Vaasa
Seinäjoki
Tampere
Turku
Vantaa
Espoo
Helsinki
Hanko
Pori
Jyväskylä
Päijänne
Hämeenlinna
Lahti
Mikkeli
Kouvola
Lappeenranta
Kotka
Vyborg
Saimaa
Imatra
Kuopio
Iisalmi
Joensuu
Nurmes
Pielinen
Kuusamo
Suomussalmi
Kajaani
Oulujärvi
Pudasjärvi

KARELIYA

Kandalaksha
Apatity
Monchegorsk
Kolskiy Poluostrov
Ponoy

Barents Sea

Kem'
Belomorsk
Segezha
Petrozavodsk
Onega
Severodvinsk
Arkhangel
Novodvinsk

Beloye More (White Sea)

Gulf of Finland
Tallinn
Haapsalu
Hiiumaa
Saaremaa
Pärnu
Rakvere
Narva
Kohtla-Järve

ESTONIA

Viljandi
Tartu
Valga
Võru
Pskov
Lake Peipus
L. Pskov

SANKT-PETERBURG (ST. PETERSBURG)
Pushkin
Gatchina
Volkhov
Tikhvin
Novgorod
Staraya Russa
Valday

LATVIA
Riga
Jūrmala
Jelgava
Ventspils
Liepāja
Talsi
Valmiera
Gulbene
Rēzekne
Jēkabpils

LITHUANIA
Klaipėda
Šiauliai
Telšiai
Panevėžys
Daugavpils
Kaunas
Marijampolė
Alytus
Vilnius

POLAND
Słupsk
Koszalin
Gdynia
Gdańsk
Tczew
Elbląg
Olsztyn
Bydgoszcz
Toruń
Grudziadz
Chojnice
Suwałki
Ełk
Włocławek
Płock
Łódź
Piotrków Trybunalski
Kalisz
Częstochowa
Radom
Katowice
Kielce
Stalowa Wola
Kraków
Tarnów
Nowy Sącz
WARSZAWA (WARSAW)
Białystok
Siedlce
Lublin
Zamość
Rzeszów
Przemyśl

RUSSIA
Kaliningrad
Chernyakhovsk

Hrodna
Lida
Navapolatsk
MINSK
Baranavichy
Brest
Kobryn
Pinsk
Salihorsk
Slutsk

BELARUS
Maladzyechna
Barysaw
Vitsyebsk
Smolensk
Orsha
Mahilyow
Babruysk
Krychaw
Homyel
Mazyr
Rechytsa
Svyetlahorsk

Velikiye Luki
Nevel
Ostashkov
Tver'
Rzhev
Vyaz'ma
Klin
Zelenograd
Noginsk
MOSKVA (MOSCOW)
Podol'sk
Serpukhov
Obninsk
Kaluga
Tula
Novomoskovsk

Bryansk
Roslavl'
Orel
Zheleznogorsk
Kursk
Shchigry
Belgorod
Staryy Oskol
Voronezh
Liski
Pavlovsk

UKRAINE
L'viv
Drohobych
Stryy
Uzhhorod
Mukacheve
Chervonohrad
Ternopil'
Khmel'nyts'kyy
Rivne
Shepetivka
Novohrad-Volyns'kyy
Zhytomyr
Berdychiv
Vinnytsya
Kam"yanets'-Podil's'kyy
Chernivtsi
Kam"yanets'
Kovel'
Luts'k
Sarny
Korosten
Ovruch
Chornobyl'
Nizhyn
KYYIV (KIEV)
Brovary
Bila Tserkva
Pryluky
Chernihiv
Konotop
Sumy
Okhtyrka
Romny
Lubny
Poltava
Cherkasy
Smila
Uman'
Kirovohrad
Oleksandriya
Kremenchuk
Krasnohrad
KHARKIV
Lozova
Pervomays'k
Dniprodzerzhyns'k
DNIPROPETROVS'K
Pavlohrad
Kryvyy Rih
Nikopol'
Zaporizhzhya
Slov"yans'k
Kramators'k
Makiyivka
Yenakiyeve
DONETS'K
Luhans'k
Lysychans'k
Stakhanov
Mariupol'

MOLDOVA
Bălţi
Rîbniţa
Ribnița
Kotovs'k
Chişinău
Tiraspol
Tighina
Bendery
Cahul

ROMANIA
Satu Mare
Oradea
Baia Mare
Bistriţa
Cluj-Napoca
Deva
Alba Iulia
Târgu Mureş
Piatra Neamţ
Sibiu
Braşov
Mediaş
Suceava
Botoşani
Iaşi
Vaslui
Bacău
Oneşti
Focşani
Brăila
Galaţi
Buzău
Ploieşti
Târgovişte
Râmnicu Vâlcea
Piteşti
Petroşani
Târgu Jiu
Craiova
BUCUREŞTI (BUCHAREST)
Alexandria
Giurgiu

SLOVAK REP.
Prešov
Košice

HUNGARY
Nyíregyháza
Debrecen

BULGARIA
Lom
Montana
Vraca
Pleven
Lovech
Ruse
Razgrad
Silistra

ODESA (ODESSA)
Mykolayiv
Kherson
Bilhorod-Dnistrovs'kyy
Izmayil
Tulcea
Armyans'k
Dzhankoy
Krym'
Yevpatoriya
Simferopol'
Sevastopol'
Balaklava
Yalta
Sudak
Feodosiya
Kerch
Berdyans'k
Melitopol'
Henichesk
Primorsko-Akhtarsk
Pavlovskaya

Sea of Azov
Taganrog
ROSTOV-NA-DONU
Novocherkassk
Shakhty
Volgodonsk
Azov
Yeysk
Temryuk
Anapa
Novorossiysk
Krasnodar
Armavir
Maykop
Stavropol'
Nevinnomyssk
Black Sea

Volgograd
Kamensk-Shakhtinskiy
Millerovo
Kalach-na-Donu

Tambov
Michurinsk
Lipetsk
Yelets
Zadonsk
Morshansk

Ryazan'
Kasimov
Vyksa
Murom
VLADIMIR
Ivanovo
Kineshma
Vichuga
Shuya
Kostroma
Yaroslavl'
Rostov
Uglich
Rybinsk
Cherepovets
Vologda
Gryazovets
Sokol
Totma

Kirov
Dzerzhinsk
NIZHNIY NOVGOROD

Petrozavodsk
Onezhskoye Ozero
Ladozhskoye Ozero (Lake Ladoga)
Olonets
Lodeynoye

metres / feet
4000 / 13120
2000 / 6560
1000 / 3280
500 / 1640
200 / 656
0 / 0
200 / 656
1000 / 3280
2000 / 6560
4000 / 13120
6000 / 19690
8000 / 26250
metres / feet

© Helicon Publishing Ltd

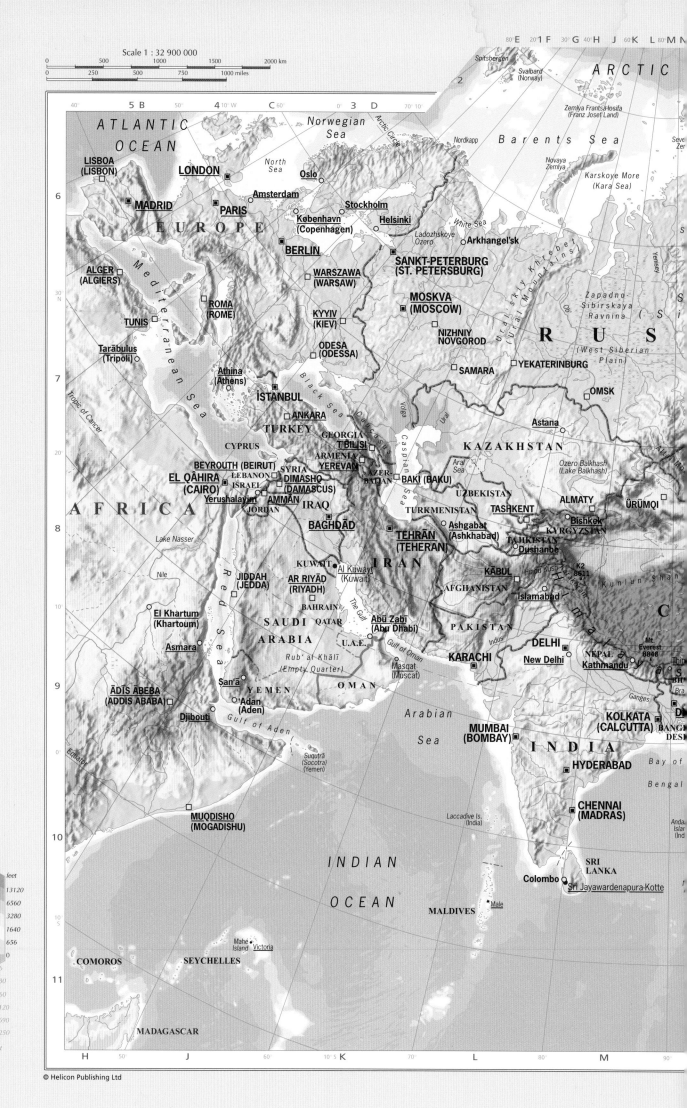

Scale 1 : 32 900 000

0   500   1000   1500   2000 km
0   250   500   750   1000 miles

ARCTIC

Spitsbergen
Svalbard
(Norway)

Zemlya Frantsa-Iosifa
(Franz Josef Land)

Seve
Zer

ATLANTIC
OCEAN

Norwegian
Sea

Barents Sea

Novaya
Zemlya

Karskoye More
(Kara Sea)

Nordkapp

LISBOA
(LISBON)

LONDON

North
Sea

Oslo

Zapadno-
Sibirskaya
Ravnina (Si

MADRID

Amsterdam

Stockholm

White Sea

(West Siberian
Plain)

PARIS

EUROPE

København
(Copenhagen)

Helsinki

Ladozhskoye
Ozero

Arkhangel'sk

RUS

RUS

BERLIN

SANKT-PETERBURG
(ST. PETERSBURG)

Ural'skiy Khrebet
(Ural Mountains)

Yenisey

ALGER
(ALGIERS)

WARSZAWA
(WARSAW)

MOSKVA
(MOSCOW)

NIZHNIY
NOVGOROD

Ob'

ROMA
(ROME)

KYYIV
(KIEV)

SAMARA

YEKATERINBURG

TUNIS

ODESA
(ODESSA)

Volga

Ural

Astana

OMSK

Tarābulus
(Tripoli)

Athina
(Athens)

Black Sea

Caucasus

Caspian Sea

KAZAKHSTAN

Ozero Balkhash
(Lake Balkhash)

İSTANBUL

Tropic of Cancer

ANKARA

TURKEY

GEORGIA
T'BILISI

Aral
Sea

Altyn Tag

CYPRUS

ARMENIA
YEREVAN

AZER-
BAIJAN

BAKI (BAKU)

UZBEKISTAN

ALMATY

ÜRÜMQI

BEYROUTH (BEIRUT)

SYRIA
DIMASHQ
(DAMASCUS)

TASHKENT

EL QÂHIRA
(CAIRO)

LEBANON
ISRAEL

TURKMENISTAN

Bishkek

KYRGYZSTAN

AFRICA

Yerushalayim
JORDAN

AMMÂN

IRAQ

BAGHDÂD

Ashgabat
(Ashkhabad)

TAJIKISTAN
Dushanbe

K2
8611

Kunlun Shan

C

Lake Nasser

Nile

TEHRÂN
(TEHERAN)

IRAN

KÂBUL

Hindu Kush

Karakoram

KUWAIT
Al Kuwayt
(Kuwait)

AFGHANISTAN

Islamabad

JIDDAH
(JEDDA)

AR RIYÂD
(RIYADH)

BAHRAIN

The Gulf

Abū Zabī
(Abu Dhabi)

PAKISTAN

Indus

DELHI

Mt.
Everest
8846

El Khartum
(Khartoum)

SAUDI

QATAR

U.A.E.

KARACHI

New Delhi

NEPAL
Kathmandu

Thi
S

Asmara

ARABIA

Rub' al Khālī
(Empty Quarter)

Gulf of Oman

Masqat
(Muscat)

Ganges

BH
Bra

ĀDĪS ĀBEBA
(ADDIS ABABA)

San'a

YEMEN

OMAN

Arabian

Sea

MUMBAI
(BOMBAY)

INDIA

KOLKATA
(CALCUTTA)

BANG
DES

D

Djibouti

Adan
(Aden)

Gulf of Aden

HYDERABAD

Bay of

Equator

Suqutrā
(Socotra)
(Yemen)

Bengal

MUQDISHO
(MOGADISHU)

Laccadive Is.
(India)

CHENNAI
(MADRAS)

And
Islar
(Ind

INDIAN

SRI
LANKA

OCEAN

Colombo

Sri Jayawardenapura-Kotte

MALDIVES

Male

COMOROS

Mahé
Island

Victoria

SEYCHELLES

MADAGASCAR

metres   feet
4000   13120
2000   6560
1000   3280
500   1640
200   656
0   0
200   656
1000   3280
2000   6560
4000   13120
6000   19690
8000   26250
metres   feet

© Helicon Publishing Ltd

32 ASIA

R | S 140° | T 150° | U 1 160° 80° V | 170° | W 2 180° | X | 70°170° E | 3 | Y | 60° | 160° | 4

AN

O. Vrangelya

Arctic Circle

Bering Strait

ALASKA
(U.S.)

St. Lawrence I.

5   40°   6

Novosibirskiye
Ostrova

Vostochno-
Sibirskoye More
(East Siberian
Sea)

Bering
Sea

Anadyr'

30°

More Laptevykh
(Laptev Sea)

Aleutian Islands (U.S.)

Aleutian Trench

International Date Line

Khrebet Kolymskiy

Verkhoyanskiy Khrebet

irskoye
or'ye

Siberian
eau)

r
r
i
a)

Lena

Kamchatka

Petropavlovsk-
Kamchatskiy

Aleutian Trench

7

I A

Yakutsk

Sea of
Okhotsk

Kuril Trench

Tropic of Cancer

20°

Stanovoy Khrebet

Sakhalin

Kuril'skiye Ostrova
(Kuril Islands)

PACIFIC

Ozero
Baykal

Amur

Hokkaidō

SAPPORO

Wake I.
(U.S.)

8

NGOLIA

Ulaanbaatar

HARBIN

Vladivostok

JAPAN

Honshū

OCEAN

SHENYANG

NORTH
KOREA

Sea of
Japan

TŌKYŌ

3776

P'YŎNGYANG

Fuji-san

Izu-
shotō

Japan Trench

10°

BEIJING
(PEKING)

SŎUL
(SEOUL)

ŌSAKA

SOUTH
KOREA

Shikoku

Ogasawara-shotō
(Japan)

QINGDAO

Nagasaki

Kyūshū

Huáng Hé

Gobi
Desert

Yellow
Sea

Kazan-rettō
(Japan)

Pohnpei

al Hu

LANZHOU

East
China
Sea

Amami-
Oshima

Marianas Trench

9

N A

SHANGHAI

WUHAN

Nansei-shotō
(Ryukyu Islands)

Okinawa

Northern
Mariana
Islands
(U.S.)

Caroline
Islands

CHONGQING

Chang Jiang

FUZHOU

T'AIPEI

Guam
(U.S.)

Equator

0°

GUANGZHOU

TAIWAN

Luzon Strait

Challenger Deep
11033

Yap

HA NỘI
(HANOI)

XIANGGANG
(HONG KONG)

Luzon

OCEANIA

Mekong

Hainan

Mt. Pulog
2929

NMAR
RMA)

Viangchan
(Vientiane)

PHILIPPINES

MANILA

Samar

Philippine Trench

Bismarck
Sea

10°

GON
GOON)

LAOS

South
China
Sea

Cebu

Mindoro

VIETNAM

Panay

THAILAND

Palawan

Negros

Mindanao

NG THEP
NGKOK)

CAMBODIA

Davao

Biak

Phnum Penh

HÔ CHI MINH
(SAIGON)

Sulu
Sea

New Guinea

Gulf of
Thailand

G.
Kinabalu
4094

Celebes
Sea

Halmahera

Puncak Jaya
5030

Irian
Jaya

Sabah

Bandar Seri
Begawan

Molucca
Sea

Torres Strait

MALAYSIA

BRUNEI

Seram

Aru

Dolak

10°

EDAN

KUALA LUMPUR

Sarawak

B o r n e o

Sulawesi
(Celebes)

Buru

Arafura
Sea

Tanimbar

11

Sumatera (Sumatra)

SINGAPORE
SINGAPORE

Selat Makassar

B a n d a
Sea

Gulf of
Carpentaria

Kepulauan
Mentawai

Banjarmasin

I N D O N E S I A

Buton

Java Sea

Flores

Timor

140°

SURABAYA

Sumba

Sumbawa

Timor Sea

JAKARTA

Jawa (Java)

Bali

Lombok

100°   P   110°   Q   120°   R   130°   S

Scale 1 : 13 800 000

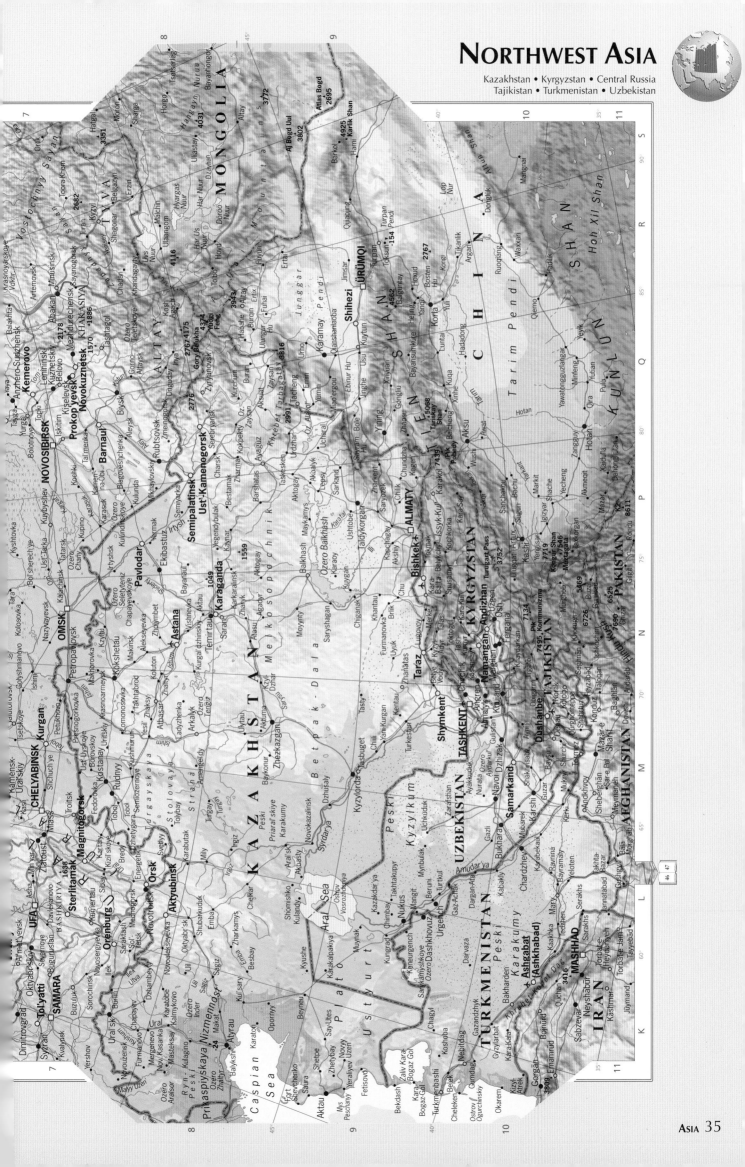

Northwest Asia

Kazakhstan • Kyrgyzstan • Central Russia
Tajikistan • Turkmenistan • Uzbekistan

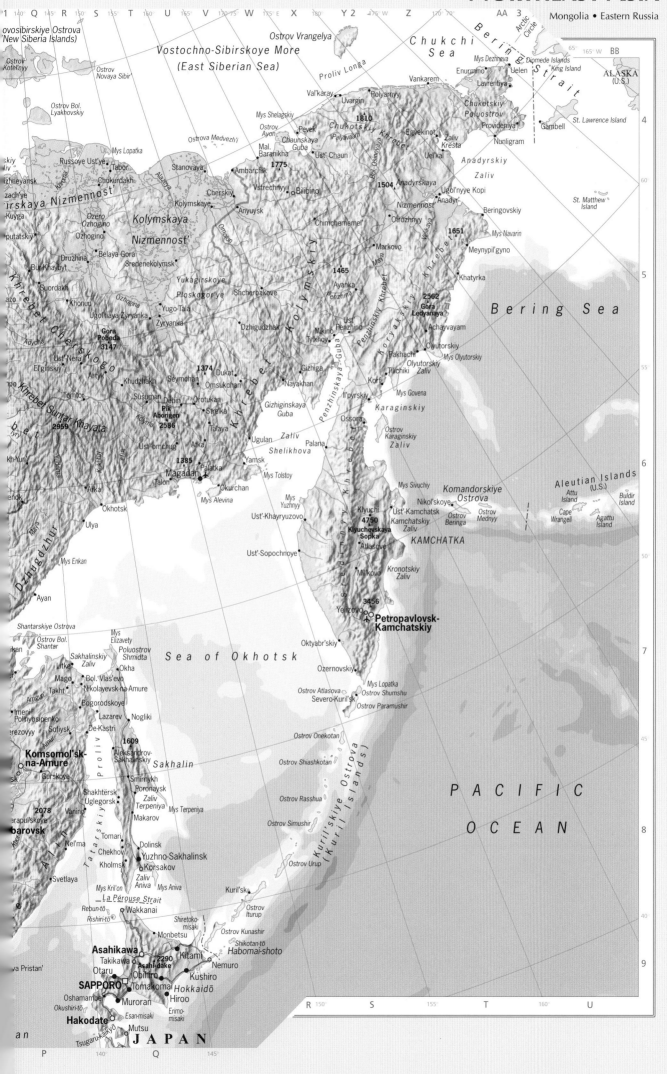

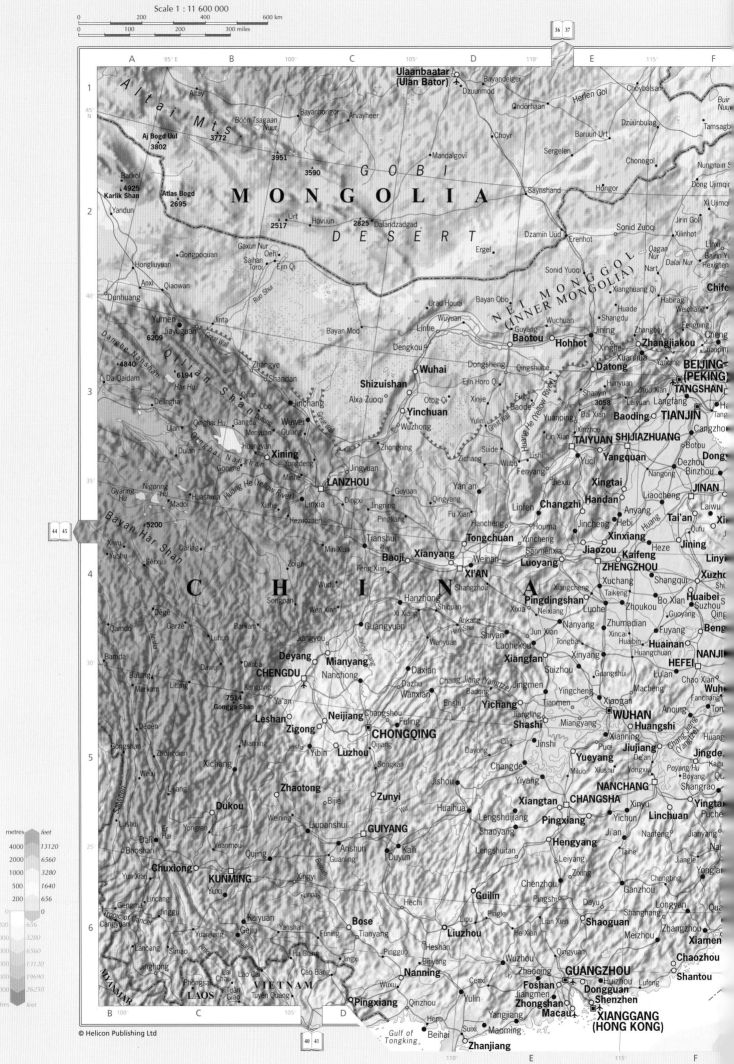

Scale 1 : 11 600 000

© Helicon Publishing Ltd

SEA OF
JAPAN

YELLOW
SEA

EAST
CHINA SEA

PACIFIC
OCEAN

HONSHŪ

HOKKAIDŌ

JAPAN

SHIKOKU

KYŪSHŪ

TAIWAN

Nansei-shotō
(Ryukyu Islands)

Tropic of Cancer

Cities and places (reading map):

QIQIHAR, Bei'an, Yichun, Hegang, Jiamusi, Suihua, Daqing, Anda, Lanxi, HARBIN, Horqin Youyi Qianqi, Baicheng, Tuquan, Tao'an, Zhaoyuan, Fuyu, Da'an, Tongyu, Taipingchuan, Acheng, Shangzhi, Wuchang, Yilan, Fangzheng, Jixi, Muling, Lesozavodsk, Svetlaya, Bikin

Tongliao, Ar Horqin Qi, Shuangliao, Kangping, Faku, Zhangwu, Jurhe, CHANGCHUN, Siping, Liaoyuan, Tieling, JILIN, Naizishan, Huadian, Hailong, Huinan, Qingyuan, Dongjingcheng, Dunhua, Antu, Tumen, Vladivostok, Nakhodka, Ussuriysk, Grodekovo, Ozero Khanka, Spassk-Dal'niy, Rudnaya Pristan', Mys Povorotnyy

Fuxin, SHENYANG, FUSHUN, Liaoyang, Benxi, Jinzhou, ANSHAN, Jinxi, Dawa, Haicheng, Yingkou, Suizhou, Dandong, Sinŭiju, Kuandian, Huanren, Manp'o, Ch'osan, Pukch'ŏng, Kimch'aek, Ch'ŏngjin, Najin, Myŏnggan, Kilchu, Kapsan, Hyesan, Linjiang, Hunjiang, NORTH KOREA, Hamhŭng, Chŏngp'yŏng, Wŏnsan, Kosŏng

Qinhuangdao, Wafangdian, Xinjin, Zhuanghe, Changhai, Lüshun, DALIAN, Nampʻo, P'YŎNGYANG, Songnim, Sariwŏn, Haeju, Kaesŏng, Kangnŭng, Sokch'o, Tonghae, Ulchin, Kimchaek

Miaodao Qundao, Yantai, Weihai, Rongcheng, Shandong Bandao, QINGDAO, Xian, SŎUL (SEOUL), INCH'ŎN, Suwŏn, Anyang, Ch'ŏngju, SOUTH KOREA, TAEJŎN, Kunsan, Ch'ŏnju, TAEGU, KWANGJU, PUSAN, P'ohang, Andong, Mokp'o, Sunch'ŏn

Ullŭng do, Tok-tō, Oki-shotō, Dōgo, Dōzen, Nanao, Toyama, Kanazawa, Fukui, Tsuruoka, Matsumoto, Nagano, Maebashi, Kōfu, Fuji-san 3776, Shizuoka, Gifu, NAGOYA, Suzuka, Hamamatsu, Matsusaka, KYOTO, OSAKA, KŌBE, Okayama, Takamatsu, Wakayama, Tokushima, Kōchi, Nakamura, Shiono-misaki

Cheju, Cheju do (South Korea), Gotō-rettō, Fukue-jima, Sasebo, Ōmuta, Omuta, KITA-KYŪSHŪ, Shimonoseki, FUKUOKA, Kurume, Ōita, Nagasaki, Yatsushiro, Kumamoto, Nobeoka, Akune, Miyazaki, Miyakonojō, Kagoshima, Makurazaki, Kanoya, Ōsumi-shotō, Tanega-shima, Yaku-shima

Yancheng, Xinghua, Taizhou, Taizhou, Nantong, Changzhou, Changshu, SHANGHAI, Jiaxing, Haining, Yuyao, Zhenhai, NINGBO, Fenghua, Ninghai, Jinhua, Linhai, Huangyan, Wenzhou, Rui'an, Fuding, Ningde

SAPPORO, Asahikawa, Asahi-dake 2290, Takikawa, Otaru, Tomakomai, Obihiro, Kushiro, Wakkanai, Esashi, Monbetsu, Abashiri, Shibetsu, Kitami, Nemuro, Shikotan-tō, Kunashir, Ostrov Iturup

Hakodate, Matsumae, Esashi, Oshima-hantō, Aomori, Hirosaki, Mutsu, Hachinohe, Ōdate, Noshiro, Morioka, Akita, Hanamaki, Kamaishi, Ichinoseki, Sakata, Furukawa, Ishinomaki, Shinjō, Yamagata, Sendai, Niigata, Fukushima, Kōriyama, Iwaki, Utsunomiya, Mito, Nagano, TOKYO, YOKOHAMA, Kashima

Chilung, T'aoyüan, T'AIPEI, Hsinchu, 3884, Hsüeh Shan, T'aichung, Chiai, 3950, Yu Shan, T'aitung, P'ingtung, KAOHSIUNG, Matsu (Taiwan), Oluanpi, Sakishima-shotō, Nago, Okinawa, Naha, Amami-Ōshima, Naze

0 100 200 300 400 600 km
0 100 200 300 miles

95 E · B · 100 · C · 105 · D · 110

BHUTAN
Tashigang · Hápoli · Pangin · Zayü · Dêgên · Gongshan · Zhongdian · Xichang · Zunyi · Huaihua
Barpeta · Itanagar · Dibrugarh · Tazungdam · Putao · Weixi · Lijiang · Bijie · Weining · Liupanshui · **GUIYANG**
Goalpara · Nagaon · Jorhat · Golaghat · Tabong · Maingkwan · **DUKOU** · Yongren · Yuanmou · Qujing · Anshun · Duyun · Kaili
I N D I A · Dimapur · Kohima · Myitkyina · Mogaung · Hopin · Lushui · Dali · **KUNMING** · Xingyi · Guanling · Guilin
Shillong · Imphal · Silchar · Chindwin · Baoshan · Yuanjiang · **Chuxiong** · Yanshan · Funing · Hechi · Yangsi
Sylhet · Mawlaik · Wandingzhen · Mong Yu · Gengma · Lincang · Simao · Lao Cai · Jingxi · Pingguo · Binyang · **Nanning**
Bhairab Bazar · Aizawl · Bhamo · Katha · Hsweni · Lashio · Cangyuan · Jinghong · Lai Chau · Cao Bang · Wuxu · Qinzhou
Comilla · Tropic of Cancer · Karnafuli Reservoir · Kalemyo · Kanbalu · Mabein · Mong Yai · Mongkung · Kunhing · Muang Sing · Phongsali · Tuyên Quang · Thai Nguyen · **Pingxiang** · Hepu · **Nanning**
Feni · Rangamati · Saiha · Haka · Chindwin · Mogok · Simao · Muang Namtha · Louang · Son La · Việt Tri · **HA NỘI (HANOI)** · Tien Yen · Beihai
CHITTAGONG · Kalewa · Monywa · Shwebo · **MANDALAY** · Amarapura · Kyaukse · Kengtung · Muang Khoua · Môc Châu · Hòn Gai · **Zhanjia**
BANGLADESH · Cox's Bazar · Paletwa 3053 Mt. Victoria · Pakokku · Myingyan · Taung-gyi · Mong Yai · Wan Hsa-la · Xam Nua · Ninh Binh · **HAI PHONG** · Haiko
Teknaf · Chauk · Meiktila · Louangphrabang · Ban Ban · Nam Dinh · Gulf of Tongking · Dan Xian · Wen
Sittwe · Magwe · Minbu · Taungdwingyi · Salween · Xianghoang · **LAOS** · Vinh · Ha Tinh · Dongfang · Hai-nan · Qiongshan
Kyaukpyu · Ramree Island · Sinbaungwe · Loikaw · Chiang Rai · Nan · **Viangchan (Vientiane)** · Muang Pakxan · Khamkkeut · Tongshi · Sanya
Bay of Bengal · Cheduba Island · Taungup · Pyè · Pasawng · Mae Hong Son · Chiang Mai · Sin Kit Dam · Chiang Khan · Nong Khai · Dông Hôi
Sandoway · Zigon · Irrawaddy · Lampang · Mae Sariang · Uttaradit · Loei · Udon Thani · Sakhon Nakhon · Muang Khammouan · Quang Tri · **Huê**
Kyeintali · Henzada · Papun · Chum Phae · Muang Phin · **Da Nẵng** · Hôi An
Bassein · Pegu · Insein · Thaton · Nam Ping · Phitsanulok · Phichit · Khon Kaen · Mukdahan · Savannakhet · Ban
Myaungmya · **YANGON (RANGOON)** · Moulmein · Tak · Chaiyaphum · Lam Chi · Khemmarat · M. Khôngxêđôn · Pakxé · **VIETNAM** · Quang Ngai
Cape Negrais · Bogale · Labutta · Kawkareik · Nakhon Sawan · Roi Et · Ban Suwannaphum · Muang Ubon Ratchathani · Attapu
Mouths of the Irrawaddy · Ye · Sangkhla Buri · Chainat · Mae Nam Mun · Surin · Det Udom · Kon Tum · Qui Nho
Preparis North Channel · Gulf of Martaban · Nakhon Ratchasima · Ayutthaya · Sara Buri · **T H A I L A N D** · Phumĭ Sâmraông · M. Không · Virôchey · Plây Cu
Preparis Island · Preparis South Channel · Tavoy · **KRUNG THEP (BANGKOK)** · Aranyaprathet · Sisôphôn · Siĕmréab · Stœ̆ng Trêng · **Buôn Mê Thuôt** · Tuy Hoa
Coco Channel · Coco Island · Rat Buri · Phet Buri · Samut Songkhram · Bight of Bangkok · Pattaya · Rayong · Bătdâmbâng · Tônlé Sab · **CAMBODIA** · Da Lat · **Nha Trang** · Ninh Hoa
North Andaman · Andaman Islands (India) · Palaw · Ban Hua Hin · Chánthaburi · Ko Chang · Kâmpóng Chhnang · Bao Lôc · Cam Ranh
Middle Andaman · Ritchie's Archipelago · Mergui · Prachuap Khiri Khan · Krŏng Kaôh Kŏng · Ta Khmau · Chon Thanh · Biên Hoa · Phan Rang
South Andaman · Port Blair · Bang Saphan Yai · **Phnum Penh** · Kâmpôt · Tay Ninh · **HÔ CHI MINH (SAIGON)** · Phan Thiêt
Duncan Passage · Little Andaman · **A n d a m a n** · Chumphon · Gulf of Thailand · Sihanoukville · Long Xuyên · My Tho · Vung Tau
Ten Degree Channel · Kawthaung · Ranong · Dao Phu Quoc · Kâmpôt · Rach Gia · **Cân Thơ** · Mouths of the Mekong
Car Nicobar · **S e a** · Takua Pa · Ko Samui · Surat Thani · **Cân Thơ** · Bac Liêu · Ca Mau · Côn Son
Katchall · Nicobar Islands (India) · Krabi · Phuket · Nakhon Si Thammarat · Nam Can
Little Nicobar · Great Nicobar · Thùng Song · Phatthalung · Trang · Thale Luang · Songkhla · Hat Yai · Pattani
Satun · Langkawi · Kangar · Yala · Narathiwat
Sabang · Alor Setar · Ban Betong · Kota Bharu
Banda Aceh · Sungei Petani · Gerik · Kuala Kerai · **M A L A Y**
Bireun · George Town · Pinang · Kuala Terengganu · Laut
Lhokseumawe · Taiping · G. Korbu 2182 · Dungun · Kemasik
Langsa · **Ipoh** · Kuala Lipis · Malay · Natuna Besar · Panarik
Takengon · **I N D I A N** · Kuantan · Kepulauan Natuna
Meulaboh · Bagun Datuk · Temerloh · Peninsula · Kepulauan Anambas (Indonesia)
S U M A T E R A (SUMATRA) 3145 Gunung Leuser · **MEDAN** · Tebingtinggi · Bentung · Subi Besar
O C E A N · Sibigo · Langsa · Takengon · Danau Toba · **KUALA LUMPUR** · Seremban · Jemaja · Natuna Tanjung Datu
Simeulue · Sinabang · Pematangsiantar · Prapat · Segamat · Mersing · Keluang
Singkilbaru · Barus · Balige · Bagansiapiapi · Melaka · Muar
Sibolga · Kotapinang · Dumai · Batu Rahat · **SINGAPORE**
Nias · Gunungsitoli · Duri · **INDONESIA** · **Johor Bahru** · **SINGAPORE** · Sambas · Pemangkat · Ku

metres / feet
4000 / 13120
2000 / 6560
1000 / 3280
500 / 1640
200 / 656
0 / 0
200 / 656
1000 / 3280
2000 / 6560
4000 / 13120
6000 / 19690
8000 / 26250
metres / feet

44 45 · 42 43

SOUTHEAST ASIA

Cambodia • Laos • Myanmar (Burma)
Philippines • Thailand • Vietnam

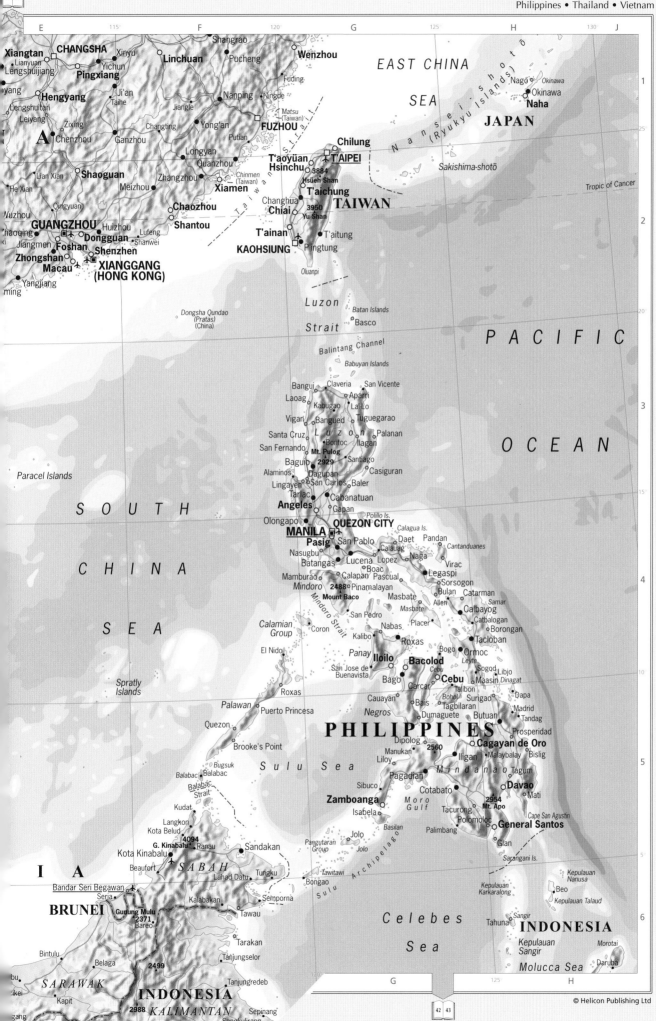

E   115°   F   120°   G   125°   H   130°   J

China / Taiwan region

Xiangtan **CHANGSHA** Xinyu Shangrao
Lianyuan **Linchuan** Pucheng **Wenzhou**
Lengshuijiang Yichun
yang **Pingxiang** Ji'an Taihe Nanping Ningde
Hengyang Changting Jiangle Fuding
Lengshuitan Zixing Ganzhou Yong'an Matsu (Taiwan) **Chilung**
A Chenzhou Longyan Putian **FUZHOU** **T'aipei**
He Xian **Shaoguan** Quanzhou Chinmen (Taiwan) 3884 **Hsinchu** **T'aoyüan**
Wuzhou Qingyuan Meizhou Zhangzhou **Xiamen** Hsüeh Shan
haoqing **GUANGZHOU** Huizhou Lufeng **Chaozhou** Changhua **T'aichung** 3950
xi Jiangmen Dongguan Shanwei **Shantou** **Chiai** Yu Shan **TAIWAN**
Zhongshan **Foshan** Shenzhen **T'ainan** T'aitung
Macau **XIANGGANG** **KAOHSIUNG** P'ingtung
Yangjiang (HONG KONG) Oluanpi
ming

EAST CHINA SEA

Nago Okinawa
Okinawa
Naha **JAPAN**

Sakishima-shotō

Tropic of Cancer

Luzon Strait Batan Islands
Basco

Balintang Channel

Babuyan Islands

PACIFIC OCEAN

Dongsha Qundao (Pratas) (China)

Paracel Islands

S O U T H

C H I N A

S E A

Bangui Claveria San Vicente
Laoag Kabugao Lal-lo Aparri
Vigan Bangued Tuguegarao
Santa Cruz *Luzon* Palanan
San Fernando Bontoc Ilagan
Baguio Mt. Pulog Santiago
Alaminos 2929 Casiguran
Lingayen Dagupan Baler
Tarlac San Carlos
Angeles Cabanatuan
Olongapo Gapan Polillo Is.
QUEZON CITY Calagua Is.
MANILA San Pablo Daet Pandan
Pasig Calauag *Cantanduanes*
Nasugbu Naga Virac
Batangas **Lucena** Lopez
Mamburao Calapan Boac Legaspi
Mindoro Pinamalayan Pascual Sorsogon
2488 Masbate Bulan Catarman
Mount Baco *Masbate* Allen *Samar*
Mindoro Strait San Pedro Calbayog
Calamian Nabas Placer Catbalogan
Group Coron Kalibo Roxas Bogo *Leyte* Borongan
El Nido *Panay* **Iloilo** *Cebu* Ormoc Tacloban
San Jose de **Bacolod** Sogod Libjo
Buenavista Bago **Cebu** Maasin Dinagat
Roxas Carcar Talibon Surigao Dapa
Spratly Islands Cauayan *Bohol* Madrid
Palawan Bais Tagbilaran Butuan Tandag
Puerto Princesa *Negros* Dumaguete Prosperidad
Quezon **PHILIPPINES** Dipolog **Cagayan de Oro**
Brooke's Point Manukan 2560 Iligan Bislig
Liloy Malaybalay
Sulu Sea Pagadian *Mindanao* **Tagum**
Bugsuk Sibuco Cotabato **Davao**
Balabac Balabac **Zamboanga** *Moro* 2954 Mati
Kudat Isabela *Gulf* Mt. Apo
Balabac Strait Jolo Tacurong Cape San Agustin
Langkon Palimbang Polomoloc **General Santos**
Kota Belud *Basilan* Glan
G. Kinabalu Ranau Jolo
Kota Kinabalu 4094 Sandakan *Pangutaran* Sarangani Is.
Beaufort *SABAH* *Group* Bongao *Kepulauan Talaud*
I   A Lahad Datu Tungku *Tawitawi* *Sulu Archipelago* Kepulauan Karkaralong Beo
Bandar Seri Begawan Kalabakan Semporna Bongao Nanusa
Seria Tawau Tahuna Sangir **INDONESIA**
BRUNEI Gurung Mulu Kalabakan *Celebes* Kepulauan Talaud
2371 Bareo *Sea* Kepulauan
Bintulu Belaga Tarakan Sangir Morotai
2499 Tanjungselor *Molucca Sea* Daruba
SARAWAK Kapit **INDONESIA** Tanjungredeb
gang 2988 *KALIMANTAN* Sepinang
Muarawahau Sangkulirang

Nansei-shotō (Ryukyu Islands)

Taiwan Strait

Calamian Group

E   115°   F   120°

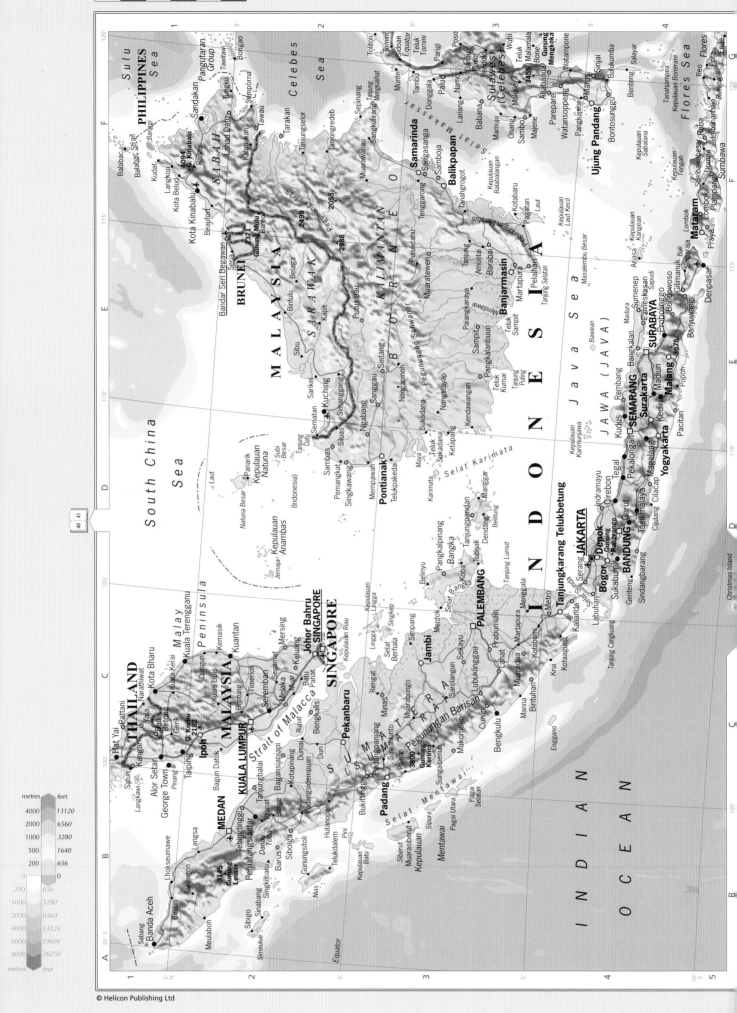

Scale 1 : 11 600 000

| 0 | 200 | 400 | 600 km |
| 0 | 100 | 200 | 300 miles |

South China Sea

Celebes Sea

Sulu Sea

INDIAN OCEAN

Java Sea

Flores Sea

PHILIPPINES

BRUNEI
Bandar Seri Begawan

MALAYSIA

SARAWAK

SABAH

KALIMANTAN

B O R N E O

INDONESIA

THAILAND

MALAYSIA
KUALA LUMPUR

SINGAPORE
Johor Bahru

SUMATRA

Pegunungan Barisan

JAWA (JAVA)

JAKARTA

Cities and towns:
Banda Aceh, Meulaboh, Lhokseumawe, Langsa, Takengon, Sibigo, Sinabang, Simeulue, Gunung Leuser 3145, Medan, Pematangsiantar, Tebingtinggi, Pematangsiantar, Rapat, Balige, Danau Toba, Sibolga, Gunungsitoli, Nias, Kepulauan Batu, Barus, Singkilbaru, Hutanopan, Padangsidempuan, Tanjungbalai, Bagansiapiapi, Kotapinang, Pekanbaru, Dumai, Bengkalis, Rupat, Duri, Minas, Padangpanjang, Bukittinggi, Padang, Gunung Kerinci 3800, Sungaipenuh, Sarolangun, Muarabungo, Rengat, Jambi, Sekayu, Lubuklinggau, Curup, Bengkulu, Lahat, Muaradua, Kotabumi, Krui, Manna, Bintuhan, Enggano, Palembang, Prabumulih, Metro, Menggala, Martapura, Kotaagung, Kalianda, Labuhan, Tanjungkarang Telukbetung, Serang, Bogor, Depok, JAKARTA, Bandung, Cianjur, Sukabumi, Garut, Tasikmalaya, Cilacap, Cirebon, Indramayu, Tegal, Pekalongan, SEMARANG, Kudus, Rembang, Magelang, Yogyakarta, Surakarta, Madiun, Kediri, Malang 3676, SURABAYA, Bangkalan, Madura, Sumenep, Pamekasan, Probolinggo, Bondowoso, Banyuwangi, Denpasar, Bali, Lombok, MATARAM, Praya, Sumbawa Besar, Plampang, Sumbawa, Flores, Ende, Reo

SATUN, Hat Yai, Pattani, Narathiwat, Yala, Kota Bharu, Kuala Terengganu, Kangar, Langkawi, Alor Setar, George Town, Pinang, Taiping, Gerik, Betong, Kuala Lipis, Kuantan, Ipoh, G. Korbu 2182, Kemasik, Dungun, Temerloh, Bentung, Seremban, Melaka, Muar, Batu Pahat, Keluang, Mersing, Segamat, Kluang, Kepulauan Riau, Pangkalpinang, Bangka, Selat Bangka, Koba, Toboali, Belinyu, Dendang, Belitung, Manggar, Tanjungpandan, Tanjung Cangkuang, Selat Sunda

Kuching, Sibu, Bintulu, Belaga, Kapit, Sarikei, Sri Aman, Gunung Mulu 2371, Miri, Serian, Simanggang, Ngabang, Sanggau, Sintang, Putussibau, Nangapinoh, Nangatayap, Ketapang, Sukadana, Pontianak, Telukpakedai, Mempawah, Singkawang, Pemangkat, Sambas, Tanjung Datu, Tanjung Sambar, Sampit, Palangkaraya, Pangkalanbuun, Kendawangan, Kuala Kapuas, Muaratewuh, Muarawahau, Banjarmasin, Martapura, Pleihari, Tanjung Selatan, Kotabaru, Amuntai, Barabai, Tanjung, Purukcahu, Pagatan, Samarinda, Sangasanga, Samboja, Balikpapan, Tanahgrogot, Tarakan, Tanjungredeb, Tanjungselor, Sangkulirang, Muarawahau

Tawau, Lahad Datu, Semporna, Tungku, Sandakan, Kudat, Langkon, Kota Belud, G. Kinabalu 4094, Kota Kinabalu, Beaufort, Balabac, Banggi, Balabac Strait, Bongao, Tawitawi, Pangutaran Group, Jolo

Tolitoli, Buol, Gorontalo, Kwandang, Tambu, Palu, Donggala, Poso, Danau Poso, Parigi, Tentena, Kolonodale, Malili, Sulawesi (Celebes), Gunung Mengkoka 2455, Gunung Mengkoka, Kendari, Wawotobi, Kolaka, Watampone, Sengkang, Pangkajene, Watansoppeng, Majene, Mamuju, Onang, Palopo, Malangke, Rantepao, Enrekang, Pinrang, Parepare, Ujung Pandang, Bontosunggu, Bulukumba, Sinjai, Watampone, Teluk Bone, Benteng, Kepulauan Salabana, Kepulauan Tengah, Selayar, Tanahjampea, Kalaotoa, Bonerate, Kepulauan Bonerate

Depth/Height legend:
metres	feet
4000	13120
2000	6560
1000	3280
500	1640
200	656
0	0
200	656
1000	3280
2000	6560
4000	13120
6000	19690
8000	26250
metres	feet

© Helicon Publishing Ltd

40 41

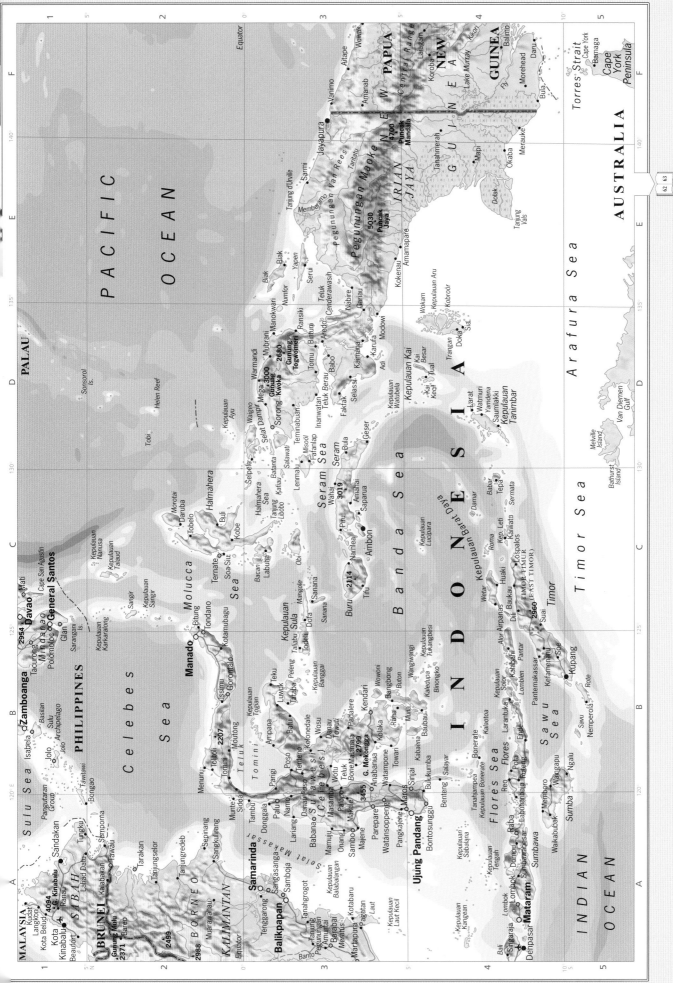

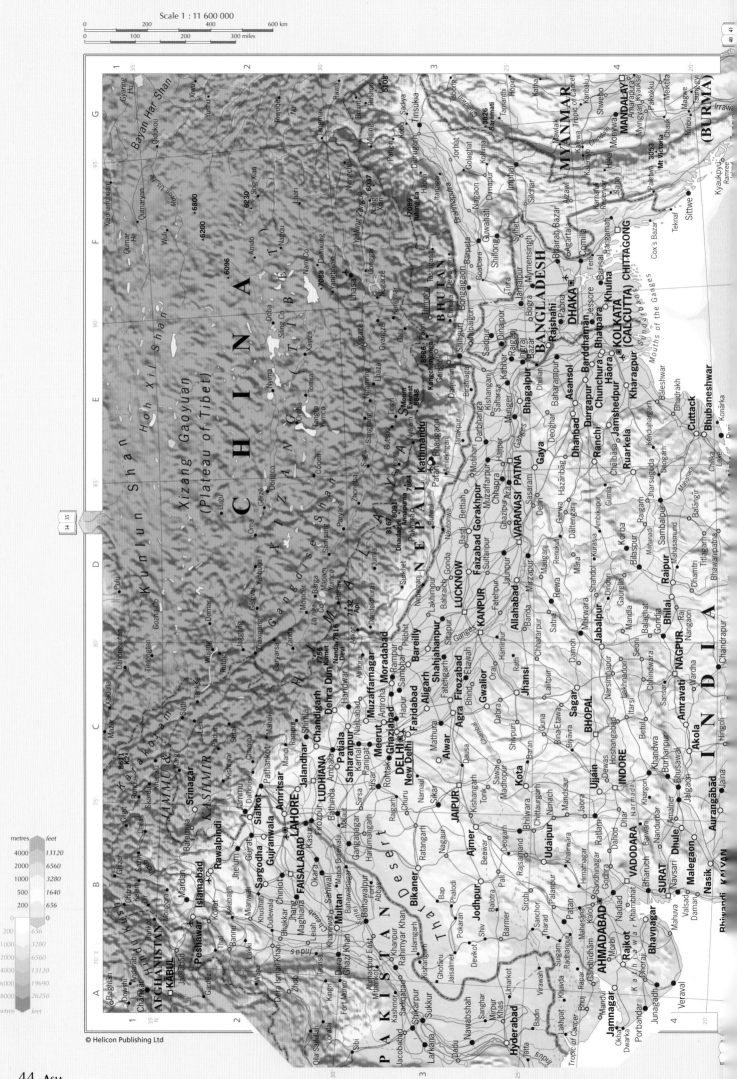

Scale 1 : 11 600 000

© Helicon Publishing Ltd

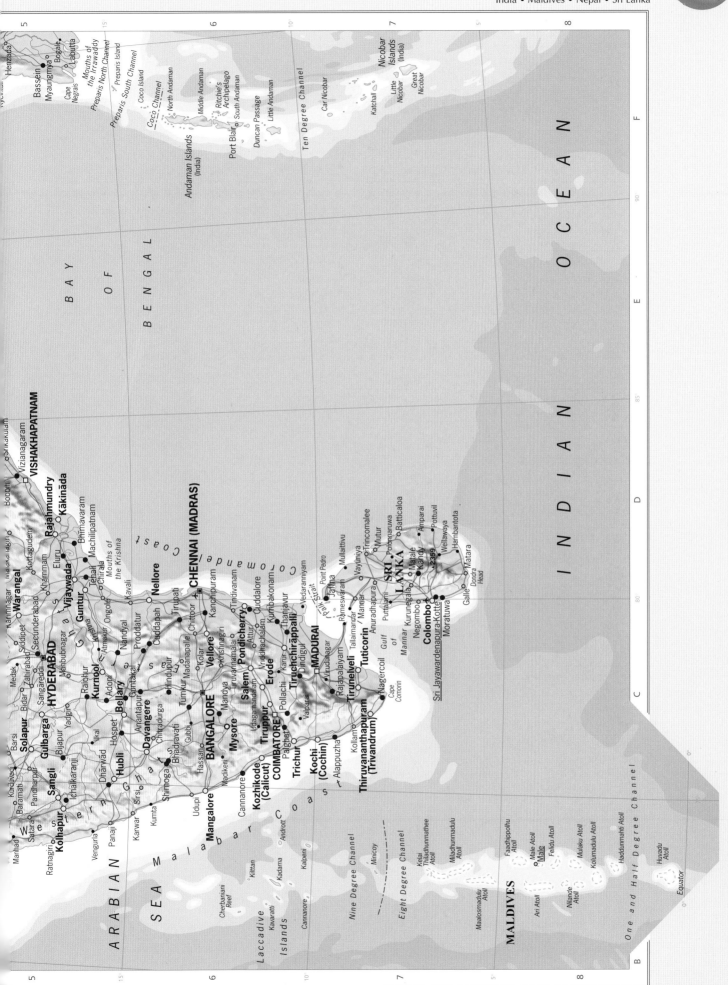

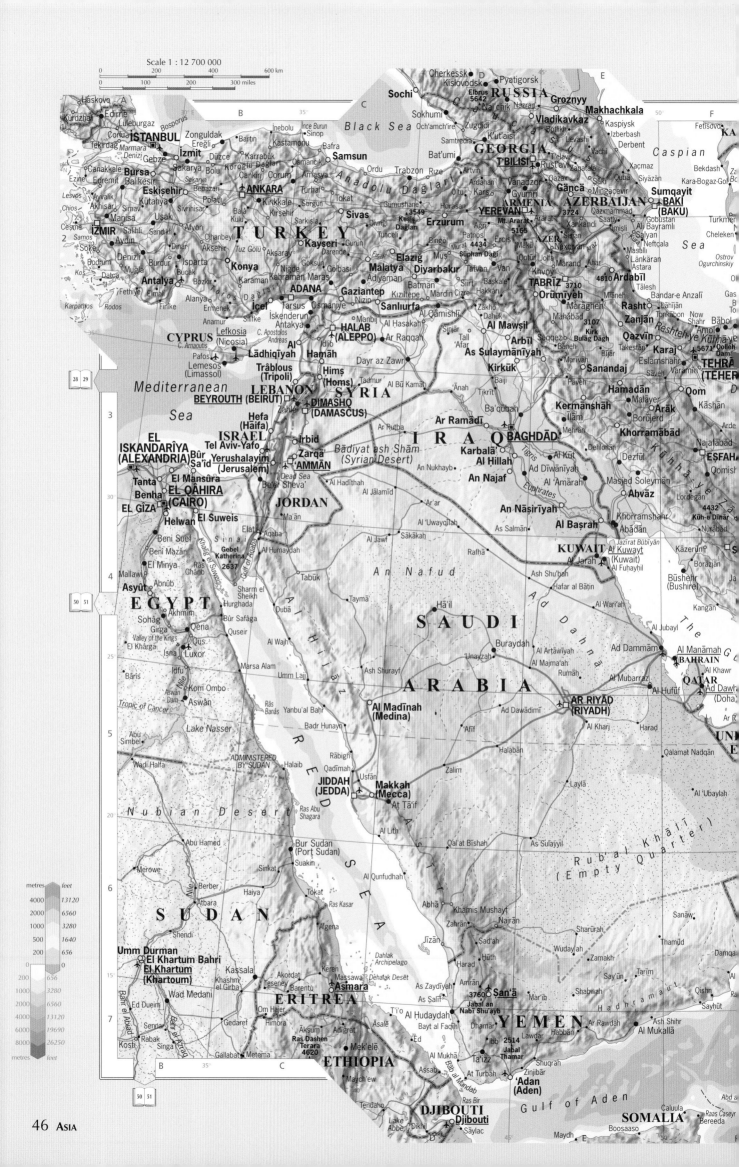

THE MIDDLE EAST

Afghanistan • Armenia • Azerbaijan • Bahrain • Cyprus • Georgia • Iran • Iraq • Israel • Jordan
Kuwait • Lebanon • Oman • Pakistan • Qatar • Saudi Arabia • Syria • Turkey • United Arab Emirates • Yemen

34 35

44 45

UZBEKISTAN

Nukus
Keneurgench
Mangit
Dashkhovuz
Beruni
Turtkul
Mynbulak
Uchkuduk
KAZAKHSTAN
Chirchik Kasansay
Tash-Kumyr
Sanchakou
Urgench
Gaz-Achak
Zarafshan
Ayakkuduk
Chardara
TASHKENT
Angren
Namangan
Uzgen
Osh
Turugart Pass
3752
Tien Shan
Bachu
Chagyl
Darvaza
Kabakly
Chardzhev
Nurata
Ozero Aydarkul'
Gulistan
Almalyk
Margilan
Andizhan
Fergana
KYRGYZSTAN
Khaydarkan
Sary-Tash
Ulugqat
Artux
Kashi
Markit
Shache
Igizyar
Yengisar
Sugun
Yarkant

Gyzylarbat
TURKMENISTAN
Karakumy
Bukhara
Samarkand
Mubarek
Shakhrisabz
Ayni
Obigarm
Jirgatol
Pik 7134
Kommunizma 7495
Kongur Shan 7719
Muztagata 7546
CHINA
Tarim Pendi
Yecheng
Zangguy

Peski
Chardzhou
Karshi
Guzar
Denau
Baysun
Dushanbe
Dangara
Qal'aikhum
Norak
Kulob
TAJIKISTAN
Murghob
5469
Khorugh
Buzai Gumbad
Mazar
Akmeqit
Xaidulla
Dahongliutan
Tianshuihai

OMAN

ARABIAN SEA

© Helicon Publishing Ltd

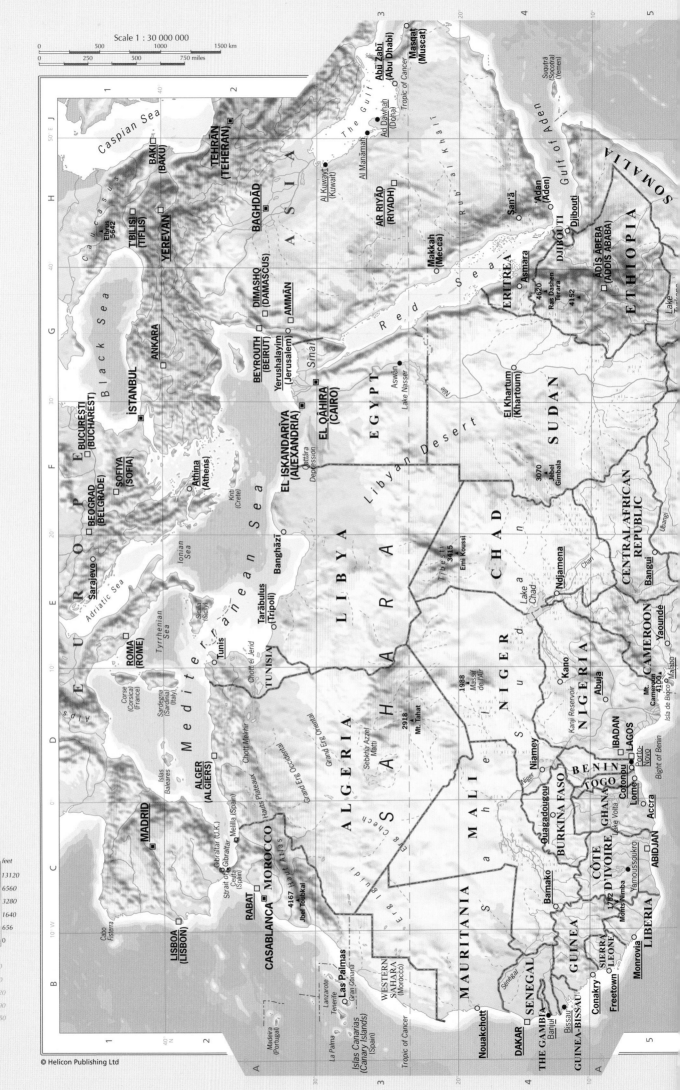

Scale 1 : 30 000 000

metres	feet
4000	13120
2000	6560
1000	3280
500	1640
200	656
0	0
200	656
1000	3280
2000	6560
4000	13120
6000	19690
8000	26250
metres	feet

© Helicon Publishing Ltd

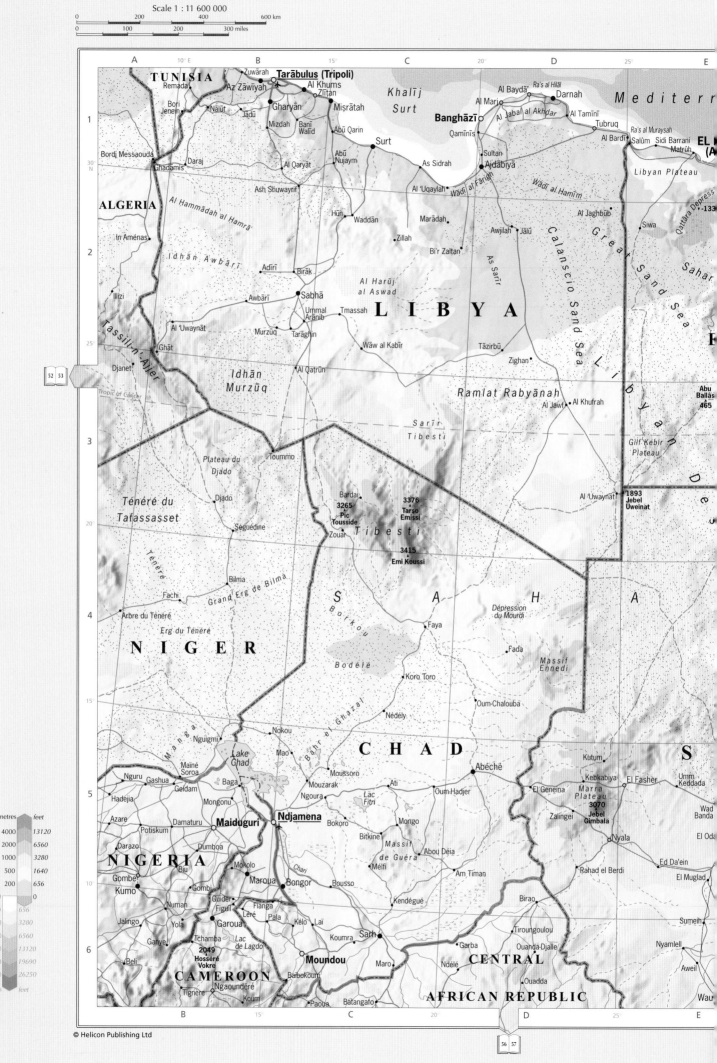

Scale 1 : 11 600 000

metres	feet
4000	13120
2000	6560
1000	3280
500	1640
200	656
0	0
200	656
1000	3280
2000	6560
4000	13120
6000	19690
8000	26250
metres	feet

© Helicon Publishing Ltd

an Sea

LEBANON Saïda
Sour
Hefa (Haifa)
SYRIA
As Suwaydā'
Badiyat ash Shām (Syrian Desert)
IRAQ
Ar Rutba
Karbalā' **Al Hillah** Al Kūt
Deztūl
Soleymān
Masjed

RÍYA
IRA)
Kafr el Dumyât
Sheikh
ISRAEL
Tel Aviv-Yafo
Irbid
Zarqā'
Yerushalayim (Jerusalem)
Gaza
AMMĀN
Negev
Dead Sea
Turayf
Al Qurayyāt
'Ar'ar
As Samāwah
An Nukhayb
An Najaf
An Nāşirīyah
Al 'Amārah
Tigris
Euphrates
Ahvāz
IRAN
Bandar-e
Ma'shur
Khorramshahr
Abādān
Al Başrah

manhûr
Tanta
Benha
Suez Canal
Ismâ'iliya
EL QÂHIRA (CAIRO)
JORDAN
Ma'ān
As Salmān
Al Busayyah
Al Kuwayt
(Kuwait)
KUWAIT
mein
Giza Pyramids
EL GÎZA
Bûr Sa'îd (Port Said)
El Mansûra
Helwan
El Suweis (Suez)
Aqaba
Elat
Sinai
Al Jawf
Rafhā
Ash Shu'bah
Hafar al Bāţin
Al Wafrā'
The Gulf

El Faiyûm
Beni Suef
Beni Mazâr
El Minya
Mallawi
Khalîg el Suweis
Ras
Ghârib
2637
Gebel Katherina
Al Humaydah
Sharm et Sheikh
Al Qalībah
Tabūk
Sharmah
An Nafud
Al 'Uwayqilah
Al Jalamīd
Ad Dawādimī
Al Mazāhimīyah
Al Jubayl

Abnûb
Asyût
Akhmîm
Sohâg
Girga
Qena
Qus
Hurghada
Dubā
Taymā'
Hā'il
Jabal Shammar
Buraydah
'Unayzah
Al Arţāwīyah
Al Majma'ah
Rumāh
Ad Dahnā

El Khârga
Bûlâq
Bâris
Isna
Idfu
Luxor
Valley of the Kings
Kom Ombo
Aswân
Aswân Dam
Lake Nasser
Abu Simbel
Qena
Marsa Alam
Quseir
Bûr Safâga
Al Wajh
Umm Lajj
Hanaĸ
Ash Shurayf
Afīf
SAUDI
ARABIA
AR RIYĀD (RIYADH)
Al Kharj
Harad
Tropic of Cancer

Rås Banâs
Yanbu' al Bahr
Al Madīnah (Medina)
Badr Hunayn
Rābigh
Halabān
Zalim
Laylā

Wâdi Halfa
Akasha
amid
Delgo
Tagab
Nubian Desert
Halaib
Ras Abu Shagara
Muhammad Qol
Dungunab
Qadīmah
Dahabān
Usfān
Makkah (Mecca)
JIDDAH (JEDDA)
At Tā'if
Qal'at Bishah
Aş Sulayyil
Dawqah

A
El Khandaq
Dongola
Ed Debba
Korti
Kerma
Abu Hamed
Keheili
Merowe
Berber
Atbara
Shendi
Al Lith
Al Qunfudhah
Red Sea
Bur Sudan (Port Sudan)
Suakin
Sinkat
Musmar
Haiya
Ras Kasar
Tokar
Derudeb
2780
Algena
Ras Abha
Khamis Mushayt
Zahrān
Najrān
Sharūrah
Sa'dah
Wuday'ah
Zamakh

'Amm Adam
ERITREA
Aroma
Keren
Akordat
Jīzān
Harad
Mīdī
Jazā'ir Farasān
Midi
As Zaydīyah
Mar'ib
Shabwah

Umm Durman (Omdurman)
El Khartum Bahri
Kassala
Khashm el Girba
Teseney
Barentu
Adi Ugri
Asmara
Massawa
Dahlak Archipelago
Dehalak Desēt
Al Hudaydah
Dhamār
San'ā
3760
Jabal an Nabī Shu'ayb
Bayt al Faqīh
YEMEN
Dhamār
Habbān
2514
Jabal Thamar
Lawdar

El Khartum (Khartoum)
Wad Medani
Gedaref
Om Hajer
Himora
Āksum
Adīgrat
Asalē
T'i'o
Subcule
1280
Ed
Ibb
Ta'izz
Al Mukhā
At Turbah
Zīnjibār
Adan (Aden)
Gulf of Aden

El Obeid
Bahr el Abiad
Kosti
Rabak
Singa
Sennar
Dabat
Metema
4620
Ras Dashen Terara
Maych'ew
Mek'elē
Assab
Bāb al Mandab
DJIBOUTI
Ras Bir
Tadjoura
Maydh
Ceerigaabo

Er Rahad
Umm Ruwaba
Gallabat
Gonder
T'ana Hāyk'
Debre Tabor
4193
Ābune Yosēf
4231
Gūna Terara
Mot'a
Bahir Dar
Guba
Tēndaho
Yoboki
Djibouti
Dikhil
Sāylac
Berbera

Ed Dueim
Ed Damazin
Er Renk
Roseires Reservoir
4152
Birhan
Burē
Dese
Gewanē
Cabdul Qaadir
Booraama
Burco

Kadugli
Melut
Kurmuk
Āsosa
Debre Markos
Abay Wenz
4000
Abuye Meda
Dirē Dawa
Hārer
Hargeysa
SOMALIA
Caynabo

N
Ghazâl
Tonga
Malakal
Mendi
Fiche
Mt'eso
Nazrēt
Degeh Bur
Haud
Geladī

Kan
Nasir
Tulu Weiel
3302
Gīmbi
Nek'emtē
Hāgere Hiywet
ĀDĪS ĀBEBA (ADDIS ABABA)
Giyon
Goba
Gīnir
K'ebrī Dehar
Werder

Duk Faiwil
Gambēla
Āgaro
Gorē
3359
Mai Gūdo
K'ech'a Terara
4193
Negele
Goba
ETHIOPIA
Āsela

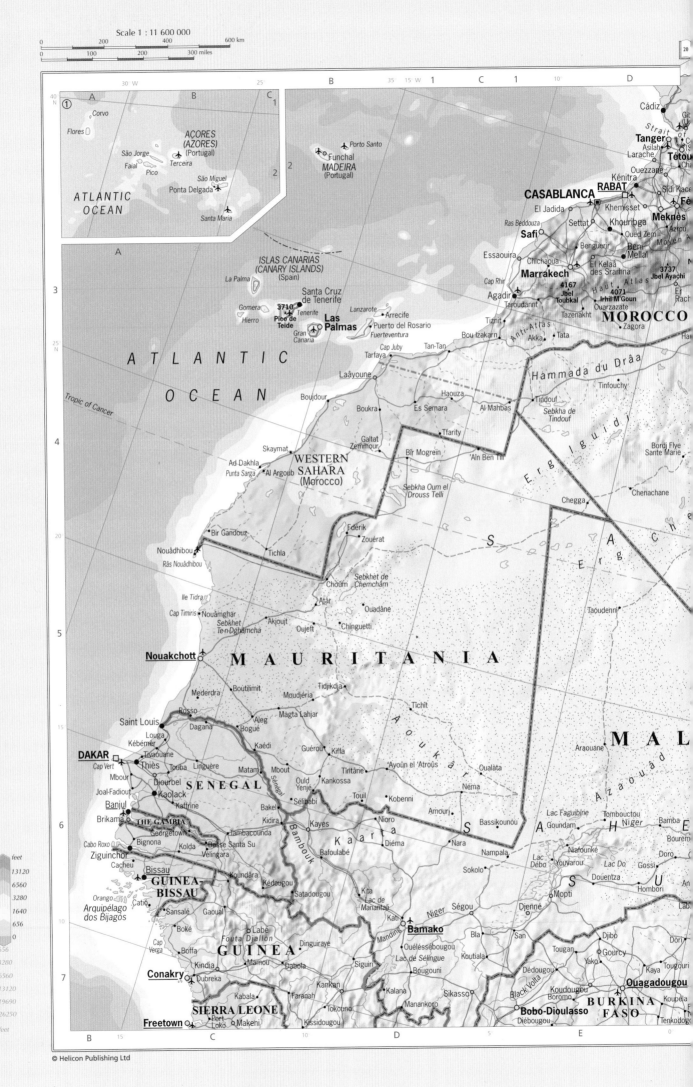

Scale 1 : 11 600 000

metres	feet
4000	13120
2000	6560
1000	3280
500	1640
200	656
0	0
200	656
1000	3280
2000	6560
4000	13120
6000	19690
8000	26250
metres	feet

①

A | B | C

40 N

Corvo

Flores

AÇORES
(AZORES)
(Portugal)

São Jorge
Faial
Pico
Terceira

São Miguel

Ponta Delgada

Santa Maria

ATLANTIC
OCEAN

Porto Santo

Funchal
MADEIRA
(Portugal)

ATLANTIC

OCEAN

ISLAS CANARIAS
(CANARY ISLANDS)
(Spain)

La Palma

Gomera
Hierro
3710
Pico de
Teide
Tenerife
Gran
Canaria

Santa Cruz
de Tenerife

Las
Palmas

Lanzarote
Arrecife

Puerto del Rosario
Fuerteventura

Cádiz

Tanger
Asilah
Larache
Tétou

Ouezzane
Kénitra
RABAT
Sidi Kace
Fè

CASABLANCA
El Jadida
Khemisset
Meknès

Ras Beddouza
Settat
Khouribga
Aztou
Moven A
Safi
Benguerir
Oued Zem

Essaouira
Chichaoua
El Kelaâ
des Srarhna
Beni
Mellal

Cap Rhir
Marrakech
3737
Jbel Ayachi

Agadir
Taroudannt
4167
Jbel
Toubkal
Irhil M'Goun
4071
Haut Atlas
Ouarzazate
Er
Rach
MOROCCO

Tiznit
Bou Izakarn
Tazenakht
Zagora

Cap Juby
Tarfaya
Tan-Tan
Akka
Tata

Anti-Atlas

Hammada du Drâa

Laâyoune
Haouza
Tinfouchy

Boujdour
Es Semara

Al Mahbas
Tindouf
Sebkha de
Tindouf

Boukra

WESTERN
SAHARA
(Morocco)

Galtat
Zemmour

Tfarity

Bîr Mogrein
Aïn Ben Tili

Skaymat

Ad Dakhla

Punta Sarga
Al Argoub

Sebkha Oum el
Drouss Telli

Erg Iguidi

Bordj Flye
Sante Marie

Chenachane

Chegga

Bir Gandouz

S

A

Erg Ach

Tichla

Fdérik
Zouérat

Nouâdhibou
Râs Nouâdhibou

Choûm

Sebkhet de
Chemchâm

Taoudenni

Ile Tidra

Atâr
Ouadâne

Cap Timiris
Nouâmghâr
Akjoujt
Oujeft
Chinguetti

Sebkhet
Te-n-Dghâmcha

Nouakchott

M A U R I T A N I A

Mederdra
Boutilimit

Moudjéria
Tidjikdja

Tichît

Rosso
Aleg
Magta Lahjar

Aoukâr

Araouane

Saint Louis

Louga
Dagana
Bogué

Guérou
Kiffa

Ayoûn el 'Atroûs
Oualâta

Kébémer
Tivaouane
Kaédi

Néma

DAKAR

Cap Vert
Thiès
Touba
Linguère
Matam
Mbout
Tîrîtâne
Kankossa

Kobenni

M A L

Mbour
Diourbel
Ould
Yenjé
Touil

Amouri
Bassikounou
Nioro

Tombouctou
Goundam
Niger
Bamba
E
Bourem

Joal-Fadiout
Kaolack
Kaffrine

SENEGAL

Sélibabi
Kobenni

Nara
Nampala

Doro

Banjul
Brikama
Bakel
Kayes
Diéma
Niafounké
Lac
Débo
Youvarou
Lac Do
Gossi

THE GAMBIA
Kidira
Kaarta
Sokolo
Douentza
Hombori

Cabo Roxo
Georgetown
Tambacounda
Bafoulabé
An

Bignona
Kolda
Basse Santa Su
Niono

Ziguinchor
Cacheu
Vélingara
Koundâra
Kédougou
Kita
Lac de
Manantali
Djenné
S
U

Bissau
Satadougou
Kati
Ségou
Mopti

GUINEA-
BISSAU
Orango
Catió
Sansalé
Gaoual
Bamako
Bla
San
Djibo

Arquipélago
dos Bijagós
Boké
Labé
Dinguiraye
Niger
Koutiala
Tougan
Gourcy

Cap
Verga
Boffa
Fouta Djallon
Ouéléssébougou
Lac de Sélingue
Yako
Kaya
Tougouri

GUINEA
Kindia
Mamou
Dabola
Siguiri
Bougouni
Dédougou
Koudougou
Boromo
Dori

Conakry
Dubreka
Kankan
Kalana
Sikasso
Ouagadougou

Kabala
Faranah
Tokouno
Manankoro
Black Volta
Koudougou
Koupèla

SIERRA LEONE
Kissidougou
Bobo-Dioulasso
BURKINA
FASO

Freetown
Port
Loko
Makeni
Diébougou
Tenkodogo

Tropic of Cancer

30 W
25
20
35 15 W
1
C
1
10
D

B

40 N
A
1
2
35 15 W

B
15
C
10
D
5
E

© Helicon Publishing Ltd

52 Africa

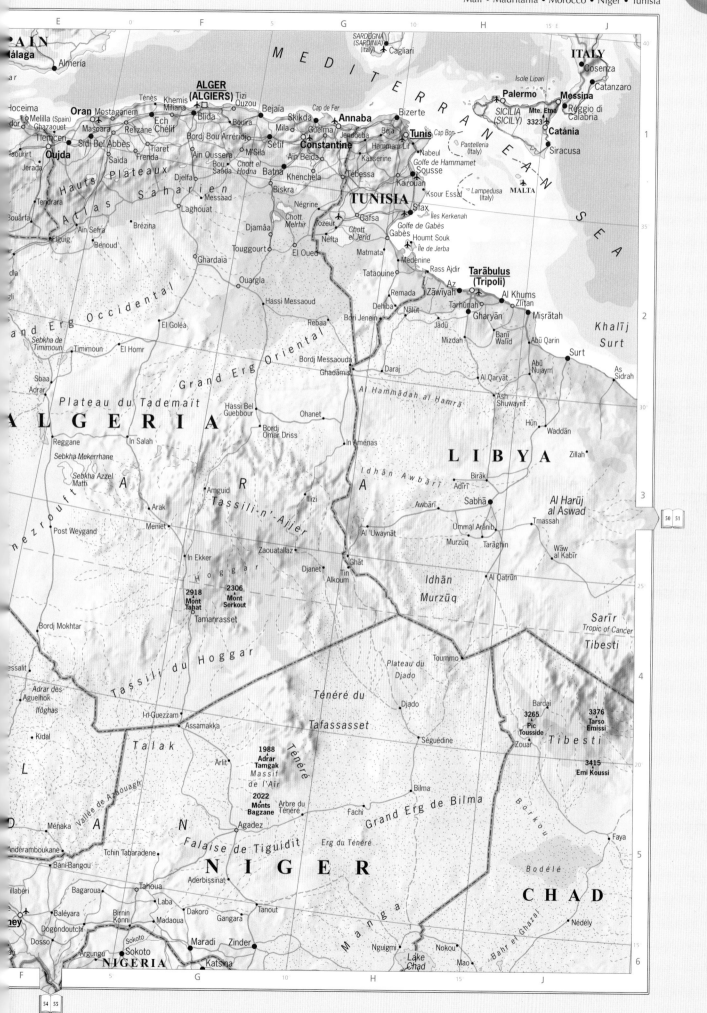

SPAIN
Málaga
Almería

MEDITERRANEAN SEA

SARDEGNA (SARDINIA) (Italy) • Cagliari

ITALY
Cosenza
Catanzaro

Isole Lipari

Palermo
Messina
Reggio di Calabria
SICILIA (SICILY)
Mte. Etna 3323
Catánia
Siracusa

Hoceima
Melilla (Spain)
Ghazaouet
Tlemcen
Oujda
Jerada
Taourirt

Oran
Mostaganem
Mascara
Relizane
Sidi Bel Abbès
Saïda
Frenda
Tiaret

TÉnès
Khemis Miliana
ALGER (ALGIERS)
Tizi Ouzou
Blida
Bouira
Bejaïa
Bordj Bou Arréridj
M'Sila
Aïn Oussera
Bou Saâda
Djelfa

Ech Chélif

Cap de Fer
Skikda
Mila
Constantine
Aïn Beïda
Sétif
Batna
Khenchela
Biskra

Annaba
Guelma
Jendouba
Béja
Hammam Lif
Kasserine
Tébessa

Bizerte
Tunis
Cap Bon
Nabeul

Pantelleria (Italy)

MALTA

Golfe de Hammamet
Sousse
Kairouan

TUNISIA
Sfax
Îles Kerkenah
Lampedusa (Italy)

Messaad
Laghouat
Brézina
Aïn Sefra
Bénoud
Figuig
Ain Sefra

Hauts Plateaux
Atlas Saharien

Djamâa
Touggourt
El Oued

Chott Melrhir
Négrine
Tozeur
Netta
Chott el Jerid

Gafsa
Gabès
Golfe de Gabès
Houmt Souk
Île de Jerba
Matmata
Medenine

Ghardaïa
Ouargla
Hassi Messaoud

Tataouine
Rass Ajdir

Tarābulus (Tripoli)
Az Zāwiyah
Al Khums
Zlīṭan
Misrātah

Grand Erg Occidental

Sebkha de Timimoun
Timimoun
El Homr

El Goléa

Rebaa
Borj Jenien
Dehiba
Nālūt
Tarhūnah
Gharyān
Jādū

Khalīj Surt

Grand Erg Oriental

Bordj Messaouda
Ghadāmis
Daraj

Mizdah
Banī Walīd
Abū Qarin

Abū Nujaym
Surt
As Sidrah

Plateau du Tademaït

Sbaa
Adrar

Hassi Bel Guebbour
Ohanet
Bordj Omar Driss

Al Hammādah al Hamrā

Al Qaryāt
Ash Shuwayrif

ALGERIA

Reggane
In Salah
Sebkha Mekerrhane
Sebkha Azzel Matti

In Aménas

LIBYA

Hūn
Waddān

Zillah

A
R
Amguid
Arak
Meniet
Tassili-n'-Ajjer
Illizi

Idhān Awbārī

Birāk
Adirī
Awbārī
Sabhā
Ummal Arānib
Murzūq
Tarāghin

Al Harūj al Aswad
Tmassah

nezrouft
Post Weygand
In Ekker
Zaouatallaz
Al 'Uwaynāt

Wāw al Kabīr

Hoggar
2918 Mont Tahat
2306 Mont Serkout
Tamanrasset

Djanet
Ghāt
Tin Alkoum

Idhān Murzūq

Al Qaṭrūn

Sarīr
Tropic of Cancer
Tibesti

Tassili du Hoggar

Bordj Mokhtar

Tessalit
Adrar des Aguelhok
Ifôghas
Kidal

In-Guezzam
Assamakka

Toummo

Plateau du Djado
Djado

Bardaï
3265 Pic Toussides
Zouar

3376 Tarso Emissi

Tibesti

Talak

Ténéré du Tafassasset

Séguédine

Arlit
1988 Adrar Tamgak
Massif de l'Aïr
2022 Monts Bagzane

Arbre du Ténéré

Ténéré

Bilma
Fachi

3415 Emi Koussi

L
MÉnaka
Vallée de l'Azaouagh

In-Guezzam

Agadez

Grand Erg de Bilma

Borkou

Andéramboukane
Bani-Bangou
tillabéri

Tchin Tabaradene

Falaise de Tiguidit

Erg du Ténéré

Faya

Bodélé

NIGER

CHAD

ney
Dogondoutchi
Dosso

Bagaroua
Birnin Konni
Laba
Madaoua
Dakoro
Gangara
Tahoua
Aderbissinat
Tanout

Nguigmi
Nokou
Mao

Bahr el Ghazal

Nédély

Argungu
NIGERIA
Maradi
Sokoto
Zinder
Katsina

Lake Chad

Manga

Scale 1 : 11 600 000

© Helicon Publishing Ltd

WEST AFRICA

Benin • Burkina Faso • Cameroon • Cape Verde • Congo • Côte d'Ivoire • Equatorial Guinea • Gabon • The Gambia
Ghana • Guinea • Guinea-Bissau • Liberia • Nigeria • São Tomé & Príncipe • Senegal • Sierra Leone • Togo

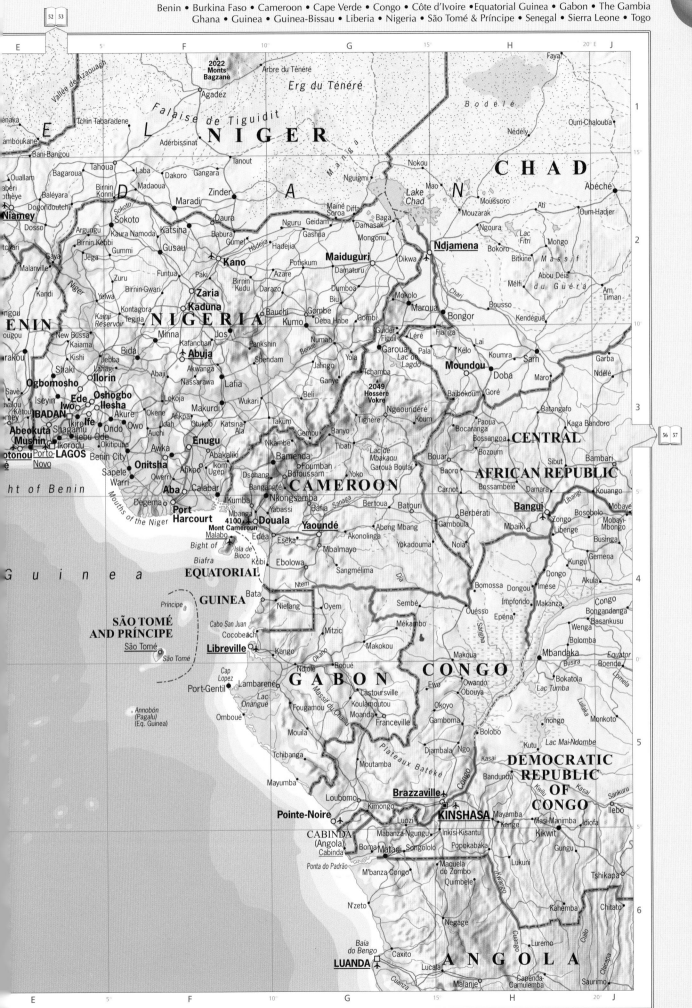

52 53
56 57

E   5°   F   10°   G   15°   H   20° E   J

NIGER

Vallée de Azaouagh
2022
Monts
Bagzane
Arbre du Ténéré
Erg du Ténéré
Faya
Bodélé

Falaise de Tiguidit
Agadez
Tchin Tabaradene
Aderbissinat
Tanout
Néde ly
Oum-Chalouba
1

Bani-Bangou
Tahoua
Laba
Dakoro
Gangara
Nguigmi
Nokou
Mao
Ati
Abéché
15°

CHAD

Ouallam
abéri
othèye
Bagaroua
Birnin
Konni
Madaoua
Zinder
Maradi
Daura
Maïné
Soroa
Diffa
Baga
Damasak
Mongonu
Ngoura
Moussoro
Mouzarak
Oum-Hadjer

Niamey
Dosso
Sokoto
Katsina
Nguru
Geidam
Gashua
Hadejia
Damaturu
Dikwa
Ndjamena
Bokoro
*Lac
Fitri*
Mongo
Bitkine
M a s s i f
2

tchari
Gaya
Malanville
Argungu
Birnin Kebbi
Jega
Kaura Namoda
Gummi
Gusau
Funtua
Paki
Birnin
Kudu
Darazo
Azare
Potiskum
Biu
Dumboa
Mokolo
Maroua
Bongor
Bousso
Kendégué
Melfi
Abou Déia
du Guéra
Am
Timan

Kandi
Kano
Zaria
Kaduna
Minna
Jos
Bauchi
Kumo
Gombe
Deba Habe
Gombi
Guider
Figuil
Garoua
Chari
Koumra
Sarh
Garba
Ndélé
3

ENIN
ougou
arakou
New Bussa
Kaiama
Kishi
Yelwa
Kontagora
Tegina
Kafanchan
Pankshin
Shendam
Numan
Yola
Léré
Pala
Lac de
Lagdo
Moundou
Doba
Maro
Batangafo
Kaga Bandoro

Shaki
Ogbomosho
Ilorin
Lafiagi
Jebba
Bida
Lafia
Nassarawa
Akwanga
Jalingo
Ganye
Beli
2049
Hossére
Vokre
Tchamba
Ngaoundéré
Koum
Paoua
Bocaranga
Bossangoa
CENTRAL

Savè
Iseyin
Ede
Oshogbo
Ilesha
Akure
Okene
Ankpa
Makurdi
Wukari
Takum
Gembu
Tibati
Banyo
Bouar
Bozoum
Bossembélé
Damara
AFRICAN REPUBLIC

IBADAN
Ife
Ikirе
Iwo
Ondo
Owo
Auchi
Katsina-
Ala
Nkambe
Bamenda
Foumban
Yoko
Baoro
Carnot
Bambari
Kouango

Abeokuta
Shagamu
Ikorodu
Okitipupa
Awka
Abakaliki
Ikom
Ugep
Dschang
Bafoussam
Bangangté
Garoua Boulaï
Berbérati
Gamboula
Mbaïki
Bangui
Zongo
Bosobolo
Mobaye
Mobayi-
Mbongo
3

Mushin
otonou
LAGOS
Benin City
Onitsha
Owerri
Afikpo
Calabar
CAMEROON
Bertoua
Batouri
Nola
Libenge
Businga
Gemena

Novo
Porto-
Sapele
Warri
Aba
Degema
Kumba
Nkongsamba
Bafia
Abong Mbang
Yokadouma
Bossambélé
Dongo
Kungu
Akula
4

**Port
Harcourt**
Mbanga
Douala
Yaoundé
Akonolinga
Mbalmayo
Carnot
Bomossa
Dongou
Imese
Makanza
Congo
Bongandanga
Basankusu

Mont Cameroun
4100
Malabo
Edéa
Eséka
Sangmélima
Ouésso
Epéna
Mbandaka
Wenga
Bolomba

*Bight of
Biafra*
EQUATORIAL
Isla de
Bioco
Kribi
Ebolowa
Dja
Impfondo
Bokatola
Boende
Busira
Equator
0°

G u i n e a
GUINEA
Bata
Niefang
Oyem
Sembé
Mékambo
Makoua
Mbandaka
Lac Tumba
Monkoto

Príncipe
**SÃO TOMÉ
AND PRÍNCIPE**
Cabo San Juan
Cocobeach
Mitzic
Makokou
Booué
Owando
Obouya
Okoyo
Inongo
Lac Mai-Ndombe
5

São Tomé
São Tomé
Libreville
Kango
GABON
Ndjolé
Boué
CONGO
Ewo
Gamboma
Bolobo
Kutu
Ilebo

Cap
Lopez
Port-Gentil
Lambaréné
Lastoursville
Koulamoutou
Moanda
Franceville
Gambома
Djambala
Ngo
Kasai
DEMOCRATIC

Annobón
(Pagalu)
(Eq. Guinea)
Omboué
*Lac
Onangué*
Massif du Chaillu
Fougamou
Mouila
Plateaux Batéké
Moutamba
Bandundu
REPUBLIC
Kwilu
Sankuru

Tchibanga
Loubomo
Kimongo
Brazzaville
Congo
Mayamba
Kenge
Masi-Manimba
Idiofa
OF
CONGO
Kikwit
5

Mayumba
Pointe-Noire
Luozi
KINSHASA
Mabanza-Ngungu
Inkisi-Kisantu
Popokabaka
Kikwit
Gungu

**CABINDA
(Angola)**
Cabinda
Boma
Matadi
Songololo
Maquela
do Zombo
Quimbele
Lukuni
Tshikapa

Ponta do Padrão
M'banza Congo
Kwango
6

N'zeto
Negage
Luremo
Chitato

*Baía
do Bengo*
Caxito
ANGOLA
Cuango
Capenda
Camulemba
Saurimo

LUANDA
Lucala
Malanje
6

E   5°   F   10°   G   15°   H   20°   J

Scale 1 : 11 600 000

© Helicon Publishing Ltd

CENTRAL AFRICA

Angola • Burundi • Central African Republic • Democratic Republic of Congo
Djibouti • Ethiopia • Kenya • Rwanda • Somalia • Tanzania • Uganda

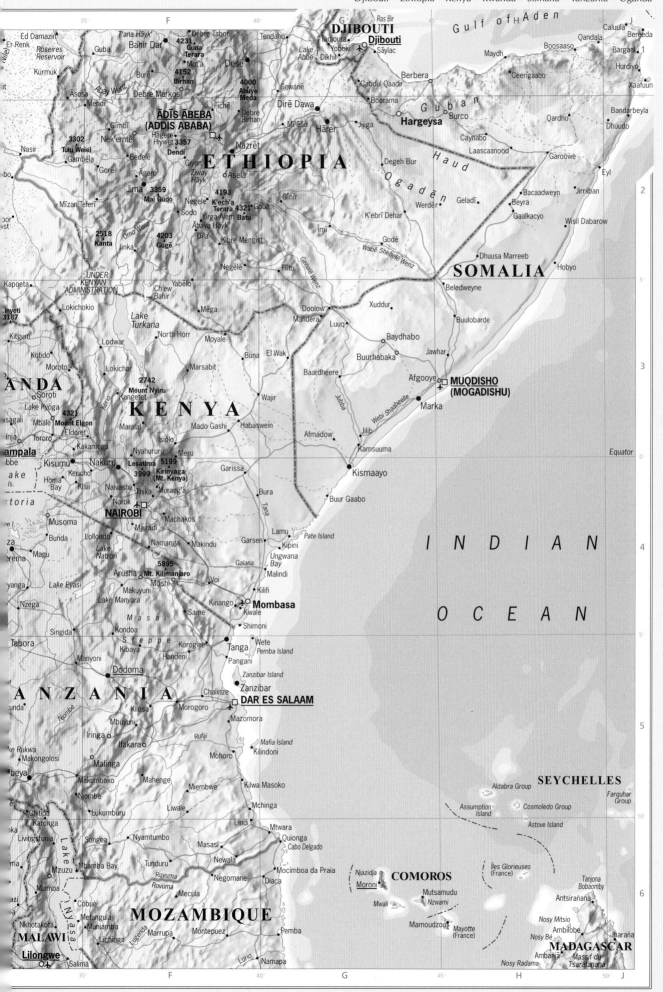

Ed Damazin
Er-Renk
Roseires Reservoir
Kurmuk
Guba
T'ana Hāyk'
Bahir Dar
4231 Guna Terara
Debre Tabor
Tendaho
Ras Bir
Tadjoura
Yoboki
DJIBOUTI
Lake Abbé
Djibouti
Dikhil
Caluula
Bereeda
Qandala
Boosaaso
Bargaal
Hurdiyo
Xaafuun

Asosa
Mendī
Bure
Debre Markos
4152 Birhan
4000 Abūye Meda
Deşē
Mot'a
Gewānē
Dire Dawa
Berbera
Cabdul Qaadir
Boorama
Maydh
Ceerigaabo
Bandarbeyla
Dhuudo

Nasir
Gīmbī
Nek'emte
3302 Tulu Weiel
Gambēla
Gorē
Bedele
Agaro
Fiche
Debre Birhan
ĀDĪS ĀBEBA (ADDIS ABABA)
Hagere Hiywet 3357
Nazrēt
Mp'eso
Harēr
Jijiga
Hargeysa
Burco
Qardho

ETHIOPIA
Mizan Teferī
Jima 3359
Maji Gudo
Negele
K'ech'a Terara 4321
Goba
4193
Gīnīr
Degeh Bur
Werdēr
Geladī
Caynabo
Laascaanood
Garoowe
Eyl

2518 Kanta
Jinka
4203 Gugē
Sodo
Yirga Alem
Ābaya Hāyk'
Batu
Dīla
Kibre Mengist
Īmī
Godē
Wabē Shebelē Wenz
K'ebrī Dehar
Beyra
Gaalkacyo
Jirriiban
Wisil Dabarow

Kapoeta
UNDER KENYAN ADMINISTRATION
Negēlē
Ch'ew Bahir
Yabēlo
Mēga
Filtu
Doolow
Mandera
Xuddur
Dhuusa Marreeb
SOMALIA
Hobyo

inyeti 3187
Lokichokio
Lake Turkana
North Horr
Moyale
Luuq
Baydhabo
Beledweyne
Buulobarde

Kitum
Kotido
Lodwar
Marsabit
El Wak
Buna
Baardheere
Buurhabaka
Jawhar
Afgooye
MUQDISHO (MOGADISHU)

Moroto
Lokichar
Wajir
2742 Mount Nyiru Kangetet
Mado Gashi
Habaswein
Jubba
Marka

Soroti
Mbale
4321 Mount Elgon
Eldoret
Kakamega
Isiolo
Meru
KENYA
Afmadow
Jilib
Kamsuuma
Webi Shabeelle

isagali
Tororo
ampala
Kisumu
Kericho
Nakuru
Nyahururu
Lesatima 5199
Kirinyaga (Mt. Kenya)
3999
Garissa
Kismaayo
Equator

bbe
ake
toria
Homa Bay
Kisii
Naivasha
Thika
Murang'a
Machakos
Bura
Tana
Buur Gaabo

Musoma
Bunda
Narok
NAIROBI
Lamu
Pate Island

za
Magu
Lollondo
Namanga
Makindu
Garsen
Kipini
Ungwana Bay
INDIAN

rema
yanga
Lake Natron
Galana
Malindi

Nzega
Lake Eyasi
5895
Arusha
Mt. Kilimanjaro
Moshi
Voi
Kilifi
OCEAN

Singida
Makuyuni
Lake Manyara
Same
Kinango
Mombasa
Kwale

Tabora
Kondoa
Masai Steppe
Korogwe
Shimoni
Wete
Pemba Island

Manyoni
Kibaya
Handeni
Tanga
Pangani

Dodoma
Kilosa
Morogoro
Zanzibar Island

nda
TANZANIA
Chalinze
Zanzibar
DAR ES SALAAM
Mazomora

Iringa
Mbuyuni
Rufiji

beya
Ifakara
Mohoro
Mafia Island
Kilindoni
SEYCHELLES

ke Rukwa
Makongolosi
Mafinga
Mahenge
Miembwe
Kilwa Masoko
Aldabra Group
Farquhar Group

Njombe
Lukumburu
Liwale
Mchinga
Assumption Island
Cosmoledo Group
Astove Island

Chitipa
Karonga
Lindi
Mtwara

Livingstonia
Songea
Nyamtumbo
Masasi
Quionga
Cabo Delgado
Îles Glorieuses (France)
Tanjona Bobaomby

Mzuzu
Mbamba Bay
Tunduru
Newala
Mocímboa da Praia
COMOROS
Antsiranana

Mzimba
Cóbuè
Mecula
Diaca
Njazidja
Moroni
Mutsamudu
Nzwani
Nosy Mitsio
Ambilobe

MALAWI
Metangula
Maniamba
Marrupa
Montepuez
Pemba
MOZAMBIQUE
Mwali
Mamoudzou
Mayotte (France)
Nosy Bé
Ambanja
MADAGASCAR

Lilongwe
Salima
Lichinga
Lúrio
Namapa
Buwali
Nosy Radama
Massif du Tsaratanana

Scale 1 : 11 600 000

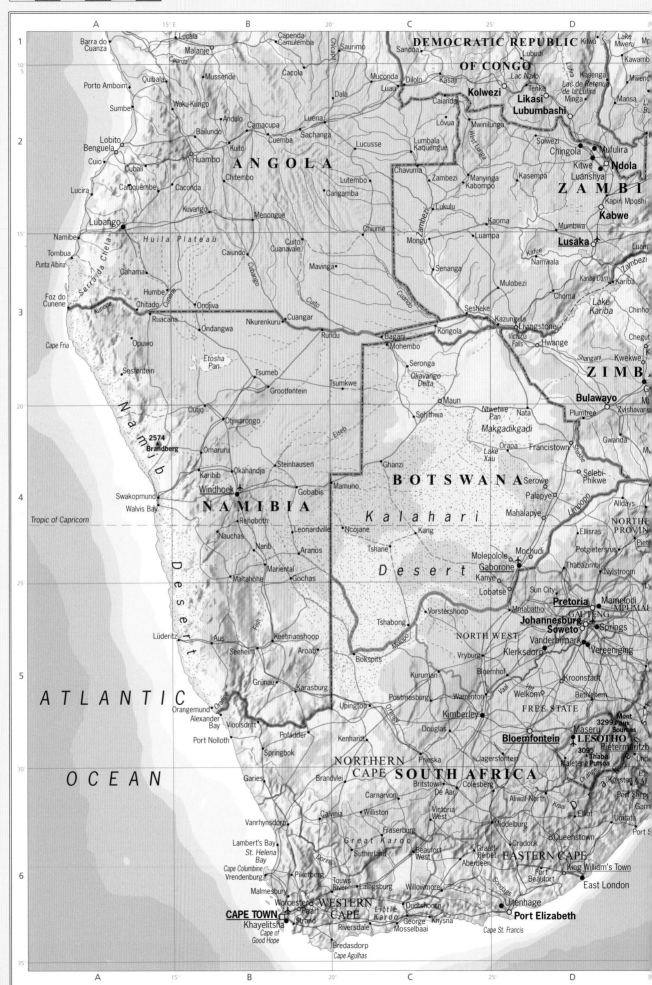

© Helicon Publishing Ltd

SOUTHERN AFRICA

Botswana • Comoros • Lesotho • Madagascar • Malawi • Mauritius
Mozambique • Namibia • Seychelles • South Africa • Swaziland • Zambia • Zimbabwe

SEYCHELLES

Aldabra Group
Assumption Island
Cosmoledo Group
Astove Island
Farquhar Group

COMOROS

Mitsamiouli
Moroni Njazidja
Fomboni
Mwali
Mutsamudu
Nzwami
Mamoudzou
Mayotte (France)

Îles Glorieuses (France)

TANZANIA

Njombe
Nakonde
Chitipa
Karonga
Livingstonia
Isoka
Kasama
Chama
Chikwa
Mzuzu
Mzimba
Mpika
Lundazi
Mfuwe
Chipata
Nkhotakota

MALAWI

Salima
Lilongwe
Dedza
Ulongue
Bene
Songo
Zomba
Lake Chilwa
Blantyre
3002
Monte Namuli
Mount Mulanje
Lichinga
Mandimba
Cuamba
Metangula
Maniamba
Marrupa
Montepuez
Pemba

Lukumburu
Liwale
Lindi
Mtwara
Nyamtumbo
Masasi
Newala
Quionga
Cabo Delgado
Mocímboa da Praia
Diaca
Mecula
Negomane
Mocuba
Moma
Pebane
Namidobe
Quelimane
Chinde

MOZAMBIQUE

Tete
Changara
Bindura
Catandica
Inhaminga
Chimoio
Cashel
Mutare
Beira
Espungabera
Nova Mambone
Mapinhane
Nhachengue
Massinga
Inhambane
Ponta Zavora
Chibuto
Xai-Xai
Maputo
Ponta Khehuene
Bela Vista
Mkuze
Lake St. Lucia
Empangeni

MADAGASCAR

ANTANANARIVO
Mahajanga
Mitsinjo
Soalala
Besalampy
Morafenobe
Maintirano
Antsalova
Miandrivazo
Belo Tsiribihina
Morondava
Mandabe
Manja
Morombe
Ankazoabo
Mahaboboka
Toliara
Betioky
Ampanihy
Beloha
Ambovombe
Tôlañaro

INDIAN OCEAN

Mauritius
Port Louis
Phoenix
St-Denis
St-Pierre
Réunion (France)

SEYCHELLES
Aldabra Islands
Cosmoledo Group
Farquhar Group

Scale 1 : 40 500 000

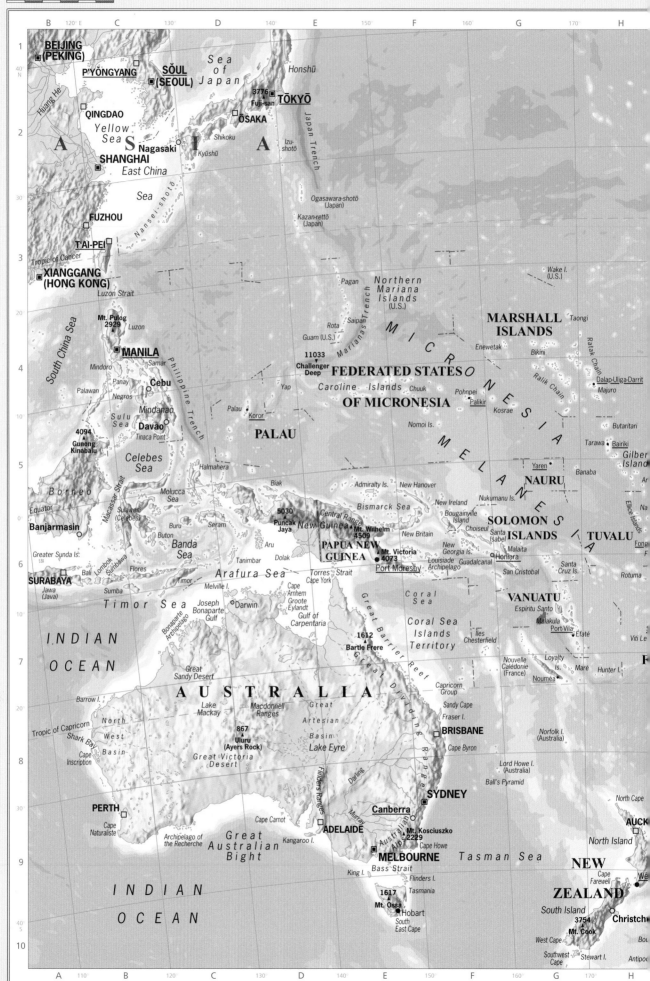

© Helicon Publishing Ltd

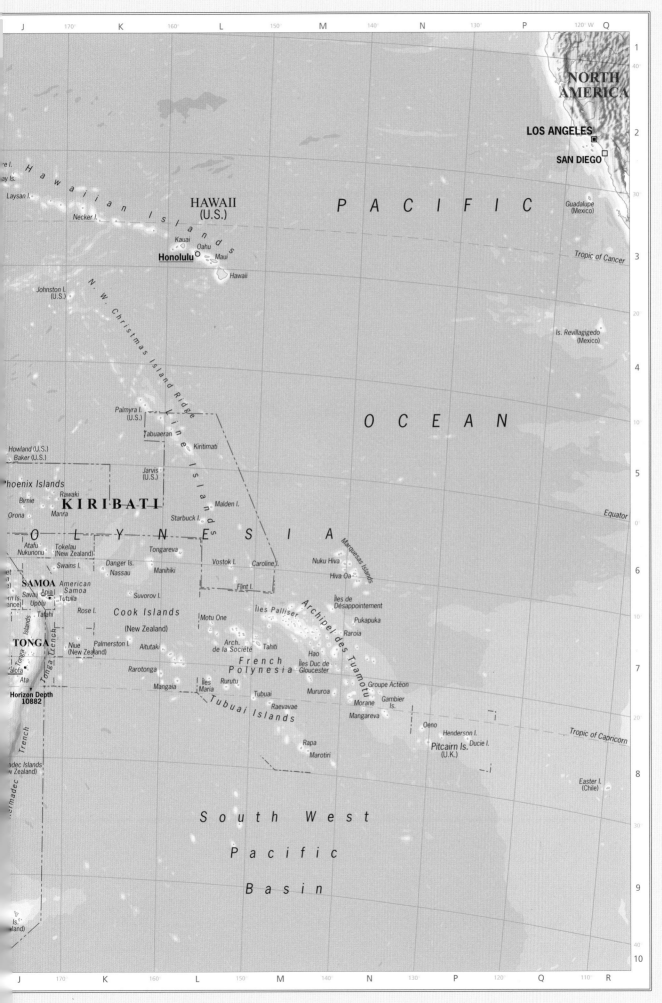

J · 170° · K · 160° · L · 150° · M · 140° · N · 130° · P · 120° W · Q

NORTH AMERICA

P A C I F I C

Guadalupe (Mexico)

LOS ANGELES ◼

SAN DIEGO ◻

re I.
ay Is.

Laysan I.

Necker I.

H a w a i i a n   I s l a n d s

HAWAII (U.S.)

Kauai
Oahu
Honolulu ○ ○ Maui
Hawaii

Tropic of Cancer

Is. Revillagigedo (Mexico)

Johnston I. (U.S.)

N. W.   C h r i s t m a s   I s l a n d   R i d g e

O C E A N

Palmyra I. (U.S.)
Tabuaeran
Kiritimati

Howland (U.S.)
Baker (U.S.)

Jarvis (U.S.)

L i n e   I s l a n d s

Phoenix Islands

Birnie
Orona   Manra

Rawaki

K I R I B A T I

Malden I.

Starbuck I.

Equator

P O L Y N E S I A

Atafu
Nukunonu

Swains I.

Tokelau (New Zealand)

Tongareva

Vostok I.

Caroline I.

Nuku Hiva

Hiva Oa

M a r q u e s a s   I s l a n d s

et I.
rn Is.
ance)

SAMOA   American Samoa
Savaii   Apia ● Tutuila
Upolu

Danger Is.
Nassau

Manihiki

Suvorov I.

Flint I.

Îles de Désappointement

Rose I.

Cook Islands
(New Zealand)

Motu One

Î l e s   P a l l i s e r

Pukapuka

Raroia

A r c h i p e l   d e s   T u a m o t u

Tafahi

TONGA

Niue
(New Zealand)

Palmerston I.

Aitutaki

Arch. de la Société   Tahiti

Hao

Îles Duc de Gloucester

álofa

Ata

T o n g a   T r e n c h

Rarotonga

Mangaia

Îles Maria

Rurutu

Tubuai

Mururoa

Groupe Actéon

Morane   Gambier Is.

Mangareva

Horizon Depth 10882

T u b u a i   I s l a n d s

Raevavae

Oeno

Henderson I.   Ducie I.

Tropic of Capricorn

adec Islands
w Zealand)

T r e n c h

Rapa

Marotiri

Pitcairn Is. (U.K.)

Easter I. (Chile)

S o u t h   W e s t

P a c i f i c

Is.
land)

B a s i n

J · 170° · K · 160° · L · 150° · M · 140° · N · 130° · P · 120° · Q · 110° · R

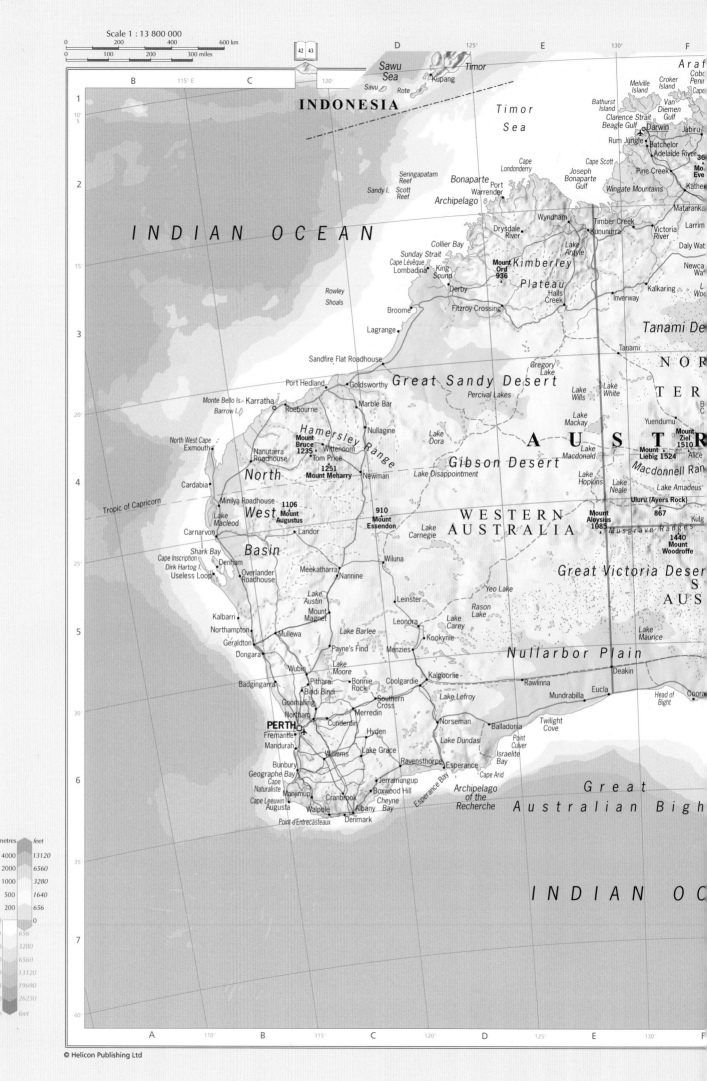

Scale 1 : 13 800 000

INDONESIA

Sawu
Sea

Timor

Savu   Rote   Kupang

Araf

Timor
Sea

Melville
Island
Bathurst
Island
Clarence Strait
Beagle Gulf
Rum Jungle
Darwin
Jabiru
Batchelor
Adelaide River
Pine Creek
Mo.
Eve

Cape
Londonderry
Bonaparte
Archipelago
Port
Warrender
Cape Scott
Joseph
Bonaparte
Gulf
Wingate Mountains

Matarank

Victoria
River
Larrim

Daly Wat

INDIAN OCEAN

Seringapatam
Reef
Scott
Reef
Sandy I.

Wyndham

Timber Creek

Kununurra

Newca
Wa

Collier Bay
Sunday Strait
Cape Lévêque
Lombadina
King
Sound
Derby

Drysdale
River

Lake
Argyle

Mount
Ord
936

Kimberley

Plateau

Halls
Creek

Kalkaring
Woo

Rowley
Shoals

Broome

Fitzroy Crossing

Inverway

Lagrange

Sandfire Flat Roadhouse

Great Sandy Desert

Gregory
Lake

Tanami De

Tanami

NOR

Port Hedland

Goldsworthy

Percival Lakes

Lake
Wills

Lake
White

TER

Monte Bello Is.
Barrow I.

Karratha
Roebourne

Marble Bar

Nullagine

Lake
Dora

Lake
Mackay

Yuendumu

Mount
Ziel
1510

AUST R

North West Cape
Exmouth

Hamersley Range

Mount
Bruce
1235
Wittenoom
Tom Price

Nanutarra
Roadhouse

Newman

Gibson Desert

Lake
Macdonald

Mount
Liebig 1524

Alice

Macdonnell Ran

Cardabia

North

West

Mount Meharry
1251

Lake Disappointment

Lake
Hopkins

Lake
Neale

Lake
Amadeus

Tropic of Capricorn

Minilya Roadhouse

Lake
Macleod

Mount
Augustus
1106

Carnarvon

Landor

Mount
Essendon
910

Lake
Carnegie

WESTERN
AUSTRALIA

Uluru (Ayers Rock)
867

Mount
Aloysius
1085

Musgrave Ranges

Kulg

Basin

Cape Inscription
Dirk Hartog I.
Useless Loop

Shark Bay

Denham

Overlander
Roadhouse

Meekatharra

Nannine

Wiluna

Yeo Lake

Great Victoria Deser

1440
Mount
Woodroffe

S

AUS

Kalbarri

Northampton

Geraldton

Dongara

Mullewa

Lake
Austin

Mount
Magnet

Lake Barlee

Payne's Find

Leinster

Leonora

Menzies

Rason
Lake

Lake
Carey

Kookynie

Lake
Maurice

Nullarbor Plain

Wubin

Pithara
Bindi Bindi

Lake
Moore

Bonnie
Rock

Southern
Cross

Coolgardie

Kalgoorlie

Deakin

Badgingarra

Goomalling
Northam

Merredin

Lake Lefroy

Rawlinna

Mundrabilla

Eucla

Head of
Bight

Coora

PERTH
Fremantle
Mandurah

Cunderdin

Hyden

Norseman

Balladonia

Twilight
Cove

Williams

Lake Grace

Ravensthorpe

Lake Dundas

Point
Culver

Israelite
Bay

Bunbury
Geographe Bay
Cape
Naturaliste
Manjimup
Cape Leeuwin
Augusta

Jerramungup
Boxwood Hill
Cranbrook
Walpole
Point d'Entrecasteaux

Cheyne
Bay
Albany
Denmark

Esperance

Esperance Bay

Cape Arid

Archipelago
of the
Recherche

Great

Australian Bigh

INDIAN OC

metres	feet
4000	13120
2000	6560
1000	3280
500	1640
200	656
0	0
200	656
1000	3280
2000	6560
4000	13120
6000	19690
8000	26250
metres	feet

© Helicon Publishing Ltd

G 135° 140° H 145° J 150°

Cape Wessel
Wessel Islands
Nangalala
Cape Arnhem
Nhulunbuy

Mulgrave I. Moa (Banks Island)
Torres Strait
Prince of Wales Cape York
Island Somerset
Bamaga

Port
Moresby
**PAPUA
NEW GUINEA**

D'Entrecasteaux
Islands
Alotau

K 155° L

1

10°

Louisiade
Archipelago

Bickerton Island
Groote
Eylandt
Numbulwar
Roper Bar

**Gulf of
Carpentaria**

Cape
Grenville
Cape
Direction

Cape
York
Peninsula

Coral Sea Islands

CORAL SEA

2

Borroloola
Cape
Crawford

Sir Edward
Pellew Group

Duifken Point
Weipa
Albatross Bay
Aurukun

Coen

Princess Charlotte Bay

Cape
Flattery
Cooktown

Osprey Reef
Shark Reef

Bougainville Reef
Holmes Reefs Diane Bank

*Territory
(Australia)*

15°

Barkly Tableland

Burketown
Karumba
Normanton

Wellesley
Islands
Mornington I.
Bertinck I.

Kowanyama

Dunbar

Laura

Silver
Plains

Willis Group

Herald
Cays
Magdelaine Cays

Diamond Islets

Turtle I.

Tregosse Islets

Ant Creek

Lake Nash
Tobermorey

Mount Isa

Cloncurry

Croydon
Georgetown
Forsayth
Greenvale

1612 Mount Bartle Frere
Mareeba Cairns
Innisfail
Ingham
Halifax Bay
Mutarnee

Port Douglas

Mount Garnet

GREAT BARRIER REEF

*PACIFIC

OCEAN*

3

Camooweal

McKinlay
Richmond
Hughenden

Townsville
Ayr
Bowen The
Whitsundays
Proserpine
Repulse Bay

20°

QUEENSLAND

Winton
Muttaburra

Charters
Towers
Dalrymple
Lake

Mackay
Sarina

Swain
Reefs

Tobermorey
Boulia

Great

Longreach
Barcaldine
Jundah

Nebo

Broad Sound
Clairview
Townshend I.

*Simpson
Desert*

Artesian

Yaraka
Blackall
Tambo

Clermont

Emerald
Blackwater
Springsure

Yeppoon
Rockhampton
Curtis I.

Capricorn
Group

Cato I.

Tropic of Capricorn

25°

Birdsville
Betoota

Windorah

Banana
Biloela

Gladstone

*Lake
Eyre
Basin*

*Sturt Stony
Desert*

Basin

Quilpie

Augathella
Charleville

Taroom
Gayndah

Eidsvold

Bundaberg
Sandy Cape
Hervey Bay Fraser I.
Maryborough

Oodnadatta

*Tirari
Desert*

Lake
Yamma
Yamma

Muckadilla
Roma
Miles
Kingaroy
Gympie
Caloundra

*Lake Eyre
North*

Marree

Thargomindah

Glenmorgan
Dalby
Moonie

Toowoomba
BRISBANE
Moreton I.

Coober Pedy
*Lake Eyre
South*

Lake
Blanche

Hungerford
Cunnamulla

St
George

Goondiwindi

North Stradbroke I.
Beenleigh
Surfers Paradise
Gold
Coast

30°

Leigh Creek
Glendambo
Pimba

Lake
Callabonna
Lake
Frome

Tibbooburra
Wanaaring

Dirranbandi
Bungunya

Boggabilla

**Mount
Roberts
1387**
Casino
Tenterfield Cape Byron
Ballina

Marree
Lake
Torrens
Hawker

Bourke

Brewarrina
Moree

Glen Innes
Grafton

**Round
Mountain
1608**

Gawler Ranges

White
Cliffs

Louth
Walgett
Narrabi
Armidale

Coffs Harbour

Whyalla
Port Augusta
Orroroo

Broken
Hill
Menindee
Wilcannia

Cobar
Coolabah
Nyngan

Gunnedah
Tamworth

Coonabarabran

**Black
Sugarloaf
1494**
Port Macquarie

Kyancutta
Cowell
Burra

**NEW
SOUTH
WALES**

Ivanhoe
Roto

Gilgandra
Quirindi
Singleton

Taree

Lord Howe I.

Morgan
Renmark

Pooncarie

Condobolin
Orange
Dubbo

1274
Lithgow
Bathurst
Katoomba

Cessnock
Newcastle

Ball's Pyramid

35°

Port Pirie
Whyalla
Eyre
Pen.

Murray River

Wentworth

Goolgowi
Marsden

1204
Cowra

SYDNEY
Wollongong

Basin
Balranald
Hay

Swan
Hill

Narrandera
Wagga Wagga

Cootamundra
Canberra
Nowra

ADELAIDE
Gawler
Murray Bridge
Tailem Bend

Ouyen
Hopetoun
Deniliquin
Finley

Tumut
A.C.T.

Batemans Bay

Inneston
Victor
Harbor

Border Town

VICTORIA

Albury
Tumut

**2229
Mount
Kosciuszko**
Cooma

Investigator Strait
Cape Borda

Kingscote
Kangaroo I.

Big Desert
*Little
Desert*

Shepparton
Seymour
Yea
Horsham
Ballarat

GREAT
**Mount Bogong
1986**
Omeo

Bombala
Eden

*Lacepede
Bay*
Cape Jaffa
Robe

Hamilton

MELBOURNE
Geelong

Bairnsdale
Cape Howe

40°

Mount Gambier
Portland

Warrnambool
Cape Nelson
Apollo
Bay

Morwell
Sale
Port Albert

Korumburra
Walkerville
Wilson's Promontory
South East Point

64 65

King Island
Currie

Bass Strait

Flinders I.
Furneaux
Group
Whitemark
Cape Barren I.

TASMAN SEA

7

Cape Grim
Stanley
Burnie
Devonport

George
Town
Banks Strait

TASMANIA
Queenstown

**1617
Mount
Ossa**
Swansea
Launceston

Cape Forestier

A.C.T. = Australian Capital Territory

Lake Gordon

Hobart
Dover
South West
Cape

Port Arthur
Storm Bay

South
East Cape

8

40°

G H 140° 145° J K 155° L 160° M

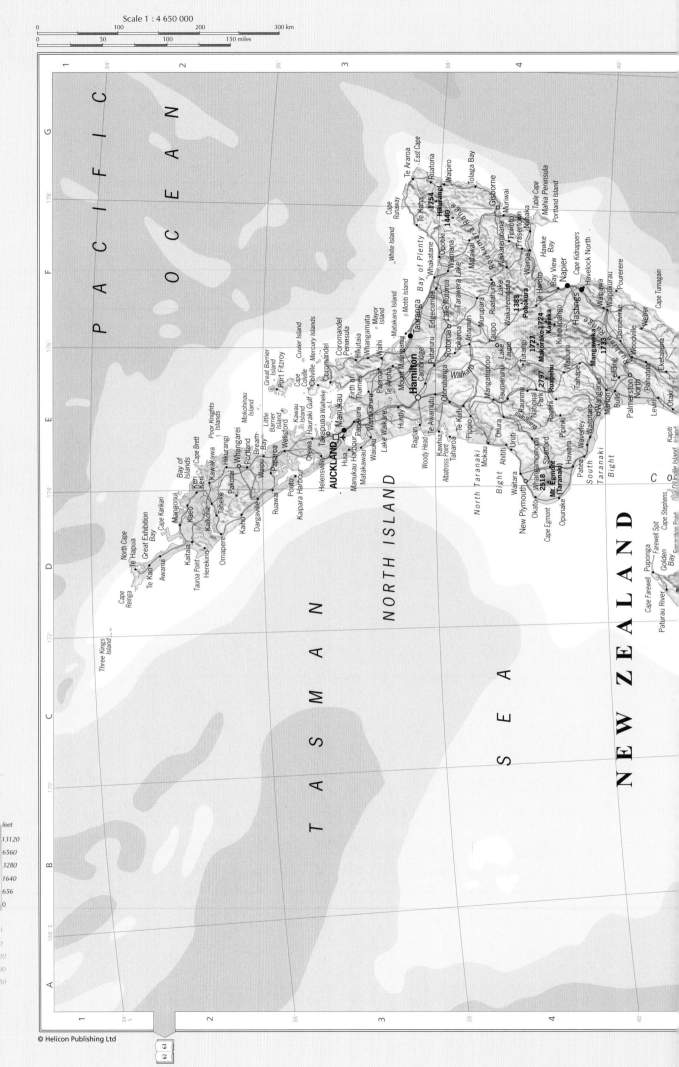

Scale 1 : 4 650 000

0	100	200	300 km	

0	50	100	150 miles	

PACIFIC OCEAN

TASMAN SEA

NORTH ISLAND

NEW ZEALAND

metres	feet
4000	13120
2000	6560
1000	3280
500	1640
200	656
0	0
200	656
1000	3280
2000	6560
4000	13120
6000	19690
8000	26250
metres	feet

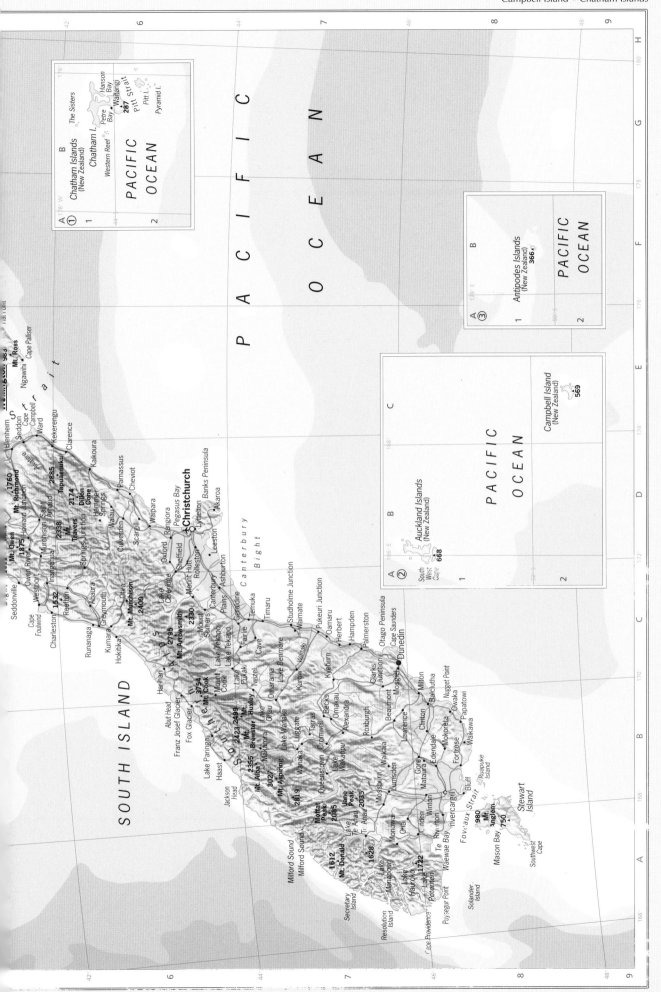

Chatham Islands (New Zealand)

The Sisters

Western Reef

Petre Bay

Hanson Bay

Waitangi

287

Pitt I.

Pyramid I.

Chatham I.

PACIFIC OCEAN

Antipodes Islands (New Zealand)

366

PACIFIC OCEAN

Auckland Islands (New Zealand)

South West Cape

668

Campbell Island (New Zealand)

569

PACIFIC OCEAN

PACIFIC OCEAN

SOUTH ISLAND

SOUTHERN ALPS

Mt. Ross

Ngawihi

Cape Palliser

Cape Campbell

Ward

Seddon

Blenheim

Kekerengu

Clarence

Kaikoura

Cheviot

Parnassus

Hanmer Springs

Waiau

Mt. Richmond
1760

Mt. Owen
1875

Murchison

Owen River

Howard Junction

Tapuaenuku
2885

Dillon Cone
2174

Mt. Arnaud
2338

Mt. Travers
2338

St. Arnaud

Springs Junction

Inangahua

Reefton

1532

Westport

Seddonville

Cape Foulwind

Charleston

Runanga

Kumara

Greymouth

Hokitika

Harihari

Otira

Lake Coleridge

Mt. Murchison
2409

Mt. Arrowsmith
2795

2330

Mount Somers

Sheffield

Oxford

Culverden

Scargill

Waipara

Rangiora

Christchurch

Lyttelton

Banks Peninsula

Akaroa

Pegasus Bay

Rolleston

Leeston

Mount Hutt

Ashburton

Geraldine

Canterbury Plains

Canterbury Bight

Temuka

Timaru

Waimate

Fairlie

Cave

Lake Tekapo

Lake Tekapo

Lake Pukaki

Mount Cook

Mt. Cook
3754

Twizel

Lake Ohau

Lake Benmore

Kurow

Waitaki

Studholme Junction

Pukeuri Junction

Oamaru

Herbert

Hampden

Palmerston

Cape Saunders

Otago Peninsula

Dunedin

Mosgiel

Clarks Junction

Milton

Balclutha

Nugget Point

Papatowai

Owaka

Kaitangata

Mokoreta

Wakawa

Fortrose

Edendale

Gore

Mataura

Clinton

Lawrence

Beaumont

Roxburgh

Alexandra

Omakau

Becks

Cromwell

Lake Hawea

Lake Wanaka

Wanaka

Luggate

Tarras

Lake Dunstan

Queenstown

Arrowtown

Lake Wakatipu

Jane Peak
2035

Mt. Aspiring
3027

Mt. Alba
2355

Mt. Brewster
2499

Mt. Huxley
2423

Franz Josef Glacier

Fox Glacier

Mount Aspiring

Abut Head

Lake Paringa

Jackson Head

Haast

Milford Sound

Milford Sound

Secretary Island

Resolution Island

Cape Providence

Puysegur Point

Solander Island

Mt. Donald
1612

1628

Moffat Peak
2085

Lake Manapouri

Lake Te Anau
2035

Lake Monowai

Lake Hauroko

Lake Poteriteri

1722

Waewae Bay

Te Anau

Manapouri

Otautau

Riverton

Winton

Ohai

Nightcaps

Mossburn

Lumsden

Kingston

Bluff

Invercargill

Foveaux Strait

Ruapuke Island

Mt. Anglem
980

Inglem
750

Stewart Island

Mason Bay

Southwest Cape

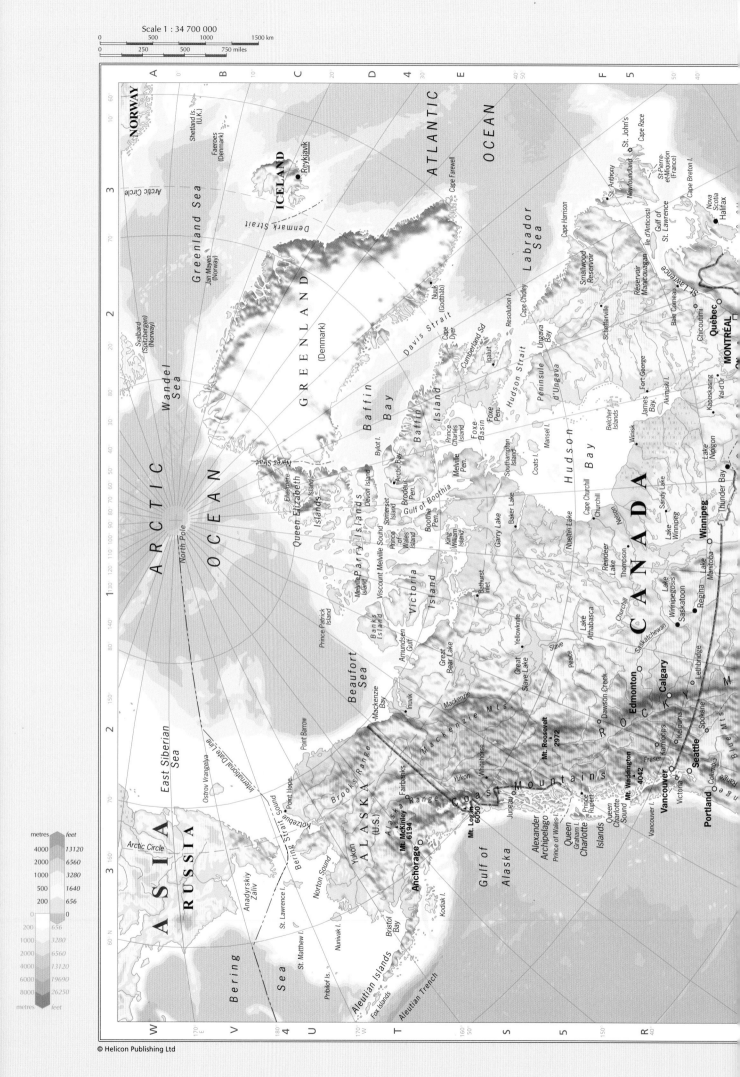

Scale 1 : 34 700 000

© Helicon Publishing Ltd

ATLANTIC OCEAN

SOUTH AMERICA

PACIFIC OCEAN

UNITED STATES

MEXICO

NEW YORK
PHILADELPHIA
Baltimore
Washington D.C.
Virginia Beach
Cape Hatteras
Bermuda (U.K.)

DETROIT
Milwaukee
CHICAGO
Cleveland
Columbus
Cincinnati
Indianapolis
St. Louis
Raleigh
Charlotte
Knoxville
Nashville
Memphis
Atlanta
Savannah
Jacksonville
Little Rock
Cape Canaveral
Tampa
Mobile
New Orleans
Miami
THE BAHAMAS
Nassau
Grand Bahama
Great Abaco
Andros

Denver
Kansas City
Oklahoma City
DALLAS
Fort Worth
Austin
SAN ANTONIO
HOUSTON
Corpus Christi
Matamoros
Abilene
Edwards Plateau

Las Vegas
Albuquerque
El Paso
Ciudad Juárez
PHOENIX
Tucson
MONTERREY
León
CIUDAD DE MÉXICO
Acapulco

Reno
Sacramento
San Francisco
San Jose
Fresno
LOS ANGELES
SAN DIEGO
Mexicali
Ensenada
Hermosillo
Ciudad Obregón
La Paz
GUADALAJARA
MÉXICO

Sierra Nevada
Death Valley
Mojave Desert
Great Basin
Grand Canyon 3951
Colorado
Salt Lake City
Great Salt Lake
Great Salt Lake Desert
4123
4011
Sierra Madre Occidental
Río Grande
Baja California
Golfo de California
Cabo San Lucas
Islas Marías
Islas Revillagigedo (Mexico)
I. Clarión
Cedros
Guadalupe (Mexico)
Channel Is.

Gulf of Mexico
Yucatán
Mérida
Veracruz
Ciudad Madero
Bahía de Campeche
Vol. Citlaltépetl 5610
Sierra Madre del Sur

CUBA
LA HABANA (HAVANA)
Santiago de Cuba
Isla de la Juventud
Isla de Cozumel
Yucatán Channel
Florida Keys
Florida Straits

Tropic of Cancer

BELIZE
Belmopán
GUATEMALA 4210
San Salvador
EL SALVADOR
HONDURAS
Tegucigalpa
NICARAGUA
Managua
Lago de Nicaragua
COSTA RICA
San José
Swan Is. (Honduras)
Cabo Gracias á Dios
Middle America Trench

JAMAICA
Kingston
HAITI
PORT-AU-PRINCE
DOMINICAN REPUBLIC
SANTO DOMINGO
Duarte 3175
Cabo Beata

PUERTO RICO (U.S.)
San Juan
Virgin Is. (U.S.)
Virgin Is. (U.K.)
Puerto Rico Trench
Turks and Caicos Is.
Great Inagua

Caribbean Sea
Greater Antilles
Lesser Antilles
Netherlands Antilles
Aruba (Neth.)
Punta Gallinas

CARACAS
Orinoco
Meta
BOGOTÁ
BARRANQUILLA
MEDELLÍN
CALI
Cristóbal Colón 5775
Cordillera Oriental
Cordillera Central
Cordillera Occidental
5750
6310
QUITO
GUAYAQUIL
Golfo de Guayaquil
Iquitos
Amazonas
Chiclayo
Equator

PANAMA
Panamá
Golfo de Panamá
Golfo del Darién
Canal de Panamá (Panama Canal)
Isla de Coiba
Isla de Malpelo (Colombia)
I. de Coco (Costa Rica)
Islas Galápagos (Galapagos Is.) (Ecuador)
Isla Isabela
Clipperton Island (France)

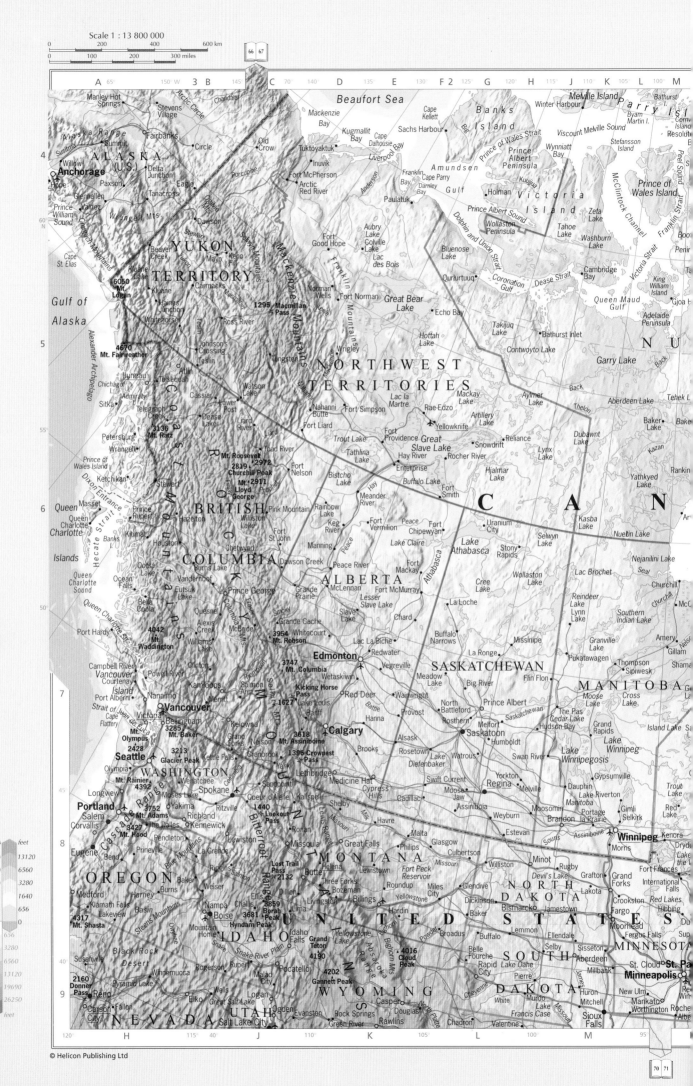

Scale 1 : 13 800 000

GREENLAND
(Denmark)

Baffin
Bay

Devon
Island

Lancaster Sound

Jones Sound

Arctic
Bay

Borden
Peninsula

Bylot
Island

Pond
Inlet

Scott Inlet

Clyde River

Cape Christian

Buchan
Gulf

Ammassalik
(Angmagssalik)

Upernavik

Kangersuatsiaq (Prøven)

Nunatuk

Uummannaq
(Umanak)

Illorsuit

Nuussuaq

Qeqertarsuaq
(Disko)

Iilissat
(Jakobshavn)

Qeqertarsuup
Tunua (Disko Bugt)

Kangaatsiaq

Gyldenløves Fjord

Kong Frederik VI Kyst

Sisimiut
(Holsteinsborg)

Maniitsoq
(Sukkertoppen)

Napasoq

Kangeq
(Kap Cort Adelaer)

Kangerlussuatsiaq
(Lindenow Fjord)

Nuuk
(Godthåb)

Kangerluarsoruseq
(Færingehavn)

Qeqertarsuatsiaat
(Fiskenæsset)

Paamiut
(Frederikshåb)

Nanortalik

Nunap Isua
(Kap Farvel)

Nittuut

Nunarsuit

Arctic Circle

Baffin Island

Boothia
Peninsula

Brodeur
Peninsula

Igloolik

Hall
Beach

Rowley
I.

Air
Force I.

Prince
Charles
Island

Nettilling
Lake

Home
Bay

Broughton
Island

Cumberland
Peninsula

Cape
Dyer

Pangnirtung

Davis Strait

Pelly Bay

Melville
Peninsula

Parry
Bay

Wales
I.

NUT

Foxe
Basin

Cape
Dominion
Bowman Bay

Amadjuak
Lake

Hall
Peninsula

Cumberland
Sound

Cape Mercy

LABRADOR
SEA

ATLANTIC
OCEAN

Repulse Bay

Wager Bay

Southampton
Island

Roes Welcome Sound

Fisher Strait

Evans
Strait

Coats
Island

Mansel
Island

Cape Dorchester

Foxe
Peninsula

Foxe
Channel

Coral Harbour

Cape Dorset

Salisbury I.

Nottingham I.

Cap de
Nouvelle-France

Hudson

Igaluit

Lake
Harbour

Frobisher Bay

Loks Land

Resolution
Island

Strait

Cape Chidley

Port Burwell

1729

A D A

HUDSON

BAY

Fort
Severn

Winisk

Esterfield

Chesterfield
Inlet

Pelly Bay

Ivujivik

Salluit

Kangiqsujuaq

Quaqtaq

Akpatok
Island

Ungava

Bay

Péninsule
d'Ungava

Akulivik

Kangirsuk

Kangiqsualujjuaq

Puvurnituq

George

Kuujjuaq

Hebron

Cod Island

Nutak

Nain

NEWFOUNDLAND

Hopedale

Lac
Payne

Lac à l'Eau
Claire

Lac
Minto

Cape Harrison
Groswater
Bay

Rigolet

Cartwright

Lake
Melville

Port Hope
Simpson

Belcher
Islands

Ottawa
Islands

Sleeper
Is.

King
George Is.

Nastapoka Is.

Long I.

Kuujjuarapik

Lac
Bienville

Scheffervile

Smallwood Reservoir

Churchill
Falls

Churchill

Labrador
City

Wabush

Ashuanipi

Ashuanipi Lake

St-Augustin

Perdi McCatina

Strait of Belle Isle

Battle Harbour
Belle Isle
Cape Bauld

St. Anthony

Roddickton

White
Bay

Fogo I.

Bonavista
Bay

Long Range Mts.

Deer Lake

Grand
Falls

Gander

Notre
Dame
Bay

St.
John's

Cape
Henrietta
Maria

Winisk

James

Bay

Ekwan

Rés. de
La Grande 4

Réservoir
Caniapiscau

QUÉBEC

1021

Monts Otish

Big Trout
Lake

Winisk
Lake

St.
Joseph

Fort Hope

Attawapiskat

Akimiski
Island

Fort
George

Charton

Rés. de
La Grande 2

Réservoir
Opinaca

Rés. de
La Grande 3

Eastmain

Réservoir
Manicouagan

Newfoundland

Harbour Breton

Fortune Bay

Grand Bank

Trepassey

Cape
Race

Albany

Moosonee

Eastmain

Fort Rupert

Rupert

L. Mistassini

Baie-du-
Poste

Chute
des Passes

Havre-St-Pierre

Natashquan

Cape
Ray

Channel-Port
aux Basques

St-Pierre-
et-Miquelon
(France)

Big Trout
Lake

Missinaibi

Lac
Evans

Chibougamau

Réservoir
Pipmuacan

Sept-
Îles

Port-
Menier

Île d'Anticosti

Gulf of
St. Lawrence

NTARIO

Armstrong

Nakina

Coral

Miquelon

Réservoir
Gouin

Les Escoumins

Rimouski

Matane

Péninsule
de Gaspé

Îles de la
Madeleine

Sydney

Cape Breton Island

Lake
Nipigon

Longlac

Hearst

Amos

Senneterre

Lac
St-Jean

Jonquière

Baie St. Paul

Chicoutimi

Bathurst

Edmundston

PRINCE EDWARD
ISLAND

Charlottetown

Port Hawkesbury

New Glasgow

Nipigon

Geraldton

Kapuskasing

Timmins

Lake
Abitibi

Val-d'Or

La Tuque

Montmagny

Presque
Isle

Houlton

NEW
BRUNSWICK

Moncton

Fredericton

Amherst

Truro

Sable I.

Thunder Bay

Isle
Royale

Lake
Superior

Marathon

Foleyet

Rouyn

Réservoir
Cabonga

Mont-Laurier

Québec

Lévis

Jackman

Stephen

St. John

Bay of Fundy

Dartmouth

Halifax

Bridgewater

NOVA SCOTIA

Copper
Harbor

Keweenaw Pen.

Wawa

Chapleau

Kirkland
Lake

Cobalt

North
Bay

Trois
Rivières

Sorel

Sherbrooke

Granby

Mt. Mts.

White

MAINE

Jackman

MONTRÉAL

Ottawa

Ottawa

Pembroke

Smiths
Falls

Cornwall

Washington

Augusta

Lewiston

Liverpool

Shelburne

Cape Sable

Yarmouth

Sault
Ste. Marie

Sudbury

1917

Blind River

Manitoulin I.

Parry Sound

Huntsville

Kingston

Plattsburgh

Burlington

Ogdensburg

Montpelier

VERMONT

NEW
HAMPSHIRE

Concord

Portsmouth

Portland

Massachusetts
Bay

Cape Cod

Ironwood

Marquette

Escanaba

MICHIGAN

Georgian
Bay

Tobermory

Orillia

Peterborough

Watertown

1629

Barrie

Oshawa

Lake
Ontario

Utica

Albany

Syracuse

MASS.

Worcester

Boston

Providence

New Bedford

Rhinelander

Manistique

Mt.
Pleasant

Alpena

Traverse City

Bay City

Saginaw

Toronto

Kitchener

Rochester

Catskill
Mts.
1295

Springfield

Hartford

CONN.

New Haven

RHODE ISLAND

Long I.

NSIN

Wausau

Appleton

Green Bay

Marinette

Iron Mountain

Grand
Rapids

Flint

Hamilton

London

St.
Catharines

Buffalo

Binghamton

NEW
YORK

Scranton

Bridgeport

Oshkosh

Sheboygan

Lake
Michigan

Muskegon

Grand
Haven

Lansing

Ann Arbor

Chatham

Sarnia

Windsor

Erie

Jamestown

Meadville

PENNSYLVANIA

Paterson

Newark

NEW
YORK

Milwaukee

DETROIT

Lake Erie

Scale 1 : 15 500 000

metres / feet
4000 / 13120
2000 / 6560
1000 / 3280
500 / 1640
200 / 656
0 / 0
200 / 656
1000 / 3280
2000 / 6560
4000 / 13120
6000 / 19690
8000 / 26250
metres / feet

© Helicon Publishing Ltd

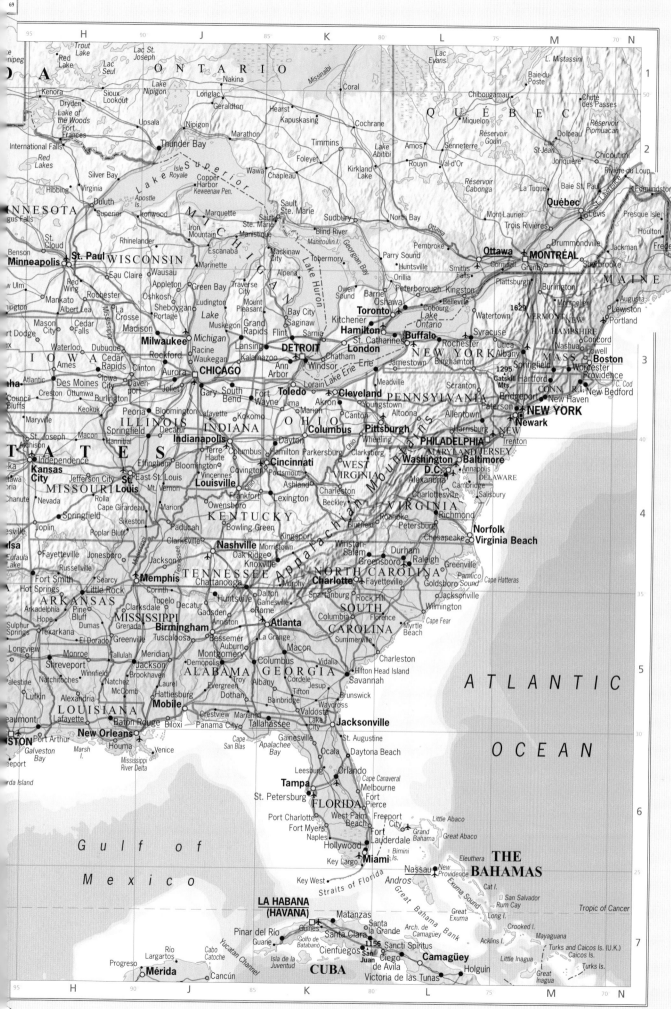

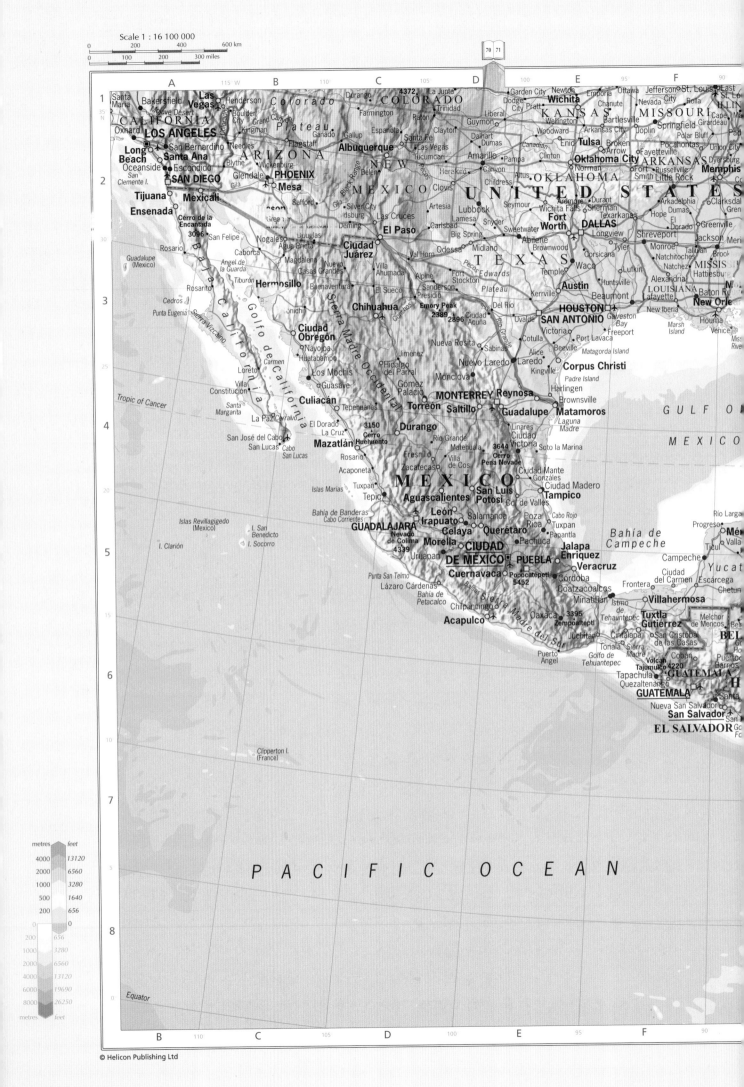

Scale 1 : 16 100 000

© Helicon Publishing Ltd

Scale 1 : 28 000 000

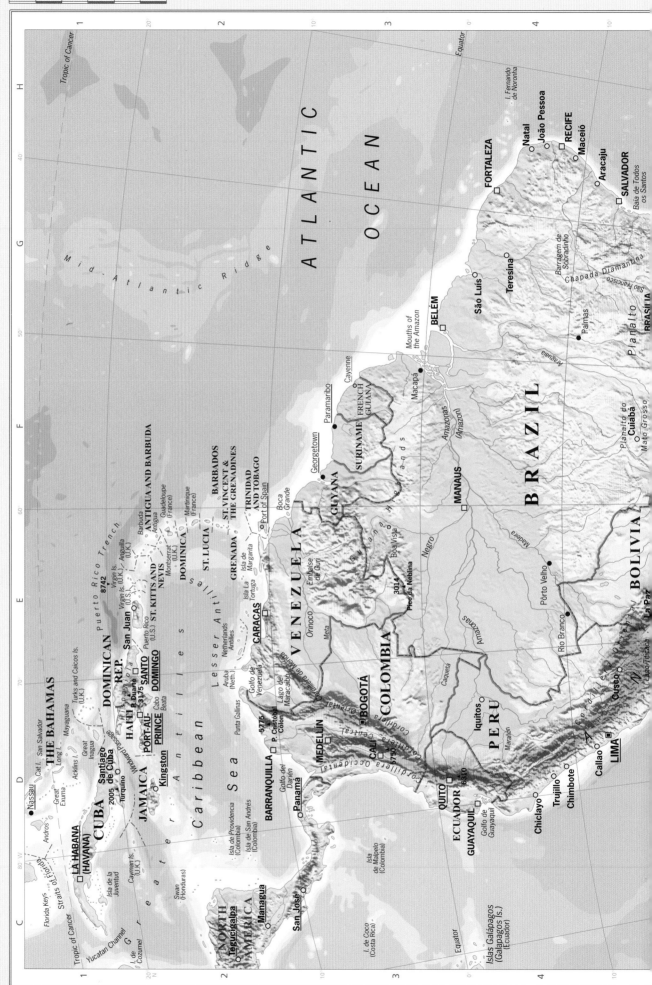

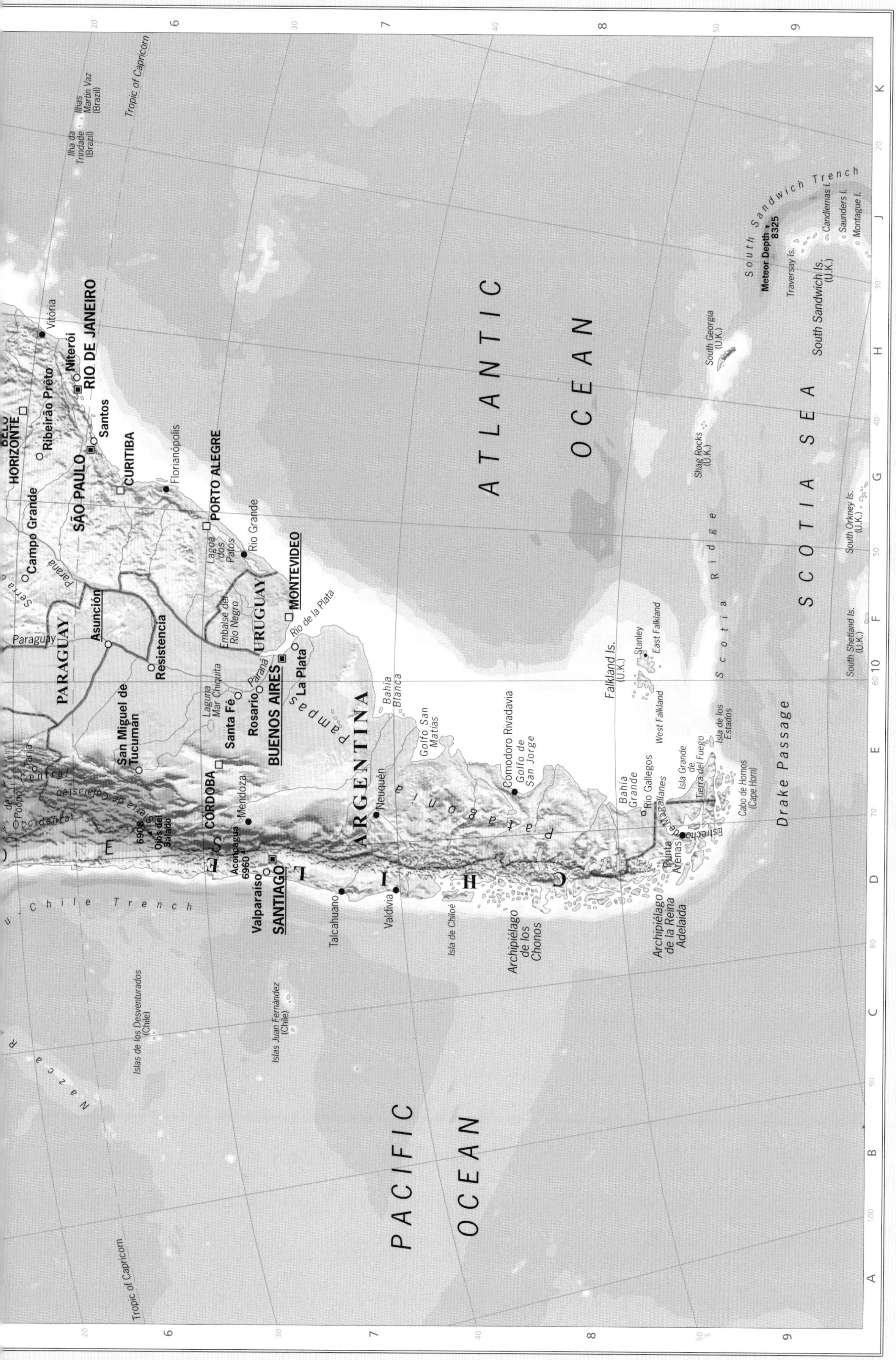
ATLANTIC
OCEAN
PACIFIC
OCEAN
SCOTIA SEA
Drake Passage
Scotia Ridge
South Sandwich Trench
Meteor Depth 8325
Chile Trench
Nazca R
Tropic of Capricorn
ARGENTINA
CHILE
PARAGUAY
URUGUAY
Paraguay
Paraná
Serra
Pampas
Patagonia
RIO DE JANEIRO
SÃO PAULO
BUENOS AIRES
SANTIAGO
MONTEVIDEO
Asunción
CURITIBA
PORTO ALEGRE
CÓRDOBA
BELO HORIZONTE
Vitória
Niterói
Ribeirão Prêto
Santos
Campo Grande
Florianópolis
Rio Grande
Lagoa dos Patos
Río de la Plata
La Plata
Rosario
Santa Fe
Resistencia
San Miguel de Tucumán
Mendoza
Aconcagua 6960
Ojos del Salado 6908
Valparaíso
Talcahuano
Valdivia
Neuquén
Bahía Blanca
Golfo San Matías
Comodoro Rivadavia
Golfo de San Jorge
Bahía Grande
Río Gallegos
Punta Arenas
Estrecho de Magallanes
Isla Grande de Tierra del Fuego
Isla de los Estados
Cabo de Hornos (Cape Horn)
Archipiélago de la Reina Adelaida
Archipiélago de los Chonos
Isla de Chiloé
Laguna Mar Chiquita
Embalse del Río Negro
Falkland Is. (U.K.)
Stanley
East Falkland
West Falkland
South Georgia (U.K.)
Shag Rocks (U.K.)
South Orkney Is. (U.K.)
South Shetland Is. (U.K.)
South Sandwich Is. (U.K.)
Traversay Is.
Candlemas I.
Saunders I.
Montague I.
Ilha da Trindade (Brazil)
Ilhas Martin Vaz (Brazil)
Islas de los Desventurados (Chile)
Islas Juan Fernández (Chile)
Poopó
Tarija
Cordillera Occidental
Central
Sierra de Calalaste

Scale 1 : 16 100 000

Islas Galápagos
(Galapagos Islands)
(Ecuador)

① A B
I. Culpepper
I. Wenman
Isla Pinta
Isla Marchena
Equator
Isla Fernandina
Isla San Salvador
Isla Santa Cruz
② Isla Isabela
Isla San Cristóbal
Isla Santa María
Isla Española

CARIBBEAN SEA

Lesser Antilles

Kingstown
ST. VINCENT & THE GRENADINES
St. George's GRENADA

NICARAGUA
Lago de Nicaragua
Isla de San Andrés (Colombia)
COSTA RICA
San José
Chirripó 3820
Volcán Barú 3475
PANAMA
Golfo de Chiriquí
Isla de Coiba
Punta Mariato
Chitré
Punta Mala
Golfo de Panamá
Panamá
Golfo de los Mosquitos
Canal de Panamá (Panama Canal)
Golfo del Darién
La Palma
Turbo
Caucasia
Quibdó
Nuquí
Cabo Corrientes
Golfo de Cupica

Punta Gallinas
Peninsula de Guajira
Aruba (Neth.)
Netherlands Antilles
Willemstad
Islas Los Roques
Isla La Tortuga
Isla de Margarita
Porlamar
Carúpano
Güiria
TRINIDAD AND TOBAGO
Port of Spain
Ríohacha
Santa Marta
BARRANQUILLA
Cartagena
Valledupar
Plato
El Banco
Sincelejo
Montería
P. Cristóbal
Colón
Maicao
Golfo de Venezuela
Coro
San Juan de los Cayos
MARACAIBO
Cabimas
Lago de Maracaibo
Maracay
CARACAS
Petare
Los Teques
Cumaná
Machiques
San Carlos del Zulia
Barquisimeto
Valencia
San Juan de los Morros
Barcelona
Maturín
Tucupita
Delta del Orinoco (Orinoco Delta)
Valera
Mérida
San Cristóbal
Cúcuta
Pamplona
Bucaramanga
4083
Bello
Puerto Berrío
5493
MEDELLÍN
La Dorada
Tunja
Sogamoso
Manizales
5399
Pereira
Armenia
Ibagué
BOGOTÁ
4560
Villavicencio
CALI
5750
Palmira
Buenaventura
Neiva
Popayán
4686
Florencia
Tumaco
Patía
Pasto
4764
N. de Cumbal
Ipiales
Esmeraldas
Volcán Cayambe
5790
Santo Domingo de los Colorados
QUITO
Volcán Cotopaxi
5896
Bahía de Manta
Chone
Ambato
Manta
Chimborazo
6310
Portoviejo
ECUADOR
Bahía de Santa Elena
GUAYAQUIL
5230
Macas
Salinas
Azogues
Isla Puná
Playas
Cuenca
Golfo de Guayaquil
Machala
Talara
Loja
Paita
Sullana
Punta Pariñas
Piura
Bahía de Sechura
Sechura
Punta Negra
Chiclayo
Cajamarca
Pacasmayo
Trujillo
Chimbote
Nevado de Huascarán
6768
Huaraz
Huarmey
Barranca
Huacho
Callao
LIMA
Chincha Alta
Bahía de Pisco
Pisco
Ica
Nazca
Lomas
Atico
Camaná
Mollendo
Ilo

Ocaña
Caucasia
La Gran Sabana
Guanare
San Cristóbal
Arauca
Apure
San Fernando de Apure
Achaguas
El Baúl
Calabozo
Zaraza
El Tigre
Puerto Nuevo
Puerto Carreño
Puerto Ayacucho
Cerro Yavi 2441
San Juan
Puerto Páez
VENEZUELA
Ciudad Bolívar
Embalse de Guri
La Paragua
El Dorado
Salto Angel
Ciudad Guayana
Mt. Roraima 2810
Sta Elena
Cerro Marahuaca 2579
La Esmeralda
Pico da Neblina 3014
San Carlos
Caracarai
RORAIMA
Orocué
San José de Ocuné
Puerto Inírida
San Fernando de Atabapo
Inírida
Guaviare
Cuiari
Içana
Uaupés
Negro
Tomar
Barcelos
Ilha Grande
Maraã
Fonte Boa
Uarini
Santo António do Içá
Alvarães
Amazonas (Amazon)
Coari
Codajás
Manacapuru
MANAUS
Airão
Coari
Juruá
AMAZONAS
Tefé
São Paulo de Olivença
Benjamin Constant
Leticia
Atalaia do Norte
Caballococha
Carauari
Arumã
Tapauá
Lábrea
Humaitá
Canutama
Calama
Pôrto Velho
Ariquemes
RONDÔNIA
Pimenta Bueno
COLOMBIA
Calamar
Miraflores
Mitú
Mesa de Yambí
lutica
Taracua
Macuje
Tres Esquinas
Caquetá
La Chorrera
La Pedrera
Puerto Leguízamo
Puerto Limón
Yari
Macaje
Japurá
El Encanto
Putumayo
Andoas
Río Tigre
Tigre
Napo
Pebas
Santa Clara
Iquitos
Nauta
Requena
Iberia
Elvira
Marari
Envira
Eirunepé
Pauini
Pauini
Boca do Acre
Madeira
Purus
Guajará
Iñapari
Cobija
Puerto Rico
Riberalta
Guayaramerín
Mirim
Rondônia
Brasiléia
Epitaciolândia
Río Branco
Sena Madureira
ACRE
Feijó
Tarauacá
Cruzeiro do Sul
BRAZIL
Contamana
Pucallpa
Bolognesi
Ucayali
PERU
Huánuco
6634
Cerro de Pasco
La Oroya
Huancayo
Huancavelica
Ayacucho
Cusco
6394
Nevado Auzangate
Abancay
Chalhuanca
Ayaviri
Nudo Coropuna
6425
Juliaca
Puno
Lago Titicaca
Arequipa
Tacna
Arica
Iquique
Tocopilla
CHILE
Maria Elena
Punta Angamos
Calama
ARGENTINA
BOLIVIA
La Paz
Cochabamba
Santa Cruz
Montero
San José de Chiquitos
Oruro
Poopó
Lago de Poopó
Challapata
Sucre
Potosí
Uyuni
Salar de Uyuni
Río Mulatos
Tupiza
Tarija
Villa Montes
Nevado Sajama 6542
Volcán San Pedro 6159
Corocoro
Guaqui
Pilaya
Boyuibe
Fortín Eugenio
PARAGUAY

Selvas
Amazonas
Marañón
Madre de Dios
Puerto Maldonado
Manú
Beni
Trinidad
San Borja
Magdalena
Exaltación
Lago Rogaguado
Puerto Heath
Cavinas
Lago Rogaguado
Yacuma
Mamoré
San Miguel
Ascensión
Concepción
San Pedro
Nevado de Illampu 6485
Santa Ana
Cerros de Pasco
Nevado de Illampu

PACIFIC OCEAN

Nazca Ridge
Peru-Chile Trench

metres feet
4000 13120
2000 6560
1000 3280
500 1640
200 656
0 0
200 656
1000 3280
2000 6560
4000 13120
6000 19690
8000 26250
metres feet

© Helicon Publishing Ltd

Equator

Volcán Chimborazo

Bolivia • Brazil • Colombia • Ecuador • French Guiana
Galapagos Islands • Guyana • Peru • Suriname • Venezuela

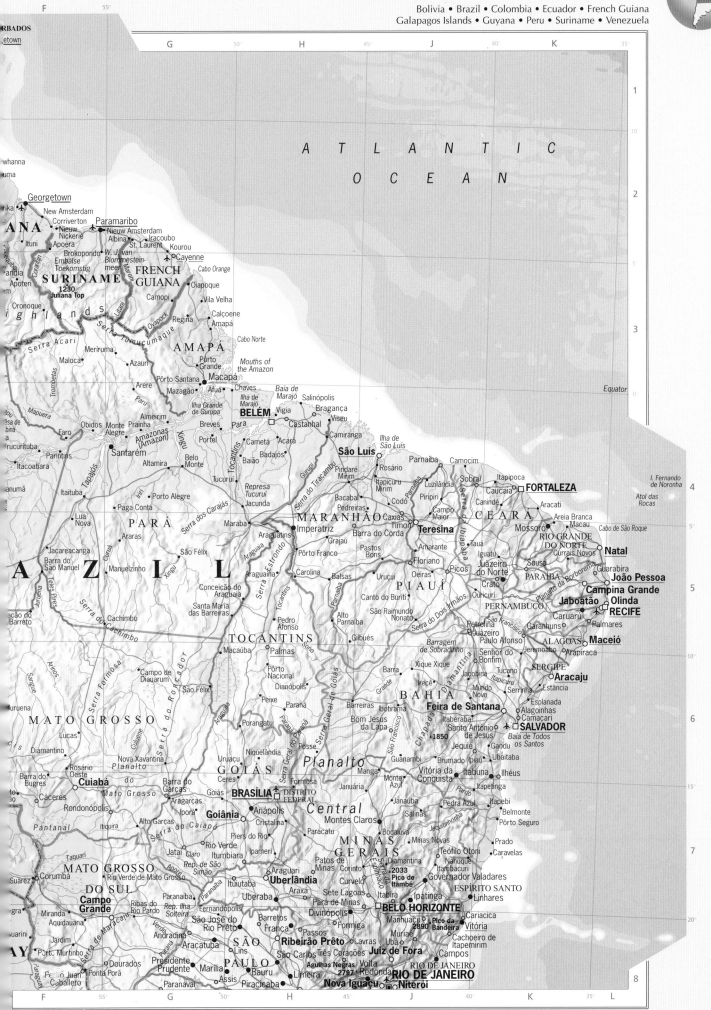

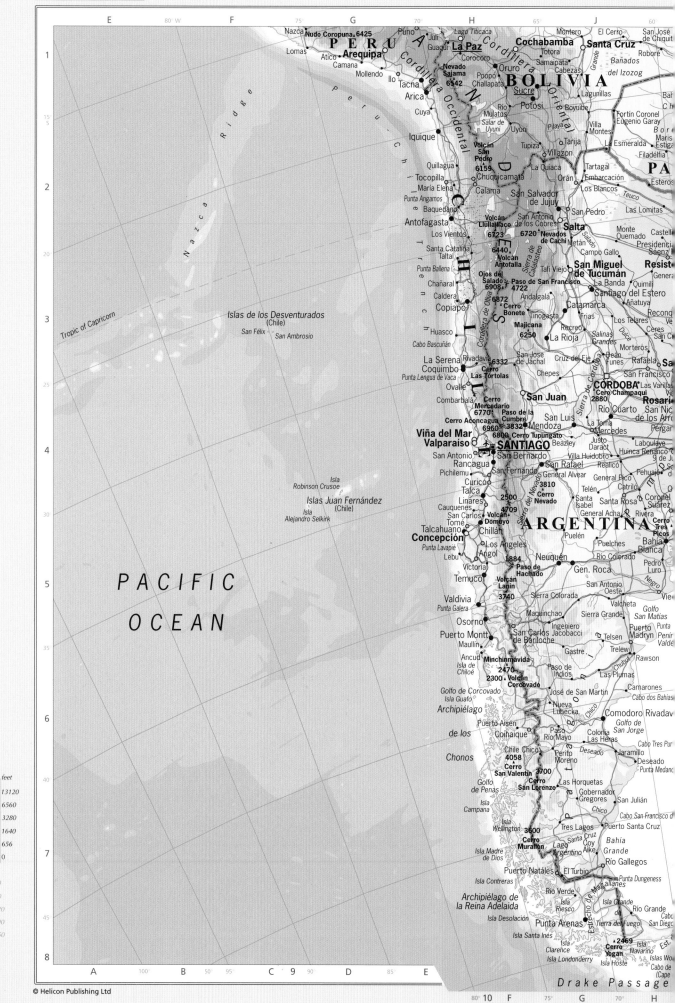

© Helicon Publishing Ltd

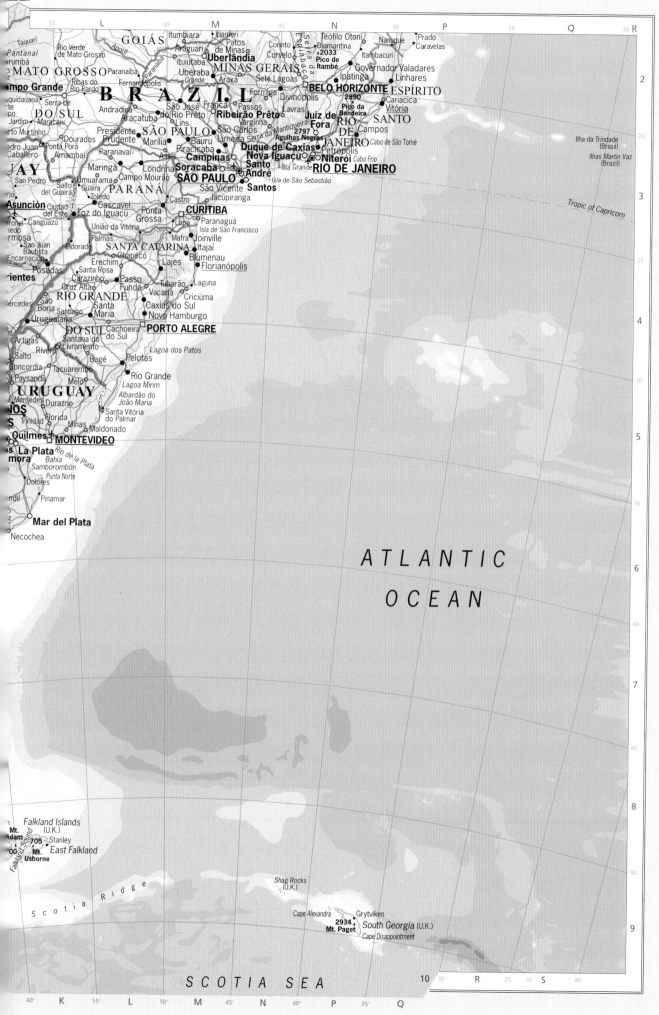

GOIÁS
Itumbiara
Ipameri
Teófilo Otoni
Nanuque
Prado
Caravelas
Taquari
Rio Verde
de Mato Grosso
Araguari
Patos
de Minas
Corinto
Diamantina
2033
Pico de
Itambé
Itambacuri
Pantanal
Ituiutaba
Curvelo
Paranaíba
Governador Valadares
rumbá
MATO GROSSO
Ribas do
Rio Pardo
Uberlândia
MINAS GERAIS
Ipatinga
Linhares
mpo Grande
Fernandópolis
Uberaba
Araxá
Sete Lagoas
BELO HORIZONTE
ESPÍRITO
quidauana
DO SUL
Serra de
Formiga
Divinópolis
2890
Cariacica
Andradina
São José
Franca
Passos
Pico da
Bandeira
Vitória
Jardim
Maçaíu
do Rio Prêto
Lavras
SANTO
to Murtinho
Dourados
Aracatuba
Lins
RIBEIRÃO PRÊTO
Varginha
2797
Juiz de
Fora
RIO
Campos
UAY
Presidente
Prudente
SÃO PAULO
Marilia
Bauru
São Carlos
Limeira
Agulhas Negras
DE
JANEIRO
Cabo de São Tomé
edro Juan
Caballero
Ponta Porã
Amambaí
Paranavaí
Assis
Piracicaba
Campinas
Duque de Caxias
Petrópolis
San Pedro
Umuarama
Maringá
Campo Mourão
Londrina
Soracaba
SÃO PAULO
Santo
André
Nova Iguaçu
Niterói
Cabo Frio
RIO DE JANEIRO
Salto
del Guairá
Guaíra
PARANÁ
São Vicente
Santos
Isla de São Sebastião
Asunción
Toledo
Castro
Jacupiranga
Ciudad
del Este
Foz do Iguaçu
Ponta
Grossa
CURITIBA
Paranaguá
Isla de São Francisco
onel
Caaguazú
União da Vitória
Lapa
iedo
Palmas
Mafra
Joinville
rmosa
Eldorado
SANTA CATARINA
Itajaí
San Juan
Bautista
Erechim
Chapecó
Lajes
Blumenau
Encarnación
Santa Rosa
Florianópolis
Posadas
Carazinho
Passo
Fundo
Vacaria
Laguna
rientes
Cruz Alta
Criciúma
mercedes
São
Borja
Santiago
Santa
Maria
Caxias do Sul
Tubarão
RIO GRANDE
Novo Hamburgo
Artigas
Uruguaiana
Cachoeira
do Sul
PORTO ALEGRE
Livramento
Rivera
Bagé
Pelotas
Salto
Santana do
Lagoa dos Patos
Concordia
Tacuarembó
Melo
Rio Grande
Paysandú
Lagoa Mirim
URUGUAY
Durazno
Albardão do
João Maria
Mercedes
Santa Vitória
do Palmar
NOS
Trinidad
Florida
Minas
S
Quilmes
Maldonado
La Plata
MONTEVIDEO
mora
Rio de la Plata
Bahía
Samborombón
Dolores
Punta Norte
ndil
Pinamar
Mar del Plata
Necochea

ATLANTIC

OCEAN

Tropic of Capricorn

Ilha da Trindade
(Brazil)

Ilhas Martin Vaz
(Brazil)

Falkland Islands
(U.K.)
Mt.
dam
705
Stanley
00
Mt.
Usborne
East Falkland

Shag Rocks
(U.K.)

Scotia Ridge

Cape Alexandra
Grytviken
2934
Mt. Paget
South Georgia (U.K.)
Cape Disappointment

SCOTIA SEA

Scale 1 : 50 700 000

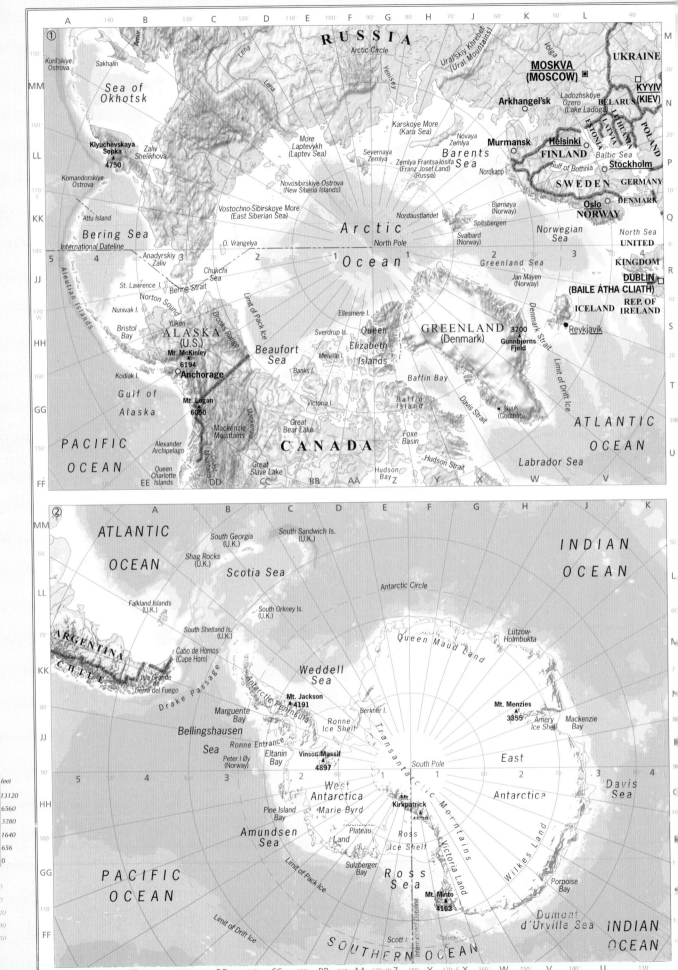

© Helicon Publishing Ltd

Nations of the World

AFGHANISTAN

Map page 46

National name: Dowlat-e Eslāmi-ye Afghānestān/Islamic State of Afghanistan
Area: 652,225 sq km/ 251,825 sq mi
Capital: Kābul
Major towns/cities: Kandahār, Herāt, Mazār-e Sharīf, Jalālābād, Konduz, Qal'eh-ye Now
Physical features: mountainous in center and northeast (Hindu Kush mountain range; Khyber and Salang passes, Wakhan salient, and Panjshir Valley), plains in north and southwest, Amu Darya (Oxus) River, Helmand River, Lake Saberi
Currency: afgháni
GNP per capita (PPP): (US$) 800 (1999 est)
Resources: natural gas, coal, iron ore, barytes, lapis lazuli, salt, talc, copper, chrome, gold, silver, asbestos, small petroleum reserves
Population: 22,720,000 (2000 est)
Population density: (per sq km) 34 (1999 est)
Language: Pashto, Dari (both official), Uzbek, Turkmen, Balochi, Pashai
Religion: Muslim (84% Sunni, 15% Shiite), other 1%
Time difference: GMT+4.5

ALBANIA

Map page 28

National name: Republika e Shqipërisë/Republic of Albania
Area: 28,748 sq km/11,099 sq mi
Capital: Tirana
Major towns/cities: Durrës, Shkodër, Elbasan, Vlorë, Korçë
Major ports: Durrës
Physical features: mainly mountainous, with rivers flowing east-west, and a narrow coastal plain
Currency: lek
GNP per capita (PPP): (US$) 2,892 (1999)
Resources: chromite (one of world's largest producers), copper, coal, nickel, petroleum and natural gas
Population: 3,113,000 (2000 est)
Population density: (per sq km) 108 (1999 est)
Language: Albanian (official), Greek
Religion: Muslim, Albanian Orthodox, Roman Catholic
Time difference: GMT +1

ALGERIA

Map page 52

National name: Al-Jumhuriyyat al-Jaza'iriyya ad-Dimuqratiyya ash-Sha'biyya/Democratic People's Republic of Algeria
Area: 2,381,741 sq km/ 919,590 sq mi
Capital: Algiers (Arabic al-Jaza'ir)
Major towns/cities: Oran, Annaba, Blida, Sétif, Constantine
Major ports: Oran (Ouahran), Annaba (Bône)
Physical features: coastal plains backed by mountains in north, Sahara desert in south; Atlas mountains, Barbary Coast, Chott Melrhir depression, Hoggar mountains
Currency: Algerian dinar
GNP per capita (PPP): (US$) 4,753 (1999)
Resources: natural gas and petroleum, iron ore, phosphates, lead, zinc, mercury, silver, salt, antimony, copper
Population: 31,471,000 (2000 est)
Population density: (per sq km) 13 (1999 est)
Language: Arabic (official), Berber, French
Religion: Sunni Muslim (state religion) 99%, Christian and Jewish 1%
Time difference: GMT +/-0

ANDORRA

Map page 20

National name: Principat d'Andorra/ Principality of Andorra
Area: 468 sq km/181 sq mi
Capital: Andorra la Vella
Major towns/cities: Les Escaldes
Physical features: mountainous, with narrow valleys; the eastern Pyrenees, Valira River
Currency: French franc and Spanish peseta
GNP per capita (PPP): (US$) 18,000 (1996 est)
Resources: iron, lead, aluminum, hydroelectric power
Population: 78,000 (2000 est)
Population density: (per sq km) 146 (1999 est)
Language: Catalan (official), Spanish, French
Religion: Roman Catholic (92%)
Time difference: GMT +1

ANGOLA

Map page 48

National name: República de Angolo/Republic of Angola
Area: 1,246,700 sq km/ 481,350 sq mi
Capital: Luanda (and chief port)
Major towns/cities: Lobito, Benguela, Huambo, Lubango, Malanje, Namibe, Kuito
Major ports: Huambo, Lubango, Malanje
Physical features: narrow coastal plain rises to vast interior plateau with rain forest in northwest; desert in south; Cuanza, Cuito, Cubango, and Cunene rivers
Currency: kwanza
GNP per capita (PPP): (US$) 632 (1999)
Resources: petroleum, diamonds, granite, iron ore, marble, salt, phosphates, manganese, copper
Population: 12,878,000 (2000 est)
Population density: (per sq km) 10 (1999 est)
Language: Portuguese (official), Bantu, other native dialects
Religion: Roman Catholic 38%, Protestant 15%, animist 47%
Time difference: GMT +1

ANTIGUA AND BARBUDA

Map page 72

Area: 440 sq km/169 sq mi (Antigua 280 sq km/108 sq mi, Barbuda 161 sq km/62 sq mi, plus Redonda 1 sq km/0.4 sq mi)
Capital: St. John's (on Antigua) (and chief port)
Major towns/cities: Codrington (on Barbuda)
Physical features: low-lying tropical islands of limestone and coral with some higher volcanic outcrops; no rivers and low rainfall result in frequent droughts and deforestation. Antigua is the largest of the Leeward Islands; Redonda is an uninhabited island of volcanic rock rising to 305 m/1,000 ft
Currency: East Caribbean dollar
GNP per capita (PPP): (US$) 8,959 (1999 est)
Population: 68,000 (2000 est)
Population density: (per sq km) 246 (1999 est)
Language: English (official), local dialects
Religion: Christian (mostly Anglican)
Time difference: GMT -4

ARGENTINA

Map page 78

National name: República Argentina/Argentine Republic
Area: 2,780,400 sq km/1,073,518 sq mi
Capital: Buenos Aires
Major towns/cities: Rosario, Córdoba, San Miguel de Tucumán, Mendoza, Santa Fé, La Plata
Major ports: La Plata and Bahía Blanca
Physical features: mountains in west, forest and savannah in north, pampas (treeless plains) in east-central area, Patagonian plateau in south; rivers Colorado, Salado, Paraná, Uruguay, Río de La Plata estuary; Andes mountains, with Aconcagua the highest peak in western hemisphere; Iguaçu Falls
Territories: disputed claim to the Falkland Islands (Islas Malvinas), and part of Antarctica
Currency: peso (= 10,000 australs, which it replaced in 1992)
GNP per capita (PPP): (US$) 11,324 (1999)
Resources: coal, crude oil, natural gas, iron ore, lead ore, zinc ore, tin, gold, silver, uranium ore, marble, borates, granite
Population: 37,032,000 (2000 est)
Population density: (per sq km) 13 (1999 est)
Language: Spanish (official) (95%), Italian (3%), English, German, French
Religion: predominantly Roman Catholic (state-supported), 2% protestant, 2% Jewish
Time difference: GMT -3

ARMENIA

Map page 46

National name: Hayastani Hanrapetoutioun/Republic of Armenia
Area: 29,800 sq km/ 11,505 sq mi
Capital: Yerevan
Major towns/cities: Gyumri (formerly Leninakan), Vanadzor (formerly Kirovakan), Hrazdan, Aboyvan
Physical features: mainly mountainous (including Mount Ararat), wooded
Currency: dram (replaced Russian ruble in 1993)
GNP per capita (PPP): (US$) 2,210 (1999)
Resources: copper, zinc, molybdenum, iron, silver, marble, granite
Population: 3,520,000 (2000 est)
Population density: (per sq km) 118 (1999 est)
Language: Armenian (official)
Religion: Armenian Orthodox
Time difference: GMT +4

AUSTRALIA

Map page 62

National name: Commonwealth of Australia
Area: 7,682,850 sq km/ 2,966,136 sq mi
Capital: Canberra
Major towns/cities: Adelaide, Alice Springs, Brisbane, Darwin, Melbourne, Perth, Sydney, Hobart, Newcastle, Wollongong
Physical features: Ayers Rock; Arnhem Land; Gulf of Carpentaria; Cape York Peninsula; Great Australian Bight; Great Sandy Desert; Gibson Desert; Great Victoria Desert; Simpson Desert; the Great Barrier Reef; Great Dividing Range and Australian Alps in the east (Mount Kosciusko, 2,229 m/7,136 ft, Australia's highest peak). The fertile southeast region is watered by the Darling, Lachlan, Murrumbridgee, and Murray rivers. Lake Eyre basin and Nullarbor Plain in the south
Territories: Norfolk Island, Christmas Island, Cocos (Keeling) Islands, Ashmore and Cartier Islands, Coral Sea Islands, Heard Island and McDonald Islands, Australian Antarctic Territory
Currency: Australian dollar
GNP per capita (PPP): (US$) 22,448 (1999)
Resources: coal, iron ore (world's third-largest producer),

bauxite, copper, zinc (world's second-largest producer), nickel (world's fifth-largest producer), uranium, gold, diamonds
Population: 18,886,000 (2000 est)
Population density: (per sq km) 2 (1999 est)
Language: English (official), Aboriginal languages
Religion: Anglican 26%, Roman Catholic 26%, other Christian 24%
Time difference: GMT +8/10

AUSTRIA
Map page 22
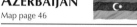

National name: Republik Österreich/Republic of Austria
Area: 83,859 sq km/32,367 sq mi
Capital: Vienna
Major towns/cities: Graz, Linz, Salzburg, Innsbruck, Klagenfurt
Physical features: landlocked mountainous state, with Alps in west and south (Austrian Alps, including Grossglockner and Brenner and Semmering passes, Lechtaler and Allgauer Alps north of River Inn, Carnic Alps on Italian border) and low relief in east where most of the population is concentrated; River Danube
Currency: schilling
GNP per capita (PPP): (US$) 23,808 (1999)
Resources: lignite, iron, kaolin, gypsum, talcum, magnesite, lead, zinc, forests
Population: 8,211,000 (2000 est)
Population density: (per sq km) 98 (1999 est)
Language: German (official)
Religion: Roman Catholic 78%, Protestant 5%
Time difference: GMT +1

AZERBAIJAN
Map page 46

National name: Azärbaycan Respublikasi/Republic of Azerbaijan
Area: 86,600 sq km/33,436 sq mi
Capital: Baku
Major towns/cities: Gäncä, Sumqayit, Naxçivan, Xankändi, Mingäçevir
Physical features: Caspian Sea with rich oil reserves; the country ranges from semidesert to the Caucasus Mountains
Currency: manat (replaced Russian ruble in 1993)
GNP per capita (PPP): (US$) 2,322 (1999)
Resources: petroleum, natural gas, iron ore, aluminum, copper, barytes, cobalt, precious metals, limestone, salt
Population: 7,734,000 (2000 est)
Population density: (per sq km) 89 (1999 est)
Language: Azeri (official), Russian
Religion: Shiite Muslim 68%, Sunni Muslim 27%, Russian Orthodox 3%, Armenian Orthodox 2%
Time difference: GMT +4

THE BAHAMAS
Map page 72

National name: Commonwealth of the Bahamas
Area: 13,880 sq km/5,383 sq mi
Capital: Nassau (on New Providence island)
Major towns/cities: Freeport (on Grand Bahama)
Physical features: comprises 700 tropical coral islands and about 1,000 cays; the Exumas are a narrow spine of 365 islands; only 30 of the desert islands are inhabited; Blue Holes of Andros, the world's longest and deepest submarine caves
Currency: Bahamian dollar
GNP per capita (PPP): (US$) 13,955 (1999 est)
Resources: aragonite (extracted from seabed), chalk, salt
Population: 307,000 (2000 est)
Population density: (per sq km) 22 (1999 est)
Language: English (official), Creole
Religion: Christian 94% (Baptist 32%, Roman Catholic 19%,

Anglican 20%, other Protestant 23%)
Time difference: GMT -5

BAHRAIN
Map page 46

National name: Dawlat al-Bahrayn/State of Bahrain
Area: 688 sq km/266 sq mi
Capital: Al Manāmah (on Bahrain island)
Major towns/cities: Sitra, Al Muharraq, Jidd Ḥafş, Madinat 'Īsá
Physical features: archipelago of 35 islands in Arabian Gulf, composed largely of sand-covered limestone; generally poor and infertile soil; flat and hot; causeway linking Bahrain to mainland Saudi Arabia
Currency: Bahraini dinar
GNP per capita (PPP): (US$) 11,527 (1999 est)
Resources: petroleum and natural gas
Population: 617,000 (2000 est)
Population density: (per sq km) 882 (1999 est)
Language: Arabic (official), Farsi, English, Urdu
Religion: 85% Muslim (Shiite 60%, Sunni 40%), Christian; Islam is the state religion
Time difference: GMT +3

BANGLADESH
Map page 44

National name: Gana Prajatantri Bangladesh/People's Republic of Bangladesh
Area: 144,000 sq km/55,598 sq mi
Capital: Dhaka
Major towns/cities: Rajshahi, Khulna, Chittagong, Sylhet, Rangpur, Narayanganj
Major ports: Chittagong, Khulna
Physical features: flat delta of rivers Ganges (Padma) and Brahmaputra (Jamuna), the largest estuarine delta in the world; annual rainfall of 2,540 mm/100 in; some 75% of the land is less than 3 m/10 ft above sea level; hilly in extreme southeast and northeast
Currency: taka
GNP per capita (PPP): (US$) 1,475 (1999)
Resources: natural gas, coal, limestone, china clay, glass sand
Population: 129,155,000 (2000 est)
Population density: (per sq km) 881 (1999 est)
Language: Bengali (official), English
Religion: Muslim 88%, Hindu 11%; Islam is the state religion
Time difference: GMT +6

BARBADOS
Map page 72

Area: 430 sq km/166 sq mi
Capital: Bridgetown
Major towns/cities: Speightstown, Holetown, Oistins
Physical features: most easterly island of the West Indies; surrounded by coral reefs; subject to hurricanes June-November; highest point Mount Hillaby 340 m/1,115 ft
Currency: Barbados dollar
GNP per capita (PPP): (US$) 12,260 (1998)
Resources: petroleum and natural gas
Population: 270,000 (2000 est)
Population density: (per sq km) 625 (1999 est)
Language: English (official), Bajan (a Barbadian English dialect)
Religion: 40% Anglican, 8% Pentecostal, 6% Methodist, 4% Roman Catholic
Time difference: GMT -4

BELARUS
Map page 30

National name: Respublika Belarus/Republic of Belarus
Area: 207,600 sq km/80,154 sq mi
Capital: Minsk (Belorussian Mensk)
Major towns/cities: Homyel', Vitsyebsk, Mahilyow, Babruysk, Hrodna, Brest
Physical features: more than 25% forested; rivers Dvina, Dnieper and its tributaries, including the Pripet and Beresina; the Pripet Marshes in the east; mild and damp climate
Currency: Belarus ruble, or zaichik
GNP per capita (PPP): (US$) 6,518 (1999)
Resources: petroleum, natural gas, peat, salt, coal, lignite
Population: 10,236,000 (2000 est)
Population density: (per sq km) 50 (1999 est)
Language: Belorussian (official), Russian, Polish
Religion: 80% Eastern Orthodox; Baptist, Roman Catholic Muslim, and Jewish minorities
Time difference: GMT +2

BELGIUM
Map page 14

National name: Royaume de Belgique (French), Koninkrijk België (Flemish)/Kingdom of Belgium
Area: 30,510 sq km/11,779 sq mi
Capital: Brussels
Major towns/cities: Antwerp, Ghent, Liège, Charleroi, Brugge, Mons, Namur, Louvain
Major ports: Antwerp, Oostende, Zeebrugge
Physical features: fertile coastal plain in northwest, central rolling hills rise eastward, hills and forest in southeast; Ardennes Forest; rivers Schelde and Meuse
Currency: Belgian franc
GNP per capita (PPP): (US$) 24,200 (1999)
Resources: coal, coke, natural gas, iron
Population: 10,161,000 (2000 est)
Population density: (per sq km) 333 (1999 est)
Language: Flemish (a Dutch dialect, known as Vlaams; official) (spoken by 56%, mainly in Flanders, in the north), French (especially the dialect Walloon; official) (spoken by 32%, mainly in Wallonia, in the south), German (0.6%; mainly near the eastern border)
Religion: Roman Catholic 75%, various Protestant denominations
Time difference: GMT +1

BELIZE
Map page 72

Area: 22,963 sq km/8,866 sq mi
Capital: Belmopan
Major towns/cities: Belize, Dangriga, Orange Walk, Corozal, San Ignacio
Major ports: Belize, Dangriga, Punta Gorda
Physical features: tropical swampy coastal plain, Maya Mountains in south; over 90% forested
Currency: Belize dollar
GNP per capita (PPP): (US$) 4,492 (1999)
Population: 241,000 (2000 est)
Population density: (per sq km) 10 (1999 est)
Language: English (official), Spanish (widely spoken), Creole dialects
Religion: Roman Catholic 62%, Protestant 30%
Time difference: GMT -6

BENIN
Map page 54

National name: République du Bénin/Republic of Benin
Area: 112,622 sq km/43,483 sq mi

Capital: Porto-Novo (official), Cotonou (de facto)

Major towns/cities: Abomey, Natitingou, Parakou, Kandi, Ouidah, Djougou, Bohicon, Cotonou

Major ports: Cotonou

Physical features: flat to undulating terrain; hot and humid in south; semiarid in north; coastal lagoons with fishing villages on stilts; Niger River in northeast

Currency: franc CFA

GNP per capita (PPP): (US$) 886 (1999)

Resources: petroleum, limestone, marble

Population: 6,097,000 (2000 est)

Population density: (per sq km) 53 (1999 est)

Language: French (official), Fon (47%), Yoruba (9%) (both in the south), six major tribal languages in the north

Religion: animist 70%, Muslim 15%, Christian 15%

Time difference: GMT +1

BHUTAN
Map page 44

National name: Druk-yul/Kingdom of Bhutan

Area: 47,500 sq km/18,147 sq mi

Capital: Thimphu

Major towns/cities: Paro, Punakha, Mongar, Phuntsholing, Tashigang

Physical features: occupies southern slopes of the Himalayas; Gangkar Punsum (7,529 m/24,700 ft) is one of the world's highest unclimbed peaks; cut by valleys formed by tributaries of the Brahmaputra; thick forests in south

Currency: ngultrum, although the Indian rupee is also accepted

GNP per capita (PPP): (US$) 1,496 (1999 est)

Resources: limestone, gypsum, coal, slate, dolomite, lead, talc, copper

Population: 2,124,000 (2000 est)

Population density: (per sq km) 44 (1999 est)

Language: Dzongkha (a Tibetan dialect; official), Tibetan, Sharchop, Bumthap, Nepali, English

Religion: 70% Mahayana Buddhist (state religion), 25% Hindu

Time difference: GMT +6

BOLIVIA
Map page 76

National name: República de Bolivia/Republic of Bolivia

Area: 1,098,581 sq km/424,162 sq mi

Capital: La Paz (seat of government), Sucre (legal capital and seat of the judiciary)

Major towns/cities: Santa Cruz, Cochabamba, Oruro, El Alto, Potosí, Tarija

Physical features: high plateau (Altiplano) between mountain ridges (cordilleras); forest and lowlands (llano) in east; Andes; lakes Titicaca (the world's highest navigable lake, 3,800 m/12,500 ft) and Poopó

Currency: boliviano

GNP per capita (PPP): (US$) 2,193 (1999)

Resources: petroleum, natural gas, tin (world's fifth-largest producer), zinc, silver, gold, lead, antimony, tungsten, copper

Population: 8,329,000 (2000 est)

Population density: (per sq km) 7 (1999 est)

Language: Spanish (official) (4%), Aymara, Quechua

Religion: Roman Catholic 90% (state-recognized)

Time difference: GMT -4

BOSNIA-HERZEGOVINA
Map page 26

National name: Bosna i Hercegovina/Bosnia-Herzegovina

Area: 51,129 sq km/19,740 sq mi

Capital: Sarajevo

Major towns/cities: Banja Luka, Mostar, Prijedor, Tuzla, Zenica, Bihac, Gorazde

Physical features: barren, mountainous country, part of the Dinaric Alps; limestone gorges; 20 km/12 mi of coastline with no harbor

Currency: dinar

GNP per capita (PPP): (US$) 450 (1996 est)

Resources: copper, lead, zinc, iron ore, coal, bauxite, manganese

Population: 3,972,000 (2000 est)

Population density: (per sq km) 75 (1999 est)

Language: Serbian, Croat, Bosnian

Religion: 40% Muslim, 31% Serbian Orthodox, 15% Roman Catholic

Time difference: GMT +1

BOTSWANA
Map page 58

National name: Republic of Botswana

Area: 582,000 sq km/224,710 sq mi

Capital: Gaborone

Major towns/cities: Mahalapye, Serowe, Francistown, Selebi-Phikwe, Molepolole, Maun

Physical features: Kalahari Desert in southwest (70-80% of national territory is desert), plains (Makgadikgadi salt pans) in east, fertile lands and Okavango Delta in north

Currency: franc CFA

GNP per capita (PPP): (US$) 6,032 (1999)

Resources: diamonds (world's third-largest producer), copper-nickel ore, coal, soda ash, gold, cobalt, salt, plutonium, asbestos, chromite, iron, silver, manganese, talc, uranium

Population: 1,622,000 (2000 est)

Population density: (per sq km) 3 (1999 est)

Language: English (official), Setswana (national)

Religion: Christian 50%, animist 50%

Time difference: GMT +2

BRAZIL
Map page 74

National name: República Federativa do Brasil/Federative Republic of Brazil

Area: 8,511,965 sq km/3,286,469 sq mi

Capital: Brasília

Major towns/cities: São Paulo, Belo Horizonte, Nova Iguaçu, Rio de Janeiro, Belém, Recife, Porto Alegre, Salvador, Curitiba, Manaus, Fortaleza

Major ports: Rio de Janeiro, Belém, Recife, Porto Alegre, Salvador

Physical features: the densely forested Amazon basin covers the northern half of the country with a network of rivers; south is fertile; enormous energy resources, both hydroelectric (Itaipú Reservoir on the Paraná, and Tucuruí on the Tocantins) and nuclear (uranium ores); mostly tropical climate

Currency: real

GNP per capita (PPP): (US$) 6,317 (1999)

Resources: iron ore (world's second-largest producer), tin (world's fourth-largest producer), aluminum (world's fourth-largest producer), gold, phosphates, platinum, bauxite, uranium, manganese, coal, copper, petroleum, natural gas, hydroelectric power, forests

Population: 170,115,000 (2000 est)

Population density: (per sq km) 20 (1999 est)

Language: Portuguese (official), Spanish, English, French, 120 Indian languages

Religion: Roman Catholic 70%; Indian faiths

Time difference: GMT -2/5

BRUNEI
Map page 42

National name: Negara Brunei Darussalam/State of Brunei

Area: 5,765 sq km/2,225 sq mi

Capital: Bandar Seri Begawan (and chief port)

Major towns/cities: Seria, Kuala Belait

Physical features: flat coastal plain with hilly lowland in west and mountains in east (Mount Pagon 1,850 m/6,070 ft); 75% of the area is forested; the Limbang valley splits Brunei in two, and its cession to Sarawak in 1890 is disputed by Brunei; tropical climate; Temburong, Tutong, and Belait rivers

Currency: Bruneian dollar, although the Singapore dollar is also accepted

GNP per capita (PPP): (US$) 24,824 (1999 est)

Resources: petroleum, natural gas

Population: 328,000 (2000 est)

Population density: (per sq km) 56 (1999 est)

Language: Malay (official), Chinese (Hokkien), English

Religion: Muslim 66%, Buddhist 14%, Christian 10%

Time difference: GMT +8

BULGARIA
Map page 26

National name: Republika Bulgaria/Republic of Bulgaria

Area: 110,912 sq km/42,823 sq mi

Capital: Sofia

Major towns/cities: Plovdiv, Varna, Ruse, Burgas, Stara Zagora, Pleven

Major ports: Burgas, Varna

Physical features: lowland plains in north and southeast separated by mountains (Balkan and Rhodope) that cover three-quarters of the country; River Danube in north

Currency: lev

GNP per capita (PPP): (US$) 4,914 (1999)

Resources: coal, iron ore, manganese, lead, zinc, petroleum

Population: 8,225,000 (2000 est)

Population density: (per sq km) 75 (1999 est)

Language: Bulgarian (official), Turkish

Religion: Eastern Orthodox Christian, Muslim, Jewish, Roman Catholic, Protestant

Time difference: GMT +2

BURKINA FASO
Map page 54

Area: 274,122 sq km/105,838 sq mi

Capital: Ouagadougou

Major towns/cities: Bobo-Dioulasso, Koudougou, Banfora, Ouahigouya, Tenkodogo

Physical features: landlocked plateau with hills in west and southeast; headwaters of the River Volta; semiarid in north, forest and farmland in south; linked by rail to Abidjan in Côte d'Ivoire, Burkina Faso's only outlet to the sea

Currency: franc CFA

GNP per capita (PPP): (US$) 898 (1999 est)

Resources: manganese, zinc, limestone, phosphates, diamonds, gold, antimony, marble, silver, lead

Population: 11,937,000 (2000 est)

Population density: (per sq km) 42 (1999 est)

Language: French (official), 50 Sudanic languages (90%)

Religion: animist 40%, Sunni Muslim 50%, Christian (mainly Roman Catholic) 10%

Time difference: GMT+/-0

BURUNDI
Map page 56

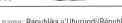

National name: Republika y'Uburundi/République du Burundi/Republic of Burundi

Area: 27,834 sq km/10,746 sq mi
Capital: Bujumbura
Major towns/cities: Bururi,
Ngozi, Ruyigi, Kayanaza
Physical features: landlocked
grassy highland straddling
watershed of Nile and Congo;
Lake Tanganyika, Great Rift Valley
Currency: Burundi franc
GNP per capita (PPP): (US$) 553 (1999 est)
Resources: nickel, gold, tungsten, phosphates, vanadium,
uranium, peat, petroleum deposits have been detected
Population: 6,695,000 (2000 est)
Population density: (per sq km) 236 (1999 est)
Language: Kirundi, French (both official), Kiswahili
Religion: Roman Catholic 62%, Pentecostalist 5%, Anglican 1%,
Muslim 1%, animist
Time difference: GMT +2

CAMBODIA

Map page 40

National name: Preah
Réaché'anachâkr
Kâmpuchéa/Kingdom of Cambodia
Area: 181,035 sq km/
69,897 sq mi
Capital: Phnum Penh
Major towns/cities:
Bâtdâmbâng, Kâmpông Cham,
Siëmréab, Prey Vêng
Major ports: Kâmpông Cham
Physical features: mostly flat, forested plains with mountains in
southwest and north; Mekong River runs north-south; Lake Tonle
Sap
Currency: Cambodian riel
GNP per capita (PPP): (US$) 1,286 (1999 est)
Resources: phosphates, iron ore, gemstones, bauxite, silicon,
manganese
Population: 11,168,000 (2000 est)
Population density: (per sq km) 66 (1999 est)
Language: Khmer (official), French
Religion: Theravada Buddhist 95%, Muslim, Roman Catholic
Time difference: GMT +7

CAMEROON

Map page 54

National name: République du
Cameroun/Republic of Cameroon
Area: 475,440 sq km/
183,567 sq mi
Capital: Yaoundé
Major towns/cities: Garoua,
Douala, Nkongsamba, Maroua,
Bamenda, Bafoussam,
Ngaoundéré
Major ports: Douala
Physical features: desert in far north in the Lake Chad basin,
mountains in west, dry savannah plateau in the intermediate area,
and dense tropical rain forest in south; Mount Cameroon 4,070
m/13,358 ft, an active volcano on the coast, west of the Adamawa
Mountains
Currency: franc CFA
GNP per capita (PPP): (US$) 1,444 (1999)
Resources: petroleum, natural gas, tin ore, limestone, bauxite,
iron ore, uranium, gold
Population: 15,085,000 (2000 est)
Population density: (per sq km) 31 (1999 est)
Language: French, English (both official; often spoken in
pidgin), Sudanic languages (in the north), Bantu languages
(elsewhere); there has been some discontent with the emphasis
on French - there are 163 indigenous peoples with their own
African languages
Religion: animist 50%, Christian 33%, Muslim 16%
Time difference: GMT +1

CANADA

Map page 68

Area: 9,970,610 sq km/
3,849,652 sq mi
Capital: Ottawa
Major towns/cities: Toronto,
Montréal, Vancouver,
Edmonton, Calgary, Winnipeg,
Québec, Hamilton, Saskatoon,
Halifax, London, Kitchener, Mississauga, Laval, Surrey
Physical features: mountains in west, with low-lying plains in
interior and rolling hills in east; St. Lawrence Seaway, Mackenzie
River; Great Lakes; Arctic Archipelago; Rocky Mountains; Great
Plains or Prairies; Canadian Shield; Niagara Falls; climate varies
from temperate in south to arctic in north; 45% of country
forested
Currency: Canadian dollar
GNP per capita (PPP): (US$) 23,725 (1999)
Resources: petroleum, natural gas, coal, copper (world's third-
largest producer), nickel (world's second-largest producer), lead
(world's fifth-largest producer), zinc (world's largest producer),
iron, gold, uranium, timber
Population: 31,147,000 (2000 est)
Population density: (per sq km) 3 (1999 est)
Language: English (60%), French (24%) (both official),
American Indian languages, Inuktitut (Inuit)
Religion: Roman Catholic 45%, various Protestant
denominations
Time difference: GMT -3.5/9

CAPE VERDE

Map page 54

National name: República de
Cabo Verde/Republic of Cape
Verde
Area: 4,033 sq km/1,557 sq mi
Capital: Praia
Major towns/cities: Mindelo,
Santa Maria
Major ports: Mindelo
Physical features: archipelago of ten volcanic islands 565
km/350 mi west of Senegal; the windward (Barlavento) group
includes Santo Antão, São Vicente, Santa Luzia, São Nicolau, Sal,
and Boa Vista; the leeward (Sotovento) group comprises Maio,
São Tiago, Fogo, and Brava; all but Santa Luzia are inhabited
Currency: Cape Verde escudo
GNP per capita (PPP): (US$) 3,497 (1999 est)
Resources: salt, pozzolana (volcanic rock), limestone, basalt,
kaolin
Population: 428,000 (2000 est)
Population density: (per sq km) 104 (1999 est)
Language: Portuguese (official), Creole
Religion: Roman Catholic 93%, Protestant (Nazarene Church)
Time difference: GMT -1

CENTRAL AFRICAN REPUBLIC

Map page 56

National name: République
Centrafricaine/Central African
Republic
Area: 622,436 sq km/
240,322 sq mi
Capital: Bangui
Major towns/cities: Berbérati,
Bouar, Bambari, Bossangoa,
Carnot, Kaga Bandoro
Physical features: landlocked flat plateau, with rivers flowing
north and south, and hills in northeast and southwest; dry in
north, rain forest in southwest; mostly wooded; Kotto and Mbali
river falls; the Oubangui River rises 6 m/20 ft at Bangui during the
wet season (June-November)
Currency: franc CFA
GNP per capita (PPP): (US$) 1,131 (1999 est)
Resources: gem diamonds and industrial diamonds, gold,
uranium, iron ore, manganese, copper
Population: 3,615,000 (2000 est)
Population density: (per sq km) 6 (1999 est)
Language: French (official), Sangho (national), Arabic, Hunsa,

Swahili
Religion: Protestant 25%, Roman Catholic 25%, animist 24%,
Muslim 15%
Time difference: GMT +1

CHAD

Map page 50

National name: République du
Tchad/Republic of Chad
Area: 1,284,000 sq km/
495,752 sq mi
Capital: Ndjamena (formerly Fort
Lamy)
Major towns/cities: Sarh,
Moundou, Abéché, Bongor, Doba,
Kélo, Koumra
Physical features: landlocked state with mountains (Tibetsi)
and part of Sahara Desert in north; moist savannah in south;
rivers in south flow northwest to Lake Chad
Currency: franc CFA
GNP per capita (PPP): (US$) 816 (1999 est)
Resources: petroleum, tungsten, tin ore, bauxite, iron ore, gold,
uranium, limestone, kaolin, titanium
Population: 7,651,000 (2000 est)
Population density: (per sq km) 6 (1999 est)
Language: French, Arabic (both official), over 100 African
languages
Religion: Muslim 50%, Christian 25%, animist 25%
Time difference: GMT +1

CHILE

Map page 78

National name: República de
Chile/Republic of Chile
Area: 756,950 sq km/
292,258 sq mi
Capital: Santiago
Major towns/cities:
Concepción, Viña del Mar,
Valparaíso, Talcahuano, Puente
Alto, Temuco, Antofagasta
Major ports: Valparaíso,
Antofagasta, Arica, Iquique, Punta Arenas
Physical features: Andes mountains along eastern border,
Atacama Desert in north, fertile central valley, grazing land and
forest in south
Territories: Easter Island, Juan Fernández Islands, part of Tierra
del Fuego, claim to part of Antarctica
Currency: Chilean peso
GNP per capita (PPP): (US$) 8,370 (1999)
Resources: copper (world's largest producer), gold, silver, iron
ore, molybdenum, cobalt, iodine, saltpeter, coal, natural gas,
petroleum, hydroelectric power
Population: 15,211,000 (2000 est)
Population density: (per sq km) 20 (1999 est)
Language: Spanish (official)
Religion: Roman Catholic 80%, Protestant 13%, atheist and
nonreligious 6%
Time difference: GMT -4

CHINA

Map page 32

National name: Zhonghua Renmin
Gongheguo (Zhongguo)/People's
Republic of China
Area: 9,572,900 sq km/
3,696,000 sq mi
Capital: Beijing (or Peking)
Major towns/cities: Shanghai,
Hong Kong, Chongqing, Tianjin,
Guangzhou (English Canton), Shenyang (formerly Mukden),
Wuhan, Nanjing, Harbin, Chengdu, Xi'an
Major ports: Tianjin, Shanghai, Hong Kong, Qingdao, Guangzhou
Physical features: two-thirds of China is mountains or desert
(north and west); the low-lying east is irrigated by rivers Huang
He (Yellow River), Chang Jiang (Yangtze-Kiang), Xi Jiang (Si
Kiang)

Territories: Paracel Islands
Currency: yuan
GNP per capita (PPP): (US$) 3,291 (1999)
Resources: coal, graphite, tungsten, molybdenum, antimony, tin (world's largest producer), lead (world's fifth-largest producer), mercury, bauxite, phosphate rock, iron ore (world's largest producer), diamonds, gold, manganese, zinc (world's third-largest producer), petroleum, natural gas, fish
Population: 1,277,558,000 (2000 est)
Population density: (per sq km) 133 (1999 est)
Language: Chinese (dialects include Mandarin (official), Yue (Cantonese), Wu (Shanghaiese), Minbai, Minnah, Xiang, Gan, and Hakka)
Religion: Taoist, Confucianist, and Buddhist; Muslim 2-3%; Christian about 1% (divided between the 'patriotic' church established in 1958 and the 'loyal' church subject to Rome); Protestant 3 million
Time difference: GMT +8

COLOMBIA
Map page 76

National name: República de Colombia/Republic of Colombia
Area: 1,141,748 sq km/440,828 sq mi
Capital: Bogotá
Major towns/cities: Medellín, Cali, Barranquilla, Cartagena, Bucaramanga, Cúcuta, Ibagué
Major ports: Barranquilla, Cartagena, Buenaventura
Physical features: the Andes mountains run north-south; flat coastland in west and plains (llanos) in east; Magdalena River runs north to Caribbean Sea; includes islands of Providencia, San Andrés, and Mapelo; almost half the country is forested
Currency: Colombian peso
GNP per capita (PPP): (US$) 5,709 (1999 est)
Resources: petroleum, natural gas, coal, nickel, emeralds (accounts for about half of world production), gold, manganese, copper, lead, mercury, platinum, limestone, phosphates
Population: 42,321,000 (2000 est)
Population density: (per sq km) 36 (1999 est)
Language: Spanish (official) (95%)
Religion: Roman Catholic
Time difference: GMT -5

COMOROS
Map page 58

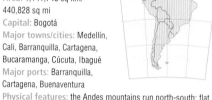

National name: Jumhuriyyat al-Qumur al-Itthadiyah al-Islamiyah (Arabic), République fédérale islamique des Comores (French)/Federal Islamic Republic of the Comoros
Area: 1,862 sq km/718 sq mi
Capital: Moroni
Major towns/cities: Mutsamudu, Domoni, Fomboni, Mitsamiouli
Physical features: comprises the volcanic islands of Njazídja, Nzwani, and Mwali (formerly Grande Comore, Anjouan, Moheli); at northern end of Mozambique Channel in Indian Ocean between Madagascar and coast of Africa
Currency: Comorian franc
GNP per capita (PPP): (US$) 1,360 (1999 est)
Population: 694,000 (2000 est)
Population density: (per sq km) 363 (1999 est)
Language: Arabic, French (both official), Comorian (a Swahili and Arabic dialect), Makua
Religion: Muslim; Islam is the state religion
Time difference: GMT +3

CONGO, DEMOCRATIC REPUBLIC OF
Map page 56

National name: République Démocratique du Congo/Democratic Republic of Congo
Area: 2,344,900 sq km/905,366 sq mi

Capital: Kinshasa
Major towns/cities: Lubumbashi, Kananga, Mbuji-Mayi, Kisangani, Kolwezi, Likasi, Boma
Major ports: Matadi, Kalemie
Physical features: Congo River basin has tropical rain forest (second-largest remaining in world) and savannah; mountains in east and west; lakes Tanganyika, Albert, Edward; Ruwenzori Range
Currency: congolese franc
GNP per capita (PPP): (US$) 731 (1999 est)
Resources: petroleum, copper, cobalt (65% of world's reserves), manganese, zinc, tin, uranium, silver, gold, diamonds (one of the world's largest producers of industrial diamonds)
Population: 51,654,000 (2000 est)
Population density: (per sq km) 21 (1999 est)
Language: French (official), Swahili, Lingala, Kikongo, Tshiluba (all national languages), over 200 other languages
Religion: Roman Catholic 41%, Protestant 32%, Kimbanguist 13%, animist 10%, Muslim 1-5%
Time difference: GMT +1/2

CONGO, REPUBLIC OF
Map page 54

National name: République du Congo/Republic of Congo
Area: 342,000 sq km/132,046 sq mi
Capital: Brazzaville
Major towns/cities: Pointe-Noire, Nkayi, Loubomo, Bouenza, Mossendjo, Ouésso, Owando
Major ports: Pointe-Noire
Physical features: narrow coastal plain rises to central plateau, then falls into northern basin; Congo River on the border with the Democratic Republic of Congo; half the country is rain forest
Currency: franc CFA
GNP per capita (PPP): (US$) 897 (1999)
Resources: petroleum, natural gas, lead, zinc, gold, copper, phosphate, iron ore, potash, bauxite
Population: 2,943,000 (2000 est)
Population density: (per sq km) 8 (1999 est)
Language: French (official), Kongo, Monokutuba and Lingala (both patois), and other dialects
Religion: Christian 50%, animist 48%, Muslim 2%
Time difference: GMT +1

COSTA RICA
Map page 72

National name: República de Costa Rica/Republic of Costa Rica
Area: 51,100 sq km/19,729 sq mi
Capital: San José
Major towns/cities: Alajuela, Cartago, Limón, Puntarenas, San Isidro, Desamparados
Major ports: Limón, Puntarenas
Physical features: high central plateau and tropical coasts; Costa Rica was once entirely forested, containing an estimated 5% of the earth's flora and fauna
Currency: colón
GNP per capita (PPP): (US$) 5,770 (1999 est)
Resources: gold, salt, hydro power
Population: 4,023,000 (2000 est)
Population density: (per sq km) 77 (1999 est)
Language: Spanish (official)
Religion: Roman Catholic 95% (state religion)
Time difference: GMT -6

CÔTE D'IVOIRE
Map page 54

National name: République de la Côte d'Ivoire/Republic of the Ivory Coast
Area: 322,463 sq km/124,502 sq mi

Capital: Yamoussoukro
Major towns/cities: Abidjan, Bouaké, Daloa, Man, Korhogo, Gagnoa
Major ports: Abidjan, San Pedro
Physical features: tropical rain forest (diminishing as exploited) in south; savannah and low mountains in north; coastal plain; Vridi canal, Kossou dam, Monts du Toura
Currency: franc CFA
GNP per capita (PPP): (US$) 1,546 (1999)
Resources: petroleum, diamonds, gold, nickel, reserves of manganese, iron ore, bauxite
Population: 14,786,000 (2000 est)
Population density: (per sq km) 45 (1999 est)
Language: French (official), over 60 ethnic languages
Religion: animist 17%, Muslim 39% (mainly in north), Christian 26% (mainly Roman Catholic in south)
Time difference: GMT +/-0

CROATIA
Map page 26

National name: Republika Hrvatska/Republic of Croatia
Area: 56,538 sq km/21,829 sq mi
Capital: Zagreb
Major towns/cities: Osijek, Split, Dubrovnik, Rijeka, Zadar, Pula
Major ports: chief port: Rijeka (Fiume); other ports: Zadar, Šibenik, Split, Dubrovnik
Physical features: Adriatic coastline with large islands; very mountainous, with part of the Karst region and the Julian and Styrian Alps; some marshland
Currency: kuna
GNP per capita (PPP): (US$) 6,915 (1999)
Resources: petroleum, natural gas, coal, lignite, bauxite, iron ore, salt
Population: 4,473,000 (2000 est)
Population density: (per sq km) 79 (1999 est)
Language: Croat (official), Serbian
Religion: Roman Catholic (Croats) 76.5%; Orthodox Christian (Serbs) 11%, Protestant 1.4%, Muslim 1.2%
Time difference: GMT +1

CUBA
Map page 72

National name: República de Cuba/Republic of Cuba
Area: 110,860 sq km/42,803 sq mi
Capital: Havana
Major towns/cities: Santiago de Cuba, Camagüey, Holguín, Guantánamo, Santa Clara, Bayamo, Cienfuegos
Physical features: comprises Cuba and smaller islands including Isle of Youth; low hills; Sierra Maestra mountains in southeast; Cuba has 3,380 km/2,100 mi of coastline, with deep bays, sandy beaches, coral islands and reefs
Currency: Cuban peso
GNP per capita (PPP): (US$) N/A
Resources: iron ore, copper, chromite, gold, manganese, nickel, cobalt, silver, salt
Population: 11,201,000 (2000 est)
Population density: (per sq km) 101 (1999 est)
Language: Spanish (official)
Religion: Roman Catholic; also Episcopalians and Methodists
Time difference: GMT -5

CYPRUS
Map page 28

National name: Kipriakí Dimokratía/Greek Republic of Cyprus (south); Kibris Cumhuriyeti/Turkish Republic of Northern Cyprus (north)
Area: 9,251 sq km/3,571 sq mi (3,335 sq km/1,287 sq mi is Turkish-occupied)

Capital: Nicosia (divided between Greek and Turkish Cypriots)
Major towns/cities: Limassol, Larnaka, Pafos, Lefkosia, Famagusta
Major ports: Limassol, Larnaka, and Pafos (Greek); Keryneia and Famagusta (Turkish)
Physical features: central plain between two east-west mountain ranges
Currency: Cyprus pound and Turkish lira
GNP per capita (PPP): (US$) 18,395 (1999 est)
Resources: copper precipitates, beutonite, umber and other ochres
Population: 786,000 (2000 est)
Population density: (per sq km) 84 (1999 est)
Language: Greek, Turkish (both official), English
Religion: Greek Orthodox 78%, Sunni Muslim 18%, Maronite, Armenian Apostolic
Time difference: GMT +2

CZECH REPUBLIC
Map page 10

National name: Ceská Republika/Czech Republic
Area: 78,864 sq km/30,449 sq mi
Capital: Prague
Major towns/cities: Brno, Ostrava, Olomouc, Liberec, Plzen, Hradec Králové, České Budějovice
Physical features: mountainous; rivers: Morava, Labe (Elbe), Vltava (Moldau)
Currency: koruna (based on the Czechoslovak koruna)
GNP per capita (PPP): (US$) 12,289 (1999)
Resources: coal, lignite
Population: 10,244,000 (2000 est)
Population density: (per sq km) 130 (1999 est)
Language: Czech (official), Slovak
Religion: Roman Catholic 39%, atheist 30%, Protestant 5%, Orthodox 3%
Time difference: GMT +1

DENMARK
Map page 8

National name: Kongeriget Danmark/Kingdom of Denmark
Area: 43,075 sq km/16,631 sq mi
Capital: Copenhagen
Major towns/cities: Århus, Odense, Ålborg, Esbjerg, Randers, Kolding, Horsens
Major ports: Århus, Odense, Ålborg, Esbjerg
Physical features: comprises the Jutland peninsula and about 500 islands (100 inhabited) including Bornholm in the Baltic Sea; the land is flat and cultivated; sand dunes and lagoons on the west coast and long inlets on the east; the main island is Sjælland (Zealand), where most of Copenhagen is located (the rest is on the island of Amager)
Territories: the dependencies of Faroe Islands and Greenland
Currency: Danish krone
GNP per capita (PPP): (US$) 24,280 (1999)
Resources: crude petroleum, natural gas, salt, limestone
Population: 5,293,000 (2000 est)
Population density: (per sq km) 123 (1999 est)
Language: Danish (official), German
Religion: Evangelical Lutheran 87% (national church), other Protestant and Roman Catholic 3%
Time difference: GMT +1

DJIBOUTI
Map page 50

National name: Jumhouriyya Djibouti/Republic of Djibouti
Area: 23,200 sq km/8,957 sq mi
Capital: Djibouti (and chief port)
Major towns/cities: Tadjoura, Obock, Dikhil, Ali-Sabieh

Physical features: mountains divide an inland plateau from a coastal plain; hot and arid
Currency: Djibouti franc
GNP per capita (PPP): (US$) 1,200 (1999 est)
Population: 638,000 (2000 est)
Population density: (per sq km) 27 (1999 est)
Language: French (official), Issa (Somali), Afar, Arabic
Religion: Sunni Muslim
Time difference: GMT +3

DOMINICA
Map page 72

National name: Commonwealth of Dominica
Area: 751 sq km/290 sq mi
Capital: Roseau
Major towns/cities: Portsmouth, Marigot, Mahaut, Atkinson, Grand Bay
Major ports: Roseau, Portsmouth, Berekua, Marigot
Physical features: second-largest of the Windward Islands, mountainous central ridge with tropical rain forest
Currency: East Caribbean dollar, although the pound sterling and French franc are also accepted
GNP per capita (PPP): (US$) 4,825 (1999)
Resources: pumice, limestone, clay
Population: 71,000 (2000 est)
Population density: (per sq km) 100 (1999 est)
Language: English (official), a Dominican patois (which reflects earlier periods of French rule)
Religion: Roman Catholic 80%
Time difference: GMT -4

DOMINICAN REPUBLIC
Map page 72

National name: República Dominicana/Dominican Republic
Area: 48,442 sq km/18,703 sq mi
Capital: Santo Domingo
Major towns/cities: Santiago, La Romana, San Pedro de Macorís, La Vega, San Juan, San Cristóbal
Physical features: comprises eastern two-thirds of island of Hispaniola; central mountain range with fertile valleys; Pico Duarte 3,174 m/10,417 ft, highest point in Caribbean islands
Currency: Dominican Republic peso
GNP per capita (PPP): (US$) 4,653 (1999 est)
Resources: ferro-nickel, gold, silver
Population: 8,495,000 (2000 est)
Population density: (per sq km) 173 (1999 est)
Language: Spanish (official)
Religion: Roman Catholic
Time difference: GMT -4

ECUADOR
Map page 76

National name: República del Ecuador/Republic of Ecuador
Area: 270,670 sq km/104,505 sq mi
Capital: Quito
Major towns/cities: Guayaquil, Cuenca, Machala, Portoviejo, Manta, Ambato, Santo Domingo
Major ports: Guayaquil
Physical features: coastal plain rises sharply to Andes Mountains, which are divided into a series of cultivated valleys; flat, low-lying rain forest in the east; Galapagos Islands; Cotopaxi, the world's highest active volcano. Ecuador is crossed by the Equator, from which it derives its name
Currency: sucre
GNP per capita (PPP): (US$) 2,605 (1999)
Resources: petroleum, natural gas, gold, silver, copper, zinc,

---

antimony, iron, uranium, lead, coal
Population: 12,646,000 (2000 est)
Population density: (per sq km) 46 (1999 est)
Language: Spanish (official), Quechua, Jivaro, other indigenous languages
Religion: Roman Catholic
Time difference: GMT -5

EGYPT
Map page 50

National name: Jumhuriyyat Misr al-'Arabiyya/Arab Republic of Egypt
Area: 1,001,450 sq km/386,659 sq mi
Capital: Cairo
Major towns/cities: El Giza, Shubrâ el Kheima, Alexandria, Port Said, El-Mahalla el-Koubra, El Mansûra, Suez
Major ports: Alexandria, Port Said, Suez, Dumyât, Shubra Al Khayma
Physical features: mostly desert; hills in east; fertile land along Nile valley and delta; cultivated and settled area is about 35,500 sq km/13,700 sq mi; Aswan High Dam and Lake Nasser; Sinai
Currency: Egyptian pound
GNP per capita (PPP): (US$) 3,303 (1999)
Resources: petroleum, natural gas, phosphates, manganese, uranium, coal, iron ore, gold
Population: 68,470,000 (2000 est)
Population density: (per sq km) 67 (1999 est)
Language: Arabic (official), Coptic (derived from ancient Egyptian), English, French
Religion: Sunni Muslim 90%, Coptic Christian and other Christian 6%
Time difference: GMT +2

EL SALVADOR
Map page 72

National name: República de El Salvador/Republic of El Salvador
Area: 21,393 sq km/8,259 sq mi
Capital: San Salvador
Major towns/cities: Santa Ana, San Miguel, Nueva San Salvador, Apopa, Delgado
Physical features: narrow coastal plain, rising to mountains in north with central plateau
Currency: US dollar (replaced Salvadorean colón in 2001)
GNP per capita (PPP): (US$) 4,048 (1999 est)
Resources: salt, limestone, gypsum
Population: 6,276,000 (2000 est)
Population density: (per sq km) 288 (1999 est)
Language: Spanish (official), Nahuatl
Religion: about 75% Roman Catholic, Protestant
Time difference: GMT -6

EQUATORIAL GUINEA
Map page 54

National name: República de Guinea Ecuatorial/Republic of Equatorial Guinea
Area: 28,051 sq km/10,830 sq mi
Capital: Malabo
Major towns/cities: Bata, Mongomo, Ela Nguema, Mbini, Campo Yaunde, Los Angeles
Physical features: comprises mainland Río Muni, plus the small islands of Corisco, Elobey Grande and Elobey Chico, and Bioko (formerly Fernando Po) together with Annobón (formerly Pagalu); nearly half the land is forested; volcanic mountains on Bioko
Currency: franc CFA
GNP per capita (PPP): (US$) 3,545 (1999 est)
Resources: petroleum, natural gas, gold, uranium, iron ore, tantalum, manganese
Population: 453,000 (2000 est)
Population density: (per sq km) 16 (1999 est)
Language: Spanish (official), pidgin English, a Portuguese

patois (on Annobón, whose people were formerly slaves of the Portuguese), Fang and other African patois (on Río Muni)
Religion: Roman Catholic, Protestant, animist
Time difference: GMT +1

ERITREA
Map page 50

National name: Hagere Eretra al-Dawla al-Iritra/State of Eritrea
Area: 125,000 sq km/48,262 sq mi
Capital: Asmara
Major towns/cities: Assab, Keren, Massawa, Adi Ugri, Ed
Major ports: Assab, Massawa
Physical features: coastline along the Red Sea 1,000 km/620 mi; narrow coastal plain that rises to an inland plateau; Dahlak Islands
Currency: Ethiopian nakfa
GNP per capita (PPP): (US$) 1,012 (1999 est)
Resources: gold, silver, copper, zinc, sulfur, nickel, chrome, potash, basalt, limestone, marble, sand, silicates
Population: 3,850,000 (2000 est)
Population density: (per sq km) 30 (1999 est)
Language: Tigre, Tigrinya, Arabic, English, Afar, Amharic, Kunama, Italian
Religion: mainly Sunni Muslim and Coptic Christian, some Roman Catholic, Protestant, and animist
Time difference: GMT +3

ESTONIA
Map page 8

National name: Eesti Vabariik/Republic of Estonia
Area: 45,000 sq km/17,374 sq mi
Capital: Tallinn
Major towns/cities: Tartu, Narva, Kohtla-Järve, Pärnu
Physical features: lakes and marshes in a partly forested plain; 774 km/481 mi of coastline; mild climate; Lake Peipus and Narva River forming boundary with Russian Federation; Baltic islands, the largest of which is Saaremaa
Currency: kroon
GNP per capita (PPP): (US$) 7,826 (1999)
Resources: oilshale, peat, phosphorite ore, superphosphates
Population: 1,396,000 (2000 est)
Population density: (per sq km) 31 (1999 est)
Language: Estonian (official), Russian
Religion: Eastern Orthodox, Evangelical Lutheran, Russian Orthodox, Muslim, Judaism
Time difference: GMT +2

ETHIOPIA
Map page 48

National name: Ya'Ityopya Federalawi Dimokrasiyawi Repeblik/Federal Democratic Republic of Ethiopia
Area: 1,096,900 sq km/423,513 sq mi
Capital: Addis Ababa
Major towns/cities: Dirē Dawa, Harar, Nazrēt, Desē, Gonder, Mek'ele, Bahir Dar
Physical features: a high plateau with central mountain range divided by Rift Valley; plains in east; source of Blue Nile River; Danakil and Ogaden deserts
Currency: Ethiopian birr
GNP per capita (PPP): (US$) 599 (1999)
Resources: gold, salt, platinum, copper, potash. Reserves of petroleum have not been exploited
Population: 62,565,000 (2000 est)
Population density: (per sq km) 56 (1999 est)
Language: Amharic (official), Arabic, Tigrinya, Orominga, about 100 other local languages
Religion: Muslim 45%, Ethiopian Orthodox Church (which has had its own patriarch since 1976) 35%, animist 12%, other Christian 8%
Time difference: GMT +3

FIJI
Map page 60

National name: Matanitu Ko Viti/Republic of the Fiji Islands
Area: 18,333 sq km/7,078 sq mi
Capital: Suva
Major towns/cities: Lautoka, Nadi, Ba, Labasa, Nausori
Major ports: Lautoka, Levuka
Physical features: comprises about 844 Melanesian and Polynesian islands and islets (about 100 inhabited), the largest being Viti Levu (10,429 sq km/4,028 sq mi) and Vanua Levu (5,556 sq km/2,146 sq mi); mountainous, volcanic, with tropical rain forest and grasslands; almost all islands surrounded by coral reefs; high volcanic peaks
Currency: Fiji dollar
GNP per capita (PPP): (US$) 4,536 (1999)
Resources: gold, silver, copper
Population: 817,000 (2000 est)
Population density: (per sq km) 44 (1999 est)
Language: English (official), Fijian, Hindi
Religion: Methodist 37%, Hindu 38%, Muslim 8%, Roman Catholic 8%, Sikh
Time difference: GMT +12

FINLAND
Map page 8

National name: Suomen Tasavalta (Finnish)/Republiken Finland (Swedish)/Republic of Finland
Area: 338,145 sq km/130,557 sq mi
Capital: Helsinki (Swedish Helsingfors)
Major towns/cities: Tampere, Turku, Espoo, Vantaa, Oulu
Major ports: Turku, Oulu
Physical features: most of the country is forest, with low hills and about 60,000 lakes; one-third is within the Arctic Circle; archipelago in south includes Åland Islands; Helsinki is the most northerly national capital on the European continent. At the 70th parallel there is constant daylight for 73 days in summer and 51 days of uninterrupted night in winter.
Currency: markka
GNP per capita (PPP): (US$) 21,209 (1999)
Resources: copper ore, lead ore, gold, zinc ore, silver, peat, hydro power, forests
Population: 5,176,000 (2000 est)
Population density: (per sq km) 15 (1999 est)
Language: Finnish (93%), Swedish (6%) (both official), Saami (Lapp), Russian
Religion: Evangelical Lutheran 87%, Greek Orthodox 1%
Time difference: GMT +2

FRANCE
Map page 18

National name: République Française/French Republic
Area: (including Corsica) 543,965 sq km/210,024 sq mi
Capital: Paris
Major towns/cities: Lyon, Lille, Bordeaux, Toulouse, Nantes, Marseille, Nice, Strasbourg, Montpellier, Rennes, Le Havre
Major ports: Marseille, Nice, Le Havre
Physical features: rivers Seine, Loire, Garonne, Rhône; mountain ranges Alps, Massif Central, Pyrenees, Jura, Vosges, Cévennes; Auvergne mountain region; Mont Blanc (4,810 m/15,781 ft); Ardennes forest; Riviera; caves of Dordogne with relics of early humans; the island of Corsica
Territories: Guadeloupe, French Guiana, Martinique, Réunion, St. Pierre and Miquelon, Southern and Antarctic Territories, New Caledonia, French Polynesia, Wallis and Futuna, Mayotte, Bassas da India, Clipperton Island, Europa Island, Glorioso Islands, Juan de Nova Island, Tromelin Island
Currency: franc
GNP per capita (PPP): (US$) 21,897 (1999)
Resources: coal, petroleum, natural gas, iron ore, copper, zinc, bauxite
Population: 59,080,000 (2000 est)
Population density: (per sq km) 108 (1999 est)
Language: French (official; regional languages include Basque, Breton, Catalan, Corsican, and Provençal)
Religion: Roman Catholic, about 90%; also Muslim, Protestant, and Jewish minorities
Time difference: GMT +1

GABON
Map page 54

National name: République Gabonaise/Gabonese Republic
Area: 267,667 sq km/103,346 sq mi
Capital: Libreville
Major towns/cities: Port-Gentil, Franceville (or Masuku), Lambaréné, Oyem, Mouila
Major ports: Port-Gentil and Owendo
Physical features: virtually the whole country is tropical rain forest; narrow coastal plain rising to hilly interior with savannah in east and south; Ogooué River flows north-west
Currency: franc CFA
GNP per capita (PPP): (US$) 5,325 (1999)
Resources: petroleum, natural gas, manganese (one of world's foremost producers and exporters), iron ore, uranium, gold, niobium, talc, phosphates
Population: 1,226,000 (2000 est)
Population density: (per sq km) 4 (1999 est)
Language: French (official), Fang (in the north), Bantu languages, and other local dialects
Religion: Christian 60% (mostly Roman Catholic), animist about 4%, Muslim 1%
Time difference: GMT +1

THE GAMBIA
Map page 54

National name: Republic of the Gambia
Area: 10,402 sq km/4,016 sq mi
Capital: Banjul
Major towns/cities: Brikama, Bakau, Farafenni, Gunjur, Basse
Physical features: consists of narrow strip of land along the River Gambia; river flanked by low hills
Currency: dalasi
GNP per capita (PPP): (US$) 1,492 (1999)
Resources: ilmenite, zircon, rutile, petroleum (well discovered, but not exploited)
Population: 1,305,000 (2000 est)
Population density: (per sq km) 122 (1999 est)
Language: English (official), Mandinka, Fula, Wolof, other indigenous dialects
Religion: Muslim 85%, with animist and Christian minorities
Time difference: GMT +/-0

GEORGIA
Map page 46

National name: Sak'art'velo/Georgia
Area: 69,700 sq km/26,911 sq mi
Capital: T'bilisi
Major towns/cities: K'ut'aisi, Rust'avi, Bat'umi, Zugdidi, Gori
Physical features: largely mountainous with a variety of landscape from the subtropical Black Sea shores to the ice and snow of the crest line of the Caucasus; chief rivers are Kura and

Rioni
Currency: lari
GNP per capita (PPP): (US$) 3,606 (1999)
Resources: coal, manganese, barytes, clay, petroleum and natural gas deposits, iron and other ores, gold, agate, marble, alabaster, arsenic, tungsten, mercury
Population: 4,968,000 (2000 est)
Population density: (per sq km) 72 (1999 est)
Language: Georgian (official), Russian, Abkazian, Armenian, Azeri
Religion: Georgian Orthodox, also Muslim
Time difference: GMT +3

GERMANY
Map page 12

National name: Bundesrepublik Deutschland/Federal Republic of Germany
Area: 357,041 sq km/ 137,853 sq mi
Capital: Berlin
Major towns/cities: Koln, Hamburg, Munich, Essen, Frankfurt am Main, Dortmund, Stuttgart, Düsseldorf, Leipzig, Dresden, Hannover
Major ports: Hamburg, Kiel, Bremerhaven, Rostock
Physical features: flat in north, mountainous in south with Alps; rivers Rhine, Weser, Elbe flow north, Danube flows southeast, Oder and Neisse flow north along Polish frontier; many lakes, including Müritz; Black Forest, Harz Mountains, Erzgebirge (Ore Mountains), Bavarian Alps, Fichtelgebirge, Thüringer Forest
Currency: Deutschmark
GNP per capita (PPP): (US$) 22,404 (1999)
Resources: lignite, hard coal, potash salts, crude oil, natural gas, iron ore, copper, timber, nickel, uranium
Population: 82,220,000 (2000 est)
Population density: (per sq km) 230 (1999 est)
Language: German (official)
Religion: Protestant (mainly Lutheran) 38%, Roman Catholic 34%
Time difference: GMT +1

GHANA
Map page 54

National name: Republic of Ghana
Area: 238,540 sq km/ 92,100 sq mi
Capital: Accra
Major towns/cities: Kumasi, Tamale, Tema, Sekondi, Takoradi, Cape Coast, Koforidua, Bolgatanga, Obuasi
Major ports: Sekondi, Tema
Physical features: mostly tropical lowland plains; bisected by River Volta
Currency: cedi
GNP per capita (PPP): (US$) 1,793 (1999 est)
Resources: diamonds, gold, manganese, bauxite
Population: 20,212,000 (2000 est)
Population density: (per sq km) 83 (1999 est)
Language: English (official), Ga, other African languages
Religion: Christian 40%, animist 32%, Muslim 16%
Time difference: GMT +/-0

GREECE
Map page 28

National name: Elliniki Dimokratia/Hellenic Republic
Area: 131,957 sq km/ 50,948 sq mi
Capital: Athens
Major towns/cities: Thessaloniki, Peiraias, Patra, Iraklion, Larisa, Peristerio, Kallithéa
Major ports: Peiraias, Thessaloniki, Patra, Iraklion

Physical features: mountainous (Mount Olympus); a large number of islands, notably Crete, Corfu, and Rhodes, and Cyclades and Ionian Islands
Currency: drachma
GNP per capita (PPP): (US$) 14,595 (1999)
Resources: bauxite, nickel, iron pyrites, magnetite, asbestos, marble, salt, chromite, lignite
Population: 10,645,000 (2000 est)
Population density: (per sq km) 81 (1999 est)
Language: Greek (official)
Religion: Greek Orthodox, over 96%; about 1% Muslim
Time difference: GMT +2

GRENADA
Map page 72

Area: (including the southern Grenadine Islands, notably Carriacou and Petit Martinique) 344 sq km/133 sq mi
Capital: St. George's
Major towns/cities: Grenville, Sauteurs, Victoria, Gouyave
Physical features: southernmost of the Windward Islands; mountainous; Grand-Anse beach; Annandale Falls; the Great Pool volcanic crater
Currency: East Caribbean dollar
GNP per capita (PPP): (US$) 5,847 (1999)
Population: 94,000 (2000 est)
Population density: (per sq km) 286 (1999 est)
Language: English (official), some French-African patois
Religion: Roman Catholic 53%, Anglican about 14%, Seventh Day Adventist, Pentecostal, Methodist
Time difference: GMT -4

GUATEMALA
Map page 72

National name: República de Guatemala/Republic of Guatemala
Area: 108,889 sq km/ 42,042 sq mi
Capital: Guatemala
Major towns/cities: Quezaltenango, Escuintla, Puerto Barrios (naval base), Chinautla
Physical features: mountainous; narrow coastal plains; limestone tropical plateau in north; frequent earthquakes
Currency: quetzal
GNP per capita (PPP): (US$) 3,517 (1999 est)
Resources: petroleum, antimony, gold, silver, nickel, lead, iron, tungsten
Population: 11,385,000 (2000 est)
Population density: (per sq km) 102 (1999 est)
Language: Spanish (official), 22 Mayan languages (45%)
Religion: Roman Catholic 70%, Protestant 10%, traditional Mayan
Time difference: GMT -6

GUINEA
Map page 54

National name: République de Guinée/Republic of Guinea
Area: 245,857 sq km/ 94,925 sq mi
Capital: Conakry
Major towns/cities: Labé, Nzérékoré, Kankan, Kindia, Mamou, Siguiri
Physical features: flat coastal plain with mountainous interior; sources of rivers Niger, Gambia, and Senegal; forest in southeast; Fouta Djallon, area of sandstone plateaus, cut by deep valleys
Currency: Guinean franc
GNP per capita (PPP): (US$) 1,761 (1999)
Resources: bauxite (world's top exporter of bauxite and second-largest producer of bauxite ore), alumina, diamonds, gold, granite, iron ore, uranium, nickel, cobalt, platinum
Population: 7,430,000 (2000 est)
Population density: (per sq km) 30 (1999 est)

Language: French (official), Susu, Pular (Fulfude), Malinke, and other African languages
Religion: Muslim 85%, Christian 6%, animist
Time difference: GMT +/-0

GUINEA-BISSAU
Map page 54

National name: República da Guiné-Bissau/Republic of Guinea-Bissau
Area: 36,125 sq km/13,947 sq mi
Capital: Bissau (and chief port)
Major towns/cities: Bafatá, Bissorã, Bolama, Gabú, Bubaque, Cacheu, Catió, Farim
Physical features: flat coastal plain rising to savannah in east
Currency: Guinean peso
GNP per capita (PPP): (US$) 595 (1999)
Resources: bauxite, phosphate, petroleum (largely unexploited)
Population: 1,213,000 (2000 est)
Population density: (per sq km) 33 (1999 est)
Language: Portuguese (official), Crioulo (a Cape Verdean dialect of Portuguese), African languages
Religion: animist 58%, Muslim 40%, Christian 5% (mainly Roman Catholic)
Time difference: GMT +/-0

GUYANA
Map page 76

National name: Cooperative Republic of Guyana
Area: 214,969 sq km/ 82,999 sq mi
Capital: Georgetown (and chief port)
Major towns/cities: Linden, New Amsterdam, Bartica, Corriverton
Major ports: New Amsterdam
Physical features: coastal plain rises into rolling highlands with savannah in south; mostly tropical rain forest; Mount Roraima; Kaietur National Park, including Kaietur Falls on the Potaro (tributary of Essequibo) 250 m/821 ft
Currency: Guyanese dollar
GNP per capita (PPP): (US$) 3,242 (1999 est)
Resources: gold, diamonds, bauxite, copper, tungsten, iron, nickel, quartz, molybdenum
Population: 861,000 (2000 est)
Population density: (per sq km) 4 (1999 est)
Language: English (official), Hindi, American Indian languages
Religion: Christian 57%, Hindu 34%, Sunni Muslim 9%
Time difference: GMT -3

HAITI
Map page 72

National name: République d'Haïti/Republic of Haiti
Area: 27,750 sq km/ 10,714 sq mi
Capital: Port-au-Prince
Major towns/cities: Cap-Haïtien, Gonaïves, Les Cayes, St. Marc, Carrefour, Delmas
Physical features: mainly mountainous and tropical; occupies western third of Hispaniola Island in Caribbean Sea
Currency: gourde
GNP per capita (PPP): (US$) 1,407 (1999 est)
Resources: marble, limestone, calcareous clay, unexploited copper and gold deposits
Population: 8,222,000 (2000 est)
Population density: (per sq km) 291 (1999 est)
Language: French (20%), Creole (both official)
Religion: Christian 95% (of which 70% are Roman Catholic), voodoo 4%
Time difference: GMT -5

HONDURAS

Map page 72

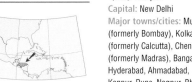

National name: República de Honduras/Republic of Honduras
Area: 112,100 sq km/ 43,281 sq mi
Capital: Tegucigalpa
Major towns/cities: San Pedro Sula, La Ceiba, El Progreso, Choluteca, Juticalpa, Danlí
Major ports: La Ceiba
Physical features: narrow tropical coastal plain with mountainous interior, Bay Islands, Caribbean reefs
Currency: lempira
GNP per capita (PPP): (US$) 2,254 (1999 est)
Resources: lead, zinc, silver, gold, tin, iron, copper, antimony
Population: 6,485,000 (2000 est)
Population density: (per sq km) 56 (1999 est)
Language: Spanish (official), English, American Indian languages
Religion: Roman Catholic 97%
Time difference: GMT -6

HUNGARY

Map page 10

National name: Magyar Köztársaság/Republic of Hungary
Area: 93,032 sq km/35,919 sq mi
Capital: Budapest
Major towns/cities: Miskolc, Debrecen, Szeged, Pécs, Győr, Nyíregyháza, Székesfehérvár, Kecskemét
Physical features: Great Hungarian Plain covers eastern half of country; Bakony Forest, Lake Balaton, and Transdanubian Highlands in the west; rivers Danube, Tisza, and Raba; more than 500 thermal springs
Currency: forint
GNP per capita (PPP): (US$) 10,479 (1999)
Resources: lignite, brown coal, natural gas, petroleum, bauxite, hard coal
Population: 10,036,000 (2000 est)
Population density: (per sq km) 108 (1999 est)
Language: Hungarian (official)
Religion: Roman Catholic 65%, Calvinist 20%, other Christian denominations, Jewish, atheist
Time difference: GMT +1

ICELAND

Map page 8

National name: Lýðveldið Ísland/ Republic of Iceland
Area: 103,000 sq km/39,768 sq mi
Capital: Reykjavík
Major towns/cities: Akureyri, Kópavogur, Hafnarfjördur, Keflavík, Vestmannaeyjar
Physical features: warmed by the Gulf Stream; glaciers and lava fields cover 75% of the country; active volcanoes (Hekla was once thought the gateway to Hell), geysers, hot springs, and new islands created offshore (Surtsey in 1963); subterranean hot water heats 85% of Iceland's homes; Sidujokull glacier moving at 100 meters a day
Currency: krona
GNP per capita (PPP): (US$) 26,283 (1999)
Resources: aluminum, diatomite, hydroelectric and thermal power, fish
Population: 281,000 (2000 est)
Population density: (per sq km) 3 (1999 est)
Language: Icelandic (official)
Religion: Evangelical Lutheran about 90%, other Protestant and Roman Catholic about 4%
Time difference: GMT +/-0

INDIA

Map page 44

National name: Bharat (Hindi)/India; Bharatiya Janarajya (unofficial)/Republic of India

---

Area: 3,166,829 sq km/ 1,222,713 sq mi
Capital: New Delhi
Major towns/cities: Mumbai (formerly Bombay), Kolkata (formerly Calcutta), Chennai (formerly Madras), Bangalore, Hyderabad, Ahmadabad, Kanpur, Pune, Nagpur, Bhopal, Jaipur, Lucknow, Surat
Major ports: Kolkata, Mumbai, Chennai
Physical features: Himalayas on northern border; plains around rivers Ganges, Indus, Brahmaputra; Deccan peninsula south of the Narmada River forms plateau between Western and Eastern Ghats mountain ranges; desert in west; Andaman and Nicobar Islands, Lakshadweep (Laccadive Islands)
Currency: rupee
GNP per capita (PPP): (US$) 2,149 (1999 est)
Resources: coal, iron ore, copper ore, bauxite, chromite, gold, manganese ore, zinc, lead, limestone, crude oil, natural gas, diamonds
Population: 1,013,662,000 (2000 est)
Population density: (per sq km) 315 (1999 est)
Language: Hindi, English, Assamese, Bengali, Gujarati, Kannada, Kashmiri, Konkani, Malayalam, Manipuri, Marathi, Nepali, Oriya, Punjabi, Sanskrit, Sindhi, Tamil, Telugu, Urdu (all official), more than 1,650 dialects
Religion: Hindu 80%, Sunni Muslim 10%, Christian 2.5%, Sikh 2%, Buddhist, Jewish
Time difference: GMT +5.5

INDONESIA

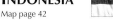

Map page 42

National name: Republik Indonesia/Republic of Indonesia
Area: 1,904,569 sq km/ 735,354 sq mi
Capital: Jakarta
Major towns/cities: Surabaya, Bandung, Medan, Semarang, Palembang, Tangerang, Tanjungkarang-Telukbetung, Ujung Pandang, Malang
Major ports: Surabaya, Semarang (Java), Ujung Pandang (Sulawesi)
Physical features: comprises 13,677 tropical islands (over 6,000 of them are inhabited): the Greater Sundas (including Java, Madura, Sumatra, Sulawesi, and Kalimantan (part of Borneo)), the Lesser Sunda Islands/Nusa Tenggara (including Bali, Lombok, Sumbawa, Flores, Sumba, Alor, Lomblen, Timor, Roti, and Savu), Maluku/Moluccas (over 1,000 islands including Ambon, Ternate, Tidore, Tanimbar, and Halmahera), and Irian Jaya (part of New Guinea); over half the country is tropical rain forest; it has the largest expanse of peatlands in the tropics
Currency: rupiah
GNP per capita (PPP): (US$) 2,439 (1999)
Resources: petroleum (principal producer of petroleum in the Far East), natural gas, bauxite, nickel (world's third-largest producer), copper, tin (world's second-largest producer), gold, coal, forests
Population: 212,107,000 (2000 est)
Population density: (per sq km) 110 (1999 est)
Language: Bahasa Indonesia (closely related to Malay; official), Javanese, Dutch, over 550 regional languages and dialects
Religion: Muslim 87%, Protestant 6%, Roman Catholic 3%, Hindu 2% and Buddhist 1% (the continued spread of Christianity, together with an Islamic revival, have led to greater religious tensions)
Time difference: GMT +7/9

IRAN

Map page 46

National name: Jomhûrî-ye Eslâmi-ye Îrân/Islamic Republic of Iran
Area: 1,648,000 sq km/ 636,292 sq mi
Capital: Teheran
Major towns/cities: Eşfahān, Mashhad, Tabrīz, Shīrāz, Ahvāz, Kermānshāh, Qom, Karaj
Major ports: Abādān
Physical features: plateau surrounded by mountains, including

---

Elburz and Zagros; Lake Rezayeh; Dasht-e-Kavir desert; occupies islands of Abu Musa, Greater Tunb and Lesser Tunb in the Gulf
Currency: rial
GNP per capita (PPP): (US$) 5,163 (1999)
Resources: petroleum, natural gas, coal, magnetite, gypsum, iron ore, copper, chromite, salt, bauxite, decorative stone
Population: 67,702,000 (2000 est)
Population density: (per sq km) 41 (1999 est)
Language: Farsi (official), Kurdish, Turkish, Arabic, English, French
Religion: Shiite Muslim (official) 91%, Sunni Muslim 8%; Zoroastrian, Christian, Jewish, and Baha'i comprise about 1%
Time difference: GMT +3.5

IRAQ

Map page 46

National name: al-Jumhuriyya al'Iraqiyya/Republic of Iraq
Area: 434,924 sq km/ 167,924 sq mi
Capital: Baghdād
Major towns/cities: Al Mawşil, Al Başrah, Kirkūk, Al Ḩillah, An Najaf, An Nāşirīyah, Arbīl
Major ports: Al Başrah
Physical features: mountains in north, desert in west; wide valley of rivers Tigris and Euphrates running northwest-southeast; canal linking Baghdād and Persian Gulf opened in 1992
Currency: Iraqi dinar
GNP per capita (PPP): (US$) N/A
Resources: petroleum, natural gas, sulfur, phosphates
Population: 23,115,000 (2000 est)
Population density: (per sq km) 52 (1999 est)
Language: Arabic (80%) (official), Kurdish (15%), Assyrian, Armenian
Religion: Shiite Muslim 60%, Sunni Muslim 37%, Christian 3%
Time difference: GMT +3

IRELAND, REPUBLIC OF

Map page 16

National name: Poblacht Na hÉireann/Republic of Ireland
Area: 70,282 sq km/27,135 sq mi
Capital: Dublin
Major towns/cities: Cork, Limerick, Galway, Waterford, Dundalk, Bray
Major ports: Cork, Dun Laoghaire, Limerick, Waterford, Galway
Physical features: central plateau surrounded by hills; rivers Shannon, Liffey, Boyne; Bog of Allen; Macgillicuddy's Reeks, Wicklow Mountains; Lough Corrib, lakes of Killarney; Galway Bay and Aran Islands
Currency: Irish pound, or punt Eireannach
GNP per capita (PPP): (US$) 19,180 (1999)
Resources: lead, zinc, peat, limestone, gypsum, petroleum, natural gas, copper, silver
Population: 3,730,000 (2000 est)
Population density: (per sq km) 53 (1999 est)
Language: Irish Gaelic, English (both official)
Religion: Roman Catholic 92%, Church of Ireland, other Protestant denominations 3%
Time difference: GMT +/-0

ISRAEL

Map page 46

National name: Medinat Israel/ State of Israel
Area: 20,800 sq km/8,030 sq mi (as at 1949 armistice)
Capital: Jerusalem (not recognized by the United Nations)
Major towns/cities: Tel Aviv-Yafo, Haifa, Bat-Yam, Ḩolon, Ramat Gan, Petah Tiqwa, Rishon le Ẕiyyon, Be'ér Sheva'
Major ports: Tel Aviv-Yafo, Haifa, 'Akko (formerly Acre), Elat
Physical features: coastal plain of Sharon between Haifa and Tel

Aviv noted since ancient times for its fertility; central mountains of Galilee, Samaria, and Judea; Dead Sea, Lake Tiberias, and River Jordan Rift Valley along the east are below sea level; Negev Desert in the south; Israel occupies Golan Heights, West Bank, East Jerusalem, and Gaza Strip (the last was awarded limited autonomy, with West Bank town of Jericho, in 1993)
Currency: shekel
GNP per capita (PPP): (US$) 16,867 (1999)
Resources: potash, bromides, magnesium, sulfur, copper ore, gold, salt, petroleum, natural gas
Population: 6,217,000 (2000 est)
Population density: (per sq km) 293 (1999 est)
Language: Hebrew, Arabic (both official), English, Yiddish, other European and west Asian languages
Religion: Israel is a secular state, but the predominant faith is Judaism 80%; also Sunni Muslim (about 15%), Christian, and Druze
Time difference: GMT +2

ITALY
Map page 24

National name: Repubblica Italiana/ Italian Republic
Area: 301,300 sq km/ 116,331 sq mi
Capital: Rome
Major towns/cities: Milan, Naples, Turin, Palermo, Genoa, Bologna, Florence
Major ports: Naples, Genoa, Palermo, Bari, Catania, Trieste
Physical features: mountainous (Maritime Alps, Dolomites, Apennines) with narrow coastal lowlands; continental Europe's only active volcanoes: Vesuvius, Etna, Stromboli; rivers Po, Adige, Arno, Tiber, Rubicon; islands of Sicily, Sardinia, Elba, Capri, Ischia, Lipari, Pantelleria; lakes Como, Maggiore, Garda
Currency: lira
GNP per capita (PPP): (US$) 20,751 (1999)
Resources: lignite, lead, zinc, mercury, potash, sulfur, fluorspar, bauxite, marble, petroleum, natural gas, fish
Population: 57,298,000 (2000 est)
Population density: (per sq km) 190 (1999 est)
Language: Italian (official), German and Ladin (in the north), French (in the Valle d'Aosta region), Greek and Albanian (in the south)
Religion: Roman Catholic 98% (state religion)
Time difference: GMT +1

JAMAICA
Map page 72

Area: 10,957 sq km/4,230 sq mi
Capital: Kingston
Major towns/cities: Montego Bay, Spanish Town, Portmore, May Pen
Physical features: mountainous tropical island; Blue Mountains (so called because of the haze over them)
Currency: Jamaican dollar
GNP per capita (PPP): (US$) 3,276 (1999)
Resources: bauxite (one of world's major producers), marble, gypsum, silica, clay
Population: 2,583,000 (2000 est)
Population density: (per sq km) 234 (1999 est)
Language: English (official), Jamaican Creole
Religion: Protestant 70%, Rastafarian
Time difference: GMT -5

JAPAN
Map page 38

National name: Nihon-koku/State of Japan
Area: 377,535 sq km/ 145,766 sq mi
Capital: Tōkyō
Major towns/cities: Yokohama, Ōsaka, Nagoya, Fukuoka, Kita-Kyūshū, Kyōto,

Sapporo, Kobe, Kawasaki, Hiroshima
Major ports: Ōsaka, Nagoya, Yokohama, Kobe
Physical features: mountainous, volcanic (Mount Fuji, volcanic Mount Aso, Japan Alps); comprises over 1,000 islands, the largest of which are Hokkaido, Honshu, Kyushu, and Shikoku
Currency: yen
GNP per capita (PPP): (US$) 24,041 (1999)
Resources: coal, iron, zinc, copper, natural gas, fish
Population: 126,714,000 (2000 est)
Population density: (per sq km) 335 (1999 est)
Language: Japanese (official), Ainu
Religion: Shinto, Buddhist (often combined), Christian (less than 1%)
Time difference: GMT +9

JORDAN
Map page 46

National name: Al-Mamlaka al-Urduniyya al-Hashemiyyah/ Hashemite Kingdom of Jordan
Area: 89,206 sq km/ 34,442 sq mi (excluding the West Bank 5,879 sq km/ 2,269 sq mi)
Capital: Ammān
Major towns/cities: Zarqā', Irbid, Ma'ān
Major ports: Aqaba
Physical features: desert plateau in east; Rift Valley separates east and west banks of River Jordan
Currency: Jordanian dinar
GNP per capita (PPP): (US$) 3,542 (1999)
Resources: phosphates, potash, shale
Population: 6,669,000 (2000 est)
Population density: (per sq km) 73 (1999 est)
Language: Arabic (official), English
Religion: over 90% Sunni Muslim (official religion), small communities of Christians and Shiite Muslims
Time difference: GMT +2

KAZAKHSTAN
Map page 34

National name: Kazak Respublikasy/Republic of Kazakhstan
Area: 2,717,300 sq km/ 1,049,150 sq mi
Capital: Astana (formerly Akmola)
Major towns/cities: Qaraghandy, Pavlodar, Semey, Petropavl, Shymkent
Physical features: Caspian and Aral seas, Lake Balkhash; Steppe region; natural gas and oil deposits in the Caspian Sea
Currency: tenge
GNP per capita (PPP): (US$) 4,408 (1999)
Resources: petroleum, natural gas, coal, bauxite, chromium, copper, iron ore, lead, titanium, magnesium, tungsten, molybdenum, gold, silver, manganese
Population: 16,223,000 (2000 est)
Population density: (per sq km) 6 (1999 est)
Language: Kazakh (related to Turkish; official), Russian
Religion: Sunni Muslim 50-60%, Russian Orthodox 30-35%
Time difference: GMT +6

KENYA
Map page 56

National name: Jamhuri ya Kenya/Republic of Kenya
Area: 582,600 sq km/ 224,941 sq mi
Capital: Nairobi
Major towns/cities: Mombasa, Kisumu, Nakuru, Eldoret, Nyeri
Major ports: Mombasa
Physical features: mountains and highlands in west and center; coastal plain in south; arid interior and tropical coast; semidesert in north; Great Rift Valley, Mount Kenya, Lake Nakuru (salt lake with world's largest colony of flamingos), Lake Turkana (Rudolf)

Currency: Kenyan shilling
GNP per capita (PPP): (US$) 975 (1999)
Resources: soda ash, fluorspar, salt, limestone, rubies, gold, vermiculite, diatonite, garnets
Population: 30,080,000 (2000 est)
Population density: (per sq km) 51 (1999 est)
Language: English, Kiswahili (both official), many local dialects
Religion: Roman Catholic 28%, Protestant 8%, Muslim 6%, traditional tribal religions
Time difference: GMT +3

KIRIBATI
Map page 60

National name: Ribaberikan Kiribati/Republic of Kiribati
Area: 717 sq km/277 sq mi
Capital: Bairiki (on Tarawa atoll)
Major towns/cities: principal islands are the Gilbert Islands, the Phoenix Islands, the Line Islands, Banaba
Major ports: Bairiki, Betio (on Tarawa)
Physical features: comprises 33 Pacific coral islands: the Kiribati (Gilbert), Rawaki (Phoenix), Banaba (Ocean Island), and three of the Line Islands including Kiritimati (Christmas Island); island groups crossed by Equator and International Date Line
Currency: Australian dollar
GNP per capita (PPP): (US$) 3,186 (1999)
Resources: phosphate, salt
Population: 83,000 (2000 est)
Population density: (per sq km) 107 (1999 est)
Language: English (official), Gilbertese
Religion: Roman Catholic, Protestant (Congregationalist)
Time difference: GMT -10/-11

KUWAIT
Map page 46

National name: Dowlat al-Kuwayt/State of Kuwait
Area: 17,819 sq km/6,879 sq mi
Capital: Kuwait (and chief port)
Major towns/cities: as-Salimiya, Al Farwānīyah, Ḥawallī, Abraq Kheetan, Al Jahrah, Al Aḥmadī, Al Fuḥayḥil
Physical features: hot desert; islands of Faylakah, Bubiyan, and Warbah at northeast corner of Arabian Peninsula
Currency: Kuwaiti dinar
GNP per capita (PPP): (US$) 24,270 (1997)
Resources: petroleum, natural gas, mineral water
Population: 1,972,000 (2000 est)
Population density: (per sq km) 106 (1999 est)
Language: Arabic (78%) (official), English, Kurdish (10%), Farsi (4%)
Religion: Sunni Muslim 45%, Shiite Muslim 40%; Christian, Hindu, and Parsi about 5%
Time difference: GMT +3

KYRGYZSTAN
Map page 34

National name: Kyrgyz Respublikasy/Kyrgyz Republic
Area: 198,500 sq km/ 76,640 sq mi
Capital: Bishkek (formerly Frunze)
Major towns/cities: Osh, Karakol, Kyzyl-Kiya, Tokmak, Djalal-Abad
Physical features: mountainous, an extension of the Tien Shan range
Currency: som
GNP per capita (PPP): (US$) 2,223 (1999)
Resources: petroleum, natural gas, coal, gold, tin, mercury, antimony, zinc, tungsten, uranium
Population: 4,699,000 (2000 est)
Population density: (per sq km) 24 (1999 est)

Language: Kyrgyz (a Turkic language; official), Russian
Religion: Sunni Muslim 70%, Russian Orthodox 20%
Time difference: GMT +5

LAOS
Map page 40

National name: Sathalanalat
Praxathipatai Paxaxôn Lao/
Democratic People's Republic of
Laos
Area: 236,790 sq km/
91,424 sq mi
Capital: Vientiane
Major towns/cities:
Louangphrabang (the former royal capital), Pakxé, Savannakhet
Physical features: landlocked state with high mountains in east;
Mekong River in west; rain forest covers nearly 60% of land
Currency: new kip
GNP per capita (PPP): (US$) 1,726 (1999)
Resources: coal, tin, gypsum, baryte, lead, zinc, nickel, potash,
iron ore; small quantities of gold, silver, precious stones
Population: 5,433,000 (2000 est)
Population density: (per sq km) 22 (1999 est)
Language: Lao (official), French, English, ethnic languages
Religion: Theravada Buddhist 85%, animist beliefs among
mountain dwellers
Time difference: GMT +7

LATVIA
Map page 8

National name: Latvijas Republika/
Republic of Latvia
Area: 63,700 sq km/24,594 sq mi
Capital: Rīga
Major towns/cities:
Daugavpils, Liepāja, Jūrmala,
Jelgava, Ventspils
Major ports: Ventspils,
Liepāja
Physical features: wooded lowland (highest point 312 m/1,024
ft), marshes, lakes; 472 km/293 mi of coastline; mild climate
Currency: lat
GNP per capita (PPP): (US$) 5,938 (1999)
Resources: peat, gypsum, dolomite, limestone, amber, gravel,
sand
Population: 2,357,000 (2000 est)
Population density: (per sq km) 38 (1999 est)
Language: Latvian (official)
Religion: Lutheran, Roman Catholic, Russian Orthodox
Time difference: GMT +2

LEBANON
Map page 46

National name: Jumhouria
al-Lubnaniya/Republic of Lebanon
Area: 10,452 sq km/4,035 sq mi
Capital: Beirut (and chief port)
Major towns/cities: Tripoli,
Zahlé, Baabda, Ba'albek,
Jezzine
Major ports: Tripoli, Soûr, Saïda, Joûnié
Physical features: narrow coastal plain; fertile Bekka valley
running north-south between Lebanon and Anti-Lebanon
mountain ranges
Currency: Lebanese pound
GNP per capita (PPP): (US$) 4,129 (1999)
Resources: there are no commercially viable mineral deposits;
small reserves of lignite and iron ore
Population: 3,282,000 (2000 est)
Population density: (per sq km) 310 (1999 est)
Language: Arabic (official), French, Armenian, English
Religion: Muslim 70% (Shiite 35%, Sunni 23%, Druze 7%, other
5%); Christian 30% (mainly Maronite 19%), Druze 3%; other
Christian denominations including Greek Orthodox, Armenian,
and Roman Catholic
Time difference: GMT +2

LESOTHO
Map page 58

National name: Mmuso oa
Lesotho/Kingdom of Lesotho
Area: 30,355 sq km/11,720 sq mi
Capital: Maseru
Major towns/cities: Qacha's
Nek, Teyateyaneng, Mafeteng,
Hlotse, Roma, Quthing
Physical features: mountainous
with plateaus, forming part of South Africa's chief watershed
Currency: loti
GNP per capita (PPP): (US$) 2,058 (1999)
Resources: diamonds, uranium, lead, iron ore; believed to have
petroleum deposits
Population: 2,153,000 (2000 est)
Population density: (per sq km) 69 (1999 est)
Language: English (official), Sesotho, Zulu, Xhosa
Religion: Protestant 42%, Roman Catholic 38%, indigenous
beliefs
Time difference: GMT +2

LIBERIA
Map page 54

National name: Republic of
Liberia
Area: 111,370 sq km/
42,999 sq mi
Capital: Monrovia (and chief
port)
Major towns/cities: Bensonville,
Gbarnga, Voinjama, Buchanan
Major ports: Buchanan, Greenville
Physical features: forested highlands; swampy tropical coast
where six rivers enter the sea
Currency: Liberian dollar
GNP per capita (PPP): (US$) N/A
Resources: iron ore, diamonds, gold, barytes, kyanite
Population: 3,154,000 (2000 est)
Population density: (per sq km) 26 (1999 est)
Language: English (official), over 20 Niger-Congo languages
Religion: animist 70%, Sunni Muslim 20%, Christian 10%
Time difference: GMT +/-0

LIBYA
Map page 50

National name: Al-Jamahiriyya
al-'Arabiyya al-Libiyya
ash-Sha'biyya al-Ishtirakiyya
al-'Uzma/Great Libyan Arab
Socialist People's State of the
Masses
Area: 1,759,540 sq km/
679,358 sq mi
Capital: Tripoli
Major towns/cities: Banghāzī, Mişrātah, Az Zāwīyah, Tubruq,
Ajdābiyā, Darnah
Major ports: Banghāzī, Mişrātah, Az Zāwīyah, Tubruq, Ajdābiyā,
Darnah
Physical features: flat to undulating plains with plateaus and
depressions stretch southward from the Mediterranean coast to
an extremely dry desert interior
Currency: Libyan dinar
GNP per capita (PPP): (US$) N/A
Resources: petroleum, natural gas, iron ore, potassium,
magnesium, sulfur, gypsum
Population: 5,605,000 (2000 est)
Population density: (per sq km) 3 (1999 est)
Language: Arabic (official), Italian, English
Religion: Sunni Muslim 97%
Time difference: GMT +1

LIECHTENSTEIN
Map page 22

National name: Fürstentum Liechtenstein/Principality of
Liechtenstein

Area: 160 sq km/62 sq mi
Capital: Vaduz
Major towns/cities: Balzers,
Schaan, Eschen
Physical features: landlocked
Alpine; includes part of Rhine
Valley in west
Currency: Swiss franc
GNP per capita (PPP): (US$) 24,000 (1998 est)
Resources: hydro power
Population: 33,000 (2000 est)
Population density: (per sq km) 199 (1999 est)
Language: German (official), an Alemannic dialect
Religion: Roman Catholic 80%, Protestant 7%
Time difference: GMT +1

LITHUANIA
Map page 8

National name: Lietuvos Respublika/
Republic of Lithuania
Area: 65,200 sq km/25,173 sq mi
Capital: Vilnius
Major towns/cities: Kaunas,
Klaipėda, Šiauliai, Panevėžys
Physical features: central
lowlands with gentle hills in
west and higher terrain in southeast; 25% forested; some 3,000
small lakes, marshes, and complex sandy coastline; River Nenumas
Currency: litas
GNP per capita (PPP): (US$) 6,093 (1999)
Resources: small deposits of petroleum, natural gas, peat,
limestone, gravel, clay, sand
Population: 3,670,000 (2000 est)
Population density: (per sq km) 56 (1999 est)
Language: Lithuanian (official)
Religion: predominantly Roman Catholic; Evangelical Lutheran,
also Russian Orthodox, Evangelical Reformist, and Baptist
Time difference: GMT +2

LUXEMBOURG
Map page 14

National name: Grand-Duché de
Luxembourg/Grand Duchy of
Luxembourg
Area: 2,586 sq km/998 sq mi
Capital: Luxembourg
Major towns/cities: Esch,
Differdange, Dudelange,
Pétange
Physical features: on the River Moselle; part of the Ardennes
(Oesling) forest in north
Currency: Luxembourg franc
GNP per capita (PPP): (US$) 38,247 (1999)
Resources: iron ore
Population: 431,000 (2000 est)
Population density: (per sq km) 165 (1999 est)
Language: Letzeburgisch (a German-Moselle-Frankish dialect;
official), English
Religion: Roman Catholic about 95%, Protestant and Jewish 4%
Time difference: GMT +1

MACEDONIA
Map page 28

National name: Republika
Makedonija/Republic of Macedonia
(official internal name); Poranesna
Jugoslovenska Republika
Makedonija/Former Yugoslav
Republic of Macedonia (official
international name)
Area: 25,700 sq km/
9,922 sq mi
Capital: Skopje
Major towns/cities: Bitola, Prilep, Kumanovo, Tetovo
Physical features: mountainous; rivers: Struma, Vardar; lakes:
Ohrid, Prespa, Scutari; partly Mediterranean climate with hot
summers

Currency: Macedonian denar
GNP per capita (PPP): (US$) 4,339 (1999)
Resources: coal, iron, zinc, chromium, manganese, lead, copper, nickel, silver, gold
Population: 2,024,000 (2000 est)
Population density: (per sq km) 78 (1999 est)
Language: Macedonian (related to Bulgarian; official), Albanian
Religion: Christian, mainly Orthodox 67%; Muslim 30%
Time difference: GMT +1

MADAGASCAR
Map page 58

National name: Repoblikan'i Madagasikara/République de Madagascar/Republic of Madagascar
Area: 587,041 sq km/ 226,656 sq mi
Capital: Antananarivo
Major towns/cities: Antsirabe, Mahajanga, Fianarantsoa, Toamasina, Ambatondrazaka
Major ports: Toamasina, Antsirañana, Mahajanga
Physical features: temperate central highlands; humid valleys and tropical coastal plains; arid in south
Currency: Malagasy franc
GNP per capita (PPP): (US$) 766 (1999)
Resources: graphite, chromite, mica, titanium ore, small quantities of precious stones, bauxite and coal deposits, petroleum reserves
Population: 15,942,000 (2000 est)
Population density: (per sq km) 26 (1999 est)
Language: Malagasy, French (both official), local dialects
Religion: over 50% traditional beliefs, Roman Catholic, Protestant about 40%, Muslim 7%
Time difference: GMT +3

MALAWI
Map page 58

National name: Republic of Malawi
Area: 118,484 sq km/ 45,735 sq mi
Capital: Lilongwe
Major towns/cities: Blantyre, Mzuzu, Zomba
Physical features: landlocked narrow plateau with rolling plains; mountainous west of Lake Nyasa
Currency: Malawi kwacha
GNP per capita (PPP): (US$) 581 (1999)
Resources: marble, coal, gemstones, bauxite and graphite deposits, reserves of phosphates, uranium, glass sands, asbestos, vermiculite
Population: 10,925,000 (2000 est)
Population density: (per sq km) 90 (1999 est)
Language: English, Chichewa (both official), other Bantu languages
Religion: Protestant 50%, Roman Catholic 20%, Muslim 2%, animist
Time difference: GMT +2

MALAYSIA
Map page 42

National name: Persekutuan Tanah Malaysia/Federation of Malaysia
Area: 329,759 sq km/ 127,319 sq mi
Capital: Kuala Lumpur
Major towns/cities: Johor Bahru, Ipoh, George Town (on Penang island), Kuala Terengganu, Kuala Bahru, Petaling Jaya, Kelang, Kuching (on Sarawak), Kota Kinabalu (on Sabah)
Major ports: Kelang
Physical features: comprises peninsular Malaysia (the nine Malay states - Johore, Kedah, Kelantan, Negri Sembilan, Pahang, Perak, Perlis, Selangor, Terengganu - plus Malacca and Penang); states of Sabah and Sarawak on the island of Borneo; and the federal territory of Kuala Lumpur; 75% tropical rain forest; central mountain range; Mount Kinabalu, the highest peak in southeast Asia, is in Sabah; swamps in east; Niah caves (Sarawak)
Currency: ringgit
GNP per capita (PPP): (US$) 7,963 (1999)
Resources: tin, bauxite, copper, iron ore, petroleum, natural gas, forests
Population: 22,244,000 (2000 est)
Population density: (per sq km) 66 (1999 est)
Language: Bahasa Malaysia (Malay; official), English, Chinese, Tamil, Iban, many local dialects
Religion: Muslim (official) about 53%, Buddhist 19%, Hindu, Christian, local beliefs
Time difference: GMT +8

MALDIVES
Map page 44

National name: Divehi Raajjeyge Jumhuriyya/Republic of the Maldives
Area: 298 sq km/115 sq mi
Capital: Malé
Physical features: comprises 1,196 coral islands, grouped into 12 clusters of atolls, largely flat, none bigger than 13 sq km/5 sq mi, average elevation 1.8 m/6 ft; 203 are inhabited
Currency: rufiya
GNP per capita (PPP): (US$) 3,545 (1999)
Resources: coral (mining was banned as a measure against the encroachment of the sea)
Population: 286,000 (2000 est)
Population density: (per sq km) 933 (1999 est)
Language: Divehi (a Sinhalese dialect; official), English, Arabic
Religion: Sunni Muslim
Time difference: GMT +5

MALI
Map page 52

National name: République du Mali/Republic of Mali
Area: 1,240,142 sq km/ 478,818 sq mi
Capital: Bamako
Major towns/cities: Mopti, Kayes, Ségou, Tombouctou, Sikasso
Physical features: landlocked state with River Niger and savannah in south; part of the Sahara in north; hills in northeast; Senegal River and its branches irrigate the southwest
Currency: franc CFA
GNP per capita (PPP): (US$) 693 (1999)
Resources: iron ore, uranium, diamonds, bauxite, manganese, copper, lithium, gold
Population: 11,234,000 (2000 est)
Population density: (per sq km) 9 (1999 est)
Language: French (official), Bambara, other African languages
Religion: Sunni Muslim 80%, animist, Christian
Time difference: GMT +/-0

MALTA
Map page 24

National name: Repubblika ta'Malta/ Republic of Malta
Area: 320 sq km/124 sq mi
Capital: Valletta (and chief port)
Major towns/cities: Rabat, Birkirkara, Qormi, Sliema
Major ports: Marsaxlokk, Valletta
Physical features: includes islands of Gozo 67 sq km/26 sq mi and Comino 3 sq km/1 sq mi
Currency: Maltese lira
GNP per capita (PPP): (US$) 15,066 (1999)
Resources: stone, sand; offshore petroleum reserves were under exploration 1988-95

Population: 389,000 (2000 est)
Population density: (per sq km) 1,206 (1999 est)
Language: Maltese, English (both official)
Religion: Roman Catholic 98%
Time difference: GMT +1

MARSHALL ISLANDS
Map page 60

National name: Majol/ Republic of the Marshall Islands
Area: 181 sq km/70 sq mi
Capital: Dalap-Uliga-Darrit (on Majuro atoll)
Major towns/cities: Ebeye (the only other town)
Physical features: comprises the Ratak and Ralik island chains in the West Pacific, which together form an archipelago of 31 coral atolls, 5 islands, and 1,152 islets
Currency: US dollar
GNP per capita (PPP): (US$) 1,860 (1999 est)
Resources: phosphates
Population: 64,000 (2000 est)
Population density: (per sq km) 343 (1999 est)
Language: Marshallese, English (both official)
Religion: Christian (mainly Protestant) and Baha'i
Time difference: GMT +12

MAURITANIA
Map page 52

National name: Al-Jumhuriyya al-Islamiyya al-Mawritaniyya/ République Islamique Arabe et Africaine de Mauritanie/Islamic Republic of Mauritania
Area: 1,030,700 sq km/ 397,953 sq mi
Capital: Nouakchott (and chief port)
Major towns/cities: Nouâdhibou, Kaédi, Zouérat, Kiffa, Rosso, Atâr
Major ports: Nouâdhibou
Physical features: valley of River Senegal in south; remainder arid and flat
Currency: ouguiya
GNP per capita (PPP): (US$) 1,522 (1999 est)
Resources: copper, gold, iron ore, gypsum, phosphates, sulfur, peat
Population: 2,670,000 (2000 est)
Population density: (per sq km) 3 (1999 est)
Language: Hasaniya Arabic (official), Pulaar, Soninke, Wolof (all national languages), French (particularly in the south)
Religion: Sunni Muslim (state religion)
Time difference: GMT +/-0

MAURITIUS
Map page 58

National name: Republic of Mauritius
Area: 1,865 sq km/720 sq mi
Capital: Port Louis (and chief port)
Major towns/cities: Beau Bassin, Rose Hill, Curepipe, Quatre Bornes, Vacoas-Phoenix
Physical features: mountainous, volcanic island surrounded by coral reefs; the island of Rodrigues is part of Mauritius; there are several small island dependencies
Currency: Mauritian rupee
GNP per capita (PPP): (US$) 8,652 (1999)
Population: 1,158,000 (2000 est)
Population density: (per sq km) 616 (1999 est)
Language: English (official), French, Creole (36%), Bhojpuri (32%), other Indian languages
Religion: Hindu over 50%, Christian (mainly Roman Catholic) about 30%, Muslim 17%
Time difference: GMT +4

MEXICO

Map page 72

National name: Estados Unidos Mexicanos/United States of Mexico
Area: 1,958,201 sq km/ 756,061 sq mi
Capital: Mexico City
Major towns/cities: Guadalajara, Monterrey, Puebla, Ciudad Juárez, Tijuana
Major ports: 49 ocean ports
Physical features: partly arid central highlands; Sierra Madre mountain ranges east and west; tropical coastal plains; volcanoes, including Popocatepetl; Rio Grande
Currency: Mexican peso
GNP per capita (PPP): (US$) 7,719 (1999)
Resources: petroleum, natural gas, zinc, salt, silver, copper, coal, mercury, manganese, phosphates, uranium, strontium sulfide
Population: 98,881,000 (2000 est)
Population density: (per sq km) 50 (1999 est)
Language: Spanish (official), Nahuatl, Maya, Zapoteco, Mixteco, Otomi
Religion: Roman Catholic about 90%
Time difference: GMT -6/8

MICRONESIA, FEDERATED STATES OF

Map page 60

National name: Federated States of Micronesia (FSM)
Area: 700 sq km/270 sq mi
Capital: Palikir (in Pohnpei island state)
Major towns/cities: Kolonia (in Pohnpei), Weno (in Truk), Lelu (in Kosrae)
Physical features: an archipelago of 607 equatorial, volcanic islands in the West Pacific
Currency: US dollar
GNP per capita (PPP): (US$) 3,860 (1999 est)
Population: 119,000 (2000 est)
Population density: (per sq km) 165 (1999 est)
Language: English (official), eight officially recognized local languages (including Trukese, Pohnpeian, Yapese, and Kosrean), a number of other dialects
Religion: Christianity (mainly Roman Catholic in Yap state, Protestant elsewhere)
Time difference: GMT +10 (Chuuk and Yap); +11 (Kosrae and Pohnpei)

MOLDOVA

Map page 26

National name: Republica Moldova/ Republic of Moldova
Area: 33,700 sq km/13,011 sq mi
Capital: Chişinău (Russian Kishinev)
Major towns/cities: Tiraspol, Bălţi, Tighina
Physical features: hilly land lying largely between the rivers Prut and Dniester; northern Moldova comprises the level plain of the Bălţi Steppe and uplands; the climate is warm and moderately continental
Currency: leu
GNP per capita (PPP): (US$) 2,358 (1999)
Resources: lignite, phosphorites, gypsum, building materials; petroleum and natural gas deposits discovered in the early 1990s were not yet exploited in 1996
Population: 4,380,000 (2000 est)
Population density: (per sq km) 130 (1999 est)
Language: Moldovan (official), Russian, Gaganz (a Turkish dialect)
Religion: Eastern Orthodox 98.5%; remainder Jewish
Time difference: GMT +2

MONACO

Map page 18

National name: Principauté de Monaco/Principality of Monaco
Area: 1.95 sq km/0.75 sq mi
Physical features: steep and rugged; surrounded landwards by French territory; being expanded by filling in the sea
Currency: French franc
GNP per capita (PPP): (US$) 27,000 (1999 est)
Population: 34,000 (2000 est)
Population density: (per sq km) 16,074 (1999 est)
Language: French (official), Monégasgne (a mixture of the French Provençal and Italian Ligurian dialects), Italian
Religion: Roman Catholic about 90%
Time difference: GMT +1

MONGOLIA

Map page 36

National name: Mongol Uls/ State of Mongolia
Area: 1,565,000 sq km/ 604,246 sq mi
Capital: Ulaanbaatar
Major towns/cities: Darhan, Choybalsan, Erdenet
Physical features: high plateau with desert and steppe (grasslands); Altai Mountains in southwest; salt lakes; part of Gobi desert in southeast; contains both the world's southernmost permafrost and northernmost desert
Currency: tugrik
GNP per capita (PPP): (US$) 1,496 (1999)
Resources: copper, nickel, zinc, molybdenum, phosphorites, tungsten, tin, fluorospar, gold, lead; reserves of petroleum discovered in 1994
Population: 2,662,000 (2000 est)
Population density: (per sq km) 2 (1999 est)
Language: Khalkha Mongolian (official), Kazakh (in the province of Bagan-Ölgiy), Chinese, Russian, Turkic languages
Religion: there is no state religion, but traditional lamaism (Mahayana Buddhism) is gaining new strength; the Sunni Muslim Kazakhs of Western Mongolia have also begun the renewal of their religious life, and Christian missionary activity has increased
Time difference: GMT +8

MOROCCO

Map page 52

National name: Al-Mamlaka al-Maghribyya/Kingdom of Morocco
Area: 458,730 sq km/ 177,115 sq mi (excluding Western Sahara)
Capital: Rabat
Major towns/cities: Casablanca, Marrakech, Fès, Oujda, Kénitra, Tétouan, Meknès
Major ports: Casablanca, Tanger, Agadir
Physical features: mountain ranges, including the Atlas Mountains northeast-southwest; fertile coastal plains in west
Currency: dirham
GNP per capita (PPP): (US$) 3,190 (1999)
Resources: phosphate rock and phosphoric acid, coal, iron ore, barytes, lead, copper, manganese, zinc, petroleum, natural gas, fish
Population: 28,351,000 (2000 est)
Population density: (per sq km) 61 (1999 est)
Language: Arabic (75%) (official), Berber dialects (25%), French, Spanish
Religion: Sunni Muslim; Christian and Jewish minorities
Time difference: GMT +/-0

MOZAMBIQUE

Map page 58

National name: República de Moçambique/Republic of Mozambique

Area: 799,380 sq km/ 308,640 sq mi
Capital: Maputo (and chief port)
Major towns/cities: Beira, Nampula, Nacala, Chimoio
Major ports: Beira, Nacala, Quelimane
Physical features: mostly flat tropical lowland; mountains in west; rivers Zambezi and Limpopo
Currency: metical
GNP per capita (PPP): (US$) 797 (1999 est)
Resources: coal, salt, bauxite, graphite; reserves of iron ore, gold, precious and semiprecious stones, marble, natural gas (all largely unexploited in 1996)
Population: 19,680,000 (2000 est)
Population density: (per sq km) 24 (1999 est)
Language: Portuguese (official), 16 African languages
Religion: animist 48%, Muslim 20%, Roman Catholic 16%, Protestant 16%
Time difference: GMT +2

MYANMAR (BURMA)

Map page 40

National name: Pyedawngsu Myanma Naingngan/Union of Myanmar
Area: 676,577 sq km/ 261,226 sq mi
Capital: Yangon (formerly Rangoon) (and chief port)
Major towns/cities: Mandalay, Moulmein, Bago, Bassein, Taung-gyi, Sittwe,
Physical features: over half is rain forest; rivers Irrawaddy and Chindwin in central lowlands ringed by mountains in north, west, and east
Currency: kyat
GNP per capita (PPP): (US$) 1,200 (1999 est)
Resources: natural gas, petroleum, zinc, tin, copper, tungsten, coal, lead, gems, silver, gold
Population: 45,611,000 (2000 est)
Population density: (per sq km) 70 (1999 est)
Language: Burmese (official), English, tribal dialects
Religion: Hinayana Buddhist 89%, Christian 5%, Muslim 4%, animist 1.5%
Time difference: GMT +6.5

NAMIBIA

Map page 58

National name: Republic of Namibia
Area: 824,300 sq km/ 318,262 sq mi
Capital: Windhoek
Major towns/cities: Swakopmund, Rehoboth, Rundu
Major ports: Walvis Bay
Physical features: mainly desert (Namib and Kalahari); Orange River; Caprivi Strip links Namibia to Zambezi River; includes the enclave of Walvis Bay (area 1,120 sq km/432 sq mi)
Currency: Namibian dollar
GNP per capita (PPP): (US$) 5,369 (1999 est)
Resources: uranium, copper, lead, zinc, silver, tin, gold, salt, semiprecious stones, diamonds (one of the world's leading producers of gem diamonds), hydrocarbons, lithium, manganese, tungsten, cadmium, vanadium
Population: 1,726,000 (2000 est)
Population density: (per sq km) 2 (1999 est)
Language: English (official), Afrikaans, German, Ovambo (51%), Nama (12%), Kavango (10%), other indigenous languages
Religion: about 90% Christian (Lutheran, Roman Catholic, Dutch Reformed Church, Anglican)
Time difference: GMT +1

NAURU

Map page 60

National name: Republic of Nauru
Area: 21 sq km/8.1 sq mi

Capital: Yaren District (seat of government)
Physical features: tropical coral island in southwest Pacific; plateau encircled by coral cliffs and sandy beaches
Currency: Australian dollar
GNP per capita (PPP): (US$) 11,800 (1994 est)
Resources: phosphates
Population: 12,000 (2000 est)
Population density: (per sq km) 524 (1999 est)
Language: Nauruan, English (both official)
Religion: majority Protestant, Roman Catholic
Time difference: GMT +12

NEPAL
Map page 44

National name: Nepál Adhirajya/Kingdom of Nepal
Area: 147,181 sq km/56,826 sq mi
Capital: Kathmandu
Major towns/cities: Biratnagar, Lalitpur, Bhadgaon, Pokhara, Birganj, Dahran Bazar
Physical features: descends from the Himalayas in the north through foothills to the River Ganges plain in the south; Mount Everest, Mount Kanchenjunga
Currency: Nepalese rupee
GNP per capita (PPP): (US$) 1,219 (1999)
Resources: lignite, talcum, magnesite, limestone, copper, cobalt
Population: 23,930,000 (2000 est)
Population density: (per sq km) 159 (1999 est)
Language: Nepali (official), Tibetan, numerous local languages
Religion: Hindu 90%; Buddhist 5%, Muslim 3%, Christian
Time difference: GMT +5.5

NETHERLANDS
Map page 14

National name: Koninkrijk der Nederlanden/Kingdom of the Netherlands
Area: 41,863 sq km/16,163 sq mi
Capital: Amsterdam (official), the Hague (legislative and judicial)
Major towns/cities: Rotterdam, the Hague (seat of government), Utrecht, Eindhoven, Groningen, Tilburg, Maastricht, Apeldoorn, Nijmegen, Breda
Major ports: Rotterdam
Physical features: flat coastal lowland; rivers Rhine, Schelde, Maas; Frisian Islands
Territories: Aruba, Netherlands Antilles (Caribbean)
Currency: guilder
GNP per capita (PPP): (US$) 23,052 (1999)
Resources: petroleum, natural gas
Population: 15,786,000 (1999 est)
Population density: (per sq km) 376 (1999 est)
Language: Dutch (official)
Religion: atheist 39%, Roman Catholic 31%, Dutch Reformed Church 14%, Calvinist 8%
Time difference: GMT +1

NEW ZEALAND
Map page 64

National name: Aotearoa/New Zealand
Area: 268,680 sq km/103,737 sq mi
Capital: Wellington
Major towns/cities: Auckland, Hamilton, Christchurch, Manukau
Major ports: Auckland, Wellington
Physical features: comprises North Island, South Island, Stewart Island, Chatham Islands, and minor islands; mainly

mountainous; Ruapehu in North Island, 2,797 m/9,180 ft, highest of three active volcanoes; geysers and hot springs of Rotorua district; Lake Taupo (616 sq km/238 sq mi), source of Waikato River; Kaingaroa state forest. In South Island are the Southern Alps and Canterbury Plains
Territories: Tokelau (three atolls transferred in 1926 from former Gilbert and Ellice Islands colony); Niue Island (one of the Cook Islands, separately administered from 1903: chief town Alafi); Cook Islands are internally self-governing but share common citizenship with New Zealand; Ross Dependency in Antarctica
Currency: New Zealand dollar
GNP per capita (PPP): (US$) 16,566 (1999)
Resources: coal, clay, limestone, dolomite, natural gas, hydroelectric power, pumice, iron ore, gold, forests
Population: 3,862,000 (2000 est)
Population density: (per sq km) 14 (1999 est)
Language: English (official), Maori
Religion: Christian (Anglican 18%, Roman Catholic 14%, Presbyterian 13%)
Time difference: GMT +12

NICARAGUA
Map page 72

National name: República de Nicaragua/Republic of Nicaragua
Area: 127,849 sq km/49,362 sq mi
Capital: Managua
Major towns/cities: León, Chinandega, Masaya, Granada, Estelí
Major ports: Corinto, Puerto Cabezas, El Bluff
Physical features: narrow Pacific coastal plain separated from broad Atlantic coastal plain by volcanic mountains and lakes Managua and Nicaragua; one of the world's most active earthquake regions
Currency: cordoba
GNP per capita (PPP): (US$) 2,154 (1999)
Resources: gold, silver, copper, lead, antimony, zinc, iron, limestone, gypsum, marble, bentonite
Population: 5,074,000 (2000 est)
Population density: (per sq km) 39 (1999 est)
Language: Spanish (official), English, American Indian languages
Religion: Roman Catholic 95%
Time difference: GMT -6

NIGER
Map page 52

National name: République du Niger/Republic of Niger
Area: 1,186,408 sq km/458,072 sq mi
Capital: Niamey
Major towns/cities: Zinder, Maradi, Tahoua, Agadez, Birnin Konni, Arlit
Physical features: desert plains between hills in north and savannah in south; River Niger in southwest, Lake Chad in southeast
Currency: franc CFA
GNP per capita (PPP): (US$) 727 (1999)
Resources: uranium (one of world's leading producers), phosphates, gypsum, coal, cassiterite, tin, salt, gold; deposits of other minerals (including petroleum, iron ore, copper, lead, diamonds, and tungsten) have been confirmed
Population: 10,730,000 (2000 est)
Population density: (per sq km) 9 (1999 est)
Language: French (official), Hausa (70%), Djerma, other ethnic languages
Religion: Sunni Muslim 95%; also Christian, and traditional animist beliefs
Time difference: GMT +1

NIGERIA
Map page 54

National name: Federal Republic of Nigeria
Area: 923,773 sq km/356,668 sq mi

Capital: Abuja
Major towns/cities: Ibadan, Lagos, Ogbomosho, Kano, Oshogbo, Ilorin, Abeokuta, Zaria, Port Harcourt
Major ports: Lagos, Port Harcourt, Warri, Calabar
Physical features: arid savannah in north; tropical rain forest in south, with mangrove swamps along coast; River Niger forms wide delta; mountains in southeast
Currency: naira
GNP per capita (PPP): (US$) 744 (1999)
Resources: petroleum, natural gas, coal, tin, iron ore, uranium, limestone, marble, forest
Population: 111,506,000 (2000 est)
Population density: (per sq km) 118 (1999 est)
Language: English, French (both official), Hausa, Ibo, Yoruba
Religion: Sunni Muslim 50% (in north), Christian 35% (in south), local religions 15%
Time difference: GMT +1

NORTH KOREA
Map page 38

National name: Chosun Minchu-chui Inmin Konghwa-guk/Democratic People's Republic of Korea
Area: 120,538 sq km/46,539 sq mi
Capital: P'yŏngyang
Major towns/cities: Hamhüng, Ch'ŏngjin, Namp'o, Wŏnsan, Sinüiji
Physical features: wide coastal plain in west rising to mountains cut by deep valleys in interior
Currency: won
GNP per capita (PPP): (US$) 950 (1999 est)
Resources: coal, iron, lead, copper, zinc, tin, silver, gold, magnesite (has 40-50% of world's deposits of magnesite)
Population: 24,039,000 (2000 est)
Population density: (per sq km) 197 (1999 est)
Language: Korean (official)
Religion: Buddhist (predominant religion), Chondoist, Christian, traditional beliefs
Time difference: GMT +9

NORWAY
Map page 8

National name: Kongeriket Norge/Kingdom of Norway
Area: 387,000 sq km/149,420 sq mi (including Svalbard and Jan Mayen)
Capital: Oslo
Major towns/cities: Bergen, Trondheim, Stavanger, Kristiansand, Drammen
Physical features: mountainous with fertile valleys and deeply indented coast; forests cover 25%; extends north of Arctic Circle
Territories: dependencies in the Arctic (Svalbard and Jan Mayen) and in Antarctica (Bouvet and Peter I Island, and Queen Maud Land)
Currency: Norwegian krone
GNP per capita (PPP): (US$) 26,522 (1999)
Resources: petroleum, natural gas, iron ore, iron pyrites, copper, lead, zinc, forests
Population: 4,465,000 (2000 est)
Population density: (per sq km) 14 (1999 est)
Language: Norwegian (official), Saami (Lapp), Finnish
Religion: Evangelical Lutheran (endowed by state) 88%; other Protestant and Roman Catholic 4%
Time difference: GMT +1

OMAN
Map page 46

National name: Saltanat `Uman/Sultanate of Oman
Area: 272,000 sq km/105,019 sq mi
Capital: Muscat

Major towns/cities: Sallālah, Ibrī, Suḥār, Al Buraymī, Nazwá, Sūr, Maṭraḥ

Physical features: mountains to the north and south of a high arid plateau; fertile coastal strip; Jebel Akhdar highlands; Kuria Muria Islands
Currency: Omani rial
GNP per capita (PPP): (US$) 8,690 (1997)
Resources: petroleum, natural gas, copper, chromite, gold, salt, marble, gypsum, limestone
Population: 2,542,000 (2000 est)
Population density: (per sq km) 9 (1999 est)
Language: Arabic (official), English, Urdu, other Indian languages
Religion: Muslim 75% (predominantly Ibadhi Muslim), about 25% Hindu
Time difference: GMT +4

PAKISTAN

Map page 46

National name: Islami Jamhuriyya e Pakistan/Islamic Republic of Pakistan
Area: 803,940 sq km/ 310,321 sq mi
Capital: Islamabad
Major towns/cities: Lahore, Rawalpindi, Faisalabad, Karachi, Hyderabad, Multan, Peshawar, Gujranwala, Quetta
Major ports: Karachi
Physical features: fertile Indus plain in east, Baluchistan plateau in west, mountains in north and northwest; the 'five rivers' (Indus, Jhelum, Chenab, Ravi, and Sutlej) feed the world's largest irrigation system; K2 mountain; Khyber Pass
Currency: Pakistan rupee
GNP per capita (PPP): (US$) 1,757 (1999)
Resources: iron ore, natural gas, limestone, rock salt, gypsum, silica, coal, petroleum, graphite, copper, manganese, chromite
Population: 156,483,000 (2000 est)
Population density: (per sq km) 189 (1999 est)
Language: Urdu (official), English, Punjabi, Sindhi, Pashto, Baluchi, other local dialects
Religion: Sunni Muslim 90%, Shiite Muslim 5%; also Hindu, Christian, Parsee, Buddhist
Time difference: GMT +5

PALAU

Map page 60

National name: Belu'u era Belau/Republic of Palau
Area: 508 sq km/196 sq mi
Capital: Koror (on Koror island)

Physical features: more than 350 (mostly uninhabited) islands, islets, and atolls in the west Pacific; warm, humid climate, susceptible to typhoons
Currency: US dollar
GNP per capita (PPP): (US$) N/A
Population: 19,000 (2000 est)
Population density: (per sq km) 39 (1999 est)
Language: Palauan, English (both official in most states)
Religion: Christian, principally Roman Catholic; Modekngei (indigenous religion)
Time difference: GMT +9

PANAMA

Map page 72

National name: República de Panamá/Republic of Panama
Area: 77,100 sq km/ 29,768 sq mi
Capital: Panamá
Major towns/cities: San Miguelito, Colón, David, La Chorrera, Santiago, Chitré,

Changuinola
Major ports: Colón, Cristóbal, Balboa
Physical features: coastal plains and mountainous interior; tropical rain forest in east and northwest; Archipelago de las Perlas in Gulf of Panama; Panama Canal
Currency: balboa
GNP per capita (PPP): (US$) 5,016 (1999)
Resources: limestone, clay, salt; deposits of coal, copper, and molybdenum have been discovered
Population: 2,856,000 (2000 est)
Population density: (per sq km) 36 (1999 est)
Language: Spanish (official), English
Religion: Roman Catholic 93%
Time difference: GMT -5

PAPUA NEW GUINEA

Map page 60

National name: Gau Hedinarai ai Papua-Matamata Guinea/Independent State of Papua New Guinea
Area: 462,840 sq km/ 178,702 sq mi
Capital: Port Moresby (on East New Guinea)
Major towns/cities: Lae, Madang, Arawa, Wewak, Goroka, Rabaul
Major ports: Port Moresby, Rabaul
Physical features: mountainous; swamps and plains; monsoon climate; tropical islands of New Ireland, New Britain, and Bougainville; Admiralty Islands, D'Entrecasteaux Islands, and Louisiade Archipelago; active volcanoes Vulcan and Tavurvur
Currency: kina
GNP per capita (PPP): (US$) 2,263 (1999 est)
Resources: copper, gold, silver; deposits of chromite, cobalt, nickel, quartz; substantial reserves of petroleum and natural gas (petroleum production began in 1992)
Population: 4,807,000 (2000 est)
Population density: (per sq km) 10 (1999 est)
Language: English (official), pidgin English, over 700 local languages
Religion: Christian 97%, of which 3% Roman Catholic; local pantheistic beliefs
Time difference: GMT +10

PARAGUAY

Map page 78

National name: República del Paraguay/Republic of Paraguay
Area: 406,752 sq km/ 157,046 sq mi
Capital: Asunción (and chief port)

Major towns/cities: Ciudad del Este, Pedro Juan Caballero, San Lorenzo, Fernando de la Mora, Lambare, Luque, Capiatá
Major ports: Concepción
Physical features: low marshy plain and marshlands; divided by Paraguay River; Paraná River forms southeast boundary
Currency: guaraní
GNP per capita (PPP): (US$) 4,193 (1999 est)
Resources: gypsum, kaolin, limestone, salt; deposits (not commercially exploited) of bauxite, iron ore, copper, manganese, uranium; deposits of natural gas discovered in 1994; exploration for petroleum deposits ongoing mid-1990s
Population: 5,496,000 (2000 est)
Population density: (per sq km) 13 (1999 est)
Language: Spanish (official), Guaraní (an indigenous Indian language)
Religion: Roman Catholic (official religion) 85%; Mennonite, Anglican
Time difference: GMT -3/4

PERU

Map page 76

National name: República del Perú/Republic of Peru
Area: 1,285,200 sq km/496,216 sq mi

Capital: Lima
Major towns/cities: Arequipa, Iquitos, Chiclayo, Trujillo, Huancayo, Piura, Chimbote
Major ports: Callao, Chimbote, Salaverry

Physical features: Andes mountains running northwest-southeast cover 27% of Peru, separating Amazon river-basin jungle in northeast from coastal plain in west; desert along coast north-south (Atacama Desert); Lake Titicaca
Currency: nuevo sol
GNP per capita (PPP): (US$) 4,387 (1999)
Resources: lead, copper, iron, silver, zinc (world's fourth-largest producer), petroleum
Population: 25,662,000 (2000 est)
Population density: (per sq km) 20 (1999 est)
Language: Spanish, Quechua (both official), Aymara, many indigenous dialects
Religion: Roman Catholic (state religion) 95%
Time difference: GMT -5

PHILIPPINES

Map page 40

National name: Republika Ñg Pilipinas/Republic of the Philippines
Area: 300,000 sq km/ 115,830 sq mi
Capital: Manila (on Luzon island) (and chief port)
Major towns/cities: Quezon City, Davao, Caloocan, Cebu, Bacolod, Cagayan de Oro, Iloilo
Major ports: Cebu, Davao (on Mindanao), Iloilo, Zamboanga (on Mindanao)
Physical features: comprises over 7,000 islands; volcanic mountain ranges traverse main chain north-south; 50% still forested. The largest islands are Luzon 108,172 sq km/41,754 sq mi and Mindanao 94,227 sq km/36,372 sq mi; others include Samar, Negros, Palawan, Panay, Mindoro, Leyte, Cebu, and the Sulu group; Pinatubo volcano (1,759 m/5,770 ft); Mindanao has active volcano Apo (2,954 m/9,690 ft) and mountainous rain forest
Currency: peso
GNP per capita (PPP): (US$) 3,815 (1999)
Resources: copper ore, gold, silver, chromium, nickel, coal, crude petroleum, natural gas, forests
Population: 75,967,000 (2000 est)
Population density: (per sq km) 248 (1999 est)
Language: Filipino, English (both official), Spanish, Cebuano, Ilocano, more than 70 other indigenous languages
Religion: Christian 94%, mainly Roman Catholic (84%), Protestant; Muslim 4%, local religions
Time difference: GMT +8

POLAND

Map page 10

National name: Rzeczpospolita Polska/Republic of Poland
Area: 312,683 sq km/ 120,726 sq mi
Capital: Warsaw
Major towns/cities: Łódź, Kraków, Wrocław, Poznań, Gdańsk, Szczecin, Katowice, Bydgoszcz, Lublin
Major ports: Gdansk (Danzig), Szczecin (Stettin), Gdynia (Gdingen)
Physical features: part of the great plain of Europe; Vistula, Oder, and Neisse rivers; Sudeten, Tatra, and Carpathian mountains on southern frontier
Currency: zloty
GNP per capita (PPP): (US$) 7,894 (1999)
Resources: coal (world's fifth-largest producer), copper, sulfur, silver, petroleum and natural gas reserves
Population: 38,765,000 (2000 est)
Population density: (per sq km) 124 (1999 est)
Language: Polish (official)
Religion: Roman Catholic 95%
Time difference: GMT +1

PORTUGAL

Map page 20

National name: República Portuguesa/Republic of Portugal
Area: 92,000 sq km/35,521 sq mi (including the Azores and Madeira)
Capital: Lisbon
Major towns/cities: Porto, Coimbra, Amadora, Setúbal, Funchal, Braga, Vila Nova de Gaia
Major ports: Porto, Setúbal
Physical features: mountainous in the north (Serra da Estrêla mountains); plains in the south; rivers Minho, Douro, Tagus (Tejo), Guadiana
Currency: escudo
GNP per capita (PPP): (US$) 15,147 (1999)
Resources: limestone, granite, marble, iron, tungsten, copper, pyrites, gold, uranium, coal, forests
Population: 9,875,000 (2000 est)
Population density: (per sq km) 107 (1999 est)
Language: Portuguese (official)
Religion: Roman Catholic 97%
Time difference: GMT +/-0

QATAR

Map page 46

National name: Dawlat Qatar/ State of Qatar
Area: 11,400 sq km/4,401 sq mi
Capital: Doha (and chief port)
Major towns/cities: Dukhān, ad Dawhah, ar-Rayyan, Umm Salal, Musay'īd, aš-Šahniyah
Physical features: mostly flat desert with salt flats in south
Currency: Qatari riyal
GNP per capita (PPP): (US$) N/A
Resources: petroleum, natural gas, water resources
Population: 599,000 (2000 est)
Population density: (per sq km) 52 (1999 est)
Language: Arabic (official), English
Religion: Sunni Muslim 95%
Time difference: GMT +3

ROMANIA

Map page 26

National name: România/Romania
Area: 237,500 sq km/91,698 sq mi
Capital: Bucharest
Major towns/cities: Brasov, Timisoara, Cluj-Napoca, Iaşi, Constanta, Galati, Craiova
Major ports: Galati, Constanta, Brăila
Physical features: mountains surrounding a plateau, with river plains in south and east. Carpathian Mountains, Transylvanian Alps; River Danube; Black Sea coast; mineral springs
Currency: leu
GNP per capita (PPP): (US$) 5,647 (1999)
Resources: brown coal, hard coal, iron ore, salt, bauxite, copper, lead, zinc, methane gas, petroleum (reserves expected to be exhausted by mid- to late 1990s)
Population: 22,327,000 (2000 est)
Population density: (per sq km) 94 (1999 est)
Language: Romanian (official), Hungarian, German
Religion: Romanian Orthodox 87%; Roman Catholic and Uniate 5%, Reformed/Lutheran 3%, Unitarian 1%
Time difference: GMT +2

RUSSIA

Map page 32

National name: Rossiiskaya Federatsiya/Russian Federation
Area: 17,075,400 sq km/6,592,811 sq mi
Capital: Moscow
Major towns/cities: St. Petersburg, Nizhniy Novgorod, Samara, Yekaterinburg, Novosibirsk, Chelyabinsk, Kazan, Omsk, Perm', Ufa
Physical features: fertile Black Earth district; extensive forests; the Ural Mountains with large mineral resources; Lake Baikal, world's deepest lake
Currency: rouble
GNP per capita (PPP): (US$) 6,339 (1999)
Resources: petroleum, natural gas, coal, peat, copper (world's fourth-largest producer), iron ore, lead, aluminum, phosphate rock, nickel, manganese, gold, diamonds, platinum, zinc, tin
Population: 146,934,000 (2000 est)
Population density: (per sq km) 9 (1999 est)
Language: Russian (official) and many East Slavic, Altaic, Uralic, Caucasian languages
Religion: traditionally Russian Orthodox; significant Muslim and Buddhist communities
Time difference: GMT +2-12

RWANDA

Map page 56

National name: Republika y'u Rwanda/Republic of Rwanda
Area: 26,338 sq km/10,169 sq mi
Capital: Kigali
Major towns/cities: Butare, Ruhengeri, Gisenyi, Kibungo, Cyangugu
Physical features: high savannah and hills, with volcanic mountains in northwest; part of lake Kivu; highest peak Mount Karisimbi 4,507 m/14,792 ft; Kagera River (whose headwaters are the source of the Nile)
Currency: Rwandan franc
GNP per capita (PPP): (US$) 690 (1998)
Resources: cassiterite (a tin-bearing ore), wolframite (a tungsten-bearing ore), natural gas, gold, columbo-tantalite, beryl
Population: 7,733,000 (2000 est)
Population density: (per sq km) 275 (1999 est)
Language: Kinyarwanda, French (both official), Kiswahili
Religion: about 50% animist; about 40% Christian, mainly Roman Catholic; 9% Muslim
Time difference: GMT +2

ST. KITTS AND NEVIS

Map page 72

National name: Federation of St. Christopher and St. Nevis
Area: 262 sq km/101 sq mi (St. Kitts 168 sq km/65 sq mi, Nevis 93 sq km/36 sq mi)
Capital: Basseterre (on St. Kitts) (and chief port)
Major towns/cities: Charlestown (Nevis), Newcastle, Sandy Point Town, Dieppe Bay Town
Physical features: both islands are volcanic; fertile plains on coast; black beaches
Currency: East Caribbean dollar
GNP per capita (PPP): (US$) 9,801 (1999)
Population: 38,000 (2000 est)
Population density: (per sq km) 160 (1999 est)
Language: English (official)
Religion: Anglican 36%, Methodist 32%, other Protestant 8%, Roman Catholic 10%
Time difference: GMT -4

ST. LUCIA

Map page 72

Area: 617 sq km/238 sq mi
Capital: Castries
Major towns/cities: Soufrière, Vieux Fort, Choiseul, Gros Islet
Major ports: Vieux-Fort
Physical features: mountainous island with fertile valleys; mainly tropical forest; volcanic peaks; Gros and Petit Pitons
Currency: East Caribbean dollar

GNP per capita (PPP): (US$) 5,022 (1999)
Resources: geothermal energy
Population: 154,000 (2000 est)
Population density: (per sq km) 252 (1999 est)
Language: English (official), French patois
Religion: Roman Catholic 85%; Anglican, Protestant
Time difference: GMT -4

ST. VINCENT AND THE GRENADINES

Map page 72

Area: 388 sq km/150 sq mi (including islets of the Northern Grenadines 43 sq km/17 sq mi)
Capital: Kingstown
Major towns/cities: Georgetown, Châteaubelair, Dovers
Physical features: volcanic mountains, thickly forested; La Soufrière volcano
Currency: East Caribbean dollar
GNP per capita (PPP): (US$) 4,667 (1999)
Population: 114,000 (2000 est)
Population density: (per sq km) 355 (1999 est)
Language: English (official), French patois
Religion: Anglican, Methodist, Roman Catholic
Time difference: GMT -4

SAMOA

Map page 60

National name: 'O la Malo Tu To'atasi o Samoa/Independent State of Samoa
Area: 2,830 sq km/1,092 sq mi
Capital: Apia (on Upolu island) (and chief port)
Major towns/cities: Lalomanu, Tuasivi, Falealupo, Falelatai, Taga
Physical features: comprises South Pacific islands of Savai'i and Upolu, with two smaller tropical islands and uninhabited islets; mountain ranges on main islands; coral reefs; over half forested
Currency: tala, or Samoan dollar
GNP per capita (PPP): (US$) 3,915 (1999)
Population: 180,000 (2000 est)
Population density: (per sq km) 63 (1999 est)
Language: English, Samoan (both official)
Religion: Congregationalist; also Roman Catholic, Methodist
Time difference: GMT -11

SAN MARINO

Map page 24

National name: Serenissima Repubblica di San Marino/Most Serene Republic of San Marino
Area: 61 sq km/24 sq mi
Capital: San Marino
Major towns/cities: Serravalle, Faetano, Fiorentino, Borgo Maggiore, Domagnano
Physical features: the slope of Mount Titano
Currency: Italian lira
GNP per capita (PPP): (US$) 20,000 (1997 est)
Resources: limestone and other building stone
Population: 27,000 (2000 est)
Population density: (per sq km) 417 (1999 est)
Language: Italian (official)
Religion: Roman Catholic 95%
Time difference: GMT +1

SÃO TOMÉ AND PRÍNCIPE

Map page 54

National name: República Democrática de São Tomé e Príncipe/Democratic Republic of São Tomé and Príncipe

Area: 1,000 sq km/386 sq mi
Capital: São Tomé
Major towns/cities: Santo
António, Sant Ana, Porto Alegre,
Neves, Santo Amaro
Physical features: comprises
two main islands and several
smaller ones, all volcanic; thickly
forested and fertile
Currency: dobra
GNP per capita (PPP): (US$) 1,335 (1999)
Population: 147,000 (2000 est)
Population density: (per sq km) 161 (1999 est)
Language: Portuguese (official), Fang (a Bantu language),
Lungwa São Tomé (a Portuguese Creole)
Religion: Roman Catholic 80%, animist
Time difference: GMT +/-0

SAUDI ARABIA
Map page 46

National name: Al-Mamlaka
al-'Arabiyya as-Sa'udiyya/
Kingdom of Saudi Arabia
Area: 2,200,518 sq km/
849,620 sq mi
Capital: Riyadh
Major towns/cities: Jedda,
Mecca, Medina, Ad Dammām, Tabūk, Buraydah
Major ports: Jedda, Ad Dammām, Jīzān, Yanbu
Physical features: desert, sloping to the Persian Gulf from a
height of 2,750 m/9,000 ft in the west
Currency: riyal
GNP per capita (PPP): (US$) 10,472 (1999 est)
Resources: petroleum, natural gas, iron ore, limestone, gypsum,
marble, clay, salt, gold, uranium, copper, fish
Population: 21,607,000 (2000 est)
Population density: (per sq km) 9 (1999 est)
Language: Arabic (official), English
Religion: Sunni Muslim 85%; there is a Shiite minority
Time difference: GMT +3

SENEGAL
Map page 54

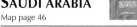

National name: République du
Sénégal/Republic of Senegal
Area: 196,200 sq km/
75,752 sq mi
Capital: Dakar (and chief port)
Major towns/cities: Thiès,
Kaolack, Saint-Louis, Ziguinchor,
Diourbel, Mbour
Physical features: plains rising to hills in southeast; swamp and
tropical forest in southwest; River Senegal; The Gambia forms an
enclave within Senegal
Currency: franc CFA
GNP per capita (PPP): (US$) 1,341 (1999)
Resources: calcium phosphates, aluminum phosphates, salt,
natural gas; offshore deposits of petroleum to be developed
Population: 9,481,000 (2000 est)
Population density: (per sq km) 47 (1999 est)
Language: French (official), Wolof, other ethnic languages
Religion: mainly Sunni Muslim; Christian 4%, animist 1%
Time difference: GMT +/-0

SEYCHELLES
Map page 58

National name: Republic of
Seychelles
Area: 453 sq km/174 sq mi
Capital: Victoria (on Mahé
island) (and chief port)
Major towns/cities: Cascade,
Anse Boileau, Takamaka
Physical features: comprises
two distinct island groups: one, the Granitic group, concentrated,
the other, the Outer or Coralline group, widely scattered; totals
over 100 islands and islets

Currency: Seychelles rupee
GNP per capita (PPP): (US$) 10,381 (1999)
Resources: guano; natural gas and metal deposits were being
explored mid-1990s
Population: 77,000 (2000 est)
Population density: (per sq km) 174 (1999 est)
Language: Creole (an Asian, African, European mixture) (95%),
English, French (all official)
Religion: Roman Catholic 90%
Time difference: GMT +4

SIERRA LEONE
Map page 54

National name: Republic of
Sierra Leone
Area: 71,740 sq km/27,698 sq mi
Capital: Freetown
Major towns/cities: Koidu, Bo,
Kenema, Makeni
Major ports: Bonthe
Physical features: mountains in
east; hills and forest; coastal mangrove swamps
Currency: leone
GNP per capita (PPP): (US$) 414 (1999)
Resources: gold, diamonds, bauxite, rutile (titanium dioxide)
Population: 4,854,000 (2000 est)
Population density: (per sq km) 66 (1999 est)
Language: English (official), Krio (a Creole language), Mende,
Limba, Temne
Religion: animist 45%, Muslim 44%, Protestant 8%, Roman
Catholic 3%
Time difference: GMT +/-0

SINGAPORE
Map page 42

National name: Republik
Singapura/Republic of Singapore
Area: 622 sq km/240 sq mi
Capital: Singapore
Physical features: comprises
Singapore Island, low and flat,
and 57 small islands; Singapore
Island is joined to the mainland
by causeway across Strait of Johore
Currency: Singapore dollar
GNP per capita (PPP): (US$) 27,024 (1999)
Resources: granite
Population: 3,567,000 (2000 est)
Population density: (per sq km) 5,662 (1999 est)
Language: Malay, Mandarin Chinese, Tamil, English (all official),
other Indian languages, Chinese dialects
Religion: Buddhist, Taoist, Muslim, Hindu, Christian
Time difference: GMT +8

SLOVAK REPUBLIC
Map page 10

National name: Slovenská
Republika/Slovak Republic
Area: 49,035 sq km/18,932 sq mi
Capital: Bratislava
Major towns/cities: Košice,
Nitra, Prešov, Banská Bystrica,
Zilina, Trnava, Martin
Physical features: Western
range of Carpathian Mountains, including Tatra and Beskids in
north; Danube plain in south; numerous lakes and mineral springs
Currency: Slovak koruna (based on Czechoslovak koruna)
GNP per capita (PPP): (US$) 9,811 (1999)
Resources: brown coal, lignite, copper, zinc, lead, iron ore,
magnesite
Population: 5,387,000 (2000 est)
Population density: (per sq km) 110 (1999 est)
Language: Slovak (official), Hungarian, Czech, other ethnic
languages
Religion: Roman Catholic (over 50%), Lutheran, Reformist,
Orthodox, atheist 10%
Time difference: GMT +1

SLOVENIA
Map page 22

National name: Republika Slovenija/
Republic of Slovenia
Area: 20,251 sq km/7,818 sq mi
Capital: Ljubljana
Major towns/cities: Maribor,
Kranj, Celje, Velenje, Koper,
Novo Mesto
Major ports: Koper
Physical features: mountainous; Sava and Drava rivers
Currency: tolar
GNP per capita (PPP): (US$) 15,062 (1999)
Resources: coal, lead, zinc; small reserves/deposits of natural
gas, petroleum, salt, uranium
Population: 1,986,000 (2000 est)
Population density: (per sq km) 98 (1999 est)
Language: Slovene (related to Serbo-Croat: official), Hungarian,
Italian
Religion: Roman Catholic 70%; Eastern Orthodox, Lutheran,
Muslim
Time difference: GMT +1

SOLOMON ISLANDS
Map page 60

Area: 27,600 sq km/
10,656 sq mi
Capital: Honiara (on
Guadalcanal island) (and chief
port)
Major towns/cities: Gizo, Auki,
Kirakira, Buala
Major ports: Yandina
Physical features: comprises all but the northernmost islands
(which belong to Papua New Guinea) of a Melanesian archipelago
stretching nearly 1,500 km/900 mi. The largest is Guadalcanal
(area 6,500 sq km/2,510 sq mi); others are Malaita, San
Cristobal, New Georgia, Santa Isabel, Choiseul; mainly
mountainous and forested
Currency: Solomon Island dollar
GNP per capita (PPP): (US$) 1,793 (1999)
Resources: bauxite, phosphates, gold, silver, copper, lead, zinc,
cobalt, asbestos, nickel
Population: 444,000 (2000 est)
Population density: (per sq km) 16 (1999 est)
Language: English (official), pidgin English, more than 80
Melanesian dialects (85%), Papuan and Polynesian languages
Religion: more than 80% Christian; Anglican 34%, Roman
Catholic 19%, South Sea Evangelical, other Protestant, animist
5%
Time difference: GMT +11

SOMALIA
Map page 56

National name: Jamhuuriyadda
Soomaaliya/Republic of Somalia
Area: 637,700 sq km/
246,215 sq mi
Capital: Mogadishu (and chief
port)
Major towns/cities: Hargeysa,
Berbera, Kismaayo, Marka
Major ports: Berbera, Marka, Kismaayo
Physical features: mainly flat, with hills in north
Currency: Somali shilling
GNP per capita (PPP): (US$) 600 (1999 est)
Resources: chromium, coal, salt, tin, zinc, copper, gypsum,
manganese, iron ore, uranium, gold, silver; deposits of petroleum
and natural gas have been discovered but remain unexploited
Population: 10,097,000 (2000 est)
Population density: (per sq km) 15 (1999 est)
Language: Somali, Arabic (both official), Italian, English
Religion: Sunni Muslim; small Christian community, mainly
Roman Catholic
Time difference: GMT +3

SOUTH AFRICA

Map page 58

National name: Republiek van Suid-Afrika/Republic of South Africa
Area: 1,222,081 sq km/ 471,845 sq mi
Capital: Cape Town (legislative), Pretoria (administrative), Bloemfontein (judicial)
Major towns/cities: Johannesburg, Durban, Port Elizabeth, Vereeniging, Pietermaritzburg, Kimberley, Soweto, Tembisa
Major ports: Cape Town, Durban, Port Elizabeth, East London
Physical features: southern end of large plateau, fringed by mountains and lowland coastal margin; Drakensberg Mountains, Table Mountain; Limpopo and Orange rivers
Territories: Marion Island and Prince Edward Island in the Antarctic
Currency: rand
GNP per capita (PPP): (US$) 8,318 (1999)
Resources: gold (world's largest producer), coal, platinum, iron ore, diamonds, chromium, manganese, limestone, asbestos, fluorspar, uranium, copper, lead, zinc, petroleum, natural gas
Population: 40,377,000 (2000 est)
Population density: (per sq km) 33 (1999 est)
Language: English, Afrikaans, Xhosa, Zulu, Sesotho (all official), other African languages
Religion: Dutch Reformed Church and other Christian denominations 77%, Hindu 2%, Muslim 1%
Time difference: GMT +2

SOUTH KOREA

Map page 38

National name: Daehan Minguk/ Republic of Korea
Area: 98,799 sq km/38,146 sq mi
Capital: Seoul
Major towns/cities: Pusan, Taegu, Inch'ŏn, Kwangju, Taejŏn, Songnam
Major ports: Pusan, Inch'ŏn
Physical features: southern end of a mountainous peninsula separating the Sea of Japan from the Yellow Sea
Currency: won
GNP per capita (PPP): (US$) 14,637 (1999)
Resources: coal, iron ore, tungsten, gold, molybdenum, graphite, fluorite, natural gas, hydroelectric power, fish
Population: 46,844,000 (2000 est)
Population density: (per sq km) 473 (1999 est)
Language: Korean (official)
Religion: Buddhist 48%, Confucian 3%, Christian 47%, mainly Protestant; Chund Kyo (peculiar to Korea, combining elements of Shaman, Buddhist, and Christian doctrines)
Time difference: GMT +9

SPAIN

Map page 20

National name: España/Spain
Area: 504,750 sq km/194,883 sq mi (including the Balearic and Canary islands)
Capital: Madrid
Major towns/cities: Barcelona, Valencia, Zaragoza, Sevilla, Málaga, Bilbao, Las Palmas (on Gran Canarias island), Murcia, Palma (on Mallorca)
Major ports: Barcelona, Valencia, Cartagena, Málaga, Cádiz, Vigo, Santander, Bilbao
Physical features: central plateau with mountain ranges, lowlands in south; rivers Ebro, Douro, Tagus, Guadiana, Guadalquivir; Iberian Plateau (Meseta); Pyrenees, Cantabrian Mountains, Andalusian Mountains, Sierra Nevada
Territories: Balearic and Canary Islands; in North Africa: Ceuta, Melilla, Alhucemas, Chafarinas Islands, Peñón de Vélez
Currency: peseta
GNP per capita (PPP): (US$) 16,730 (1999)
Resources: coal, lignite, anthracite, copper, iron, zinc, uranium, potassium salts
Population: 39,630,000 (2000 est)

Population density: (per sq km) 79 (1999 est)
Language: Spanish (Castilian; official), Basque, Catalan, Galician
Religion: Roman Catholic 98%
Time difference: GMT +1

SRI LANKA

Map page 44

National name: Sri Lanka Prajatantrika Samajavadi Janarajaya/Democratic Socialist Republic of Sri Lanka
Area: 65,610 sq km/25,332 sq mi
Capital: Sri Jayewardenepura Kotte
Major towns/cities: Colombo, Kandy, Dehiwala-Mount Lavinia, Moratuwa, Jaffna, Galle
Major ports: Jaffna, Galle, Negombo, Trincomalee
Physical features: flat in north and around coast; hills and mountains in south and central interior
Currency: Sri Lankan rupee
GNP per capita (PPP): (US$) 3,056 (1999)
Resources: gemstones, graphite, iron ore, monazite, rutile, uranium, iemenite sands, limestone, salt, clay
Population: 18,827,000 (2000 est)
Population density: (per sq km) 284 (1999 est)
Language: Sinhala, Tamil (both official), English
Religion: Buddhist 69%, Hindu 15%, Muslim 8%, Christian 8%
Time difference: GMT +5.5

SUDAN

Map page 50

National name: Al-Jumhuryyat es-Sudan/Republic of Sudan
Area: 2,505,800 sq km/ 967,489 sq mi
Capital: Khartoum
Major towns/cities: Omdurman, Port Sudan, Juba, Wad Medani, El Obeid, Kassala, Gedaref, Nyala
Major ports: Port Sudan
Physical features: fertile Nile valley separates Libyan Desert in west from high rocky Nubian Desert in east
Currency: Sudanese dinar
GNP per capita (PPP): (US$) 1,298 (1999)
Resources: petroleum, marble, mica, chromite, gypsum, gold, graphite, sulfur, iron, manganese, zinc, fluorspar, talc, limestone, dolomite, pumice
Population: 29,490,000 (2000 est)
Population density: (per sq km) 12 (1999 est)
Language: Arabic (51%) (official), 100 local languages
Religion: Sunni Muslim 70%; also animist 25%, and Christian 5%
Time difference: GMT +2

SURINAME

Map page 76

National name: Republiek Suriname/Republic of Suriname
Area: 163,820 sq km/ 63,250 sq mi
Capital: Paramaribo
Major towns/cities: Nieuw Nickerie, Moengo, Brokopondo, Nieuw Amsterdam, Albina, Groningen
Physical features: hilly and forested, with flat and narrow coastal plain; Suriname River
Currency: Suriname guilder
GNP per capita (PPP): (US$) 3,820 (1998 est)
Resources: petroleum, bauxite (one of the world's leading producers), iron ore, copper, manganese, nickel, platinum, gold, kaolin
Population: 417,000 (2000 est)
Population density: (per sq km) 3 (1999 est)
Language: Dutch (official), Spanish, Sranan (Creole), English, Hindi, Javanese, Chinese, various tribal languages

Religion: Christian 47%, Hindu 28%, Muslim 20%
Time difference: GMT -3.5

SWAZILAND

Map page 58

National name: Umbuso waka Ngwane/Kingdom of Swaziland
Area: 17,400 sq km/6,718 sq mi
Capital: Mbabane (administrative), Lobamba (legislative)
Major towns/cities: Manzini, Big Bend, Mhlume, Nhlangano
Physical features: central valley; mountains in west (Highveld); plateau in east (Lowveld and Lubombo plateau)
Currency: lilangeni
GNP per capita (PPP): (US$) 4,200 (1999)
Resources: coal, asbestos, diamonds, gold, tin, kaolin, iron ore, talc, pyrophyllite, silica
Population: 1,008,000 (2000 est)
Population density: (per sq km) 56 (1999 est)
Language: Swazi, English (both official)
Religion: about 60% Christian, animist
Time difference: GMT +2

SWEDEN

Map page 8

National name: Konungariket Sverige/Kingdom of Sweden
Area: 450,000 sq km/ 173,745 sq mi
Capital: Stockholm
Major towns/cities: Göteborg, Malmö, Uppsala, Norrköping, Västerås, Linköping, Örebro, Helsingborg
Major ports: Helsingborg, Malmö, Göteborg, Stockholm
Physical features: mountains in west; plains in south; thickly forested; more than 20,000 islands off the Stockholm coast; lakes, including Vänern, Vättern, Mälaren, and Hjälmaren
Currency: Swedish krona
GNP per capita (PPP): (US$) 20,824 (1999)
Resources: iron ore, uranium, copper, lead, zinc, silver, hydroelectric power, forests
Population: 8,910,000 (2000 est)
Population density: (per sq km) 20 (1999 est)
Language: Swedish (official), Finnish, Saami (Lapp)
Religion: Evangelical Lutheran, Church of Sweden (established national church) 90%; Muslim, Jewish
Time difference: GMT +1

SWITZERLAND
Map page 22

National name: Schweizerische Eidgenossenschaft (German)/ Confédération Suisse (French)/ Confederazione Svizzera (Italian)/ Confederaziun Svizra (Romansch)/ Swiss Confederation
Area: 41,300 sq km/15,945 sq mi
Capital: Bern
Major towns/cities: Zürich, Geneva, Basel, Lausanne, Luzern, St. Gallen, Winterthur
Major ports: river port Basel (on the Rhine)
Physical features: most mountainous country in Europe (Alps and Jura mountains); highest peak Dufourspitze 4,634 m/15,203 ft in Apennines
Currency: Swiss franc
GNP per capita (PPP): (US$) 27,486 (1999)
Resources: salt, hydroelectric power, forest
Population: 7,386,000 (2000 est)
Population density: (per sq km) 178 (1999 est)
Language: German (65%), French (18%), Italian (10%), Romansch (1%) (all official)
Religion: Roman Catholic 46%, Protestant 40%
Time difference: GMT +1

SYRIA
Map page 46

National name: al-Jumhuriyya al-Arabiyya as-Suriyya/Syrian Arab Republic
Area: 185,200 sq km/ 71,505 sq mi
Capital: Damascus
Major towns/cities: Aleppo, Homs, Al Lādhiqīyah, Hamāh, Ar Raqqah, Dayr az Zawr
Major ports: Al Lādhiqīyah
Physical features: mountains alternate with fertile plains and desert areas; Euphrates River
Currency: Syrian pound
GNP per capita (PPP): (US$) 2,761 (1999)
Resources: petroleum, natural gas, iron ore, phosphates, salt, gypsum, sodium chloride, bitumen
Population: 16,125,000 (2000 est)
Population density: (per sq km) 85 (1999 est)
Language: Arabic (89%) (official), Kurdish (6%), Armenian (3%), French, English, Aramaic, Circassian
Religion: Sunni Muslim 74%; other Islamic sects 16%, Christian 10%
Time difference: GMT +2

TAIWAN
Map page 38

National name: Chung-hua Min-kuo/Republic of China
Area: 36,179 sq km/13,968 sq mi
Capital: T'aipei
Major towns/cities: Kaohsiung, T'aichung, T'ainan, Panch'iao, Chungho, Sanch'ung
Major ports: Kaohsiung, Chilung
Physical features: island (formerly Formosa) off People's Republic of China; mountainous, with lowlands in west; Penghu (Pescadores), Jinmen (Quemoy), Mazu (Matsu) islands
Currency: New Taiwan dollar
GNP per capita (PPP): (US$) 18,950 (1998 est)
Resources: coal, copper, marble, dolomite; small reserves of petroleum and natural gas
Population: 22,113,000 (1999 est)
Population density: (per sq km) 685 (1999 est)
Language: Chinese (dialects include Mandarin (official), Min, and Hakka)
Religion: officially atheist; Buddhist 23%, Taoist 18%, I-Kuan Tao 4%, Christian 3%, Confucian and other 3%
Time difference: GMT +8

TAJIKISTAN
Map page 34

National name: Jumhurii Tojikston/Republic of Tajikistan
Area: 143,100 sq km/ 55,250 sq mi
Capital: Dushanbe
Major towns/cities: Khūjand, Qūrghonteppa, Kūlob, Ūroteppa, Kofarnihon
Physical features: mountainous, more than half of its territory lying above 3,000 m/10,000 ft; huge mountain glaciers, which are the source of many rapid rivers
Currency: Tajik ruble
GNP per capita (PPP): (US$) 981 (1999)
Resources: coal, aluminum, lead, zinc, iron, tin, uranium, radium, arsenic, bismuth, gold, mica, asbestos, lapis lazuli; small reserves of petroleum and natural gas
Population: 6,188,000 (2000 est)
Population density: (per sq km) 43 (1999 est)
Language: Tajik (related to Farsi; official), Russian
Religion: Sunni Muslim; small Russian Orthodox and Jewish communities
Time difference: GMT +5

TANZANIA
Map page 56

National name: Jamhuri ya Muungano wa Tanzania/United Republic of Tanzania
Area: 945,000 sq km/ 364,864 sq mi
Capital: Dodoma (official), Dar es Salaam (administrative)
Major towns/cities: Zanzibar, Mwanza, Mbeya, Tanga, Morogoro
Major ports: (former capital) Dar es Salaam
Physical features: central plateau; lakes in north and west; coastal plains; lakes Victoria, Tanganyika, and Nyasa; half the country is forested; comprises islands of Zanzibar and Pemba; Mount Kilimanjaro, 5,895 m/19,340 ft, the highest peak in Africa; Olduvai Gorge; Ngorongoro Crater, 14.5 km/9 mi across, 762 m/2,500 ft deep
Currency: Tanzanian shilling
GNP per capita (PPP): (US$) 478 (1999)
Resources: diamonds, other gemstones, gold, salt, phosphates, coal, gypsum, tin, kaolin (exploration for petroleum in progress)
Population: 33,517,000 (2000 est)
Population density: (per sq km) 35 (1999 est)
Language: Kiswahili, English (both official), Arabic (in Zanzibar), many local languages
Religion: Muslim, Christian, traditional religions
Time difference: GMT +3

THAILAND
Map page 40

National name: Ratcha Anachak Thai/Kingdom of Thailand
Area: 513,115 sq km/ 198,113 sq mi
Capital: Bangkok (and chief port)
Major towns/cities: Chiang Mai, Hat Yai, Khon Kaen, Songkhla, Nakhon Ratchasima, Nonthaburi, Udon Thani
Major ports: Nakhon Sawan
Physical features: mountainous, semiarid plateau in northeast, fertile central region, tropical isthmus in south; rivers Chao Phraya, Mekong, and Salween
Currency: baht
GNP per capita (PPP): (US$) 5,599 (1999)
Resources: tin ore, lignite, gypsum, antimony, manganese, copper, tungsten, lead, gold, zinc, silver, rubies, sapphires, natural gas, petroleum, fish
Population: 61,399,000 (2000 est)
Population density: (per sq km) 119 (1999 est)
Language: Thai, Chinese (both official), English, Lao, Malay, Khmer
Religion: Buddhist 95%; Muslim 5%
Time difference: GMT +7

TOGO
Map page 54

National name: République Togolaise/Togolese Republic
Area: 56,800 sq km/21,930 sq mi
Capital: Lomé
Major towns/cities: Sokodé, Kpalimé, Kara, Atakpamé, Bassar, Tsévié
Physical features: two savannah plains, divided by range of hills northeast-southwest; coastal lagoons and marsh; Mono Tableland, Oti Plateau, Oti River
Currency: franc CFA
GNP per capita (PPP): (US$) 1,346 (1999 est)
Resources: phosphates, limestone, marble, deposits of iron ore, manganese, chromite, peat; exploration for petroleum and uranium was under way in the early 1990s
Population: 4,629,000 (2000 est)
Population density: (per sq km) 79 (1999 est)
Language: French (official), Ewe, Kabre, Gurma, other local languages
Religion: animist about 50%, Catholic and Protestant 35%, Muslim 15%
Time difference: GMT +/-0

TONGA
Map page 60

National name: Pule'anga Fakatu'i 'o Tonga/Kingdom of Tonga
Area: 750 sq km/290 sq mi
Capital: Nuku'alofa (on Tongatapu island)
Major towns/cities: Neiafu, Vaini
Physical features: three groups of islands in southwest Pacific, mostly coral formations, but actively volcanic in west; of the 170 islands in the Tonga group, 36 are inhabited
Currency: pa'anga, or Tongan dollar
GNP per capita (PPP): (US$) 4,281 (1999)
Population: 99,000 (2000 est)
Population density: (per sq km) 131 (1999 est)
Language: Tongan (official), English
Religion: mainly Free Wesleyan Church; Roman Catholic, Anglican
Time difference: GMT +13

TRINIDAD AND TOBAGO
Map page 72

National name: Republic of Trinidad and Tobago
Area: 5,130 sq km/1,980 sq mi (Trinidad 4,828 sq km/ 1,864 sq mi and Tobago 300 sq km/115 sq mi)
Capital: Port of Spain (and chief port)
Major towns/cities: San Fernando, Arima, Point Fortin
Major ports: Scarborough
Physical features: comprises two main islands and some smaller ones in Caribbean Sea; coastal swamps and hills east-west
Currency: Trinidad and Tobago dollar
GNP per capita (PPP): (US$) 7,262 (1999)
Resources: petroleum, natural gas, asphalt (world's largest deposits of natural asphalt)
Population: 1,295,000 (2000 est)
Population density: (per sq km) 251 (1999 est)
Language: English (official), Hindi, French, Spanish
Religion: Roman Catholic 33%, Hindu 25%, Anglican 15%, Muslim 6%, Presbyterian 4%
Time difference: GMT -4

TUNISIA
Map page 52

National name: Al-Jumhuriyya at-Tunisiyya/Tunisian Republic
Area: 164,150 sq km/ 63,378 sq mi
Capital: Tunis (and chief port)
Major towns/cities: Sfax, L'Ariana, Bizerte, Gabès, Sousse, Kairouan
Major ports: Sfax, Sousse, Bizerte
Physical features: arable and forested land in north graduates toward desert in south; fertile island of Jerba, linked to mainland by causeway (identified with island of lotus-eaters); Shott el Jerid salt lakes
Currency: Tunisian dinar
GNP per capita (PPP): (US$) 5,478 (1999)
Resources: petroleum, natural gas, phosphates, iron, zinc, lead, aluminum fluoride, fluorspar, sea salt
Population: 9,586,000 (2000 est)
Population density: (per sq km) 58 (1999 est)
Language: Arabic (official), French
Religion: Sunni Muslim (state religion); Jewish and Christian minorities
Time difference: GMT +1

TURKEY
Map page 46

National name: Türkiye Cumhuriyeti/Republic of Turkey
Area: 779,500 sq km/300,964 sq mi

Capital: Ankara
Major towns/cities: İstanbul, İzmir, Adana, Bursa, Gaziantep, Konya, Mersin, Antalya, Diyarbakduringr
Major ports: İstanbul and İzmir

Physical features: central plateau surrounded by mountains, partly in Europe (Thrace) and partly in Asia (Anatolia); Bosporus and Dardanelles; Mount Ararat (highest peak Great Ararat, 5,137 m/16,854 ft); Taurus Mountains in southwest (highest peak Kaldi Dag, 3,734 m/12,255 ft); sources of rivers Euphrates and Tigris in east
Currency: Turkish lira
GNP per capita (PPP): (US$) 6,126 (1999)
Resources: chromium, copper, mercury, antimony, borax, coal, petroleum, natural gas, iron ore, salt
Population: 66,591,000 (2000 est)
Population density: (per sq km) 84 (1999 est)
Language: Turkish (official), Kurdish, Arabic
Religion: Sunni Muslim 99%; Orthodox, Armenian churches
Time difference: GMT +3

TURKMENISTAN
Map page 34

National name: Türkmenistan/ Turkmenistan
Area: 488,100 sq km/ 188,455 sq mi
Capital: Ashkhabad
Major towns/cities: Chardzhev, Mary, Nebitdag, Dashkhovuz, Turkmenbashi
Major ports: Turkmenbashi
Physical features: about 90% of land is desert including the Kara Kum 'Black Sands' desert (area 310,800 sq km/120,000 sq mi)
Currency: manat
GNP per capita (PPP): (US$) 3,099 (1999)
Resources: petroleum, natural gas, coal, sulfur, magnesium, iodine-bromine, sodium sulfate and different types of salt
Population: 4,459,000 (2000 est)
Population density: (per sq km) 9 (1999 est)
Language: Turkmen (a Turkic language; official), Russian, Uzbek, other regional languages
Religion: Sunni Muslim
Time difference: GMT +5

TUVALU
Map page 60

National name: Fakavae Aliki-Malo i Tuvalu/ Constitutional Monarchy of Tuvalu
Area: 25 sq km/9.6 sq mi
Capital: Fongafale (on Funafuti atoll)
Physical features: nine low coral atolls forming a chain of 579 km/650 mi in the Southwest Pacific
Currency: Australian dollar
GNP per capita (PPP): (US$) 970 (1998 est)
Population: 12,000 (2000 est)
Population density: (per sq km) 423 (1999 est)
Language: Tuvaluan, English (both official), a Gilbertese dialect (on Nui)
Religion: Protestant 96% (Church of Tuvalu)
Time difference: GMT +12

UGANDA
Map page 56

National name: Republic of Uganda
Area: 236,600 sq km/91,351 sq mi
Capital: Kampala
Major towns/cities: Jinja, Mbale, Entebbe, Masaka, Mbarara, Soroti
Physical features: plateau with mountains in west (Ruwenzori Range, with Mount Margherita, 5,110 m/16,765 ft); forest and

grassland; 18% is lakes, rivers, and wetlands (Owen Falls on White Nile where it leaves Lake Victoria; Lake Albert in west); arid in northwest
Currency: Ugandan new shilling
GNP per capita (PPP): (US$) 1,136 (1999 est)

Resources: copper, apatite, limestone; believed to possess the world's second-largest deposit of gold (hitherto unexploited); also reserves of magnetite, tin, tungsten, beryllium, bismuth, asbestos, graphite
Population: 21,778,000 (2000 est)
Population density: (per sq km) 89
Language: English (official), Kiswahili, other Bantu and Nilotic languages
Religion: Christian 65%, animist 20%, Muslim 15%
Time difference: GMT +3

UKRAINE
Map page 30

National name: Ukrayina/ Ukraine
Area: 603,700 sq km/ 233,088 sq mi
Capital: Kiev
Major towns/cities: Kharkiv, Donets'k, Dnipropetrovs'k, L'viv, Kryvyy Rih, Zaporizhzhya, Odessa
Physical features: Russian plain; Carpathian and Crimean Mountains; rivers: Dnieper (with the Dnieper dam 1932), Donetz, Bug
Currency: hryvna
GNP per capita (PPP): (US$) 3,142 (1999)
Resources: coal, iron ore (world's fifth-largest producer), crude oil, natural gas, salt, chemicals, brown coal, alabaster, gypsum
Population: 50,456,000 (2000 est)
Population density: (per sq km) 84 (1999 est)
Language: Ukrainian (a Slavonic language; official), Russian (also official in Crimea), other regional languages
Religion: traditionally Ukrainian Orthodox; also Ukrainian Catholic; small Protestant, Jewish, and Muslim communities
Time difference: GMT +2

UNITED ARAB EMIRATES
Map page 46

National name: Dawlat Imarat al-'Arabiyya al Muttahida/State of the Arab Emirates (UAE)
Area: 83,657 sq km/ 32,299 sq mi
Capital: Abu Dhabi
Major towns/cities: Dubai, Sharjah, Ra's al Khaymah, Ajmān, Al 'Ayn
Major ports: Dubai
Physical features: desert and flat coastal plain; mountains in east
Currency: UAE dirham
GNP per capita (PPP): (US$) 18,825 (1999 est)
Resources: petroleum and natural gas
Population: 2,441,000 (2000 est)
Population density: (per sq km) 29 (1999 est)
Language: Arabic (official), Farsi, Hindi, Urdu, English
Religion: Muslim 96% (of which 80% Sunni); Christian, Hindu
Time difference: GMT +4

UNITED KINGDOM
Map page 16

National name: United Kingdom of Great Britain and Northern Ireland (U.K.)
Area: 244,100 sq km/ 94,247 sq mi
Capital: London
Major towns/cities: Birmingham, Glasgow, Leeds, Sheffield, Liverpool, Manchester, Edinburgh, Bradford, Bristol, Coventry, Belfast, Cardiff

Major ports: London, Grimsby, Southampton, Liverpool
Physical features: became separated from European continent in about 6000 BC; rolling landscape, increasingly mountainous toward the north, with Grampian Mountains in Scotland, Pennines in northern England, Cambrian Mountains in Wales; rivers include Thames, Severn, and Spey
Territories: Anguilla, Bermuda, British Antarctic Territory, British Indian Ocean Territory, British Virgin Islands, Cayman Islands, Falkland Islands, Gibraltar, Montserrat, Pitcairn Islands, St. Helena and Dependencies (Ascension, Tristan da Cunha), South Georgia, South Sandwich Islands, Turks and Caicos Islands; the Channel Islands and the Isle of Man are not part of the U.K. but are direct dependencies of the crown
Currency: pound sterling
GNP per capita (PPP): (US$) 20,883 (1999)
Resources: coal, limestone, crude petroleum, natural gas, tin, iron, salt, sand and gravel
Population: 58,830,000 (2000 est)
Population density: (per sq km) 240 (1999 est)
Language: English (official), Welsh (also official in Wales), Gaelic
Religion: about 46% Church of England (established church); other Protestant denominations, Roman Catholic, Muslim, Jewish, Hindu, Sikh
Time difference: GMT +/-0

UNITED STATES OF AMERICA
Map page 70

National name: United States of America (U.S.A.)
Area: 9,372,615 sq km/ 3,618,766 sq mi
Capital: Washington, D.C.
Major towns/cities: New York, Los Angeles, Chicago, Philadelphia, Detroit, San Francisco, Dallas, San Diego, San Antonio, Houston, Boston, Phoenix, Indianapolis, Honolulu, San José
Physical features: topography and vegetation from tropical (Hawaii) to arctic (Alaska); mountain ranges parallel with east and west coasts; the Rocky Mountains separate rivers emptying into the Pacific from those flowing into the Gulf of Mexico; Great Lakes in north; rivers include Hudson, Mississippi, Missouri, Colorado, Columbia, Snake, Rio Grande, Ohio
Territories: the commonwealths of Puerto Rico and Northern Marianas; Guam, the U.S. Virgin Islands, American Samoa, Wake Island, Midway Islands, Johnston Atoll, Baker Island, Howland Island, Jarvis Island, Kingman Reef, Navassa Island, Palmyra Island
Currency: US dollar
GNP per capita (PPP): (US$) 30,600 (1999)
Resources: coal, copper (world's second-largest producer), iron, bauxite, mercury, silver, gold, nickel, zinc (world's fifth-largest producer), tungsten, uranium, phosphate, petroleum, natural gas, timber
Population: 278,357,000 (2000 est)
Population density: (per sq km) 29 (1999 est)
Language: English, Spanish
Religion: Protestant 58%; Roman Catholic 28%; atheist 10%; Jewish 2%; other 4% (1998)
Time difference: GMT -5-11

URUGUAY
Map page 78

National name: República Oriental del Uruguay/Eastern Republic of Uruguay
Area: 176,200 sq km/ 68,030 sq mi
Capital: Montevideo
Major towns/cities: Salto, Paysandú, Las Piedras, Rivera, Tacuarembó
Physical features: grassy plains (pampas) and low hills; rivers Negro, Uruguay, Río de la Plata
Currency: Uruguayan peso
GNP per capita (PPP): (US$) 8,280 (1999)
Resources: small-scale extraction of building materials, industrial minerals, semiprecious stones; gold deposits are being

developed
Population: 3,337,000 (2000 est)
Population density: (per sq km) 19 (1999 est)
Language: Spanish (official), Brazilero (a mixture of Spanish and Portuguese)
Religion: mainly Roman Catholic
Time difference: GMT -3

UZBEKISTAN
Map page 34

National name: Özbekiston Respublikasi/Republic of Uzbekistan
Area: 447,400 sq km/
172,741 sq mi
Capital: Tashkent
Major towns/cities:
Samarkand, Bukhara, Namangan, Andijon, Nukus, Karshi
Physical features: oases in deserts; rivers: Amu Darya, Syr Darya; Fergana Valley; rich in mineral deposits
Currency: som
GNP per capita (PPP): (US$) 2,092 (1999)
Resources: petroleum, natural gas, coal, gold (world's seventh-largest producer), silver, uranium (world's fourth-largest producer), copper, lead, zinc, tungsten
Population: 24,318,000 (2000 est)
Population density: (per sq km) 54 (1999 est)
Language: Uzbek (a Turkic language; official), Russian, Tajik
Religion: predominantly Sunni Muslim; small Wahhabi, Sufi, and Orthodox Christian communities
Time difference: GMT +5

VANUATU
Map page 60

National name: Ripablik blong Vanuatu/République de Vanuatu/Republic of Vanuatu
Area: 14,800 sq km/
5,714 sq mi
Capital: Port-Vila (on Efate island) (and chief port)
Major towns/cities: Luganville (on Espíritu Santo)
Physical features: comprises around 70 inhabited islands, including Espíritu Santo, Malekula, and Efate; densely forested, mountainous; three active volcanoes; cyclones on average twice a year
Currency: vatu
GNP per capita (PPP): (US$) 2,771 (1999 est)
Resources: manganese; gold, copper, and large deposits of petroleum have been discovered but have hitherto remained unexploited
Population: 190,000 (2000 est)
Population density: (per sq km) 13 (1999 est)
Language: Bislama (82%), English, French (all official)
Religion: Christian 80%, animist about 8%
Time difference: GMT +11

VATICAN CITY STATE
Map page 24

National name: Stato della Città del Vaticano/Vatican City State
Area: 0.4 sq km/0.2 sq mi
Physical features: forms an enclave in the heart of Rome, Italy
Currency: Vatican City lira and Italian lira
GNP per capita (PPP): see Italy
Population: 1,000 (2000 est)
Population density: (per sq km) 2,500 (2000 est)
Language: Latin (official), Italian
Religion: Roman Catholic
Time difference: GMT +1

VENEZUELA
Map page 76

National name: República de Venezuela/Republic of Venezuala
Area: 912,100 sq km/
352,161 sq mi
Capital: Caracas
Major towns/cities: Maracaibo, Maracay, Barquisimeto, Valencia, Ciudad Guayana, Petare
Major ports: Maracaibo
Physical features: Andes Mountains and Lake Maracaibo in northwest; central plains (llanos); delta of River Orinoco in east; Guiana Highlands in southeast
Currency: bolívar
GNP per capita (PPP): (US$) 5,268 (1999)
Resources: petroleum, natural gas, aluminum, iron ore, coal, diamonds, gold, zinc, copper, silver, lead, phosphates, manganese, titanium
Population: 24,170,000 (2000 est)
Population density: (per sq km) 26 (1999 est)
Language: Spanish (official), Indian languages (2%)
Religion: Roman Catholic 92%
Time difference: GMT -4

VIETNAM
Map page 40

National name: Công-hòa xã-hôi chu-nghia Viêt Nam/Socialist Republic of Vietnam
Area: 329,600 sq km/
127,258 sq mi
Capital: Hanoi
Major towns/cities: Ho Chi Minh (formerly Saigon), Hai Phong, Da Năng, Cân Tho, Nha Trang, Biên Hoa, Huê
Major ports: Ho Chi Minh (formerly Saigon), Da Năng, Hai Phong
Physical features: Red River and Mekong deltas, center of cultivation and population; tropical rain forest; mountainous in north and northwest
Currency: dong
GNP per capita (PPP): (US$) 1,755 (1999)
Resources: petroleum, coal, tin, zinc, iron, antimony, chromium, phosphate, apatite, bauxite
Population: 79,832,000 (2000 est)
Population density: (per sq km) 237 (1999 est)
Language: Vietnamese (official), French, English, Khmer, Chinese, local languages
Religion: mainly Buddhist; Christian, mainly Roman Catholic (8-10%); Taoist, Confucian, Hos Hoa, and Cao Dai sects
Time difference: GMT +7

YEMEN
Map page 46

National name: Al-Jumhuriyya al Yamaniyya/Republic of Yemen
Area: 531,900 sq km/
205,366 sq mi
Capital: Şan'ā
Major towns/cities: Aden, Ta'izz, Al Mukallā, Al Ḥudaydah, Ibb, Dhamār
Major ports: Aden
Physical features: hot, moist coastal plain, rising to plateau and desert
Currency: riyal
GNP per capita (PPP): (US$) 688 (1999)
Resources: petroleum, natural gas, gypsum, salt; deposits of copper, gold, lead, zinc, molybdenum
Population: 18,112,000 (2000 est)
Population density: (per sq km) 33 (1999 est)
Language: Arabic (official)
Religion: Sunni Muslim 63%, Shiite Muslim 37%
Time difference: GMT +3

YUGOSLAVIA
Map page 26

National name: Savezna Republika Jugoslavija/Federal Republic of Yugoslavia
Area: 58,300 sq km/
22,509 sq mi
Capital: Belgrade
Major towns/cities: Priština, Novi Sad, Niš, Kragujevac, Podgorica (formerly Titograd), Subotica
Physical features: federation of republics of Serbia and Montenegro and two former autonomous provinces, Kosovo and Vojvodina
Currency: new Yugoslav dinar
GNP per capita (PPP): (US$) 5,880 (1997 est)
Resources: petroleum, natural gas, coal, copper ore, bauxite, iron ore, lead, zinc
Population: 10,640,000 (2000 est)
Population density: (per sq km) 182 (1999 est)
Language: Serbo-Croat (official), Albanian (in Kosovo)
Religion: Serbian and Montenegrin Orthodox; Muslim in southern Serbia
Time difference: GMT +1

ZAMBIA
Map page 58

National name: Republic of Zambia
Area: 752,600 sq km/
290,578 sq mi
Capital: Lusaka
Major towns/cities: Kitwe, Ndola, Kabwe, Mufulira, Chingola, Luanshya, Livingstone
Physical features: forested plateau cut through by rivers; Zambezi River, Victoria Falls, Kariba Dam
Currency: Zambian kwacha
GNP per capita (PPP): (US$) 686 (1999)
Resources: copper (world's fourth-largest producer), cobalt, zinc, lead, coal, gold, emeralds, amethysts and other gemstones, limestone, selenium
Population: 9,169,000 (2000 est)
Population density: (per sq km) 12 (1999 est)
Language: English (official), Bantu languages
Religion: about 64% Christian, animist, Hindu, Muslim
Time difference: GMT +2

ZIMBABWE
Map page 58

National name: Republic of Zimbabwe
Area: 390,300 sq km/
150,694 sq mi
Capital: Harare
Major towns/cities: Bulawayo, Gweru, Kwekwe, Mutare, Kadoma, Chitungwiza
Physical features: high plateau with central high veld and mountains in east; rivers Zambezi, Limpopo; Victoria Falls
Currency: Zimbabwe dollar
GNP per capita (PPP): (US$) 2,470 (1999)
Resources: gold, nickel, asbestos, coal, chromium, copper, silver, emeralds, lithium, tin, iron ore, cobalt
Population: 11,669,000 (2000 est)
Population density: (per sq km) 30 (1999 est)
Language: English, Shona, Ndebele (all official)
Religion: 50% follow a syncretic (part Christian, part indigenous beliefs) type of religion, Christian 25%, animist 24%, small Muslim minority
Time difference: GMT +2

Index

HOW TO USE THE INDEX

This is an alphabetically arranged index of the places and features that can be found on the maps in this atlas. Each name is generally indexed to the largest scale map on which it appears. If that map covers a double page, the name will always be indexed by the left-hand page number.

Names composed of two or more words are alphabetized as if they were one word.

All names appear in full in the index, except for 'St.' and 'Ste.', which, although abbreviated, are indexed as though spelled in full.

Where two or more places have the same name, they can be distinguished from each other by the country or province name that immediately follows the entry. These names are indexed in the alphabetical order of the country or province.

Alternative names, such as English translations, can also be found in the index and are cross-referenced to the map form by the '=' sign. In these cases the names also appear in brackets on the maps.

Settlements are indexed to the position of the symbol; all other features are indexed to the position of the name on the map.

Abbreviations used in this index are explained in the list opposite.

FINDING A NAME ON THE MAP

Each index entry contains the name, followed by a symbol indicating the feature type (for example, settlement, river), a page reference, and a grid reference:

Name	Owerri .... ⊙ 54 F3
	Owo .... ⊙ 54 F3
	Owyhee .... ↗ 46 C3
	Oxford *N.Z.* .... ⊙ 64 D6
Symbol	Oxford *U.K.* .... ■ 14 A3
	Oxnard .... ⊙ 70 C5
	Oyapock .... ↗ 76 G3
	Oyem .... ⊙ 54 G4
Page reference	Oyen .... ✦ **70** D1
	Oyonnax .... ⊙ 22 A4
	Ozd .... ⊙ 10 K9
	Ozernovskiy .... ⊙ 36 T6
Grid reference	Ozero Alakol .... ↗ 34 Q8

The grid reference locates a place or feature within a rectangle formed by the network of lines of longitude and latitude. A name can be found by referring to the letters and numbers placed around the maps. First find the letter, which appears along the top and bottom of the map, and then the number, down the sides. The name will be found within the rectangle uniquely defined by that letter and number. A number in brackets preceding the grid reference indicates that the name is to be found within an inset map.

ABBREVIATIONS

Ak.	Alaska	N.D.	North Dakota
Al.	Alabama	Nebr.	Nebraska
Arg.	Argentina	Nev.	Nevada
Ariz.	Arizona	Nfld.	Newfoundland
Ark.	Arkansas	N.H.	New Hampshire
Aus.	Australia	N. Ire.	Northern Ireland
B.C.	British Columbia	N.J.	New Jersey
Calif.	California	N. Mex.	New Mexico
Can.	Canada	N.W.T.	Northwest Territories
C.A.R.	Central African Republic	N.Y.	New York
Col.	Colombia	N.Z.	New Zealand
Colo.	Colorado	Oh.	Ohio
Conn.	Connecticut	Okla.	Oklahoma
Czech Rep.	Czech Republic	Ont.	Ontario
Del.	Delaware	Oreg.	Oregon
Dem. Rep. of Congo		Orkney Is.	Orkney Islands
	Democratic Republic of Congo	Pa.	Pennsylvania
Eng.	England	Phil.	Philippines
Fla.	Florida	P.N.G.	Papua New Guinea
Ga.	Georgia	Rep. of I.	Republic of Ireland
Ia.	Iowa	R.G.S.	Rio Grande do Sul
Id.	Idaho	R.I.	Rhode Island
Ill.	Illinois	S.A.	South Africa
Ind.	Indiana	S.C.	South Carolina
It.	Italy	Scot.	Scotland
Kans.	Kansas	S.D.	South Dakota
Ky.	Kentucky	Shetland Is.	Shetland Islands
La.	Louisiana	Tenn.	Tennessee
Man.	Manitoba	Tex.	Texas
Mass.	Massachusetts	U.K.	United Kingdom
Md.	Maryland	U.S.	United States
Me.	Maine	Ut.	Utah
M.G.	Mato Grosso	Va.	Virginia
Mich.	Michigan	Vt.	Vermont
Minn.	Minnesota	Wash.	Washington
Miss.	Mississippi	Wis.	Wisconsin
Mo.	Missouri	W. Va.	West Virginia
Mont.	Montana	Wyo.	Wyoming
N.B.	New Brunswick	Y.T.	Yukon Territory
N.C.	North Carolina		

SYMBOLS

☒ Continent name	⬨ River, canal
⒜ Country name	⬨ Lake, salt lake
ⓐ State or province name	⬨ Gulf, strait, bay
■ Country capital	⬚ Sea, ocean
⬓ State or province capital	⬨ Cape, point
⦿ Settlement	⬨ Island or island group,
▲ Mountain, volcano, peak	rocky or coral reef
⬟ Mountain range	✳ Place of interest
⬰ Physical region or feature	⬨ Historical or cultural region

102

A

Aachen 14 J4
Aalen 12 F8
Aalst 14 G4
Aarau 22 D3
Aare 22 C3
Aarschot 14 G4
Aba 54 F3
Ābādān 46 E3
Abadla 52 E2
Abaji 54 F3
Abakaliki 54 F3
Abakan 34 S7
Abancay 76 C6
Abano Terme 22 G5
Abashiri 38 L2
Abava 8 M8
Ābaya Hāyk' 56 F2
Abay Wenz 50 G5
Abbeville 14 D4
Abd al Kūrī 46 F7
Abéché 50 D5
Abengourou 54 D3
Abenójar 20 F6
Åbenrå 12 E1
Abensberg 12 G8
Abeokuta 54 E3
Aberaeron 16 H9
Aberdeen, S.A. 58 C6
Aberdeen, U.K. 16 K4
Aberdeen, S.D., U.S. 70 G2
Aberdeen, Wash., U.S. 70 B2
Aberdeen Lake 68 M4
Aberystwyth 16 H9
Abez' 30 M1
Abhā 50 H4
Abidjan 54 D3
Abilene 70 G5
Abingdon 14 A3
Abnūb 50 F2
Aboisso 54 D3
Abomey 54 E3
Abong Mbang 54 G4
Abou Déia 50 C5
Abrantes 20 B5
Abrud 26 L3
Absaroka Range 70 D2
Abu Ballās 50 E3
Abu Dhabi = Abū Ẕabī 46 G5
Abu Hamed 50 F4
Abuja 54 F3
Abumombazi 56 C3
Ābune Yosēf 50 G5
Abū Nujaym 50 C1
Abū Qarin 50 C1
Aburo 56 E3
Abu Simbel 50 F3
Abut Head 64 B6
Abū Ẕabī 46 G5
Acaponeta 70 E7
Acapulco 72 E5
Acará 76 H4
Acarigua 76 D2
Accra 54 D3
Achaguas 72 L7
Achayvayam 36 W4
Acheng 38 H1
Achenkirch 22 G3
Achen See 22 G3
Achill Island 16 B8
Achim 12 E3
Achinsk 34 S6
Achit 30 L3
Aci Göl 28 M7
A Cihanbeyli 28 Q6
Acireale 24 K11
Acklins Island 72 K4
Aconcagua 74 D7
Açores 52 (1)B2
A Coruña 20 B1
Acquarossa 22 D4
Acqui Terme 22 D6
Acre 76 C5
Acri 24 L9
Ada 10 K12
Adam 46 G5
Adamas 28 G8
Adams Island 64 (2)B1
'Adan 46 E7
Adana 46 C2
Adda 22 E5
Ad Dakhla 46 E4
Ad Dakhla 52 B4
Ad Dammām 46 F4
Ad Dawādimī 46 D5
Ad Dawḥah 46 F4
Addis Ababa = Ādīs Ābeba 56 F2
Ad Dīwānīyah 46 D3
Adelaide 62 G6
Adelaide Peninsula 68 M3
Adelaide River 62 F2
Aden = Adan 46 E7
Aderbissinat 54 F1
Adi 43 D3
Adige 22 G5
Adīgrat 50 G5
Adilabad 44 C5
Adīrī 50 B2
Ādīs Ābeba 56 F2
Adi Ugri 50 G5
Adiyaman 46 C2
Adjud 26 Q3
Admiralty Island 68 E5
Admiralty Islands 60 E6
Adoni 44 C5
Adour 18 F10
Adra 20 H8
Adrano 24 J11
Adrar 52 E3
Adrar des Ifôghas 52 F5
Adrar Tamgak 52 G5

Adria 22 H5
Adriatic Sea 24 H4
Adycha 36 P3
Adygeya 30 H6
Adzopé 54 D3
Adz'vavom 30 L1
Aegean Sea 28 H5
A Estrada 20 B2
Afghanistan 46 H3
Afgooye 56 H3
'Afīf 50 H3
Afikpo 54 F3
Afmadow 56 G3
A Fonsagrada 20 C1
Afragola 24 J8
Africa 48 F5
Afuá 76 G4
Afyon 28 N6
Agadez 52 G5
Agadir 52 D2
Agadyr' 34 N8
Agalega Islands 48 J7
Agan 36 B4
Ägaro 56 F2
Agartala 44 F4
Agathonisi 28 J7
Agattu Island 36 W6
Agde 18 J10
Agen 18 F9
Agia Triada 28 D7
Aginskoye 34 S6
Agiokampos 28 E5
Agios Efstratios 28 H5
Agios Georgios 28 F7
Agios Nikolaos 28 H9
Agnibilekrou 54 D3
Agnita 26 M4
Agra 44 C3
Ağrı 46 D2
Agri 24 L8
Agrigento 24 H11
Agrinio 28 D6
Agropoli 24 J8
Agryz 30 K3
Agua Prieta 70 E5
Aguascalientes 72 D4
A Gudiña 20 C2
Aguelhok 52 F5
Águilas 20 J7
Agulhas Negras 76 H8
Ağva 28 M3
Ahar 46 E2
Ahaura 64 C6
Ahaus 14 K2
Ahititi 64 E4
Ahlen 14 K3
Ahmadabad 44 B4
Ahmadnagar 44 B5
Ahmadpur East 44 B3
Ahr 12 B6
Ahrensburg 12 F3
Ahväz 46 E3
Aichach 12 G8
Aigialousa 28 S9
Aigina 28 F7
Aigina 28 F7
Aigio 28 E6
Aigosthena 28 F6
Aiguillon 18 F9
Aihui 36 M6
Aim 36 N5
Ain 18 L7
Aïn Beïda 52 G1
'Aïn Ben Tili 52 D3
Aïn Bessem 20 P8
Aïn el Hadjel 20 P9
Ain Oussera 52 F1
Ainsa 20 L2
Aïn Sefra 52 E2
Ain Taya 20 P8
Aïn-Tédéles 20 L8
Aïn-Témouchent 20 J9
Airão 76 E4
Aire 16 L8
Air Force Island 68 S3
Airolo 22 D4
Airpanas 43 C4
Aisne 14 F5
Aitape 43 F3
Aitutaki 60 K7
Aiud 26 L3
Aix-en-Provence 18 L10
Aix-les-Bains 18 L8
Aizawl 44 F4
Aizkraukle 8 N8
Aizpute 8 L8
Ajaccio 24 C7
Aj Bogd Uul 38 B2
Ajdābiyā 50 D1
Ajka 10 G10
Ajmer 44 B3
Ajtos 26 Q7
Akaroa 64 D6
Akasha 50 F3
Akbalyk 34 P8
Akçakoca 28 P3
Aken 12 H5
Aketi 56 C3
Akhisar 28 K6
Akhmim 50 F2
Akimiski Island 68 Q6
Akita 38 L3
Akjoujt 52 C5
Akka 52 D3
Akkajaure 8 J3
Akmeqit 46 L2
Akobo 56 E2
Akola 44 C4
Akonolinga 54 G4
Akordat 50 G4
Akpatok Island 68 T4
Akqi 34 P9
Akra Drepano 28 G5
Akranes 8 (1)B2
Akra Sounio 28 G7
Akra Spatha 28 F9

Akra Trypiti 28 G9
Åkrehamn 8 C7
Akron 70 K3
Aksaray 28 R6
Aksarka 34 M4
Akşehir 28 P6
Akseki 28 P7
Aksha 36 J6
Akshiy 34 P9
Aksu 34 Q9
Aksuat 34 Q8
Āksum 50 G5
Aktau, Kazakhstan 6 K3
Aktau, Kazakhstan 34 N7
Aktogay, Kazakhstan 34 N8
Aktogay, Kazakhstan 34 P8
Aktuma 34 M8
Aktyubinsk 30 L4
Akula 56 C3
Akulivik 68 R4
Akune 38 J4
Akure 54 F3
Akureyri 8 (1)E2
Akwanga 54 F3
Alabama 70 J5
Alaejos 20 E3
Alagoas 76 K5
Alagoinhas 76 K6
Alagón 20 J3
Al 'Amārah 46 E3
Alaminos 40 F3
Åland 8 K6
Alanya 28 Q8
Alappuzha 44 C7
Al Argoub 52 B4
Al Arţāwīyah 46 E4
Alaşehir 28 L6
Al 'Ashurīyah 50 H1
Alaska 66 S3
Alaska Range 66 R3
Alatri 24 H7
Alatyr' 30 J4
Alavus 8 M5
Al 'Ayn 46 G5
Alazeya 36 S2
Alba, It. 22 D6
Alba, Spain 20 E4
Albacete 20 J5
Alba Iulia 26 L3
Albania 28 B3
Albany 68 Q6
Albany, Aus. 62 C6
Albany, Ga., U.S. 70 K5
Albany, N.Y., U.S. 70 M3
Albany, Oreg., U.S. 70 B3
Albardão do João Maria 78 L4
Al Bardī 50 D1
Al Başrah 46 E3
Albatross Bay 62 H2
Albatross Point 64 E4
Al Baydā 50 D1
Albenga 22 D6
Albert 14 E4
Alberta 68 H6
Albertirsa 10 J10
Albert Kanaal 14 G3
Albert Lea 70 H3
Albert Nile 56 E3
Albertville 18 M8
Albi 18 H10
Albina 76 G2
Albino 22 E5
Ålborg 8 E8
Ålborg Bugt 8 F8
Albox 20 H7
Albstadt 12 E8
Albufeira 20 B7
Āl Bū Kamāl 46 D3
Albuquerque 70 E4
Al Buraymī 46 G5
Alburquerque 20 D5
Albury 62 J7
Al Buşayyah 50 G1
Alcácer do Sal 20 B6
Alcala de Guadaira 20 E7
Alcala de Henares 20 G4
Alcalá la Real 20 G7
Alcañiz 20 K3
Alcantarilla 20 J7
Alcaraz 20 H6
Alcaudete 20 F7
Alcazar de San Juan 20 G5
Alcobendas 20 G4
Alcoi 20 K6
Alcolea del Pinar 20 H3
Alcorcón 20 G4
Alcoutim 20 C7
Aldabra Islands 58 (2)A2
Aldan 36 M5
Aldan 36 N5
Aldeburgh 14 D2
Alderney 18 C4
Aldershot 14 B3
Aleg 52 C5
Aleksandrov-Sakhalinskiy 36 Q6
Aleksandrovskiy Zavod 36 K6
Aleksandrovskoye 30 Q2
Alekseyevka 34 N7
Aleksinac 26 J6
Alençon 18 F5
Aleppo = Ḥalab 46 G5
Aléria 24 D6
Alès 18 K9
Aleşd 10 M10
Alessandria 22 D6
Ålesund 8 D5
Aleutian Islands 66 T4
Aleutian Trench 60 W5
Alexander Archipelago 68 D5
Alexander Bay 58 B5
Alexandra 64 B7
Alexandreia 28 E4

Alexandria = El Iskandarîya, Egypt 50 E1
Alexandria, Romania 26 N6
Alexandria, La., U.S. 70 H5
Alexandria, Va., U.S. 70 L4
Alexandroupoli 28 H4
Alexis Creek 68 G6
Aley 34 Q7
Aleysk 34 Q7
Alfeld 12 E5
Alföld 26 H2
Alfonsine 22 H6
Alfreton 14 A1
Al Fuḥayḥil 46 E4
Al-Fujayrah 46 G4
Algeciras 20 E8
Algemesi 20 K5
Algena 50 G4
Alger 52 F1
Algeria 52 E3
Algiers = Alger 52 F1
Al Hadīthah 46 C3
Alhama de Murcia 20 J7
Al Harūj al Aswad 50 C2
Alhaurmín el Grande 20 F8
Al Ḥijāz 50 G2
Al Ḥillah 46 D3
Al Ḥudaydah 50 H5
Al Hufūf 46 E4
Al Ḥumaydah 46 C4
Aliağa 28 J6
Aliakmonas 28 E4
Āli Bayramlı 46 E2
Alicante 20 K6
Alice 70 G6
Alice Springs 62 F4
Alicudi 24 J10
Aligarh 44 C3
Alindao 56 C2
Alingsås 8 G8
Aliwal North 58 D6
Al Jabal al Akhḍar 50 D1
Al Jaghbūb 50 D2
Al Jālamīd 50 G1
Al Jarah 46 E4
Al Jawf, Libya 50 D3
Al Jawf, Saudi Arabia 50 G2
Aljezur 20 B7
Al Jubayl 46 E4
Aljustrel 20 B7
Al Kāmil 46 G5
Al Kharj 46 E5
Al Khaşab 46 G4
Al Khawr 46 F4
Al Khufrah 50 D3
Al Khums 52 H2
Alkmaar 14 G2
Al Kūt 46 E3
Al Kuwayt 46 E4
Al Lādhiqīyah 46 C2
Allahabad 44 D3
Allakh-Yun' 36 P4
Alldays 58 D4
Allen 40 G4
Allentown 70 L3
Aller = Cabañaquinta 20 E1
Aller 12 F4
Alliance 70 F3
Allier 18 J8
Allinge 10 D2
Al Lith 50 H3
Almada 20 A6
Almadén 20 F5
Al Madīnah 50 G3
Al Mahbas 52 D3
Al Majma'ah 46 E4
Almalyk 34 M9
Al Manāmah 46 F4
Almansa 20 J6
Al Marj 50 D1
Almaty 34 P9
Al Mawşil 46 D2
Al Mazāhimīyah 50 J3
Almazán 20 H3
Almeirim 76 G4
Almelo 14 J2
Almendralejo 20 D6
Almería 20 H8
Al'met'yevsk 34 J7
Almiros 28 E5
Almodôvar 20 D7
Almonte 44 D4
Almora 44 D3
Al Mubarraz 46 E4
Al Mukallā 46 E5
Al Mukhā 50 H5
Almuñécar 20 G8
Al Qalībah 50 D1
Al Qāmishlī 46 D2
Al Qaryāt 50 B1
Al Qaţrūn 50 H4
Al Qunfudhah 50 G4
Al Quwayrah 50 G1
Als 8 K6
Alsask 68 K6
Alsasua 20 H2
Alsfeld 12 E6
Alta 8 M2
Altaelva 8 M2
Altai Mountains 38 A1
Al Tamīnī 50 D1

Altamira 76 G4
Altamura 24 L8
Altanbulag 36 H6
Altay, China 34 R8
Altay, Mongolia 38 B1
Altdorf 22 D4
Alte Mellum 12 D3
Altenberg 12 J6
Altenburg 12 H6
Altenkirchen 12 J2
Altkirch 22 C3
Alto Garças 76 G7
Alto Molócuè 58 F3
Altoona 70 L3
Alto Parnaiba 76 H5
Altötting 22 H2
Altun Shan 34 S10
Altus 70 G5
Al 'Ubaylah 46 F5
Alūksne 8 P8
Al 'Uqaylah 50 C1
Al 'Uwaynāt, Libya 50 B2
Al 'Uwaynāt, Libya 50 H1
Al 'Uwayqīlah 50 H1
Alvarães 76 E4
Älvdalen 8 H6
Älvsbyn 8 L4
Al Wajh 50 G2
Alwar 44 C3
Al Wari'ah 46 E4
Alxa Zouqi 38 D3
Alytus 10 P3
Alzey 12 D7
Alzira 20 K5
Amadi 56 E2
Amadjuak Lake 68 S4
Amadora 20 A6
Amahai 43 C3
Amaliada 28 D7
Amalner 44 C4
Amamapare 43 E3
Amambaí 78 K3
Amami-Ōshima 32 S7
Amanab 43 F3
Amandola 24 H6
Amantea 24 L9
Amapá 76 G3
Amapá 76 G3
Amarante 76 J5
Amarapura 40 B2
Amareleja 20 C6
Amarillo 70 F4
Amasya 46 C1
Amay 34 L6
Amazar 36 L6
Amazon = Amazonas 74 F4
Amazonas 76 D4
Amazonas 76 E4
Ambala 44 C2
Ambanjā 58 H2
Ambarchik 36 U3
Ambato 76 B4
Ambato Boeny 58 H3
Ambatondrazaka 58 H3
Amberg 12 G7
Ambikapur 44 D4
Ambilobe 58 H2
Ambohimahasoa 58 H4
Amboise 18 G6
Ambon 43 C3
Ambositra 58 H4
Ambovombe 58 H5
Amderma 34 L4
Amdo 44 F2
Ameland 14 H1
Amengel'dy 34 M7
American Samoa 60 J7
Amersfoort 14 H2
Amery 68 N5
Amery Ice Shelf 80 (2)M2
Ames 70 H3
Amfilochia 28 D6
Amfissa 28 E6
Amga 36 M4
Amga 36 N4
Amguid 52 G3
Amgun' 36 P6
Amherst 68 U7
Amiens 14 E5
Amirante Islands 58 (2)B2
Amlekhganj 44 D3
Åmli 8 E7
'Amm Adam 50 G4
Ammān 46 C3
Ammassalik 68 Z3
Ammerland 14 K1
Ammersee 22 G2
Ammochostos 28 R9
Amo 40 C2
Amol 46 F2
Amorgos 28 H8
Amos 70 L2
Amour 52 D5
Ampana 43 B3
Ampanihy 58 H4
Amparai 44 D7
Ampezzo 22 H4
Amposta 20 L4
Amrān 50 H4
Amravati 44 C4
Amriswil 22 E3
Amritsar 44 B2
Amroha 44 C3
Amrum 12 D2
Amstetten 22 K2
Am Timan 50 D5
Amudar'y 34 L9
Amundsen Gulf 68 G2
Amundsen Sea 80 (2)GG3
Amungen 8 H6
Amuntai 42 F3
Amur 36 P6
Amursk 36 P6
Amvrosiyivka 30 G5
Amvrakikos Kolpos 28 D6
Anabanua 43 B3
Anabar 36 J2

Anaconda 70 D2
Anadolu Dağları 46 C1
Anadyr' 36 X4
Anadyrskaya Nizmennost' 36 X3
Anadyrskiy Zaliv 36 Y3
Anafi 28 H8
'Ānah 46 D3
Analalava 58 H2
Anamur 28 Q8
Anantapur 44 C6
Anan'yiv 26 T2
Anapa 30 G6
Anápolis 76 H7
Anār 46 G3
Anārak 46 F3
Anardara 46 H3
Anatolia 46 M6
Añatuya 78 J4
Anchorage 66 H4
Ancona 24 H5
Ancud 78 G7
Anda 38 H1
Andalgalá 78 H4
Åndalsnes 8 D5
Andaman Islands 40 A4
Andaman Sea 40 A4
Andapa 58 H2
Andarāb 46 J2
Andenne 14 H4
Andéramboukane 54 E1
Andermatt 22 D4
Andernach 14 K4
Anderson 68 F3
Andes 74 D5
Andfjorden 8 J2
Andilamena 58 H3
Andipsara 28 H6
Andizhan 46 N9
Andkhvoy 46 J2
Andoas 76 B4
Andong 38 H3
Andorra 20 L2
Andorra la Vella 20 M2
Andover 14 A3
Andøya 8 H2
Andradina 78 L3
Andria 24 L7
Andriamena 58 H3
Andros, Greece 28 G7
Andros, The Bahamas 72 J4
Andrott 44 B6
Andrychów 10 J8
Andújar 20 F6
Andulo 58 B2
Aneto 20 L2
Angara 36 G5
Angarsk 36 G6
Ånge 8 H5
Angel de la Guarda 70 D6
Angeles 40 G3
Ängelholm 8 G8
Angeln 12 E2
Angermünde 12 K4
Angern 22 M2
Angers 18 E6
Anglesey 16 H8
Angmagssalik = Ammassalik 68 Z3
Ango 56 D3
Angoche 58 F3
Angol 78 G6
Angola 48 E7
Angoulême 18 F8
Angren 34 M9
Anguilla 72 M5
Anina 26 J4
Ankang 38 D4
Ankara 28 R5
Ankazoabo 58 G4
Anklam 12 J3
Ankpa 54 F3
Ånn 8 G5
Anna 30 H4
Annaba 52 G1
Annaberg-Buchholz 12 H6
An Nafud 50 G2
An Nāiriyah 46 E3
An Najaf 46 D3
Annapolis 70 L4
Annapurna 44 D3
Ann Arbor 70 K3
An Nāşiriyah 50 J1
Annecy 22 B5
Annemasse 22 B4
Anniston 70 J5
Annobón 48 F5
Annonay 18 K8
An Nukhayb 46 D3
Anqing 38 F4
Ansbach 12 F7
Anshan 38 G2
Anshun 38 D5
Ansongo 52 F5
Antakya 46 C2
Antalaha 58 J2
Antalya 28 N8
Antalya Körfezi 28 N8
Antananarivo 58 H3
Antarctic Peninsula 80 (2)LL3
Antequera 20 F7
Anti-Atlas 52 D3
Antibes 22 C7
Antigua 72 M5
Antigua and Barbuda 72 M5
Antikythira 28 F9
Antiparos 28 G7
Antipaxoi 28 C5
Antipayuta 34 P4
Antipodes Islands 64 (3)A1
Antofagasta 78 G3
Antrim 16 F7
Antropovo 30 H3
Antsalova 58 G3
Antsirabe 58 H3

Bansko 28 F3
Bantry 16 C10
Banyo 54 G3
Banyoles 20 N2
Banyuwangi 42 E4
Baode 38 E3
Baoding 38 F3
Baoji 38 D4
Bao Lôc 40 D4
Baoro 56 B2
Baoshan 40 B1
Baotou 38 E2
Baoying 38 F4
Bap 44 B3
Bapaume 14 E4
Ba'qūbah 46 D3
Baquedano 78 H3
Bar 26 G7
Barabai 42 F3
Barakaldo 20 H1
Baramati 44 B5
Baramula 44 B2
Baran 44 C3
Baranavichy 30 E4
Baraolt 26 N3
Barbados 76 F1
Barbastro 20 L2
Barbate 20 E8
Barbuda 72 M5
Barcaldine 62 J4
Barcău 26 K2
Barcellona Pozzo di Gotto 24 K10
Barcelona, *Spain* 20 N3
Barcelona, *Venezuela* 72 M6
Barcelos, *Brazil* 76 E4
Barcelos, *Spain* 20 B3
Barclayville 54 C4
Barco de Valdeorras = O Barco 20 D2
Barcs 26 E4
Bardai 50 C3
Barddhamān 44 E4
Bardejov 10 L8
Bardonecchia 22 B5
Bareilly 44 C3
Barentin 14 C5
Barents Sea 34 E3
Barentu 50 G4
Bareo 42 F2
Barga 44 D2
Bargaal 56 J1
Bargteheide 12 F3
Barguzin 36 H6
Bari 24 L7
Barikot 44 B1
Barinas 76 C2
Bārīs 50 F3
Barisal 44 F4
Barito 43 A3
Barkam 38 C4
Barkava 8 P8
Barkly Tableland 62 F3
Barkol 34 S9
Bârlad 26 Q3
Bârlad 26 Q3
Bar-le-Duc 14 H6
Barletta 24 L7
Barmer 44 B3
Barmouth Bay 16 H9
Barnaul 34 Q7
Barnsley 16 L8
Barnstaple 16 H10
Barnstaple Bay 16 H10
Barpeta 44 F3
Barquisimeto 76 D1
Barr 22 C2
Barra, *Brazil* 76 J6
Barra, *U.K.* 16 E4
Barracão do Barreto 76 G5
Barracas 20 K5
Barra do Bugres 76 F7
Barra do Corda 76 H5
Barra do Cuanza 56 A5
Barra do Garças 76 G7
Barra do São Manuel 76 G5
Barragem de Santa Clara 20 B7
Barragem de Sobradinho 76 J5
Barragem do Castelo de Bode 20 B5
Barragem do Maranhão 20 C6
Barranca, *Peru* 76 B4
Barranca, *Peru* 76 B6
Barranquilla 72 K6
Barreiras 76 H6
Barreiro 20 A6
Barretos 76 H8
Barrie 70 L3
Barrow Creek 62 F4
Barrow-in-Furness 16 J7
Barrow Island 62 B4
Barrow Strait 68 N2
Barshatas 34 P8
Barsi 44 C5
Bar-sur-Aube 18 K5
Bar-sur-Seine 18 K5
Barth 12 H2
Bartın 28 Q3
Bartle Frere 60 E7
Bartlesville 70 G4
Bartoszyce 10 K3
Barus 42 B2
Baruun Urt 38 E1
Barwani 44 B4
Barysaw 30 E4
Basankusu 56 B3
Basarabeasca 26 R3
Basarabi 26 R5
Basca 24 C2
Basco 40 G2
Basel 22 C3
Bashkiriya 30 K4
Basilan 43 B1
Basildon 14 C3
Basiluzzo 24 K10
Basingstoke 16 L10
Başkale 46 D2
Basoko 56 C3
Bassano 70 D1
Bassano del Grappa 22 G5
Bassar 54 E3
Bassas da India 58 F4
Bassein 40 A3
Basse Santa Su 52 C6
Basse-Terre 72 M5
Bassikounou 52 D5
Bass Strait 62 H7
Bassum 12 D4
Bastak 46 F4
Basti 44 D3
Bastia 24 D6
Bastogne 14 H4
Bata 54 F4
Batagay 36 N3
Batagay-Alyta 36 N3
Batak 28 G3
Batamay 36 M4
Batang 38 B5
Batangas 40 G4
Batan Islands 40 G2
Batanta 43 C3
Batchelor 62 F2
Batemans Bay 62 K7
Bath 16 K10
Bathinda 44 B2
Bathurst, *Aus.* 62 J6
Bathurst, *Can.* 68 T7
Bathurst Inlet 68 K3
Bathurst Island, *Aus.* 62 E2
Bathurst Island, *Can.* 68 M1
Batman 46 D2
Batna 52 G1
Baton Rouge 70 H5
Bátonyterenye 26 G2
Batouri 54 G4
Batticaloa 44 D7
Battipaglia 24 J8
Battle 68 J6
Battle Harbour 68 V6
Batu 56 F2
Batui 43 B3
Bat'umi 46 D1
Batu Pahat 42 C2
Baturino 34 R6
Baubau 43 B4
Bauchi 54 F2
Baukau 43 C4
Baume-les-Dames 18 M6
Bauru 78 M3
Bauska 8 N8
Bautzen 10 D6
Bawean 42 E4
Bawiti 50 E2
Bawku 54 D2
Bayamo 72 J4
Bayanaul 34 P7
Bayandelger 36 H7
Bayan Har Shan 38 B4
Bayanhongor 38 C1
Bayan Mod 38 C2
Bayan Obo 38 D2
Bayansumküre 34 Q9
Bay City 70 K3
Baydhabo 56 G3
Bayerische Alpen 22 G3
Bayeux 14 B5
Bayındır 28 K6
Baykit 34 T5
Baykonur 34 M8
Bay of Bengal 44 E5
Bay of Biscay 18 C9
Bay of Fundy 68 T8
Bay of Islands 64 E2
Bay of Plenty 64 F3
Bayonne 18 D10
Bayramaly 46 H2
Bayramiç 28 J5
Bayreuth 12 G7
Baysun 46 J2
Bayt al Faqīh 50 H5
Bay View 64 F4
Baza 20 H7
Bazas 18 E9
Bazdar 46 J4
Beachy Head 14 C4
Beagle Gulf 62 E2
Bealanana 58 H2
Bear Island = Bjørnøya, *Norway* 34 B3
Bear Island, *Rep. of I.* 16 B10
Beasain 20 H1
Beas de Segura 20 H6
Beaufort 42 F1
Beaufort Sea 66 Q2
Beaufort West 58 C6
Beaumont, *N.Z.* 64 B7
Beaumont, *U.S.* 70 H5
Beaune 18 K6
Beauvais 14 E5
Beaver Creek 68 C4
Beawar 44 B3
Beazley 78 H5
Bebra 12 E6
Bečej 26 H4
Béchar 52 E2
Beckley 70 K4
Becks 64 B7
Beckum 14 L3
Beclean 26 M2
Bedelē 56 F2
Bedford 16 M9
Bedworth 14 A2
Beenleigh 62 K5
Be'ér Sheva' 46 B3
Beeville 70 G6
Bei'an 36 M7
Beihai 40 D2
Beijing 38 F3
Beipan 38 D5
Beipiao 38 G2
Beira 58 E3
Beirut = Beyrouth 46 C3
Beiuş 26 K3
Béja 52 G1
Bejaïa 52 G1
Béjar 20 E4
Bekdash 46 F1
Békés 10 L11
Békéscsaba 26 J3
Bekily 58 H4
Bela 46 J4
Bela Crkva 26 J5
Belaga 42 E2
Belarus 6 G2
Bela Vista 58 E5
Belaya 30 K3
Belaya Gora 36 R3
Bełchatów 10 J6
Belcher Islands 68 Q5
Beledweyne 56 H3
Belek 34 J10
Belém 76 H4
Belen 72 C2
Belfast 16 G7
Belfort 22 B3
Belgazyn 34 T7
Belgium 14 G4
Belgorod 30 G4
Belgrade = Beograd 26 H5
Beli 54 G3
Belice 24 H11
Beli Manastir 26 F4
Belinyu 42 D3
Belitung 42 D3
Belize 72 G5
Belize 72 G5
Bellac 18 G7
Bella Coola 68 F6
Bellary 44 C5
Belle Fourche 70 F3
Belle Île 18 B6
Belle Isle 68 V6
Bellême 18 F5
Belleville 70 L3
Bellingham 70 B2
Bellingshausen Sea 80 (2)JJ4
Bellinzona 22 E4
Bello 76 B2
Belluno 22 H4
Bellyk 36 E6
Belmonte, *Brazil* 76 K7
Belmonte, *Spain* 20 H5
Belmopan 72 G5
Belmullet 16 B7
Belogorsk 36 M6
Belogradčik 26 K6
Beloha 58 H5
Belo Horizonte 76 J7
Belo Monte 76 G4
Belomorsk 30 F2
Beloretsk 30 L4
Belo Tsiribihina 58 G3
Belovo 34 R7
Beloyarskiy 34 M5
Beloye More 30 G1
Belozersk 30 G2
Belozerskoye 30 N3
Belye Vody 34 M9
Belyy Yar 34 Q6
Belzig 12 H4
Bembibre 20 D2
Bena Dibele 56 C4
Benavente 20 E3
Benbecula 16 E4
Bend 70 B3
Bendorf 14 K4
Bene 58 E3
Benešov 10 D8
Benevento 24 J7
Bengbu 38 F4
Bengkalis 42 C2
Bengkulu 42 C3
Benguela 58 A2
Benguerir 52 D2
Benha 50 F1
Beni 56 D3
Beni 76 D6
Beni Abbès 52 E2
Benicarló 20 L4
Benidorm 20 K6
Benī Mazâr 50 F2
Beni Mellal 52 D2
Benin 54 E2
Benin City 54 F3
Beni Saf 20 J9
Beni Slimane 20 P8
Beni Suef 50 F2
Benito Juaréz 78 K6
Benjamin Constant 76 D4
Benkovac 22 L6
Ben More Assynt 16 H3
Ben Nevis 16 H5
Benoud 52 F2
Bensheim 12 D7
Benson, *Ariz., U.S.* 70 D5
Benson, *Minn., U.S.* 70 G2
Benteng 43 B4
Bentinck Island 62 G3
Bentung 42 C2
Benue 54 G3
Benxi 38 G2
Beo 40 H6
Beograd 26 H5
Berat 28 B4
Beravina 58 H3
Berber 50 F4
Berbera 50 H5
Berbérati 56 B3
Berchtesgaden 22 J3
Berck 14 D4
Berdigestyakh 36 M4
Berdyans'k 30 G5
Berdychiv 30 E5
Bereeda 56 J1
Berehove 26 K1
Bererreá 20 C2
Berettyóújfalu 26 J2
Berettys 10 L10
Bereznik 30 H2
Berezniki 30 L3
Berezovo 30 N2
Berezovyy 36 P6
Berga 20 M2
Bergama 28 K5
Bergamo 22 E5
Bergara 20 H1
Bergby 8 J6
Bergedorf 12 F3
Bergen, *Germany* 12 J2
Bergen, *Germany* 12 E4
Bergen, *Netherlands* 14 G2
Bergen, *Norway* 8 C6
Bergen op Zoom 14 G3
Bergerac 18 F9
Bergheim 14 J4
Bergisch Gladbach 12 C6
Bergsfjordhalvøya 8 L1
Beringen 14 H3
Beringovskiy 36 X4
Bering Sea 66 V4
Bering Strait 66 T3
Berkner Island 80 (2)A2
Berkovica 26 L6
Berlin 12 J4
Bermejo 78 K4
Bermeo 20 H1
Bermuda 66 H6
Bern 22 C4
Bernalda 24 L8
Bernau 12 J4
Bernay 14 C5
Bernburg 12 G5
Berner Alpen 22 C4
Beroun 10 D8
Berounka 12 J7
Berovo 28 E3
Berrouaghia 20 N8
Bertoua 54 G4
Beruni 34 L9
Berwick-upon-Tweed 16 L6
Besalampy 58 G3
Besançon 18 M6
Besbay 34 K8
Bessemer 70 J5
Bestamak 34 P8
Bestuzhevo 30 H2
Bestyakh, *Russia* 36 L3
Bestyakh, *Russia* 36 M4
Betanzos 20 B1
Bětdâmbâng 40 C4
Bethlehem 58 D5
Béthune 14 E4
Betioky 58 G4
Betoota 62 H5
Betpak-Dala 34 M8
Betroka 58 H4
Bettiah 44 D3
Betul 44 C4
Betzdorf 12 C6
Beverley 16 M8
Beverungen 12 E5
Bexhill 14 C4
Bey Dağlari 28 M8
Beykoz 28 M3
Beyla 54 C3
Beyneu 34 J8
Beypazarı 28 P4
Beyra 56 H2
Beyrouth 46 C3
Beyşehir 28 P7
Beyşehir Gölü 28 P7
Bezhetsk 30 G3
Béziers 18 J10
Bhadgaon 44 E3
Bhadrakh 44 E4
Bhadravati 44 C6
Bhagalpur 44 E3
Bhairab Bazar 44 F4
Bhakkar 44 B2
Bhamo 40 B2
Bharuch 44 B4
Bhatpara 44 E4
Bhavnagar 44 B4
Bhawanipatna 44 D5
Bhilai 44 D4
Bhilwara 44 B3
Bhīmavaram 44 D5
Bhind 44 C3
Bhiwandi 44 B5
Bhopal 44 C4
Bhubaneshwar 44 E4
Bhuj 44 A4
Bhusawal 44 C4
Bhutan 44 E3
Biak 43 E3
Biak 43 E3
Biała 10 K8
Biała Podlaska 10 N5
Białogard 10 F3
Białystok 10 N4
Biarritz 18 D10
Biasca 22 D4
Bibbiena 22 G7
Biberach 22 E2
Bicaz 26 P3
Bicester 14 A3
Bickerton Island 62 G2
Bicske 26 F2
Bida 54 F3
Bidar 44 C5
Bideford 16 H10
Biedenkopf 12 D6
Biel 22 C3
Bielefeld 12 D4
Biella 22 D5
Bielsko-Biała 10 J8
Bielsk Podlaski 10 N5
Biên Hoa 40 D4
Bietigheim-Bissingen 22 E2
Big 68 G2
Biga 28 K4
Bigadiç 28 L5
Big Desert 62 H7
Bighorn 70 E2
Bighorn Mountains 70 E3
Bight of Bangkok 40 C4
Bight of Benin 54 E3
Bight of Biafra 54 F4
Bignona 52 B6
Big River 68 K6
Big Spring 70 F5
Big Trout Lake 68 P6
Bihać 22 L6
Bijapur 44 C5
Bījār 46 E2
Bijeljina 26 G5
Bijelo Polje 26 G6
Bijie 38 D5
Bikaner 44 B3
Bikin 36 N7
Bikini 60 G4
Bilaspur 44 D4
Bila Tserkva 30 F5
Bilbao 20 H1
Bileća 26 F7
Bilecik 28 M4
Bilečko Jezero 26 F7
Biled 26 H4
Biłgoraj 10 M7
Bilhorod-Dnistrovs'kyy 30 F5
Bilibino 36 V3
Bílina 12 J6
Billings 70 E2
Bill of Portland 16 K11
Bilma 50 B4
Biloela 62 K4
Biloxi 70 J5
Bimini Islands 70 L6
Bina-Etawa 44 C4
Binche 14 G4
Bindi Bindi 62 C6
Bindura 58 E3
Bingen 12 C7
Binghamton 70 L3
Bingöl 46 D2
Binongko 43 B4
Bintuhan 42 C3
Bintulu 42 E2
Bintuni 43 D3
Binyang 40 D2
Binzhou 38 F3
Biograd 22 L7
Birāk 52 H3
Birao 50 D5
Biratnagar 44 E3
Birdsville 62 G5
Bireun 42 B1
Bir Gandouz 52 B4
Birhan 50 G5
Bīrjand 46 G3
Birkenfeld 14 K5
Birmingham, *U.K.* 16 L9
Birmingham, *U.S.* 70 J5
Bîr Mogreïn 52 C3
Birnie 60 J6
Birnin-Gwari 54 F2
Birnin Kebbi 54 E2
Birnin Konni 54 F2
Birnin Kudu 54 F2
Birobidzhan 36 N7
Birsk 30 L3
Biržai 10 P1
Bi'r Zalţan 50 C2
Bisceglie 24 L7
Bischofshofen 22 J3
Bischofswerda 10 D6
Biševo 24 L6
Bishkek 34 N9
Bishop Auckland 16 L7
Bishop's Stortford 14 C3
Biskra 52 G2
Bislig 40 H5
Bismarck 70 F2
Bismarck Sea 60 E6
Bissau 52 B6
Bistcho Lake 68 H5
Bistriţa 26 M2
Bistriţa 26 P3
Bitburg 14 J5
Bitche 12 C7
Bitkine 50 C5
Bitola 28 D3
Bitonto 24 L7
Bitterfeld 12 H5
Bitterroot Range 70 C2
Bitti 24 D8
Bitung 43 C2
Biu 54 G2
Biyāvra 44 C4
Biysk 34 R7
Bizerte 52 G1
Bjala, *Bulgaria* 26 N6
Bjala, *Bulgaria* 26 Q7
Bjala Slatina 26 L6
Bjelovar 26 D4
Bjerkvik 8 J2
Bjørnøya 34 B3
B-Köpenick 12 J4
Bla 54 C2
Blackall 62 J4
Blackburn 16 K8
Blackpool 16 J8
Black Range 70 E5
Black Rock Desert 46 C3
Black Sea 6 H3
Black Sugarloaf 62 K6
Black Volta 54 D3
Blackwater 16 D9
Blackwater 62 J4
Blagoevgrad 28 F3
Blagoveshchenka 34 P7
Blagoveshchensk 36 M6
Blain 18 D6
Blaj 26 L3
Blanco 76 E6
Blangy-sur-Bresle 14 D5
Blankenberge 14 F3
Blankenburg 12 F5
Blankenheim 14 J4
Blantyre 58 F3
Blasket Islands 16 B9
Blaubeuren 22 E2
Blaye-et-Sainte-Luce 18 E8
Bled 22 K4
Blenheim 64 D5
Blevands Huk 12 D1
Blida 52 F1
Blind River 70 K2
Bloemfontein 58 D5
Bloemhof 58 D5
Blois 18 G6
Blönduós 8 (1)C2
Błonie 10 K5
Bloomington, *Ill., U.S.* 70 J3
Bloomington, *Ind., U.S.* 70 J4
Bludenz 22 E3
Bluefield 70 K4
Bluefields 72 H6
Blue Mountains 46 C3
Blue Nile = Bahr el Azraq 50 F5
Bluenose Lake 68 H3
Bluff 64 B8
Blumenau 78 M4
Blythe 70 D5
Bo 54 B3
Boac 40 G4
Boa Vista, *Brazil* 76 E3
Boa Vista, *Cape Verde* 54 (1)B1
Bobbili 44 D5
Bobbio 22 E6
Bobigny 14 E6
Bobingen 22 F2
Böblingen 22 E2
Bobo-Dioulasso 54 D2
Bobolice 10 F4
Bobr 10 E6
Bobrov 30 H4
Bôca do Acre 76 D5
Boca Grande 72 M7
Boca Grande 74 E3
Bocaiúva 76 J7
Bocaranga 56 B2
Bochnia 10 K8
Bocholt 12 B5
Bochum 12 C5
Bockenem 12 F4
Bodaybo 36 J5
Bode 12 G4
Bodélé 50 C4
Boden 8 L4
Bodham 44 C5
Bodmin 16 H11
Bodø 8 H3
Bodrog 10 L9
Bodrum 28 K7
Boende 56 C4
Boffa 54 B2
Bogale 40 B3
Boggabilla 62 K5
Boghni 20 P8
Bognor Regis 14 B4
Bogo 40 G4
Bogor 42 D4
Bogorodskoye 36 Q6
Bogotá 76 C3
Bogotol 34 R6
Bogra 44 E4
Boguchany 36 F5
Bogué 52 C5
Bo Hai 38 F3
Bohmerwald 12 H7
Bohol 40 G5
Bohumin 10 H8
Boiaçu 76 E4
Boise 46 C3
Bojnūrd 34 K10
Bokatola 56 B4
Boké 54 B2
Bokoro 54 H2
Bokspits 58 C5
Bokungu 56 C4
Bolbec 14 C5
Boldu 26 Q4
Bole, *China* 34 Q9
Bole, *Ghana* 54 D3
Bolechiv 10 N8
Bolesławiec 10 E6
Bolgatanga 54 D2
Bolhrad 26 R4
Bolintin-Vale 26 N5
Bolivia 76 D7
Bollène 18 K9
Bollnäs 8 J6
Bolmen 8 G8
Bolobo 54 H5
Bologna 22 G6
Bolognesi 76 C5
Bolomba 54 H4
Bolotnoye 34 Q6
Bol'shaya Pyssa 30 J2
Bol'sherech'ye 30 P3
Bol'shezemel'skaya Tundra 34 J4
Bol Shirta 36 C4
Bolshoy Atlym 30 N2
Bol'shoy Osinovaya 36 W3
Bol'shoy Vlas'evo 36 Q6
Bolshoy Yugan 30 P2
Bolsover 14 A1
Bolton 16 K8
Bolu 28 P4
Bolvadin 28 P6
Bolzano 22 G4
Boma 54 G6
Bombala 62 J7
Bombay = Mumbai 44 B5
Bomili 56 D3
Bom Jesus da Lapa 76 J6
Bømlo 8 C7
Bomnak 36 M6
Bomossa 54 H4
Bonaparte Archipelago 62 B2
Bonavista Bay 68 W7
Bondeno 22 G6

Bondo 56 C3
Bondokodi 62 C1
Bondoukou 54 D3
Bondowoso 42 E4
Bonerate 43 B4
Bongaigaon 44 F3
Bongandanga 56 C3
Bongao 43 A1
Bongor 54 H2
Bonifacio 24 D7
Bonn 12 C6
Bonneville 22 B4
Bonnie Rock 62 C6
Bonorva 24 C8
Bonthe 54 B3
Bontoc 40 G3
Bontosunggu 43 A4
Bonyhád 26 F3
Boorama 56 G2
Boosaaso 56 H1
Boothia Peninsula 68 M2
Booué 54 G5
Boppard 12 C6
Bor, *Russia* 36 D4
Bor, *Sudan* 56 E2
Bor, *Turkey* 28 S7
Bor, *Yugoslavia* 26 K5
Borah Peak 70 D3
Borås 8 G8
Borāzjān 46 F4
Bordeaux 18 E9
Bordeira 20 B7
Borden Peninsula 68 Q2
Border Town 62 H7
Bordj Bou Arréridj 52 F1
Bordj Bounaam 20 M9
Bordj Flye Sante Marie 52 E3
Bordj Messaouda 52 G2
Bordj Mokhtar 52 F4
Bordj Omar Driss 52 G3
Borgarnes 8 (1)C2
Borgholm 8 J8
Borgomanero 22 D5
Borgo San Dalmazzo 22 C6
Borgo San Lorenzo 22 G7
Borgosesia 22 D5
Borgo Val di Taro 22 E6
Bori Jenein 52 H2
Borislav 10 N8
Borisoglebsk 30 H4
Borken 14 J3
Borkou 50 C4
Borkum 14 J1
Borkum 14 J1
Borlänge 8 H6
Bormida 22 D6
Bormio 22 F4
Borna 12 H5
Borne 14 J2
Borneo 42 E3
Bornholm 8 H9
Borodino 34 R5
Borodinskoye 8 Q6
Boromo 54 D2
Borongan 40 H4
Borovichi 30 F3
Borovskoy 30 M4
Borriana 20 K5
Borroloola 62 G3
Borşa 26 M2
Borshchiv 26 P1
Borshchovochnyy Khrebet 36 J7
Borðeyri 8 (1)C2
Borūjerd 46 E3
Borzya 36 K6
Bosa 24 C8
Bosanska Dubica 26 D4
Bosanska Gradiška 26 E4
Bosanska Kostajnica 22 M5
Bosanska Krupa 26 D5
Bosanski Brod 26 F4
Bosanski Novi 26 D4
Bosanski Petrovac 26 D5
Bosansko Grahovo 22 M6
Boşca 26 J4
Bose 40 D2
Bosilegrad 26 K7
Boskovice 10 F8
Bosna 26 F5
Bosnia-Herzegovina 26 E5
Bosobolo 56 B3
Bosporus 46 A1
Bosporus = İstanbul Boğazı 28 M3
Bossambélé 56 B2
Bossangoa 56 B2
Bosten Hu 34 R9
Boston, *U.K.* 16 M9
Boston, *U.S.* 70 M3
Botevgrad 26 L7
Botlikh 46 E1
Botna 26 R3
Botoşani 26 P2
Botou 38 F3
Botrange 14 J4
Botswana 58 C4
Bottrop 14 J3
Bou Ahmed 20 F9
Bouaké 54 C3
Bouar 56 B2
Bouârfa 52 E2
Boufarik 20 N8
Bougainville Island 60 F6
Bougainville Reef 62 J3
Bougouni 54 C2
Bougzoul 20 N9
Bouira 52 F1
Bou Ismaïl 20 N8
Bou Izakarn 52 D3
Boujdour 52 C3
Bou Kadir 20 M8
Boukra 52 C3
Boulder 70 E3
Boulder City 70 D4
Boulia 62 G4
Boulogne-sur-Mer 14 D4
Bouna 54 D3
Boundiali 54 C3
Bounty Islands 60 H10
Bourem 52 E5
Bourg 18 E8
Bourg-de-Piage 18 L9
Bourg-en-Bresse 18 L7
Bourges 18 H6
Bourgoin-Jallieu 18 L8
Bourke 62 J6
Bournemouth 16 L11
Bou Saâda 52 F1
Bousso 50 C5
Boussu 14 F4
Boutilimit 52 C5
Bouzghaïa 20 M8
Bowen 62 J4
Bowling Green 70 J4
Bowman Bay 68 R3
Bo Xian 38 F4
Boxwood Hill 62 C6
Boyang 38 F5
Boyarka 36 F2
Boyle 16 D8
Boyuibe 78 J3
Bozcaada 28 H5
Boz Dağ 28 M7
Bozkır 28 Q7
Bozoum 56 B2
Bozüyük 28 N5
Bra 22 C6
Brač 26 D6
Bracciano 24 G6
Bräcke 8 H5
Bracknell 14 B3
Brad 26 K3
Bradano 24 L8
Bradford 16 L8
Brady 70 G5
Braga 20 B3
Bragança, *Brazil* 76 H4
Bragança, *Portugal* 20 D3
Brahmapur 44 D5
Brahmaputra 44 F3
Brăila 26 Q4
Braintree 14 C3
Brake 12 D3
Bramming 12 D1
Bramsche 12 D4
Branco 76 E3
Brandberg 58 A4
Brandenburg 12 H4
Brandon 68 M7
Brandvlei 58 C5
Brandýs 10 D7
Braniewo 10 J3
Brasileia 76 D6
Brasília 76 H7
Braslaw 8 P9
Braşov 26 N4
Bratislava 10 G9
Bratsk 36 G5
Bratskoye Vodokhranilishche 36 G5
Braţul 26 R4
Bratunac 26 G5
Braunau 22 J2
Braunschweig 12 F4
Bray 16 F8
Brazil 74 F4
Brazzaville 56 B4
Brčko 26 F5
Brda 10 G4
Bream Bay 64 E2
Břeclav 10 F9
Breda 14 G3
Bredasdorp 58 C6
Bredstedt 12 E2
Bredy 30 M4
Bree 14 H3
Bree 18 L2
Bregenz 22 E3
Breiðafjörður 8 (1)A2
Bremangerlandet 8 B6
Bremen 12 D3
Bremerhaven 12 D3
Bremervörde 12 E3
Brenham 70 G5
Brennero 22 G4
Breno 22 F5
Brentwood 14 C3
Brescia 22 F5
Breslau = Wrocław 10 G6
Bressanone 22 G4
Bressay 16 M1
Bressuire 18 E7
Brest, *Belarus* 30 D4
Brest, *France* 18 A5
Breteuil 14 E5
Bretten 12 D7
Breves 76 G4
Brewarrina 62 J5
Brežice 26 C4
Brézina 52 F2
Brezno 10 J9
Bria 56 C2
Briançon 22 B6
Briceni 26 Q1
Bridgend 16 J10
Bridgeport 70 M3
Bridgetown 76 F1
Bridgewater 68 U8
Bridgwater 16 J10
Bridlington 16 M7
Brienzer See 22 D4
Brig 22 C4
Brighton 14 B4
Brignoles 22 B7
Brikama 54 A2
Brilon 12 D5
Brindisi 24 M8
Brisbane 62 K5
Bristol 16 K10
Bristol Bay 66 S4
Bristol Channel 16 H10
British Columbia 68 F5
Britstown 58 C6
Brive-la-Gaillarde 18 G8
Briviesca 20 G2
Brixham 16 J11
Brlik 34 N9
Brno 10 F8
Broad Sound 62 J4
Broadus 70 E2
Brod 26 J9
Brodeur Peninsula 68 P2
Brodick 16 G6
Brodnica 10 J4
Broken Arrow 72 E1
Broken Hill 62 H6
Brokopondo 76 F2
Bromölla 10 D1
Bromsgrove 16 K9
Brønderslev 8 E8
Broni 22 E5
Brooke's Point 40 F5
Brookhaven 70 H5
Brooks 68 J6
Brooks Range 66 S3
Broome 62 D3
Brora 16 J3
Brösarp 8 H9
Broughton Island 68 U3
Brovary 30 F4
Brownsville 70 G6
Brownwood 70 G5
Bruchsal 12 D7
Bruck, *Austria* 22 L3
Bruck, *Austria* 22 M2
Bruck an der Mur 26 C2
Brugge 14 F3
Brühl 14 J4
Bruint 44 G3
Brumado 76 J6
Brumath 22 C2
Brunei 42 E2
Brunflo 8 H5
Brunico 24 F2
Brunsbüttel 12 E3
Brunswick 70 K5
Bruntal 10 G8
Brussels = Bruxelles 14 G4
Bruxelles 14 G4
Bryan 70 G5
Bryanka 34 S6
Bryansk 30 F4
Brzeg 10 G7
Brzeg Dolny 10 F6
Brzeziny 10 J6
B-Spandau 10 C5
Bubi 58 E4
Bucak 28 N7
Bucaramanga 76 C2
Buchanan 54 B3
Buchan Gulf 68 S2
Bucharest = Bucureşti 26 P5
Buchen 12 E7
Buchholz 12 E3
Buchy 18 M5
Bückeburg 12 E4
Bučovice 10 F8
Bucureşti 26 P5
Budapest 26 G2
Bude 16 H11
Budennovsk 30 H6
Büdingen 12 E6
Budoni 24 D8
Budrio 22 G6
Budva 26 F7
Buenaventura, *Col.* 76 B3
Buenaventura, *Mexico* 70 E6
Buenos Aires 78 K5
Buffalo, *N.Y., U.S.* 70 L3
Buffalo, *S.D., U.S.* 70 F2
Buffalo Lake 68 J4
Buffalo Narrows 68 K5
Buftea 26 N5
Bug 10 L5
Bugojno 26 E5
Bugrino 34 H4
Bugsuk 40 F5
Bugul'ma 30 K4
Buguruslan 30 K4
Buhuşi 26 P3
Builth Wells 16 J9
Buinsk 30 J3
Buir Nuur 38 F1
Bujanovac 26 J7
Buje 22 J5
Bujumbura 56 D4
Bukachacha 36 K6
Bukavu 56 D4
Bukhara 46 H2
Bukittinggi 42 C3
Bukoba 56 E4
Bula, *Indonesia* 43 D3
Bula, *P.N.G.* 43 F4
Bülach 22 D3
Bulan 40 G4
Bûlâq 50 F2
Bulawayo 58 D4
Buldir Island 36 X6
Bulgan 36 G7
Bulgaria 26 M7
Buli 43 C2
Bulle 22 C4
Bulls 64 E5
Bulukumba 43 B4
Bulun 36 M2
Bumba 56 C3
Bumbeşti Jiu 26 L4
Buna 56 F3
Bunbury 62 C6
Buncrana 16 E6
Bunda 56 E4
Bundaberg 62 K4
Bünde 12 D4
Bungunya 62 J5
Bunia 56 E3
Buôn Mê Thuột 40 D4
Buotama 36 M4
Bura 56 F4
Buran 34 R8
Buranj 44 D2
Buraydah 46 D4
Burco 56 H2
Burdur 28 N7
Burdur Gölü 28 N7
Burë 50 G5
Büren 14 L3
Burg 12 G4
Burgas 26 Q7
Burgaski Zaliv 26 Q7
Burgdorf 22 C3
Burghausen 22 H2
Burglengenfeld 12 H7
Burgos 20 G2
Burgsvik 8 K8
Burhaniye 28 K5
Burhanpur 44 C4
Burjassot 20 K5
Burketown 62 G3
Bur-Khaybyt 36 P3
Burkina Faso 54 D2
Burlin 30 K4
Burlington, *Colo., U.S.* 70 F4
Burlington, *Ia., U.S.* 70 H3
Burlington, *Vt., U.S.* 70 M3
Burma = Myanmar 40 B2
Burnet 70 G5
Burnie 62 J8
Burns 46 C3
Burns Lake 68 F6
Burqin 34 R8
Burra 62 G6
Burrel 28 C3
Bursa 28 M4
Bûr Safâga 50 F2
Bûr Sa'îd 50 F1
Bur Sudan 50 G4
Burtnieks 8 N8
Burton-upon-Trent 16 L9
Buru 43 C3
Burundi 56 D4
Bururi 56 D4
Buryatiya 36 J6
Bury St. Edmunds 14 C2
Būshehr 46 F4
Bushire = Būshehr 46 F4
Businga 56 C3
Busira 56 C4
Bussum 14 H2
Busto Arsizio 22 D5
Buta 56 C3
Butare 56 D4
Butaritari 60 H5
Bute 16 G6
Butembo 56 D3
Búðardalur 8 (1)C2
Buton 43 B3
Butte 70 D2
Butuan 40 H5
Butwal 44 D3
Butzbach 12 D6
Bützow 12 G3
Buulobarde 56 H3
Buur Gaabo 56 G4
Buurhabaka 56 G3
Buxtehude 12 E3
Buxton 14 A1
Buy 30 H3
Büyükada 28 L4
Büyükçekmece 28 L4
Buzai Gumbad 46 K2
Buzançais 18 G7
Buzău 26 P4
Buzău 26 Q4
Buzuluk 30 K4
Byam Martin Island 68 L2
Byaroza 8 N10
Bydgoszcz 10 H4
Bygdin 8 D6
Bygland 8 D7
Bykovskiy 36 M2
Bylot Island 68 R2
Byskeälven 8 L4
Bystřice 10 G8
Bystrzyca Kłodzka 10 F7
Bytča 10 H8
Bytom 10 H7
Bytów 10 G3
Bzura 10 J5

C

Caaguazú 78 K4
Caballococha 76 C5
Cabañaquinta 20 E1
Cabanatuan 40 G3
Cabdul Qaadir 50 H5
Cabeza del Buey 20 E6
Cabezas 76 E7
Cabimas 76 C1
Cabinda 54 G6
Cabinda 54 G6
Cabo Bascuñán 78 G4
Cabo Beata 72 K5
Cabo Camarón 72 G5
Cabo Carvoeiro 20 A5
Cabo Catoche 72 G4
Cabo Corrientes, *Col.* 76 B2
Cabo Corrientes, *Mexico* 72 C4
Cabo Corrubedo 20 A2
Cabo Cruz 72 J5
Cabo de Espichel 20 A6
Cabo de Gata 20 H8
Cabo de Hornos 78 H10
Cabo de la Nao 20 L6
Cabo Delgado 58 G2
Cabo de Palos 20 K7
Cabo de São Roque 76 K5
Cabo de Sao Tomé 78 N3
Cabo de São Vicente 20 A7
Cabo de Trafalgar 20 D8
Cabo dos Bahías 78 H8
Cabo Fisterra 20 A2
Cabo Frio 78 N3
Cabo Gracias a Dios 72 H6
Cabo Mondego 20 A4
Cabo Norte 76 H3
Cabo Orange 76 G3
Cabo Ortegal 20 B1
Cabo Peñas 20 E1
Caborca 70 D5
Cabo Rojo 72 E4
Cabo Roxo 54 A2
Cabo San Diego 78 H9
Cabo San Francisco de Paula 78 H8
Cabo San Juan 54 F4
Cabo San Lucas 70 D7
Cabo Santa Elena 72 J7
Cabo Tortosa 20 L4
Cabo Tres Puntas 78 H8
Cabot Strait 68 U7
Cabrera 20 N5
Čačak 26 H6
Cáceres, *Brazil* 76 F7
Cáceres, *Spain* 20 D5
Cacheu 54 A2
Cachimbo 76 G5
Cachoeira do Sul 78 L4
Cachoeiro de Itapemirim 76 J8
Cacola 58 B2
Caconda 58 B2
Čadca 10 H8
Cadillac 70 E2
Cádiz 20 D8
Caen 14 B5
Caernarfon 16 H8
Cagayan de Oro 40 G5
Cagli 22 H7
Cagliari 24 D9
Cagnes-sur-Mer 22 C7
Caguas 72 L5
Cahama 58 A3
Cahersiveen 16 B10
Cahir 16 E9
Cahors 18 G9
Cahuapanas 76 B5
Cahul 26 R4
Caia 58 F3
Caianda 58 C2
Caicos Islands 72 K4
Cairns 62 J3
Cairo = El Qâhira 50 F1
Cairo Montenotte 22 D6
Caiundo 58 B3
Cajamarca 76 B5
Čakovec 26 D3
Calabar 54 F3
Calabozo 76 D2
Calabro 24 L9
Calafat 26 K6
Calagua Islands 40 G4
Calahorra 20 J2
Calais 14 D4
Calama, *Brazil* 76 E5
Calama, *Peru* 78 H3
Calamar 76 C3
Calamian Group 40 F4
Calamocha 20 J4
Călan 26 L4
Calanscio Sand Sea 50 D2
Calapan 40 G4
Călăraşi, *Moldova* 26 R2
Călăraşi, *Romania* 26 Q5
Calatafim 24 G11
Calatayud 20 J3
Calauag 40 G4
Calbayog 40 G4
Calçoene 76 G3
Calcutta = Kolkata 44 E4
Caldas da Rainha 20 A5
Caldera 78 G4
Calf of Man 16 H7
Calgary 68 J6
Cali 76 B3
Calicut = Kozhikode 44 C6
Caliente 70 D4
California 70 B4
Callao 76 B6
Caloundra 62 K5
Caltagirone 24 J11
Caltanissetta 24 J11
Caluquembe 58 A2
Caluula 56 J1
Calvi 24 C6
Calvinia 58 B6
Calw 22 D2
Camaçari 76 K6
Camacupa 58 B2
Camagüey 72 J4
Camaiore 22 F7
Camana 76 C7
Camargue 18 K10
Camariñas 20 A1
Camarones 78 H7
Ca Mau 40 D5
Camberley 16 M10
Cambodia 40 C4
Cambrai 14 F4
Cambre 20 B1
Cambrian Mountains 16 H10
Cambridge, *N.Z.* 64 E3
Cambridge, *U.K.* 16 N9
Cambridge, *U.S.* 70 L4
Cambridge Bay 68 K3
Cambrils 20 M3
Cameroon 54 G3
Cametá 76 H4
Çamiçigölü 28 K7
Caminha 20 B3
Camiranga 76 H4
Camocim 76 J4
Camooweal 62 G3
Camopi 76 G3
Campbell Island 64 (2)C2
Campbell River 68 F7
Campbeltown 16 G6
Campeche 72 F5
Câmpeni 26 L3
Câmpia Turzii 26 L3
Câmpina 26 N4
Campina Grande 76 L5
Campinas 78 M3
Campobasso 24 J7
Campo de Criptana 20 G5
Campo de Diauarum 76 G6
Campo Gallo 78 J4
Campo Grande 78 L3
Campo Maior 76 J4
Campo Mourão 78 L3
Campos 78 N3
Câmpulung 26 N4
Câmpulung Moldovenesc 26 N2
Cam Ranh 40 D4
Çan 28 K4
Canada 66 M4
Canadian 70 F4
Çanakkale 28 J4
Çanakkale Boğazı 28 J4
Canal de Panamá 72 J7
Canary Islands = Islas Canarias 52 B3
Cañaveras 20 H4
Canberra 62 J7
Cancún 72 G4
Çandarli Körfezi 28 J6
Candelaro 26 C8
Candlemas Island 74 J9
Cangamba 58 B2
Cangas 20 B2
Cangas de Narcea 20 D1
Cangyuan 40 B2
Cangzhou 38 F3
Canicattì 24 H11
Canindé 76 K4
Çankiri 28 R4
Canna 16 F4
Cannanore 44 B6
Cannanore 44 C6
Cannes 22 C7
Cannock 14 A2
Cantanduanes 40 G4
Canterbury 14 D3
Canterbury Bight 64 C7
Canterbury Plains 64 C6
Cân Tho 40 D5
Canto do Buriti 76 J5
Canton 70 K3
Canumã 76 F4
Canumã 76 F5
Canutama 76 E5
Canyon 70 F5
Cao Băng 40 D2
Caorle 22 H5
Cap Blanc 24 D11
Cap Bon 52 H1
Cap Corse 24 D5
Cap d'Agde 18 J10
Cap d'Antifer 14 C5
Cap de Fer 52 G1
Cap de Formentor 20 P5
Cap de la Hague 18 D4
Cap de Nouvelle-France 68 S4
Cap de ses Salines 20 P5
Cap des Trois Fourches 20 H9
Cape Agulhas 58 C6
Cape Alexandra 78 P9
Cape Apostolos Andreas 46 B2
Cape Arid 62 D6
Cape Arnaoutis 28 Q9
Cape Arnhem 62 G2
Cape Barren Island 62 J8
Cape Bauld 68 V6
Cape Blanco 70 B3
Cape Borda 62 G7
Cape Breton Island 68 U7
Cape Brett 64 E2
Cape Byron 62 K5
Cape Campbell 64 E5
Cape Canaveral 70 K6
Cape Carnot 62 F6
Cape Chidley 68 U4
Cape Christian 68 T2
Cape Churchill 68 N5
Cape Clear 16 C10
Cape Coast 54 D3
Cape Cod 66 H5
Cape Columbine 58 B6
Cape Colville 64 E3
Cape Comorin 44 C7
Cape Crawford 62 G3
Cape Croker 62 F2
Cape Dalhousie 68 F2
Cape Direction 62 H2
Cape Disappointment 78 P9
Cape Dominion 68 R3
Cape Dorchester 68 R3
Cape Dorset 68 R4
Cape Dyer 68 U3
Cape Egmont 64 D4
Cape Farewell, *Greenland* 66 F4
Cape Farewell, *N.Z.* 64 D5
Cape Fear 70 L5
Cape Finisterre = Cabo Fisterra 20 A2
Cape Flattery, *Aus.* 62 J2
Cape Flattery, *U.S.* 70 B2
Cape Forestier 62 J8
Cape Foulwind 64 C5
Cape Fria 58 A3
Cape Girardeau 70 J4
Cape Greko 28 S10
Cape Grenville 62 H2
Cape Grim 62 H8
Cape Harrison 68 V6
Cape Hatteras 70 L4
Cape Henrietta Maria 68 Q5
Cape Horn = Cabo de Hornos 78 H10

Donegal 16 D7
Donegal Bay 16 D7
Donets 6 H3
Donets'k 30 G5
Dongara 62 B5
Dongco 44 D2
Dongfang 40 D3
Donggala 43 A3
Dongguan 40 E2
Dông Hôi 40 D3
Dongjingcheng 38 H2
Donglük 34 R10
Dongo 54 H4
Dongola 50 F4
Dongou 54 H4
Dongsha Qundao 40 F2
Dongsheng 38 E3
Dong Ujimqin Qi 38 F1
Dongying 38 F3
Donji Vakuf 22 N6
Donner Pass 70 C4
Donostia 20 J1
Donousa 28 H7
Doolow 56 G3
Dora 22 C5
Dorchester 16 K11
Dordrecht 14 G3
Dorfen 22 H2
Dori 54 D2
Doring 58 B6
Dormagen 14 J3
Dornbirn 22 E3
Doro 54 D1
Dorog 10 H10
Dorohoi 26 P2
Döröö Nuur 34 S8
Dorotea 8 J4
Dorsten 14 J3
Dortmund 12 C5
Doruma 56 D3
Dos Hermanas 20 E7
Dosse 12 H4
Dosso 54 E2
Dothan 70 J5
Douai 14 F4
Douala 54 F4
Douarnenez 18 A5
Doubs 22 B3
Douentza 54 C2
Douglas, *S.A.* 58 C5
Douglas, *U.K.* 16 H7
Douglas, *Ariz., U.S.* 70 E5
Douglas, *Wyo., U.S.* 70 E3
Doullens 14 E4
Dourados 78 L3
Douro 20 B3
Dover, *U.K.* 14 D3
Dover, *Aus.* 62 J8
Downpatrick 16 G7
Dowshī 46 J2
Drac 22 B6
Drachten 14 J1
Dragan 8 H4
Drăgănești-Olt 26 M5
Drăgășani 26 M5
Draguignan 22 B7
Drakensberg 58 D6
Drake Passage 78 G10
Drama 28 G3
Drammen 8 F7
Drasenhofen 22 M2
Drau 22 J4
Drava 26 E4
Dravograd 24 K2
Drawsko Pomorskie 10 E4
Dresden 12 J5
Dreux 14 D6
Drezdenko 10 E5
Drina 26 G5
Driva 8 E5
Drjanovo 26 N7
Drniš 26 D6
Drobeta-Turnu
Severin 26 K5
Drochia 26 Q1
Drogheda 16 F8
Drohobych 10 N8
Drôme 18 K9
Dronne 18 F8
Dronten 14 H2
Drummondville 70 M2
Druskininkai 8 M9
Druzhina 36 Q3
Drvar 26 D5
Dryden 70 H2
Drysdale River 62 E3
Dschang 54 G3
Ḑubā 50 G2
Dubai = Dubayy 46 G4
Dubăsari 26 S2
Dubawnt Lake 68 L4
Dubayy 46 G4
Dubbo 62 J6
Dübendorf 22 D3
Dublin 16 F8
Dublin Bay 16 F8
Dubna 30 G3
Dubnica 10 H9
Dubovskoye 30 H5
Dubreka 54 B3
Dubrovnik 26 F7
Dubuque 70 H3
Ducie Island 60 P8
Dudelange 14 J5
Duderstadt 12 F5
Dudinka 34 R4
Dudley 16 K9
Duero 20 F3
Dugi Otok 26 B6
Duifken Point 62 H2
Duisburg 14 J3
Duiveland 14 F3
Dukat 36 T4
Duk Faiwil 56 E2
Dukla 10 L8
Dukou 38 C5
Dulan 38 B3
Dulce 78 J4
Dul'Durga 36 J6
Dullewala 44 B2
Dülmen 12 C5
Dulovo 26 Q6
Duluth 70 H2
Dumaguete 40 G5
Dumai 42 C2
Dumas, *Ark., U.S.* 70 H5
Dumas, *Tex., U.S.* 70 F4
Dumbarton 16 H5
Ďumbier 10 J9
Dumboa 54 G2
Dumfries 16 J6
Dümmer 12 D4
Dumont d'Urville Sea 80 (2)U3
Dumyât 50 F1
Duna = Danube 26 E2
Dunaj = Danube 10 G10
Dunajská Streda 26 E2
Dunakeszi 26 G2
Dunărea = Danube 26 K5
Dunaújváros 26 F3
Dunav = Danube 26 J5
Dunayivtsi 30 E5
Dunbar, *Aus.* 62 H3
Dunbar, *U.K.* 16 K6
Duncan Passage 40 A4
Dundaga 8 M8
Dundalk 16 F7
Dundalk Bay 16 F8
Dundee, *S.A.* 58 E5
Dundee, *U.K.* 16 K5
Dunedin 64 C7
Dunfermline 16 J5
Dungarvan 16 E9
Dungeness 14 C4
Dungu 56 D3
Dungun 40 C6
Dungunab 50 G3
Dunhua 38 H2
Dunhuang 38 A2
Dunkerque 14 E3
Dunkwa 54 D3
Dun Laoghaire 16 F8
Dunnet Head 16 J3
Duque de Caxias 78 N3
Durance 18 L10
Durango, *Mexico* 70 F7
Durango, *Spain* 20 H1
Durango, *U.S.* 70 E4
Durankurak 26 R6
Durant 70 G5
Durazno 78 K5
Durban 58 E5
Durban-Corbières 18 H10
Düren 14 J4
Durgapur 44 E4
Durham, *U.K.* 16 L7
Durham, *U.S.* 70 L4
Duri 42 C2
Durmanec 26 C3
Durmitor 26 G6
Durness 16 H3
Durrës 28 B3
Dursey 16 B10
Dursunbey 28 L5
D'Urville Island 64 D5
Dushanbe 46 J2
Düsseldorf 14 J3
Duvno 22 N7
Duyun 38 D5
Düzce 28 P4
Dvina 6 H2
Dvinskaya Guba 30 G1
Dwarka 44 A4
Dyat'kovo 30 F4
Dyersburg 72 G1
Dyje 22 M2
Dzamïn Üüd 36 J8
Dzavhan 34 S8
Dzerzhinsk 30 H3
Dzhalinda 36 L6
Dzhambeyty 30 K4
Dzhankoy 30 F5
Dzhardzhan 36 L3
Dzharkurgan 46 J2
Dzhetygara 30 M4
Dzhezkazgan 30 N5
Dzhigudzhak 36 T4
Dzhizak 34 M9
Dzhusaly 30 M5
Działdowo 10 K4
Dzüünbulag 38 F1
Dzuunmod 38 D1

E

Eagle 68 C4
East Antarctica 80 (2)P2
Eastbourne 14 C4
East Cape 64 G3
East China Sea 38 H4
East Dereham 14 C2
Easter Island 60 Q8
Eastern Cape 58 D6
Eastern Ghats 44 C6
Easter Ross 16 H4
East Falkland 78 K9
East Grinstead 14 C3
East Kilbride 16 H6
Eastleigh 14 A4
East London 58 D6
Eastmain 68 R6
Eastmain 68 S6
East Retford 14 B1
East St. Louis 70 H4
East Siberian Sea =
Vostochno-Sibirskoye
More 36 U2
East Timor = Timor
Timur 43 C4
Eau Claire 70 H3
Ebbw Vale 16 J10
Ebensee 22 J3
Eberbach 12 D7
Ebersbach 10 D6
Ebersberg 22 G2
Eberswalde 12 J4
Ebinur Hu 34 Q9
Eboli 24 K8
Ebolowa 54 G4
Ebro 20 K3
Eceabat 28 J4
Ech Chélif 52 F1
Echinos 28 G3
Echo Bay 68 H3
Écija 20 E7
Eckernförde 12 E2
Ecuador 76 B4
Ed 50 H5
Edam 14 H2
Eday 16 K2
Ed Da'ein 50 E5
Ed Damazin 50 F5
Ed Debba 50 F4
Ed Dueim 50 F5
Ede, *Netherlands* 14 H2
Ede, *Nigeria* 54 E3
Edéa 54 G4
Edelény 10 K9
Eden 62 J7
Edendale 64 B8
Eder 12 D5
Edersee 12 E5
Edessa 28 E4
Edgecumbe 64 F3
Edinburgh 16 J6
Edineț 26 Q1
Edirne 28 J3
Edmonton 68 J6
Edmundston 68 T7
Edolo 22 F4
Edremit 28 J5
Edremit Körfezi 28 H5
Edwards Plateau 70 F5
Eeklo 14 F3
Eemshaven 14 J1
Éfaté 60 G7
Eferding 10 D9
Effingham 70 J4
Eger 12 G6
Eger 26 H2
Egersund 8 D7
Eggenfelden 22 H2
Egilsstaðir 8 (1)F2
Eğridir 28 N7
Eğridir Gölü 28 N6
Egvekinot 36 Y3
Egypt 50 E2
Ehingen 22 E2
Eibar 20 H1
Eichstätt 22 G2
Eider 12 D2
Eidfjord 8 D6
Eidsvold 62 K5
Eidsvoll 8 F6
Eifel 14 J4
Eigg 16 F5
Eight Degree Channel 44 B7
Eilenburg 12 H5
Einbeck 12 E5
Eindhoven 14 H3
Eirunepé 76 D5
Eiseb 58 C4
Eisenach 12 F6
Eisenerz 22 K3
Eisenhüttenstadt 10 D5
Eisenstadt 22 M3
Eisleben 12 G5
Eivissa 20 M5
Eivissa 20 M6
Ejea de los
Caballeros 20 J2
Ejido Insurgentes 70 D6
Ejin Horo Qi 38 D3
Ejin Qi 38 C2
Ekenäs 8 M7
Eketahuna 64 E5
Ekibastuz 34 P7
Ekimchan 36 N6
Ekonda 34 V4
Eksjo 8 H8
Ekwan 68 Q6
Elafonisos 28 E8
El 'Alamein 50 E1
El Amria 20 J9
Elat 46 B4
Elazığ 46 C2
Elba 24 E6
El Banco 76 C2
Elbasan 28 C3
El Baúl 76 D2
Elbe 12 F3
Elbeuf 14 D5
Elbląg 10 J3
El Borj 20 E9
Elbow 70 E1
Elbrus 6 J3
El Burgo de Ebro 20 K3
El Burgo de Osma 20 G3
El Callao 76 E2
El Centro 70 C5
El Cerro 76 E7
Elch 20 K6
Elda 20 K6
El'dikan 36 P4
Eldorado 78 L4
El Dorado, *Mexico* 70 E7
El Dorado, *U.S.* 70 H5
El Dorado, *Venezuela* 76 E2
Eldoret 56 F3
Elefsína 28 F6
Elektrėnai 10 P3
El Encanto 76 C4
Eleuthera 70 L6
El Fahs 24 D12
El Faiyûm 50 F2
El Fasher 50 E5
El Geneina 50 D5
Elgin 16 J4
El'ginskiy 36 Q4
El Gîza 50 F1
El Goléa 52 F2
El Homr 52 F3
Elhovo 28 J2
El Iskandarîya 50 E1
Elista 30 H5
El Jadida 52 D2
Ełk 10 M4
Ełk 10 M4
El Kala 24 C12
El Kef 24 C12
El Kelaâ des Srarhna 52 D2
El Khandaq 50 F4
El Khârga 50 F2
El Khartum 50 F4
El Khartum Bahri 50 F4
Elko 46 C3
Ellendale 70 G2
Ellesmere Island 66 K1
Ellice Islands 60 H6
Elliot 58 D6
Ellis 68 J8
Ellisras 58 D4
Elliston 62 F6
Ellwangen 22 F2
Elmadağ 28 R5
Elmali 28 M8
El Mansûra 50 F1
El Minya 50 F2
Elmshorn 12 E3
El Muglad 50 E5
El Nido 40 F4
El Obeid 50 F5
El Odaiya 50 E5
El Oued 52 G2
El Paso 70 E5
El Prat de Llobregat 20 N3
El Puerto de Santa
María 20 D8
El Qâhira 50 F1
El Qasr 50 E2
El Salvador 72 F6
Elster 12 H5
Elsterwerda 12 J5
El Sueco 70 E6
El Suweis 50 F2
Eltanin Bay 80 (2)JJ2
El Tarf 24 C12
El Tigre 76 E2
El Turbio 78 G9
Eluru 44 D5
Elvas 20 C6
Elverum 8 F6
Elvira 76 C5
El Wak 56 G3
Ely, *U.K.* 16 N9
Ely, *U.S.* 70 D4
Emajõgi 8 P7
Emāmrūd 46 F2
Emba 30 L5
Emba 30 L5
Embalse de Alarcon 20 H5
Embalse de Alcántara
Uno 20 D5
Embalse de
Almendra 20 D3
Embalse de
Contreras 20 J5
Embalse de Gabriel y
Galán 20 D4
Embalse de Garcia
Sola 20 E5
Embalse de
Guadalhorce 20 F8
Embalse de
Guadalmena 20 G6
Embalse de Guri 76 E2
Embalse de la
Serena 20 E6
Embalse de la
Sotonera 20 K2
Embalse del
Bembézar 20 E6
Embalse del Ebro 20 G1
Embalse del Río
Negro 74 F7
Embalse de Negratín 20 G7
Embalse de
Ricobayo 20 E3
Embalse de Santa
Teresa 20 E4
Embalse de Yesa 20 J2
Embalse Toekomstig 76 F3
Embarcación 78 J3
Emden 12 C3
Emerald 62 J4
Emi Koussi 50 C4
Emin 34 Q8
Emirdağ 28 P5
Emmeloord 14 H2
Emmen 14 J2
Emmendingen 22 C2
Emmerich 14 J3
Emory Peak 70 F6
Empangeni 58 E5
Empoli 22 F7
Emporia 70 G4
Empty Quarter =
Rub' al Khālī 46 E6
Ems 14 J1
Ems-Jade-Kanal 12 C3
Enafors 30 B2
Encarnación 78 K4
Encs 26 J1
Ende 43 B4
Enderby Island 64 (2)B1
Energetik 30 L4
Enewetak 60 F4
Enez 28 J4
Enfida 24 E12
Enfield 14 B3
Engel's 30 J4
Enggano 42 C4
Enghien 14 G4
England 16 L9
English Channel 16 J12
Engozero 8 S4
Enid 70 G4
Enkhuizen 14 H2
Enköping 8 J7
Enna 24 J11
En Nahud 50 E5
Enngonia 62 J5
Ennis 16 D9
Enniscorthy 16 F9
Enniskillen 16 E7
Enns 22 K2
Enns 22 K3
Enschede 14 J2
Ensenada 70 C5
Enshi 38 D4
Entebbe 56 E3
Entrevaux 22 B7
Entroncamento 20 B5
Enugu 54 F3
Enurmino 36 Z3
Envira 76 C5
Enz 22 D2
Enza 22 F6
Epanomi 28 E4
Epéna 56 B3
Épernay 18 J4
Épinal 22 B2
Episkopi 28 Q10
Epsom 14 B3
Equatorial Guinea 54 F4
Erbach 12 D7
Erciş 46 D2
Ercolano 24 J8
Érd 26 F2
Erdek 28 K4
Erdemli 28 S8
Erdenet 36 G7
Erding 22 G2
Erechim 78 L4
Ereğli, *Turkey* 28 P3
Ereğli, *Turkey* 28 S7
Ereikoussa 28 B5
Erenhot 38 E2
Erfurt 12 G6
Erg Chech 52 D4
Erg du Ténéré 52 H5
Ergel 38 D2
Ergene 28 J3
Erg Iguidi 52 D3
Er Hai 38 C5
Erie 70 K3
Erimo-misaki 38 L2
Eriskay 16 E4
Eritrea 50 G4
Erlangen 12 G7
Ermenek 28 Q8
Ermoupoli 28 G7
Erode 44 C6
Er Rachidia 52 E2
Er Rahad 50 F5
Er Renk 56 E1
Ersekë 28 C4
Ertai 34 S8
Ertix 34 R8
Erzgebirge 12 H6
Erzin 34 S7
Erzurum 46 D2
Esan-misaki 38 L2
Esashi, *Japan* 38 L2
Esashi, *Japan* 38 L2
Esbjerg 8 E9
Escanaba 70 J2
Escárcega 72 F5
Esch 14 J5
Eschwege 12 F5
Eschweiler 14 J4
Escondido 70 C5
Eséka 54 G4
Eşfahān 46 F3
Eskifjörður 8 (1)G2
Eskilstuna 8 J7
Eskişehir 28 N5
Esla 20 E3
Eslamshahr 46 F2
Esler Dağ 28 M7
Eslö 10 C2
Esmeraldas 76 B3
Esneux 14 H4
Espalion 18 H9
Espanola 70 E4
Espelkamp 12 D4
Esperance 62 D6
Esperance Bay 62 D6
Esperanza 76 C5
Espinho 20 B4
Espírito Santo 76 J7
Espíritu Santo 60 G7
Esplanada 76 K6
Espoo 8 N6
Espungebera 58 E4
Essaouira 52 D2
Es Semara 52 C3
Essen, *Belgium* 14 G3
Essen, *Germany* 14 K3
Essequibo 76 F2
Esslingen 22 E2
Este 22 G5
Estella 20 H2
Estepona 20 E8
Esteros 78 J3
Estevan 70 F2
Estonia 8 M7
Estoril 20 A6
Estrecho de Le Maire 78 H10
Estrecho de
Magallanes 78 G9
Estrela 20 C4
Estremoz 20 C6
Estuário do Rio
Amazonaz 76 H3
Esztergom 26 F2
Étain 14 H5
Étampes 18 H5
Étang de Berre 18 L10
Étaples 14 D4
Etawah 44 C3
Ethiopia 48 G5
Etosha Pan 58 B3
Étretat 14 C5
Ettelbruck 12 B7
Ettlingen 12 D8
Eucla 62 E6
Eufaula Lake 70 G4
Eugene 70 B3
Eupen 12 B6
Euphrates = Firat 46 E3
Eure 14 D6
Eureka, *Calif., U.S.* 70 B3
Eureka, *Mont., U.S.* 70 C2
Europe 6 G2
Europoort 14 F3
Euskirchen 12 B6
Eutin 12 F2
Eutsuk Lake 68 F6
Evans Strait 68 Q4
Evanston 70 D3
Everett 70 B2
Evergreen 70 J5
Evesham 14 A2
Évora 20 C6
Évreux 14 D5
Evron 18 E5
Evvoia 28 F6
Ewo 54 G5
Exaltación 76 D6
Exe 16 J11
Exeter 16 J11
Exmouth, *Aus.* 62 B4
Exmouth, *U.K.* 16 J11
Exuma Sound 70 L7
Eyl 56 H2
Eyre Peninsula 62 G2
Ezine 28 J5

F

Faadippolu Atoll 44 B8
Fåborg 12 F1
Fabriano 22 H7
Fachi 52 H5
Fada 50 D4
Fada Ngourma 54 E2
Faenza 22 G6
Færingehavn =
Kangerluarsoruseq 68 W4
Faeroes 6 D1
Fafanlap 43 D3
Făgăraș 26 M4
Fagernes 8 E6
Fagersta 8 H6
Făget 26 K4
Fagurhólsmýri 8 (1)E3
Faial 52 (1)B2
Fairbanks 68 B4
Fair Isle 16 L2
Fairlie 64 C7
Faisalabad 44 B2
Faizabad 44 D3
Fakfak 43 D3
Fakse 12 H1
Fakse Bugt 8 G9
Faku 38 G2
Falaise 14 B6
Falaise de Tiguidit 52 G5
Falconara Marittima 22 J7
Falcon Lake 70 G6
Fălești 26 Q2
Falkenberg 8 G8
Falkensee 12 J4
Falkland Islands 78 K9
Falkland Sound 78 J9
Falköping 8 G7
Fallingbostel 12 E4
Fallon 70 C4
Falls City 70 G3
Falmouth 16 G11
Falster 12 H2
Fălticeni 26 P2
Falun 8 H6
Famagusta =
Ammochostos 28 R9
Fanchang 38 F4
Fandriana 58 H4
Fangzheng 38 H1
Fannūj 46 G4
Fano 22 J7
Fanø 12 D1
Fanø Bugt 12 D1
Faradje 56 D3
Farafangana 58 H4
Farāh 46 H3
Farah Rud 46 H3
Faranah 54 B2
Fareham 14 A4
Farewell Spit 64 D5
Fargo 70 G2
Faridabad 44 C3
Farihy Alaotra 58 H3
Färjestaden 10 F1
Farmington 70 E4
Farnborough 14 B3
Farne Islands 16 L6
Fårö 8 K8
Faro, *Brazil* 76 F4
Faro, *Portugal* 20 C7
Fårösund 8 K8
Farquhar Group 58 (2)B3
Fasano 24 M8
Fatehgarh 44 C3
Fatehpur 44 D3
Făurei 26 Q4
Fauske 8 H3
Fauville-en-Caux 14 C5
Favara 24 H11
Faversham 14 C3
Favignana 24 G11
Faxaflói 8 (1)B2
Faya 50 C4
Fayetteville, *Ark.,*
U.S. 70 H4
Fayetteville, *N.C.,*
U.S. 70 L4
Fažana 24 H4

Fdérik 52 C4
Featherston 64 E5
Fécamp 14 C5
Federated States of
Micronesia 60 E5
Fedorovka 30 M4
Fehmarn 12 G2
Feijó 76 C5
Feilding 64 E5
Feira de Santana 76 K6
Feistritz 22 L3
Fejø 12 G2
Feldbach 22 L4
Feldkirch 22 E3
Feldkirchen 22 K4
Felidu Atoll 44 B8
Felixstowe 14 D3
Feltre 22 G4
Femø 12 G2
Femund 8 F5
Fenghua 38 G5
Fengning 38 F2
Feng Xian 38 D4
Feni 44 F4
Fenyang 38 E3
Feodosiya 30 G5
Feres 28 J4
Fergana 46 K1
Fergus Falls 70 G2
Ferkessédougou 54 C3
Ferlach 22 K4
Fermo 24 H5
Fernandópolis 78 L3
Ferrara 22 G6
Ferreira do Alentejo 20 B7
Ferrol 20 B1
Fès 52 E2
Feteşti 26 Q5
Fethiye 28 M8
Fetisovo 46 F1
Fetlar 16 M1
Feucht 12 G7
Feuchtwangen 12 F7
Feyzābād 46 K2
Fianarantsoa 58 H4
Fianga 56 B2
Fichē 56 F2
Fidenza 22 F6
Fieni 26 N4
Fier 28 B4
Figari 24 D7
Figeac 18 G9
Figline Valdarno 22 G7
Figueira da Foz 20 B4
Figueres 20 N2
Figuig 52 E2
Figuil 54 G3
Fiji 60 H8
Filadélfia 78 J3
Fil'akovo 10 J9
Filiaşi 26 L5
Filicudi 24 J10
Filtu 56 G2
Finale Ligure 22 D6
Fingoè 58 E3
Finike 28 N8
Finland 8 P3
Finlay 68 F5
Finley 62 J7
Finnsnes 8 K2
Finsterwalde 12 J5
Frat 46 E3
Firenze 22 G7
Firminy 18 K8
Firozabad 44 C3
Firozpur 44 B2
Firth of Clyde 16 G6
Firth of Forth 16 K5
Firth of Lorn 16 G5
Firth of Thames 64 E3
Fish 58 B5
Fisher Strait 68 Q4
Fishguard 16 H9
Fiskenæsset =
Qeqertarsuatsiaat 68 W4
Fismes 14 F5
Fitzroy Crossing 62 E3
Fivizzano 22 F6
Fizi 56 D4
Flå 8 E6
Flannan Islands 16 E3
Flåsjön 8 H4
Flateyri 8 (1)B1
Flathead Lake 70 D2
Flat Point 64 E5
Flekkefjord 8 D7
Flensburg 12 E2
Flensburg Fjord 12 E2
Flers 14 B6
Flinders Island 62 J7
Flinders Ranges 62 G6
Flinders Reefs 62 J3
Flin Flon 68 L6
Flint 70 K3
Flint Island 60 L7
Flirey 22 A2
Flöha 12 J6
Florac 18 J9
Florence = Firenze, *It.* 22 G7
Florence, *U.S.* 70 L5
Florencia 76 B3
Florennes 14 G4
Florenville 14 H5
Flores, *Azores* 52 (1)A2
Flores, *Indonesia* 43 B4
Flores Sea 43 A4
Floreşti 26 R2
Floriano 76 J5
Florianópolis 78 M4
Florida 70 K6
Florida 78 K5
Florida Keys 66 K7
Florina 28 D4
Florø 8 C6
Flumendosa 24 D9
Fly 43 F4
Foça 28 J6
Foča 26 F6
Focşani 26 Q4
Foggia 24 K7
Fogo 54 (1)B1
Fogo Island 68 W7
Fohnsdorf 22 K3
Föhr 12 D2
Foix 18 G11
Folegandros 28 G8
Foleyet 70 K2
Foligno 24 G6
Folkestone 14 D3
Follonica 24 E6
Fomboni 58 G2
Fondi 24 H7
Fongafale 60 H6
Fontainebleau 18 H5
Fontana 24 M8
Fonte Boa 76 D4
Fontenay-le-Comte 18 E7
Fontur 8 (1)F1
Fonyód 24 M2
Forbach, *France* 14 J5
Forbach, *Germany* 14 L6
Forchheim 12 G7
Førde 8 C6
Forfar 16 K5
Forges-les-Eaux 14 D5
Forlì 22 H6
Formazza 22 D4
Formentera 20 M6
Formia 24 H7
Formiga 78 M3
Formosa, *Brazil* 76 H7
Formosa, *Paraguay* 78 K4
Fornovo di Taro 22 F6
Forsayth 62 H3
Forssa 8 M6
Forst 12 K5
Fort Abbas 44 B3
Fortaleza 76 K4
Fort Augustus 16 H4
Fort Beaufort 58 D6
Fort Chipewyan 68 J5
Fort-de-France 72 M6
Fort Dodge 70 H3
Forte dei Marmi 22 F7
Fortezza 22 G4
Fort Frances 70 H2
Fort George 68 R6
Fort Good Hope 68 F3
Forth 16 H5
Fort Hope 68 P6
Fortín Coronel
Eugenio Garay 78 J3
Fort Lauderdale 70 K6
Fort Liard 68 G4
Fort Mackay 68 J5
Fort McMurray 68 J5
Fort McPherson 68 D3
Fort Munro 46 J4
Fort Myers 70 K6
Fort Nelson 68 G5
Fort Norman 68 F4
Fort Peck Reservoir 70 E2
Fort Pierce 70 K6
Fort Portal 56 E3
Fort Providence 68 H4
Fortrose 64 B8
Fort Rupert 68 R6
Fort St. John 68 G5
Fort Severn 68 P5
Fort Shevchenko 34 J9
Fort Simpson 68 G4
Fort Smith, *Can.* 68 J4
Fort Smith, *U.S.* 70 H4
Fort Stockton 70 F5
Fortune Bay 68 V7
Fort Vermilion 68 H5
Fort Wayne 70 G3
Fort William 16 G5
Fort Worth 70 G5
Foshan 40 E2
Fosna 8 F5
Fossano 22 C6
Fossombrone 22 H7
Fougamou 54 G5
Fougères 18 D5
Foula 16 K1
Foulness 14 C3
Foumban 54 G3
Fourmies 14 G4
Fournoi 28 J7
Fouta Djallon 54 B2
Foveaux Strait 64 A8
Foxe Basin 68 R3
Foxe Channel 68 R4
Foxe Peninsula 68 R4
Fox Glacier 64 B6
Fox Islands 66 T4
Foz 20 C1
Foz do Cunene 58 A3
Foz do Iguaçu 78 L4
Fraga 20 L3
Franca 78 M3
Francavilla al Mare 24 J6
France 18 G7
Franceville 54 G5
Francistown 58 D4
Franeker 14 H1
Frankenberg 12 D5
Frankenthal 12 D7
Frankfort 70 K4
Frankfurt, *Germany* 12 K4
Frankfurt, *Germany* 12 D6
Franklin Bay 68 F2
Franklin D. Roosevelt
Lake 70 C2
Franklin Mountains 68 F3
Franklin Strait 68 M2
Franz Josef Glacier 64 C6
Franz Josef Land =
Zemlya
Frantsa-Iosifa 34 J2
Fraser 68 G6
Fraserburg 58 C6
Fraserburgh 16 L4
Fraser Island 62 K5
Frasertown 64 F4
Frauenfeld 22 D3
Fredensborg 10 B2
Fredericton 68 T7
Frederikshåb =
Paamiut 68 X4
Frederikshavn 8 F8
Frederikssund 10 B2
Frederiksværk 8 G9
Fredrikstad 8 F7
Freeport 70 G6
Freeport City 72 J3
Free State 58 D5
Freetown 54 B3
Fregenal de la Sierre 20 D6
Freiberg 12 J6
Freiburg 22 C3
Freilassing 22 H3
Freising 22 G2
Freistadt 22 K2
Fréjus 18 M10
Fremantle 62 C6
Fremont 70 G3
French Guiana 76 G3
French Pass 64 D5
French Polynesia 60 L7
Frenda 52 F1
Fresnes-sur-Apances 22 A3
Fresnillo 72 D4
Fresno 70 C4
Freudenstadt 22 D2
Freyung 12 J8
Frias 78 H4
Fribourg 22 C4
Friedburg 22 G2
Friedrichshafen 22 E3
Friesach 22 K4
Friesoythe 12 C3
Frisian Islands 14 H1
Fritzlar 12 E5
Frobisher Bay 68 T4
Frolovo 30 H5
Frome 16 K10
Frontera 72 F5
Frontignan 18 J10
Frosinone 24 H7
Frøya 8 D5
Fruges 14 E4
Frýdek Místek 10 H8
Fuding 38 G5
Fuengirola 20 F8
Fuentesauco 20 E3
Fuerte Olimpo 78 K3
Fuerteventura 52 C3
Fugu 38 E3
Fuhai 34 R8
Fujin 36 N7
Fuji-san 38 K3
Fukue-jima 38 H4
Fukui 38 K3
Fukuoka 38 J4
Fukushima 38 L3
Fulda 12 E6
Fulda 12 E6
Fuling 38 D5
Funafuti 60 H6
Funchal 52 B2
Fundão 20 C4
Funing 40 D2
Funtua 54 F2
Furmanovka 34 N9
Furmanovo 30 J5
Furneaux Group 62 J8
Fürstenberg 12 J3
Fürstenfeldbruck 22 G2
Fürstenwalde 12 K4
Fürth 12 F7
Furukawa 38 L3
Fushun 38 G2
Fusong 36 M8
Füssen 22 F3
Futog 26 G4
Fuxhou 38 F5
Fu Xian 38 D3
Fuxin 38 G2
Fuyang 38 F4
Fuyu 38 G1
Fuyun 34 R8
Fuzhou 40 F1
Fyn 12 F1
Fynshav 12 F2

G

Gaalkacyo 56 H2
Gabès 52 H2
Gabon 54 G5
Gaborone 58 D4
Gabrovo 26 N7
Gacé 14 C6
Gacko 26 F6
Gäddede 8 H4
Gadsden 70 J5
Găeşti 26 N5
Gaeta 24 H7
Gafsa 52 G2
Gaggenau 22 D2
Gagnoa 54 C3
Gaildorf 22 E2
Gaillac 18 G10
Gainesville, *Fla., U.S.* 70 K6
Gainesville, *Ga., U.S.* 70 K5
Gala 44 E3
Gălăbovo 28 H2
Galana 56 F4
Galanta 22 N2
Galapagos Islands =
Islas Galápagos 76 (1)B1
Galashiels 16 K6
Galatas 28 F7
Galaţi 26 R4
Galdhøpiggen 8 D6
Galich 30 H3
Gallabat 50 G5
Galle 44 D7
Gallipoli 24 N8
Gällivare 8 L3
Gallup 70 E4
Galtat Zemmour 52 C3
Galveston Bay 70 G6
Galway 16 C8
Galway Bay 16 C8
Gamalakhe 58 E6
Gamběla 56 E2
Gambell 36 Z4
Gambier Islands 60 N8
Gamboma 56 B4
Gamboula 56 B3
Gan 36 L7
Ganado 70 E4
Găncă 46 E1
Gandajika 56 C5
Gander 68 W7
Ganderkesee 12 D3
Gandesa 20 L3
Gāndhīdhām 44 B4
Gandhinagar 44 B4
Gandia 20 K6
Gandu 76 K6
Ganganagar 44 B3
Gangara 54 F2
Gangdise Shan 44 D2
Ganges 18 J10
Ganges 44 E3
Gangi 24 J11
Gangtok 44 E3
Gannett Peak 70 E3
Ganta 54 C3
Ganye 54 G3
Ganzhou 38 E5
Gao 52 E5
Gaoual 52 C6
Gap 22 B6
Gapan 40 G3
Garanhuns 76 K5
Garba 54 J3
Garbsen 12 E4
Gardelegen 12 G4
Garden City 70 F4
Gardēz 46 J3
Gardone Val Trompia 22 F5
Gargždai 10 L2
Gariau 43 D3
Garies 58 B6
Garissa 56 F4
Garlasco 22 D5
Garliava 10 N3
Garmisch-
Partenkirchen 22 G3
Garonne 18 E9
Garoowe 56 H2
Garoua 54 G3
Garoua Boulaï 54 G3
Garry Lake 68 L3
Garsen 56 G4
Garut 42 D4
Garwa 44 D4
Garwolin 10 L6
Gary 70 J3
Garyarsa 44 D2
Garzē 38 B4
Gasan Kuli 46 F2
Gasht 46 H4
Gashua 54 G2
Gastre 78 H7
Gatchina 30 F3
Gateshead 16 L7
Gauja 8 N8
Gaula 8 F5
Gaurella 44 D4
Gauteng 58 D5
Gava 20 N3
Gavdos 28 G10
Gävle 8 J6
Gawler 62 G6
Gawler Ranges 62 G6
Gaxun Nur 38 C2
Gaya, *India* 44 E4
Gaya, *Niger* 54 E2
Gayndah 62 K5
Gayny 30 K2
Gaza 50 F1
Gaz-Achak 34 L9
Gazandzhyk 34 K10
Gaziantep 46 C2
Gazipaşa 28 Q8
Gazli 34 L9
Gbaaka 54 C3
Gbarnga 54 C3
Gdańsk 10 H3
Gdov 8 P7
Gdyel 20 K9
Gdynia 10 H3
Gebel Katherina 50 F2
Gebze 28 M4
Gedaref 50 G5
Gediz 28 K6
Gediz 28 M6
Gedser 12 G2
Geel 14 H3
Geelong 62 H7
Geesthacht 12 F3
Gê'gyai 44 D2
Geidam 54 G2
Geilenkirchen 14 J4
Geilo 8 E6
Geinhausen 12 E6
Geislingen 22 E2
Geita 56 E4
Gejiu 40 C2
Gela 24 J11
Geladī 56 H2
Geldern 14 J3
Geleen 14 H4
Gelibolu 28 J4
Gelibolu Yarimadasi 28 J4
Gelsenkirchen 14 K3
Gembloux 14 G4
Gembu 54 G3
Gemena 56 B3
Gemlik 28 M4
Gemlik Körfezi 28 L4
Gemona del Friuli 22 J4
Genalē Wenz 56 G2
General Acha 78 J6
General Alvear 78 H6
General Pico 78 J6
General Pinedo 78 J4
General Roca 78 H6
General Santos 40 H5
Genève 22 B4
Gengma 40 B2
Genil 20 F7
Genk 14 H4
Genoa = Genova 22 D6
Genova 22 D6
Gent 14 F3
Genteng 42 D4
Genthin 12 H4
Geographe Bay 62 B6
George 58 C6
George 68 T5
George Town, *Aus.* 62 J8
George Town,
Malaysia 42 C1
Georgetown, *Aus.* 62 H3
Georgetown, *Gambia* 54 B2
Georgetown, *Guyana* 76 F2
Georgia 46 D1
Georgia 70 K5
Georgian Bay 70 K2
Gera 12 H6
Geraldine 64 C7
Geraldton, *Aus.* 62 B5
Geraldton, *Can.* 70 J2
Gérardmer 22 B2
Gerede 28 Q4
Gerefsried 22 G3
Gereshk 46 H3
Gérgal 20 H7
Gerik 40 C5
Germany 12 E6
Germencik 28 K7
Germering 22 G2
Germersheim 14 L5
Gernika 20 H1
Gerolzhofen 12 F7
Gērzê 44 D2
Geser 43 D3
Getafe 20 G4
Getxo 20 H1
Geugnon 18 K7
Gevgelija 28 E3
Gewanē 50 H5
Geyik Dağ 28 Q8
Geyve 28 N4
Ghadāmis 52 G2
Ghana 54 D3
Ghanzi 58 C4
Ghardaïa 52 F2
Gharo 46 J5
Gharyān 52 H2
Ghāt 50 B2
Ghazaouet 52 E1
Ghaziabad 44 C3
Ghazipur 44 D3
Ghazn 46 J3
Gheorgheni 26 N3
Gherla 26 L2
Ghizar 44 B1
Ghotāru 44 B3
Giannitsa 28 E4
Giannutri 24 F6
Giarre 24 K11
Gibraleón 20 D7
Gibraltar 20 E8
Gibson Desert 62 D4
Gideån 8 K5
Gien 18 H6
Gießen 12 D6
Gifhorn 12 F4
Gifu 38 K3
Gigha 16 G6
Giglio 24 E6
Giglio Castello 24 E6
Gijón 20 E1
Gila Bend 70 D5
Gilău 26 L3
Gilbert Islands 60 H5
Gilbués 76 H5
Gilching 22 G2
Gilf Kebir Plateau 50 E3
Gilgandra 62 J6
Gilgit 44 B1
Gilimanuk 42 E4
Gillam 68 N5
Gillette 70 E3
Gillingham 14 C3
Gīmbī 56 F2
Gimli 68 M6
Gimol'skoe Ozero 8 R5
Gīnīr 56 G2
Gioia del Colle 24 L8
Gioia Tauro 24 K10
Gioura 28 F5
Girga 50 F2
Girona 20 N3
Gironde 18 E8
Girvan 16 H6
Gisborne 64 G4
Gisenyi 56 D4
Gitega 56 D4
Giurgiu 26 N6
Givet 14 G4
Givors 18 K8
Giyon 56 F2
Gizhiga 36 U4
Gizhiginskaya Guba 36 T4
Giżycko 10 L3
Gjiri i Vlorës 28 B4
Gjirokaster 28 C4
Gjoa Haven 68 M3
Gjøvik 8 F6
Glacier Peak 70 B2
Gladstone 62 K4
Glamoč 26 D5
Glan 12 C7
Glan 43 C1
Glarner Alpen 22 D4
Glasgow, *U.K.* 16 H6
Glasgow, *U.S.* 70 E2
Glauchau 12 H6
Glazov 34 J6
Gleisdorf 22 L3
Glendale 70 D5
Glendambo 62 G6
Glendive 70 F2
Glenmorgan 62 J5
Glennallen 68 B4
Glenn Innes 62 K5
Glenrothes 16 J5
Glina 22 M5
Gliwice 10 H7
Glodeni 26 Q2
Głogów 10 F6
Glomfjord 8 H3
Glomma 8 F5
Glorieuses 48 H7
Gloucester 16 K10
Głowno 10 J6
Głuchołazy 10 G7
Glückstadt 12 E3
Gmünd, *Austria* 22 J4
Gmünd, *Austria* 22 L2
Gmunden 22 J3
Gniezno 10 G5
Gnjilane 28 D2
Gnoien 12 H3
Goalpara 44 F3
Goba 56 F2
Gobabis 58 B4
Gobernador
Gregores 78 G8
Gobi Desert 38 C2
Gobustan 46 E1
Goce Delčev 28 F3
Goch 14 J3
Gochas 58 B4
Godé 56 G2
Godhra 44 B4
Gödöllő 26 G2
Gods Lake 68 N6
Godthåb = Nuuk 68 W4
Goeree 14 F3
Goes 14 F3
Goiânia 76 H7
Goiás 76 G6
Goiás 76 G7
Gökçeada 28 H4
Gökova Körfezi 28 K8
Göksun 46 C2
Golaghat 44 F3
Gölbāf 46 G4
Gölbasi 46 C2
Gol'chikha 34 Q3
Gölcük 28 K5
Goldap 10 M3
Gold Coast 62 K5
Golden Bay 64 D5
Goldsboro 70 L4
Goldsworthy 62 C4
Goleniów 10 D4
Golfe d'Ajaccio 24 C7
Golfe de Gabès 52 H2
Golfe de Hammamet 52 H1
Golfe de Porto 24 C6
Golfe de Sagone 24 C6
Golfe de Saint-Malo 18 C5
Golfe de Tunis 24 E11
Golfe de Valinco 24 C7
Golfe du Lion 18 J10
Golfo de Almería 20 H8
Golfo de Batabanó 72 H4
Golfo de Cádiz 20 C7
Golfo de California 72 B3
Golfo de Chiriquí 72 H7
Golfo de Corcovado 78 F7
Golfo de Cupica 76 B2
Golfo de Fonseca 72 G6
Golfo de Guayaquil 76 A4
Golfo de Honduras 72 G5
Golfo del Darién 76 B2
Golfo dell' Asinara 24 C7
Golfo de los
Mosquitos 76 A2
Golfo de Mazarrón 20 J7
Golfo de
Morrosquillo 76 B1
Golfo de Panamá 72 J7
Golfo de Penas 78 F8
Golfo de San Jorge 78 H8
Golfo de
Tehuantepec 72 E5
Golfo de València 20 L5
Golfo de Venezuela 76 C1
Golfo di Augusta 24 K11
Golfo di Catania 24 K11
Golfo di Gaeta 24 H7
Golfo di Gela 24 J11
Golfo di Genova 24 C4
Golfo di Manfredonia 24 L7
Golfo di Olbia 24 D8
Golfo di Oristano 24 C9
Golfo di Orosei 24 D8
Golfo di Palmas 24 C10
Golfo di Policastro 24 K9
Golfo di Salerno 24 J8
Golfo di
Sant'Eufemia 24 K10
Golfo di Squillace 24 L10
Golfo di Taranto 24 L8
Golfo di Trieste 22 J5
Golfo di Venezia 22 H5
Golfo San Matías 78 J6
Gölhisar 28 M8
Gölmarmara 28 K6
Golyshmanovo 34 M6
Goma 56 D4
Gombe 54 G2
Gombi 54 G2
Gomera 52 B3
Gómez Palacio 70 F6
Gonam 36 M5
Gonbad-e Kavus 46 G2
Gonda 44 D3

Gonder 50 G5
Gondia 44 D4
Gondomar 20 B3
Gönen 28 K4
Gonfreville-Orcher 14 C5
Gongga Shan 38 C5
Gonghe 38 C3
Gongliu 34 Q9
Gongpoquan 38 B2
Gongshan 40 B1
Gonzáles 70 G7
González 70 G7
Goolgowi 62 J6
Goomalling 62 C6
Goondiwindi 62 K5
Göppingen 22 E2
Góra 10 F6
Gora Kamen 34 S4
Gorakhpur 44 D3
Gora Ledyanaya 36 W4
Gora Pobeda 36 R4
Gora Yenashimskiy Polkan 34 S6
Goražde 26 F6
Gorbitsa 36 K6
Gorë 56 F2
Gore 64 B8
Goré 54 H3
Gorgān 46 F2
Gorgona 22 E7
Gorinchem 14 H3
Gorizia 22 J5
Gorki 30 N1
Gorlice 10 L8
Görlitz 10 D6
Gorna Orjakhovica 26 N6
Gornji Milanovac 26 H5
Gorno-Altaysk 34 R7
Gorodets 30 H3
Gorontalo 43 B2
Gory Belukha 34 R8
Gory Ulutau 30 N5
Gorzów Wielkopolski 10 E5
Goslar 12 F5
Gospić 24 K4
Gosport 18 D3
Gossau 22 E3
Gossi 54 D1
Gostivar 28 C3
Gostyń 10 G6
Gostynin 10 J5
Göteborg 8 F8
Gotha 12 F6
Gothèye 54 E2
Gotland 8 K8
Gotō-rettō 38 H4
Gotska Sandön 8 K7
Göttingen 12 E5
Gouda 14 G2
Gough Island 48 B10
Goundam 52 E5
Gouraya 20 M8
Gourcy 54 D2
Gourdon 18 G9
Gournay-en-Bray 14 D5
Governador Valadares 76 J7
Govorovo 36 M3
Gowārān 46 J4
Goya 78 K4
Gozha Co 44 D1
Gozo = Gwardex 24 J12
Graaff-Reinet 58 C6
Grabovica 26 K5
Gračac 22 L6
Gračanica 26 F5
Gradačac 26 F5
Gräfenhainichen 12 H5
Grafton, *Aus.* 62 K5
Grafton, *U.S.* 70 G2
Grajaú 76 H5
Grajewo 10 M4
Gram 12 E1
Gramat 18 G9
Grampian Mountains 16 H5
Granada, *Nicaragua* 72 G6
Granada, *Spain* 20 G7
Granby 70 M2
Gran Canaria 52 B3
Grand Bahama 72 J3
Grand Ballon 18 N6
Grand Bank 68 V7
Grand Canyon 70 D4
Grande, *Bolivia* 76 E7
Grande, *Brazil* 76 J6
Grande Cache 68 H6
Grande Prairie 68 H5
Grand Erg de Bilma 52 H5
Grand Erg Occidental 52 E3
Grand Erg Oriental 52 F3
Grand Falls 68 V7
Grand Forks, *Can.* 70 C2
Grand Forks, *U.S.* 70 G2
Grand Island 70 G3
Grand Junction 70 E4
Grândola 20 B6
Grand Rapids, *Can.* 68 M6
Grand Rapids, *U.S.* 70 J3
Grand Teton 70 D3
Granollers 20 N3
Gran Paradiso 22 C5
Grantham 16 M9
Grants 70 E4
Grants Pass 70 B3
Granville 18 D5
Granville Lake 68 M5
Gräsö 8 K6
Grasse 22 B7
Graulhet 18 G10
Graus 20 L2
Gravelines 14 E3
Gravesend 14 C3
Gravina in Puglia 24 L8
Gray 18 L6
Grays 14 C3
Graz 22 L3
Great Abaco 72 J3
Great Artesian Basin 62 H4
Great Australian Bight 62 E6
Great Bahama Bank 72 J4
Great Barrier Island 64 E3
Great Barrier Reef 62 J2
Great Basin 70 C4
Great Bear Lake 68 G3
Great Dividing Range 62 J4
Greater Antilles 72 J5
Greater Sunda Islands 60 B6
Great Exhibition Bay 64 D2
Great Exuma 70 L7
Great Falls 70 D2
Great Inagua 72 K4
Great Karoo 58 C6
Great Malvern 16 K9
Great Nicobar 44 F7
Great Ouse 16 N9
Great Plains 70 F2
Great Rift Valley 56 E5
Great Salt Lake 70 D3
Great Salt Lake Desert 70 D3
Great Sand Sea 50 D2
Great Sandy Desert 62 D4
Great Slave Lake 66 N3
Great Victoria Desert 62 E5
Great Wall 38 C3
Great Yarmouth 16 P9
Greece 28 D5
Greeley 70 F3
Green 70 E4
Green Bay 70 J3
Greenland 66 G2
Greenland Sea 66 B2
Greenock 16 H6
Green River, *Wyo., U.S.* 70 E3
Green River, *Ut., U.S.* 70 D4
Greensboro 70 L4
Greenvale 62 J3
Green Valley 72 B2
Greenville, *Liberia* 54 C3
Greenville, *Miss., U.S.* 70 H5
Greenville, *N.C., U.S.* 70 L4
Gregory Lake 62 E4
Greifswald 12 J2
Greifswalder Bodden 12 J2
Greiz 12 H6
Grenada 70 J5
Grenada 76 E1
Grenchen 22 C3
Grenoble 18 L8
Greve in Chianti 22 G7
Greven 14 K2
Grevena 28 D4
Grevenbroich 14 J3
Grevesmühlen 12 G3
Greymouth 64 C6
Grey Range 62 H5
Griesheim 12 D7
Grieskirchen 22 J2
Grigoriopol 26 S2
Grimma 12 H5
Grimmen 12 J2
Grimsby 16 M8
Grímsey 8 (1)D1
Grímsstaðir 8 (1)E2
Grímsvötn 8 (1)E2
Grindsted 8 E9
Grobina 10 L1
Gröbming 22 J3
Grodekovo 38 J2
Grodzisk Wielkopolski 10 F5
Grójec 10 K6
Gronau 12 C4
Groningen 12 B3
Groote Eylandt 62 G2
Grootfontein 58 B3
Großenhain 12 J5
Großer Arber 12 J7
Großer Beerberg 12 F6
Grosseto 24 F6
Groß-Gerau 12 D7
Großglockner 22 H3
Groß Mohrdorf 12 H2
Groswater Bay 68 V6
Grottaglie 24 M8
Groupe Actéon 60 N8
Groznyy 46 L2
Grubišno Polje 26 E4
Grudovo 28 K2
Grudziądz 10 H4
Grünau 58 B5
Grünberg 12 D6
Gryazi 30 G4
Gryazovets 30 H3
Gryfice 10 E4
Gryfino 12 K3
Grytøya 8 J2
Grytviken 78 P9
Gstaad 22 C4
Guadalajara, *Mexico* 72 D4
Guadalajara, *Spain* 20 G4
Guadalcanal 60 F7
Guadalope 20 K4
Guadalquivir 20 E7
Guadalupe 72 A3
Guadalupe 72 E3
Guadeloupe 74 E2
Guadiana 20 C7
Guadix 20 G7
Guaíra 78 L3
Guajará Mirim 76 D6
Guajarraã 76 D5
Guam 60 E4
Guanambi 76 J6
Guanare 76 D2
Guane 72 H4
Guangshui 38 E4
Guangyuan 38 D4
Guangzhou 40 E2
Guanipa 76 E2
Guanling 38 D5
Guantánamo 72 J4
Guanyun 38 F4
Guaporé 76 E6
Guaqui 76 D7
Guarabira 76 K5
Guarda 20 C4
Guardo 20 F2
Guasave 70 E6
Guastalla 22 F6
Guatemala 72 F5
Guatemala 72 F6
Guaviare 76 D3
Guayaquil 76 B4
Guayaramerín 76 D6
Guba, *Dem. Rep. of Congo* 56 D6
Guba, *Ethiopia* 50 G5
Guba Buorkhaya 36 N2
Gubakha 30 L3
Guban 56 G2
Gubbi 44 C6
Gubbio 22 H7
Guben 12 K5
Gubin 10 D6
Gudbransdalen 8 E6
Gudvangen 8 D6
Guebwiller 12 C9
Guéckédou 54 B3
Guelma 52 G1
Guérande 18 C6
Guéret 18 B7
Guernsey 18 C4
Guérou 52 C5
Gugē 56 F2
Güh Küh 46 G4
Guiana 72 L7
Guiana Highlands 76 F3
Guider 54 G3
Guiglo 54 C3
Guijuelo 20 E4
Guildford 16 M10
Guilianova 24 H6
Guilin 40 E1
Guillaumes 22 B6
Guillestre 22 B6
Guimarães 20 B3
Guinea 54 B2
Guinea-Bissau 54 A2
Güines 72 H4
Guingamp 18 B5
Güiria 76 E1
Guise 14 F5
Guitiriz 20 C1
Guiyang 38 D5
Gujranwala 44 B2
Gujrat 44 B2
Gulang 38 C3
Gulbarga 44 C5
Gulbene 8 P8
Gulf of Aden 46 E7
Gulf of Alaska 66 R4
Gulf of Aqaba 46 B4
Gulf of Boothia 68 N2
Gulf of Bothnia 8 K6
Gulf of Carpentaria 62 G2
Gulf of Finland 8 M7
Gulf of Gdansk 10 J3
Gulf of Guinea 54 D4
Gulf of Mannar 44 C7
Gulf of Martaban 40 B3
Gulf of Mexico 72 F3
Gulf of Oman 46 G5
Gulf of Riga 8 M8
Gulf of St. Lawrence 68 U7
Gulf of Thailand 40 C4
Gulf of Tongking 40 D3
Gulistan 34 M9
Gülşehir 28 S6
Gulu 56 E3
Gumdag 46 F2
Gumel 54 F2
Gumla 44 D4
Gummersbach 14 K3
Gummi 54 F2
Gümüşhane 46 D1
Guna 44 C4
Guna Terara 50 G5
Gungu 56 B5
Gunnbjørns Fjeld 80 (1)U2
Gunnedah 62 K6
Gunong Kinabalu 42 F1
Guntakal 44 C5
Guntur 44 D5
Gunung Kerinci 42 C3
Gunung Korbu 42 C2
Gunung Kwoka 43 D3
Gunung Leuser 42 B2
Gunung Mekongga 43 B3
Gunung Mulu 42 E2
Gunung Pangrango 42 D4
Gunungsitoli 42 B2
Gunung Togwomeri 43 D3
Günzburg 22 F2
Gunzenhausen 12 F7
Guoyang 38 F4
Gura Humorului 26 N2
Gurk 22 K4
Gurskoye 36 P6
Gürün 46 C2
Gurupi 76 H4
Gusau 54 F2
Gusev 10 M3
Gushgy 46 H2
Gusinoozersk 36 H6
Guspini 24 C9
Güssing 22 M3
Güstrow 10 B4
Gütersloh 12 D5
Gutsuo 44 E3
Guwahati 44 F3
Guyana 76 F2
Guyang 38 E2
Guymon 70 F4
Guyuan 38 D3
Guzar 46 J2
Gvardeysk 10 L3
Gwadar 46 H4
Gwalior 44 C3
Gwanda 58 D4
Gwardex 24 J12
Gwda 10 F4
Gweebarra Bay 16 C7
Gweru 58 D3
Gyangzê 44 E3
Gyaring Hu 38 B4
Gyaros 28 G7
Gyda 34 P3
Gydanskiy Poluostrov 34 P3
Gyirong 44 E3
Gyldenløves Fjord 68 Y4
Gympie 62 K5
Gyomaendrőd 26 H3
Gyöngyös 26 G2
Győr 26 E2
Gypsumville 68 M6
Gytheio 28 E8
Gyula 26 J3
Gyumri 46 D1
Gyzylarbat 46 G2

H

Haapajärvi 8 N5
Haapsalu 8 M7
Haar 22 G2
Haarlem 14 G2
Haast 64 B6
Habahe 34 R8
Habarūt 46 F6
Habaswein 56 F3
Habbān 46 E7
Habirag 38 F2
Habomai-Shoto 36 R8
Haboro 38 L2
Hachijō-jima 38 L4
Hachinohe 38 L2
Hadadong 34 Q9
Haddunmahti Atoll 44 B8
Hadejia 54 F2
Hadejia 54 G2
Haderslev 12 E1
Ḩaḑramaut 46 E6
Hadilik 34 R10
Hadjout 20 N8
Haeju 38 H3
Ḩafar al Bāţin 46 E4
Hafnarfjörður 8 (1)C2
Hagen 14 K3
Hagenow 12 G3
Hägere Hiywet 56 F2
Ha Giang 38 C6
Haguenau 14 K6
Haicheng 38 G2
Haifa = Ḩefa 46 B3
Haikou 40 E3
Hā'il 46 D4
Hailar 36 K7
Hailong 38 H2
Hailuoto 8 N4
Hainan 40 D3
Haines Junction 68 D4
Haining 38 G4
Hai Phong 40 D2
Haiti 72 K5
Haiya 50 G4
Hajdúböszörmény 26 J2
Hajdúhadház 10 L10
Hajdúnánás 10 L10
Hajdúszoboszló 10 L10
Hajipur 44 E3
Hajmah 46 G6
Hajnówka 10 N5
Haka 44 F4
Hakkâri 46 D2
Hakodate 38 L2
Ḩalab 46 C2
Ḩalabān 50 H3
Halaib 50 G3
Halberstadt 12 G5
Halden 8 F7
Haldensleben 12 G4
Halifax 68 U8
Halifax Bay 62 J3
Hall 22 G3
Hall Beach 68 Q3
Halle 14 G4
Hallein 22 J3
Halligen 12 D2
Hall Peninsula 68 T4
Halls Creek 62 E3
Halmahera 43 C2
Halmahera Sea 43 C3
Halmstad 10 B1
Haltern 14 K3
Hamada 38 J4
Hamadān 46 E3
Hamaguir 52 E2
Ḩamāh 46 C2
Hamamatsu 38 K4
Hamar 8 F6
Hamarøy 8 H2
Hambantota 44 D7
Hamburg 12 E3
Hämeenlinna 8 N6
Hameln 12 E4
Hamersley Range 62 C4
Hamhŭng 38 H2
Hami 34 S9
Hamid 50 F3
Hamilton, *Aus.* 62 H7
Hamilton, *Bermuda* 72 M2
Hamilton, *Can.* 70 L3
Hamilton, *N.Z.* 64 E3
Hamilton, *U.S.* 70 K4
Hamina 8 P6
Hamirpur 44 D3
Hamm 12 C5
Hammada du Drâa 52 D3
Hammam Bou Hadjar 20 K9
Hammamet 24 E12
Hammam Lif 52 H1
Hammelburg 12 E6
Hammerfest 8 M1
Hammer Springs 64 D6
Hampden 64 C7
Ḩanalc 50 G2
Hanamaki 38 L3
Hanau 12 D6
Hancheng 38 E3
Handan 38 E3
Handeni 56 F5
Handerslev 8 E9
Handlová 10 H9
Hangayn Nuruu 34 T8
Hangu 38 F3
Hangzhou 38 F4
Hanko 8 M7
Hanna 68 K6
Hannibal 70 H4
Hannover 12 E4
Hanö 10 D2
Hanöbukten 10 D2
Ha Nôi 40 D2
Hanoi = Ha Nôi 40 D2
Han Shui 38 D4
Hanson Bay 64 (1)B1
Hanumangarh 44 B3
Hanzhong 38 D4
Hao 60 M7
Häora 44 E4
Haouza 52 C3
Haparanda 8 N4
Hāpoli 44 F3
Hapur 44 C3
Ḩaraḑ, *Saudi Arabia* 46 E5
Ḩaraḑ, *Yemen* 50 H4
Harare 58 E3
Harbin 38 H1
Harbour Breton 68 V7
Harburg 12 F3
Hardangerfjorden 8 C7
Hardangervidda 8 D6
Hardenberg 14 J2
Harderwijk 14 H2
Hardin 70 E2
Haren 14 K2
Härer 56 G2
Hargeysa 56 G2
Har Hu 38 B3
Haridwar 44 C3
Harihari 64 C6
Hari Rud 46 H3
Hărlău 26 P2
Harlingen, *Netherlands* 14 H1
Harlingen, *U.S.* 70 G6
Harlow 16 N10
Harmanli 28 H3
Harney Basin 70 B3
Härnösand 8 J5
Har Nur 36 K7
Har Nuur 34 S8
Haro 20 H2
Harricanaw 68 R6
Harrisburg 70 L3
Harrogate 16 L8
Hârşova 26 Q5
Harstad 8 J2
Hartberg 22 L3
Hartford 70 M3
Hartland Point 16 H10
Hartlepool 16 L7
Har Us Nuur 34 S8
Harwich 14 D3
Harz 12 F5
Haselünne 12 C4
Hāsik 46 G6
Haskovo 28 H3
Haslemere 14 B3
Hassan 44 C6
Hasselfelde 12 F5
Hasselt 14 H4
Haßfurt 12 F6
Hassi Bel Guebbour 52 G3
Hassi Messaoud 52 G2
Hässleholm 8 G8
Hastings, *N.Z.* 64 F4
Hastings, *U.K.* 14 C4
Hastings, *Nebr., U.S.* 70 G3
Haţeg 26 K4
Hatgal 36 G6
Ha Tinh 40 D3
Hattiesburg 70 J5
Hatvan 26 G2
Hat Yai 40 C5
Haud 50 H6
Haud Ogadēn 56 G2/H2
Haugesund 8 C7
Hauraki Gulf 64 E3
Haut Atlas 52 D2
Hauts Plateaux 52 E2
Havana = La Habana 72 H4
Havant 16 M11
Havel 10 C5
Havelock 64 D5
Havelock North 64 F4
Havenby 12 D1
Haverfordwest 16 H10
Havlíčkův Brod 10 E8
Havre 70 E2
Havre-St-Pierre 68 U6
Havrylivtsi 26 P1
Hawaii 60 L3
Hawaii 60 L4
Hawaiian Islands 60 J3
Hawera 64 E4
Hawick 16 K6
Hawke Bay 64 F4
Hawker 62 G6
Hay 62 H6
Hay 68 H5
Hayange 14 J5
Hayrabolu 28 K3
Hay River 68 H4
Hazārībāg 44 E4
Hazebrouck 14 E4
Hazelton 68 F5
Head of Bight 62 F6
Hearst 70 K2
Hebi 38 E3
Hebron 68 U5
Hecate Strait 68 E6
Hechi 40 D2
Hechingen 22 D2
Hede 8 G5
Heerenveen 14 H2
Heerlen 14 J4
Ḩefa 46 B3
Hefei 38 F4
Hegang 38 J1
Hegyfalu 22 M3
Heide 12 E2
Heidelberg 12 D7
Heidenheim 22 F2
Heilbad Heiligenstadt 12 F5
Heilbronn 12 E7
Heiligenhafen 12 F2
Heimaey 8 (1)C3
Heinola 8 N6
Hejing 34 R9
Hekla 8 (1)D3
Helagsfjället 8 G5
Helena 70 D2
Helen Reef 43 D2
Helensville 64 E3
Helgea 10 D1
Helgoland 12 C2
Helgoländer Bucht 12 D2
Hellín 20 J6
Helmand 46 H3
Helmond 14 H3
Helmsdale 16 J3
Helmstedt 12 G4
Helodrano Antongila 58 H3
Helsingborg 8 G8
Helsinge 10 B1
Helsingør 8 G8
Helsinki 8 N6
Helston 16 G11
Helwan 50 F2
Hemel Hempstead 16 M10
Hendek 28 N4
Henderson 70 C4
Henderson Island 60 P8
Hengelo 14 J2
Hengyang 38 E5
Henichesk 30 F5
Hénin-Beaumont 14 E4
Hennebont 18 B6
Hennigsdorf 12 J4
Henzada 40 B3
Heppenheim 12 D7
Hepu 40 D2
Herald Cays 62 J3
Herāt 46 H3
Héraðsflói 8 (1)F2
Herbert 64 C7
Herborn 12 D6
Herceg-Novi 26 F7
Hereford, *U.K.* 16 K9
Hereford, *U.S.* 72 D2
Herekino 64 D2
Herentals 14 G3
Herford 12 D4
Herisau 22 E3
Herlen Gol 38 E1
Hermagor 22 J4
Herma Ness 16 M1
Hermosillo 70 D6
Hernád 10 L9
Herne 12 C5
Herne Bay 14 D3
Herning 8 E8
Hérouville-St-Clair 14 B5
Herrenberg 22 D2
Hersbruck 12 G7
Herstal 14 H4
Hertlay 14 E6
Hervey Bay 62 K5
Herzberg 12 F5
Hesdin 14 E4
Heshan 40 D2
Hesselø 10 A1
Hessisch-Lichtenau 12 E5
Hettstedt Lutherstadt 12 G5
Heves 10 K10
He Xian 40 E2
Hexigten Qi 38 F2
Heze 38 F3
Hezuozhen 38 C3
Hibbing 70 H2
Hidalgo del Parral 72 C3
Hiddensee 12 H2
Hierro 52 B3
Higashi-suidō 38 J3
High Wycombe 14 B3
Hiiumaa 8 M7
Hikurangi 64 E2
Hikurangi 64 G3
Hikutaia 64 E3
Hildburghausen 12 F6
Hildesheim 12 E4
Hillsboro 70 G5
Hillswick 16 L1
Hilton Head Island 70 K5
Hilversum 14 H2
Himalayas 32 L6
Himarë 28 B4
Himatnagar 44 B4
Himora 50 G5
Ḩimş 46 C3
Hînceşti 26 R3
Hindu Kush 44 A1
Hindupur 44 C6
Hingoli 44 C5
Hinnøya 8 H2
Hiroo 38 L2
Hirosaki 38 L2
Hiroshima 38 J4
Hirschaid 12 F7
Hirson 14 G5
Hirtshals 8 E8
Hisar 44 C3
Hischberg 12 G6
Hisdal 8 C6
Hispaniola 74 D2
Hitra 8 D5
Hiva Oa 60 M6
Hjälmaren 8 H7

Japan 38 K4
Japan Trench 60 E2
Japurá 76 D4
Jaramillo 78 H8
Jardim 78 K3
Jarosław 10 M7
Järpen 8 G5
Jarud Qi 38 G2
Järvenpää 8 N6
Jarvis 60 K6
Jasel'da 8 N10
Jäsk 46 G4
Jason Islands 78 J9
Jastrebarsko 22 L5
Jászberény 26 G2
Jataí 76 G7
Jatapu 76 F4
Jaunpur 44 D3
Java = Jawa 42 E4
Javarthushuu 36 J7
Java Sea 42 E4
Javoriv 10 N8
Jawa 42 E4
Jawhar 56 H3
Jayapura 43 F3
Jaza'ir Farasān 50 H4
Jazīrat Būbīyān 46 E4
Jbel Ayachi 52 E2
Jbel Bou Naceur 52 E2
Jbel Toubkal 52 D2
Jebba 54 E3
Jebel Gimbala 50 D5
Jebel Uweinat 50 E3
Jedburgh 16 K6
Jedda = Jiddah 46 C5
Jedeida 24 D12
Jędrzejów 10 K7
Jefferson City 70 H4
Jega 54 E2
Jēkabpils 8 N8
Jelgava 8 M8
Jemaja 42 D2
Jena 12 G6
Jendouba 52 G1
Jequié 76 J6
Jequitinhonha 76 J7
Jerada 52 E2
Jeremoabo 76 K6
Jerez de la Frontera 20 D8
Jerez de los
Caballeros 20 D6
Jericho 62 J4
Jerramungup 62 C6
Jersey 18 C4
Jerusalem =
Yerushalayim 46 C3
Jesenice 26 B3
Jeseník 10 G7
Jesi 22 J7
Jessore 44 E4
Jesup 70 K5
Jeumont 14 G4
Jever 12 C3
Jeypore 44 D5
Jezioro 10 D4
Jezioro Gardno 8 J9
Jezioro Jeziorsko 10 H6
Jezioro Łebsko 10 F3
Jezioro Śniardwy 10 L4
Jezioro Wigry 10 N2
Jhang Maghiana 44 B2
Jhansi 44 C3
Jharsuguda 44 D4
Jhelum 44 B2
Jialing Jiang 38 D4
Jiamusi 38 J1
Ji'an 38 E5
Jiangle 38 F5
Jiangling 38 E4
Jiangmen 38 E6
Jiangyou 38 C4
Jianyang 38 F5
Jiaonan 38 F3
Jiaozou 38 E3
Jiaxing 38 G4
Jiayuguan 38 B3
Jibou 26 L2
Jičín 10 E7
Jiddah 46 C5
Jiesjavrre 8 N2
Jiexiu 38 E3
Jihlava 10 E8
Jijia 26 Q2
Jijiga 56 G2
Jilib 56 G3
Jilin 38 H2
Jima 56 F2
Jimbolia 26 H4
Jiménez 70 F6
Jimsar 34 R9
Jinan 38 F3
Jinchang 38 C3
Jincheng 38 E3
Jindřichův Hradec 10 E8
Jingdezhen 38 F5
Jinggu 38 C6
Jinghe 34 Q9
Jinghong 38 C6
Jingmen 38 E4
Jingning 38 D3
Jingxi 38 D6
Jingyuan 38 C3
Jinhua 38 F5
Jining, *China* 38 E2
Jining, *China* 38 F3
Jinja 56 E3
Jinka 56 F2
Jinsha 38 C5
Jinshi 38 E5
Jinta 38 B2
Jinxi 38 G2
Jinzhou 38 G2
Jirgatol 46 K2
Jirin Gol 38 F2
Jirkov 12 J6
Jīroft 46 G4
Jirriiban 56 H2
Jishou 38 D5
Jiu 26 L4
Jiujiang 38 F5
Jiwani 46 H4
Jixi 38 J1
Jīzān 50 H4
Jizera 10 D7
J. J. Castelli 76 D4
Joal-Fadiout 52 B6
João Pessoa 76 L5
Jódar 20 G7
Jodhpur 44 B3
Joensuu 30 E2
Jōetsu 38 K3
Jõgeva 8 P7
Johannesburg 58 D5
John o' Groats 16 J3
Johnson's Crossing 68 E4
Johnston Island 60 J4
Johor Bahru 42 C2
Joigny 18 J5
Joinville, *Brazil* 78 M4
Joinville, *France* 18 L5
Jokkmokk 8 K3
Jökulsá-á Fjöllum 8 (1)E1
Jolfa 46 E2
Joliet 70 J3
Jolo 43 B1
Jolo 43 B1
Jonava 10 P2
Jonesboro 70 H4
Jones Sound 68 P1
Jonglei Canal 56 E2
Jongunjärvi 8 P4
Joniškis 10 N1
Jönköping 8 H8
Jonquière 70 M2
Joplin 70 H4
Jordan 46 C3
Jorhat 44 F3
Jörn 8 L4
Jos 54 F3
José de San Martin 78 G7
Joseph Bonaparte
Gulf 62 E2
Joure 14 H2
Juan de Nova 58 G3
Juàzeiro 76 J5
Juàzeiro do Norte 76 K5
Juba 56 E3
Jubba 56 G3
Júcar 20 J5
Juchitán 72 F5
Judenburg 22 K3
Juhre 36 L8
Juist 12 B3
Juiz de Fora 78 N3
Juli 76 C7
Juliaca 76 C7
Juliana Top 76 F3
Jülich 14 J4
Jullouville 14 A6
Jumilla 20 J6
Jumla 44 D3
Junagadh 44 B4
Junction City 70 G4
Jundah 62 H4
Juneau 68 E5
Jungfrau 22 C4
Junggar Pendi 34 R8
Junsele 8 J5
Jun Xian 38 E4
Jūra 10 M2
Jura 16 G5
Jura 22 B4
Jurbarkas 10 M2
Jurhe 38 G2
Jurilovca 26 R5
Jūrmala 8 M8
Jūrmala 30 D3
Juruá 76 D4
Juruena 76 F6
Juruena 76 F6
Justo Daract 78 H5
Jutaí 76 D5
Jüterbog 12 J5
Juwain 46 H3
Ju Xian 38 F3
Jüymand 46 G3
Juzur al Halaniyat 46 G6
Jylland 8 E8
Jyväskylä 30 E2
Jyväskylä 8 N5

K

K2 44 C1
Kaakhka 46 G2
Kaamanen 8 P2
Kaarta 52 C6
Kabaena 43 B4
Kabakly 46 H2
Kabala 54 B3
Kabale 56 E4
Kabalo 56 D5
Kåbdalis 8 L3
Kabompo 58 C2
Kabongo 56 D5
Kabugao 40 G3
Kābul 46 J3
Kabwe 58 D2
Kachikattsy 36 M4
Kachug 36 H6
Kadama 44 B6
Kadaň 10 C7
Kadınhanı 28 Q6
Kadoka 70 F3
Kadoma 58 D3
Kadugli 50 E5
Kaduna 54 F2
Kadzherom 30 L2
Kaédi 52 C5
Kaeo 64 D2
Kaesŏng 38 H3
Kafanchan 54 F3
Kaffrine 54 A2
Kafiau 43 C3
Kåfjord 8 N1
Kafr el Sheikh 50 F1
Kafue 58 D3
Kaga Bandoro 56 B2
Kagoshima 38 J4
Kahemba 56 B5
Kahnūj 46 G4
Kahraman Maraş 46 C2
Kahurangi Point 64 C5
Kaiama 54 E3
Kai Besar 43 D4
Kaifeng 38 E4
Kaihu 64 D2
Kaihua 38 F5
Kai Kecil 43 D4
Kaikohe 64 D2
Kaikoura 64 D6
Kaili 38 D5
Kaimana 43 D3
Käina 8 M7
Kainji Reservoir 54 E2
Kaipara Harbour 64 D3
Kairouan 52 H1
Kaiserslautern 12 C7
Kaišiadorys 10 P3
Kaitaia 64 D2
Kaiwatu 43 C4
Kaiyuan 40 C2
Kajaani 8 P4
Kakamega 56 E3
Kakata 54 B3
Kakhovs'ke
Vodoskhovyshche 30 F5
Kākināda 44 D5
Kalabagh 44 B2
Kalabahi 43 B4
Kalabakan 42 F2
Kalach 30 H4
Kalachinsk 30 P3
Kalach-na-Donu 30 H5
Kalahari Desert 58 C4
Kalajoki 8 M4
Kalakan 36 K5
Kalam 44 B1
Kalamata 28 E7
Kalamazoo 70 J3
Kalampaka 28 D5
Kalana 54 C2
Kalaotoa 43 B4
Kalavryta 28 E6
Kalbarri 62 B5
Kale 28 L7
Kaledupa 43 B4
Kalemie 56 D5
Kalemyo 44 F4
Kalevala 8 R4
Kalewa 44 F4
Kalgoorlie 62 D6
Kalianda 42 D4
Kalibo 40 G4
Kalima 56 D4
Kalimantan 42 E2
Kaliningrad 10 K3
Kaliningradskiy Zaliv 10 J3
Kalispell 70 D2
Kalisz 10 H6
Kalixälven 8 M3
Kalkan 28 M8
Kalkaring 62 F3
Kallavesi 8 P5
Kallsjön 8 G5
Kalmar 8 J8
Kalmykiya 30 J5
Kalmykovo 30 K5
Kalocsa 26 F3
Kalol 44 B4
Kalpakio 28 C5
Kalpeni 44 B6
Kaltenkirchen 12 E3
Kaluga 30 G4
Kalyan 44 B5
Kalymnos 28 J7
Kalymnos 28 J8
Kama 6 K1
Kama 56 D4
Kamaishi 38 L3
Kaman 28 R5
Kamande 56 D4
Kamango 34 U6
Kamares 28 G8
Kambarka 30 K3
Kamchatka 36 U6
Kamchatskiy Zaliv 36 U5
Kamenica 28 E2
Kamenka, *Russia* 30 H1
Kamenka, *Russia* 30 H4
Kamen'-na-Obi 34 Q7
Kamensk-
Shakhtinskiy 30 H5
Kamensk-Ural'skiy 30 M3
Kamenz 10 D6
Kamet 44 C2
Kamina 56 C5
Kamituga 56 D4
Kamloops 68 G6
Kampala 56 E3
Kampen 14 H2
Kâmpóng Cham 40 D4
Kâmpóng Chhnăng 40 C4
Kâmpot 40 C4
Kamsuuma 56 G3
Kam"yanets'-
Podil's'kyy 30 E5
Kamyanyets 8 M10
Kamyshin 30 J4
Kamyzyak 30 J5
Kan 50 F6
Kananga 56 C5
Kanazawa 38 K3
Kanbalu 44 G4
Kanchipuram 44 C6
Kandahār 46 J3
Kandalaksha 8 S3
Kandalakshskiy Zaliv 30 F1
Kandi 54 E2
Kandira 28 N3
Kandy 44 D7
Kang 58 C4
Kangaatsiaq 68 W3
Kangān 46 F4
Kangar 42 C1
Kangaroo Island 62 G7
Kangchenjunga 44 E3
Kangding 38 C4
Kangeq 68 Y4
Kangerluarsoruseq 68 W4
Kangerlussuatsiaq 68 Y4
Kangersuatsiaq 68 W2
Kangetet 56 F3
Kangiqsualujjuaq 68 T5
Kangiqsujuaq 68 S4
Kangirsuk 68 S4
Kangmar 44 E3
Kangnŭng 38 H3
Kango 54 G4
Kangping 38 G2
Kaniama 56 C5
Kanin Nos 34 G4
Kanji Reservoir 48 D4
Kanjiža 26 H3
Kankaanpää 8 M6
Kankan 54 C2
Kankossa 52 C5
Kano 54 F2
Kanoya 38 J4
Kanpur 44 D3
Kansas 70 G4
Kansas City 70 H4
Kansk 34 T6
Kanta 56 F2
Kantchari 54 E2
Kantemirovka 30 G5
Kanye 58 C4
Kaohsiung 38 G6
Kaolack 52 B6
Kaoma 58 C2
Kapanga 56 C5
Kap Arkona 10 C3
Kapchagay 34 P9
Kap Cort Adelaer =
Kangeq 68 Y4
Kap Farvel =
Nunap Isua 68 Y5
Kapfenberg 22 L3
Kapidağı Yarimadası 28 K4
Kapiri Mposhi 58 D2
Kapit 42 E2
Kapiti Island 64 E5
Kaplice 22 K2
Kapoeta 56 E3
Kaposvár 26 E3
Kappel 12 C6
Kappeln 12 E2
Kappl 22 F3
Kapsan 38 H2
Kapuskasing 70 K2
Kapuvár 26 E2
Kara 34 M4
Kara, *Russia* 34 M4
Kara, *Togo* 54 E3
Kara Ada 28 K8
Kara-Balta 34 N9
Karabekaul 46 H2
Kara-Bogaz-Gol 46 F1
Karabutak 30 M5
Karacabey 28 L4
Karacaköy 28 L3
Karacal Tepe 28 Q8
Karachayevo-
Cherkesiya 30 H6
Karachi 46 J5
Karaganda 34 N8
Karaginskiy Zaliv 36 V5
Karaj 46 F2
Kara-Kala 46 G2
Karakalpakiya 34 K9
Karakol 34 P9
Karakoram 32 L6
Karaksar 36 K6
Kara-Kul' 34 N9
Karam 36 H5
Karaman 28 R7
Karamay 34 R8
Karamea 64 D5
Karamea Bight 64 C5
Karamürsel 28 M4
Karaoy 34 N8
Karapınar 28 R7
Kara-Say 34 P9
Karasburg 58 B5
Kara Sea = Karskoye
More 34 L3
Karasu 28 N3
Karasuk 34 P7
Karasuk 34 P7
Karatal 34 P8
Karatobe 30 K5
Karaton 30 K5
Karazhal 30 P5
Karbalā' 46 D3
Karcag 26 H2
Karditsa 28 D5
Kärdla 8 M7
Kărdžali 28 H3
Kareliya 8 R4
Karepino 30 L2
Karesuando 8 M2
Kargasok 34 Q6
Kargat 34 P6
Kargil 44 C2
Kargopol' 30 G2
Kariba 58 D3
Kariba Dam 58 D3
Karibib 58 B4
Karimata 42 D3
Karimnagar 44 C5
Karkaralinsk 34 P8
Karkinits'ka Zatoka 30 F5
Karlik Shan 38 A2
Karlovac 26 C4
Karlovasi 28 J7
Karlovo 28 G2
Karlovy Vary 12 H6
Karlshamn 10 D1
Karlskoga 8 H7
Karlskrona 8 H8
Karlsruhe 12 D8
Karlstad 8 G7
Karlstadt 12 E7
Karmala 44 C5
Karmøy 8 C7
Karnafuli Reservoir 44 F4
Karnal 44 C3
Karnische Alpen 22 H4
Karnobat 28 J2
Karodi 46 J4
Karonga 56 E5
Karpathos 28 K9
Karpathos 28 K9
Karpenisi 28 D6
Karpogory 30 H2
Karrabük 28 Q3
Karratha 62 C4
Kars 46 D1
Karsakpay 30 N5
Kärsava 8 P8
Karshi 46 J2
Karskoye More 34 L3
Karslyaka 28 K6
Karstula 8 N5
Kartal 28 M4
Kartaly 30 M4
Kartayel' 30 K2
Kartuzy 10 H3
Karufa 43 D3
Karumba 62 H3
Karur 44 C6
Karvina 10 H8
Karwar 44 B6
Karystos 28 G6
Kasai 56 B4
Kasaji 58 C2
Kasama 58 E2
Kasansay 34 N9
Kasba Lake 68 L4
Kasempa 58 D2
Kasenga 58 D2
Kāshān 46 F3
Kashi 46 L2
Kashima 38 L3
Kāshmar 46 G2
Kashmor 46 J4
Kasimov 30 H4
Kasli 30 M3
Kasongo 56 D4
Kasos 28 K9
Kaspiysk 46 E1
Kassala 50 G4
Kassandreia 28 F4
Kassel 12 E5
Kasserine 52 G1
Kastamonu 28 R3
Kastelli 28 F9
Kastoria 28 D4
Kasulu 56 E4
Kasur 44 B2
Kata 36 G5
Katchall 44 F7
Katerini 28 E4
Katete 58 E2
Katha 44 G4
Katherine 62 F2
Kathiawar 46 K5
Kathmandu 44 E3
Kati 54 C2
Katihar 44 E3
Katiola 54 C3
Kato Nevrokopi 28 F3
Katonga 56 E3
Katoomba 62 K6
Katowice 10 J7
Katrineholm 8 J7
Katsina 54 F2
Katsina-Ala 54 F3
Kattakurgan 46 J2
Kattavia 28 K9
Kattegat 8 F8
Katun' 34 R7
Katwijkaan Zee 14 G2
Kauai 60 L3
Kaufbeuren 22 F3
Kauhajoki 8 M5
Kaunas 10 N3
Kauno 10 P3
Kaunus 6 G2
Kaura Namoda 54 F2
Kavadarci 28 D3
Kavajë 28 B3
Kavala 28 G4
Kavali 44 C5
Kavaratti 44 B6
Kavarna 26 R6
Kawakawa 64 E2
Kawambwa 56 D5
Kawau Island 64 E3
Kaweka 64 F4
Kawhia 64 E4
Kawkareik 40 B3
Kawthaung 40 B4
Kaya 54 D2
Kayak 34 U3
Kayes 54 B2
Kaymaz 28 P5
Kaynar 34 P8
Kayseri 46 C2
Kayyerkan 34 R4
Kazachinskoye 36 E5
Kazach'ye 36 P2
Kazakdar'ya 34 K9
Kazakhstan 34 L8
Kazan 68 M4
Kazan' 30 J3
Kazanlăk 28 H2
Kazan-rettō 60 E3
Kāzerūn 46 F4
Kazincbarcika 26 H1
Kazungula 58 D3
Kazymskiy Mys 34 M5
Kea 28 G7
Kea 28 G7
Kearney 70 G3
Kébémèr 52 B5
Kebkabiya 50 D5
Kebnekaise 8 K3
K'ebrī Dehar 56 G2
K'ech'a Terara 56 F2
Keçiborlu 28 N7
Kecskemet 26 G3
Kėdainiai 10 N2
Kediri 42 E4
Kédougou 54 B2
Kędzierzyn-Koźle 10 H7
Keele 68 F4
Keetmanshoop 58 B5
Kefallonia 28 C6
Kefamenanu 43 B4
Keflavík 8 (1)B2
Kegen' 34 P9
Keg River 68 H5
Keheili 50 F4
Kehl 22 C2
Keila 8 N7
Keitele 8 N5
Kekerengu 64 D5
Kékes 26 H2
Kelai Thiladhunmathee
Atoll 44 B7
Kelheim 22 G2
Kelibia 24 F12
Kells 16 F8
Kelmë 10 M2
Kélo 54 H3
Kelowna 68 H7
Keluang 42 C2
Kem' 30 F2
Kemalpaşa 28 K6
Kemasik 42 C2
Kemer, *Turkey* 28 M8
Kemer, *Turkey* 28 N8
Kemerovo 34 R6
Kemi 8 N4
Kemijärvi 8 P3
Kemijärvi 8 P3
Kemijoki 8 P3
Kemmuna 24 J12
Kemnath 12 G7
Kempten 22 F3
Kendal 16 K7
Kendari 43 B3
Kendawangan 42 E3
Kendégué 54 H2
Kendujhargarh 44 E4
Kenema 54 B3
Keneurgench 46 G1
Kenge 56 B4
Kengtung 40 B2
Kenhardt 58 C5
Kénitra 52 D2
Kenmare 16 C10
Kennewick 70 C2
Keno Hill 68 D4
Kenora 70 H2
Kentau 34 M9
Kentucky 70 J4
Kenya 48 G5
Keokuk 70 H3
Kępno 10 H6
Kepulauan Anambas 42 D2
Kepulauan Aru 43 E4
Kepulauan Ayu 43 D2
Kepulauan
Balabalangan 42 F3
Kepulauan Banggai 43 B3
Kepulauan Barat
Daya 43 C4
Kepulauan Batu 42 B3
Kepulauan Bonerate 43 A4
Kepulauan Kai 43 D4
Kepulauan Kangean 42 F4
Kepulauan
Karimunjawa 42 D4
Kepulauan
Karkaralong 43 B2
Kepulauan Laut Kecil 42 F3
Kepulauan Leti 43 C4
Kepulauan Lingga 42 C2
Kepulauan Lucipara 43 C4
Kepulauan Mentawai 42 B3
Kepulauan Nanusa 43 C2
Kepulauan Natuna 42 D2
Kepulauan Riau 42 C2
Kepulauan Sabalana 42 F4
Kepulauan Sangir 43 C2
Kepulauan Solor 43 B4
Kepulauan Sula 43 B3
Kepulauan Talaud 43 C2
Kepulauan Tanimbar 43 D4
Kepulauan Tengah 42 F4
Kepulauan Togian 43 B3
Kepulauan
Tukangbesi 43 B4
Kepulauan Watubela 43 D3
Kerch 30 G5
Kerchevskiy 30 L3
Kerempe Burnu 28 R2
Keren 50 G4
Kericho 56 F4
Keri Keri 64 D2
Kerio 56 F3
Kerki 46 J2
Kerkrade 14 J4
Kerkyra 28 B5
Kerkyra 28 B5
Kerma 50 F4
Kermadec Islands 60 H8
Kermadec Trench 60 J9
Kermān 46 G3
Kermānshāh 46 E3
Keros 28 H8
Kerpen 14 J4
Kerrville 70 G6
Kerulen 36 J7
Keryneia 28 R9
Keşan 28 J4
Keşiş Dağları 46 C2
Keszthely 26 E3

Keta 54 E3
Ketapang 42 D3
Ketchikan 68 E5
Kētou 54 E3
Kętrzyn 10 L3
Kettering 16 M9
Kettle Falls 70 C2
Keweenaw Peninsula 70 J2
Key Largo 70 K6
Key West 70 K7
Kezhma 36 G5
Kežmarok 10 K8
Khabarovsk 36 P7
Khairwāra 44 B4
Khakasiya 34 R7
Khalîg el Suweis 50 F2
Khalīj Surt 50 C1
Khalūf 46 G5
Khambhat 44 B4
Khamis Mushay 46 D6
Khamis Mushayţ 50 H4
Khamkkeut 40 C3
Khampa 36 L4
Khamrà 36 J4
Khandagayty 34 S7
Khandwa 44 C4
Khanewal 44 B2
Khannya 34 X4
Khanpur 44 B3
Khantau 34 N9
Khantayka 36 D3
Khanty-Mansiysk 30 N2
Khapalu 44 C1
Kharabali 30 J5
Kharagpur 44 E4
Kharampur 36 B4
Kharan 46 J4
Khargon 44 C4
Kharkiv 30 G5
Kharlu 8 R6
Kharnmam 44 D5
Kharovsk 30 H3
Khartoum = El Khartum 50 F4
Khāsh 46 H4
Khashgort 30 N1
Khashm el Girba 50 G4
Khatanga 36 G2
Khatyrka 36 X4
Khavda 46 J5
Khaydarkan 46 K2
Khayelitsha 58 B6
Khemis Miliana 52 F1
Khemisset 52 D2
Khenchela 52 G1
Kherson 30 F5
Kheta 34 T3
Kheta 34 T3
Kheygiyakha 30 P2
Khilok 36 J6
Khmel'nyts'kyy 30 E5
Kholmsk 36 Q7
Khonj 46 F4
Khon Kaen 40 C3
Khonuu 36 Q3
Khoper 30 H4
Khor 36 P7
Khor 36 P7
Khoreyver 30 L1
Khorinsk 36 H6
Khorramābād 46 E3
Khorramshahr 46 E3
Khorugh 46 K2
Khoseda Khard 30 L1
Khouribga 52 D2
Khrebet Cherskogo 36 P3
Khrebet Dzhagdy 36 N6
Khrebet Dzhugdzhur 36 N5
Khrebet Khamar Daban 36 G6
Khrebet Kolymskiy 32 U3
Khrebet Kopet Dag 46 G2
Khrebet Suntar Khayata 36 P4
Khrebet Tarbagatay 34 Q8
Khroma 36 Q2
Khudoseya 36 C3
Khudzhakh 36 R4
Khujand 46 J1
Khulna 44 E4
Khushab 44 B2
Khust 26 L1
Khuwei 50 E5
Khuzdar 46 J4
Khvoy 46 E2
Khyber Pass 46 K3
Kibaya 56 F4
Kibombo 56 D4
Kibondo 56 E4
Kibre Mengist 56 F2
Kičevo 28 C3
Kichmengskiy Gorodok 30 J3
Kicking Horse Pass 68 H6
Kidal 52 F5
Kidderminster 16 K9
Kidira 54 B2
Kiel 12 F2
Kielce 10 K7
Kieler Bucht 12 F2
Kiev = Kyyiv 30 F4
Kiffa 52 C5
Kigali 56 E4
Kigoma 56 D4
Kihnu 8 M7
Kıkıköy 28 L3
Kikinda 26 H4
Kikori 43 F4
Kikwit 56 B5
Kilchu 38 H2
Kilifi 56 F4
Kilindoni 56 F5
Kilingi-Nõmme 8 N7
Kiliya 26 S4
Kilkenny 16 E9
Kilkis 28 E4
Killarney 16 C9
Kilmarnock 16 H6
Kil'mez 30 K3
Kilosa 56 F5
Kilrush 16 C9
Kilttan 44 B6
Kilwa 56 D5
Kilwa Masoko 56 F5
Kimberley 58 C5
Kimberley Plateau 62 E3
Kimch'aek 38 H2
Kimolos 28 G8
Kimongo 54 G5
Kimry 30 G3
Kinango 56 F4
Kinda 56 C5
Kindia 54 B2
Kindu 56 D4
Kineshma 30 H3
King George Islands 68 R5
Kingisepp 8 Q7
King Island, *Aus.* 62 H7
King Island, *Can.* 36 AA3
Kingman 70 D4
Kingri 46 J3
Kingscote 62 G7
King's Lynn 16 N9
King Sound 62 D3
Kings Peak 70 D3
Kingsport 70 K4
Kingston, *Can.* 70 L3
Kingston, *Jamaica* 72 J5
Kingston-upon-Hull 16 M8
Kingston upon Thames 14 B3
Kingstown 76 E1
Kingsville 70 G6
Kingville 72 E3
King William Island 68 M3
King William's Town 58 D6
Kinik 28 K5
Kinna 8 G8
Kinsale 16 D10
Kinshasa 56 B4
Kintampo 54 D3
Kintyre 16 G6
Kinyeti 56 E3
Kinzig 12 E6
Kipini 56 G4
Kirchheim 22 E2
Kirchheimbolanden 14 L5
Kirenga 36 H5
Kirensk 36 H5
Kiribati 60 J6
Kırıkkale 28 R5
Kirillov 30 G3
Kirinyaga 56 F4
Kirishi 30 F3
Kiritimati 60 L5
Kirkağaç 28 K5
Kirk Bulāg Dāgh 46 E2
Kirkcaldy 16 J5
Kirkcudbright 16 H7
Kirkjubæjarklaustur 8 (1)E3
Kirkland Lake 70 K2
Kırklareli 28 K3
Kirkūk 46 D2
Kirkwall 16 K3
Kirov, *Russia* 30 F4
Kirov, *Russia* 30 J3
Kirovo-Chepetsk 30 K3
Kirovohrad 30 F5
Kirriemuir 16 K5
Kirs 30 K3
Kirsanov 30 H4
Kırşehir 28 S5
Kiruna 8 L3
Kisangani 56 D3
Kisbér 26 E2
Kiselevsk 34 R7
Kishanganj 44 E3
Kishangarh, *India* 44 B3
Kishangarh, *India* 44 B3
Kishi 54 E3
Kishtwar 44 C2
Kisii 56 E4
Kiskőrös 26 G3
Kiskunfélegyháza 26 G3
Kiskunhalas 26 G3
Kiskunmajsa 26 G3
Kislovodsk 46 D1
Kismaayo 56 G4
Kissidougou 54 B3
Kisumu 56 E4
Kisvárda 26 K1
Kita 54 C2
Kita-Kyūshū 38 H4
Kita-Kyūshū 38 J4
Kitami 38 L2
Kitchener 70 K3
Kitgum 56 E3
Kitimat 68 F6
Kittilä 8 N3
Kitunda 56 E5
Kitwe 58 D2
Kitzingen 12 F7
Kiuruvesi 8 P5
Kivijärvi 8 N5
Kivik 10 D2
Kiya 36 D5
Kıyıköy 28 L3
Kizel 30 L3
Kizilalan 28 R8
Kızılcahamam 28 Q4
Kızılırmak 28 R4
Kızılkaya 28 N7
Kizil'skoye 30 L4
Kızıltepe 46 D2
Kizyl-Atrek 34 J10
Kjustendil 28 E2
Kladanj 26 F5
Kladno 10 D7
Klagenfurt 22 K4
Klaipėda 8 L9
Klamath 70 B3
Klamath Falls 70 B3
Klarälven 8 G6
Klatovy 12 J7
Klaus 22 K3
Klerksdorp 58 D5
Kleve 12 B5
Klin 30 G3
Klingenthal 12 H6
Klínovec 12 H6
Klintsy 30 F4
Ključ 22 M6
Kłobuck 10 H7
Kłodzko 10 F7
Kløfta 8 F6
Klosterneuburg 22 M2
Klosters 22 E4
Kluane 68 D4
Kluane Lake 68 D4
Kluczbork 10 H7
Klyuchevskaya Sopka 36 U5
Klyuchi 36 U5
Kneža 26 M6
Knin 26 D5
Knittelfeld 26 B2
Knjaževac 26 K6
Knokke-Heist 14 F3
Knoxville 70 K4
Knysna 58 C6
Koba 42 D3
Kōbe 38 K4
Kobe 43 C2
København 8 G9
Kobenni 52 D5
Koblenz 12 C6
Kobo 44 G3
Kobroör 43 E4
Kobryn 10 P5
Kočani 28 E3
Koçarli 28 K7
Kočevje 26 B4
Ko Chang 40 C4
Kochechum 36 F3
Kōchi 38 J4
Kochi 44 C7
Kochki 34 Q7
Kochkorka 34 P9
Kochubey 30 J6
Kodiak Island 66 S4
Kodino 30 G2
Kodinsk 36 F5
Kodyma 26 S1
Köflach 26 C2
Kōfu 38 K3
Køge 10 B2
Køge Bugt 10 B2
Kohat 44 B2
Kohima 44 F3
Koh-i-Qaisir 46 H3
Koh-i-Sangan 46 J3
Kohtla-Järve 8 P7
Koidu 54 B3
Koitere 8 R5
Kokenau 43 E3
Kokkola 8 M5
Kokomo 70 J3
Kokpekty 34 Q8
Kokshetau 30 N4
Kokstad 58 D6
Kolaka 43 B3
Kolar 44 C6
Kolari 8 M3
Kolašin 26 G7
Kolda 54 B2
Kolding 8 E9
Kole 56 C4
Kolhapur 44 B5
Kolin 10 E7
Kolkata 44 E4
Kollam 44 C7
Köln 12 B6
Kolno 10 L4
Koło 10 H5
Kołobrzeg 10 E3
Kologriv 30 H3
Kolomna 30 G3
Kolomyya 26 N1
Kolonedale 43 B3
Kolosovka 30 P3
Kolpashevo 34 Q6
Kolpos Agiou Orous 28 F4
Kolpos Kassandras 28 F4
Kolpos Murampelou 28 H9
Kolskijzaliv 8 S2
Kolskiy Poluostrov 30 G1
Kolumadulu Atoll 44 B8
Koluton 30 N4
Kolva 30 L2
Kolwezi 58 D2
Kolyma 36 R4
Kolymskaya Nizmennost' 36 S3
Kolymskoye 36 T3
Komandorskiye Ostrova 36 V5
Komárno 26 F2
Komárom 26 F2
Kombe 56 D4
Komi 30 K2
Komló 26 F3
Kom Ombo 50 F3
Komotini 28 H3
Komsa 34 R5
Komsomol'skiy 30 J5
Komsomol'sk-na-Amure 36 P6
Konārka 44 E5
Konda 30 N3
Kondagaon 44 D5
Kondinskoye 30 N3
Kondoa 56 F4
Kondopoga 30 F2
Kondrat'yeva 34 V5
Kondūz 46 J2
Kong Frederick VI Kyst 68 Y4
Kongi 34 R9
Kongola 58 C3
Kongolo 56 D5
Kongsberg 8 E7
Kongur Shan 34 N10
Königsberg = Kaliningrad 10 K3
Königswinter 12 C6
Königs-Wusterhausen 12 J4
Konin 10 H5
Konispol 28 C5
Konitsa 28 C4
Köniz 22 C4
Konjic 26 E6
Konosha 30 H2
Konotop 30 F4
Konstanz 22 E3
Kontagora 54 F2
Kon Tum 40 D4
Konya 28 Q7
Konz 12 B7
Kookynie 62 D5
Kootenay Lake 70 C2
Kópasker 8 (1)E1
Kópavogur 8 (1)C2
Koper 22 J5
Kopeysk 30 M3
Köping 8 J7
Koplik 26 G7
Koprivnica 26 D3
Korba, *India* 44 D4
Korba, *Tunisia* 24 E12
Korbach 12 D5
Korçë 28 C4
Korčula 26 D7
Korea Bay 38 G3
Korea Strait 38 H4
Korf 36 V4
Korhogo 54 C3
Korinthiakos Kolpos 28 E6
Korinthos 28 E7
Kōriyama 38 L3
Korkino 30 M4
Korkuteli 28 N7
Korla 34 R9
Korliki 36 C4
Körmend 26 D2
Kornat 26 C6
Koroba 43 F4
Köroğlu Dağları 28 Q4
Köroğlu Tepesi 28 P4
Korogwe 56 F5
Koronowo 10 G4
Koror 60 D5
Korosten' 30 E4
Koro Toro 50 C4
Korsakov 36 Q7
Korsør 12 G1
Korti 50 F4
Kortrijk 14 F4
Korumburra 62 J7
Koryakskiy Khrebet 36 V4
Koryazhma 34 H5
Kos 28 K8
Kos 28 K8
Kosa 30 L3
Ko Samui 40 C5
Kościan 10 F5
Kościerzyna 10 H3
Kosh Agach 34 R8
Koshoba 46 F1
Košice 10 L9
Koslan 30 J2
Kosŏng 38 H3
Kosovo 28 C2
Kosovska Mitrovica 28 C2
Kosrae 60 G5
Kostajnica 22 M5
Kostanay 30 M4
Kostenec 28 F2
Kosti 50 F5
Kostinbrod 26 L7
Kostino 36 D3
Kostomuksha 8 R4
Kostroma 30 H3
Kostrzyn 10 D5
Kos'yu 30 L1
Koszalin 10 F3
Kőszeg 26 D2
Kota 44 C3
Kotaagung 42 C4
Kotabaru 42 F3
Kota Belud 42 F1
Kota Bharu 42 C1
Kotabumi 42 C3
Kota Kinabalu 42 F1
Kotamubagu 43 B2
Kotapinang 42 B2
Kotel'nich 30 J3
Kotel'nikovo 30 H5
Köthen 12 G5
Kotido 56 E3
Kotka 8 P6
Kotlas 30 J2
Kotor Varoš 26 E5
Kotov'sk 30 E5
Kottagudem 44 D5
Kotte 44 D7
Kotto 56 C2
Kotuy 36 G3
Kotzebue Sound 66 T3
Kouango 54 H3
Koudougou 54 D2
Koulamoutou 54 G5
Koum 54 G3
Koumra 54 H3
Koundâra 54 B2
Koupéla 52 C6
Kourou 76 G2
Koutiala 54 C2
Kouvola 8 P6
Kovdor 8 R3
Kovel' 30 D4
Kovin 26 H5
Kovrov 30 H3
Kowanyama 62 H3
Köyceğiz 28 L8
Koygorodok 30 K2
Koynas 30 J2
Kozani 28 D4
Kozheynikovo 34 W3
Kozhikode 44 C6
Kozienice 10 L6
Kozloduy 26 L6
Kozlu 28 P3
Kpalimé 54 E3
Kraai 58 D6
Krabi 40 B5
Kradeljevo 24 M5
Kragujevac 26 H5
Kraków 10 J7
Kraljeviča 22 K5
Kraljevo 26 H6
Kralovice 10 C8
Kramators'k 30 G5
Kramfors 8 J5
Kranj 26 B3
Krapina 24 K2
Krapinske Toplice 22 L4
Krasino 34 J3
Krāslava 8 P9
Kraśnik 10 M7
Krasnoarmeysk 30 N4
Krasnoborsk 30 J2
Krasnodar 30 G5
Krasnohrad 30 G5
Krasnokamensk 36 K6
Krasnosel'kup 36 C3
Krasnotur'insk 30 M3
Krasnoufimsk 30 L3
Krasnovishersk 30 L2
Krasnoyarsk 36 E5
Krasnoyarskoye Vodokhranilishche 34 S6
Krasnoznamensk 10 M3
Krasnystaw 10 N7
Krasnyy Chikoy 36 H6
Krasnyy Kut 30 J4
Krasnyy Yar 30 J5
Kratovo 28 E2
Krefeld 14 J3
Kremenchuk 30 F5
Krems 22 L2
Kremsmünster 22 K2
Krestovka 30 K1
Krestyakh 36 K4
Kretinga 10 L2
Kribi 54 F4
Kričim 28 G2
Krieglach 22 L3
Krishna 44 C5
Krishnagiri 44 C6
Kristiansand 8 E7
Kristianstad 8 H8
Kristiansund 8 D5
Kristinehamn 8 H7
Kristinestad 8 L5
Kriti 28 H10
Kriva Palanka 28 E2
Križevci 26 D3
Krk 22 K5
Krk 22 K5
Kroměříž 10 G8
Kronach 12 G6
Krŏng Kaôh Kŏng 40 C4
Kronotskiy Zaliv 36 U6
Kroonstadt 58 D5
Kroper 24 H3
Kropotkin 30 H5
Krosno 10 L8
Krško 22 L5
Krugë 28 B3
Krui 42 C4
Krumbach 22 F2
Krung Thep 40 C4
Krusă 12 E2
Kruševac 26 J6
Krychaw 30 F4
Krym' 6 H3
Krynica 10 L8
Krytiko Pelagos 28 G9
Kryve Ozero 26 T2
Kryvyy Rih 30 F5
Krzna 10 N5
Ksar el Boukhari 20 N9
Ksen'yevka 36 K6
Ksour Essaf 52 H1
Kuala Kerai 42 C1
Kuala Lipis 42 C2
Kuala Lumpur 42 C2
Kuala Terengganu 42 C1
Kuandian 38 G2
Kuantan 42 C2
Kuçadasi 28 K7
Kučevo 26 J5
Kuching 42 E2
Kucovë 28 B4
Kudat 42 F1
Kudus 42 E4
Kudymkar 30 K3
Kufstein 22 H3
Kugmallit Bay 68 E2
Kūh-e Bābā 46 J3
Kūh-e Dīnār 46 F3
Kūh-e Fūrgun 46 G4
Kūh-e Hazārān 46 G4
Kūh-e Kalat 46 G3
Kūh-e Taftān 46 H4
Kūhhā-ye Zāgros 46 F3
Kuhmo 8 Q4
Kuito 58 B2
Kukës 26 H7
Kukhtuy 36 Q4
Kula 26 K6
Kulagino 30 K5
Kulandy 34 K8
Kuldīga 8 L8
Kulgera 62 F5
Kulmbach 12 G6
Kŭlob 46 J2
Kul'sary 30 K5
Kultsjön 8 H4
Kulu 28 R5
Kulunda 34 P7
Kulynigol 36 C4
Kuma 30 N3
Kumanovo 26 J7
Kumara, *N.Z.* 64 C6
Kumara, *Russia* 36 M6
Kumasi 54 D3
Kumba 54 F4
Kumbağ 28 K4
Kumbakonam 44 C6
Kumeny 30 K3
Kumertau 30 L4
Kumla 8 H7
Kumluca 28 N8
Kummerower See 12 H3
Kumo 54 G3
Kumta 44 B6
Kunene 58 A3
Kungälv 8 F8
Kungrad 34 K9
Kungu 56 B3
Kungur 30 L3
Kunhing 40 B2
Kunlun Shan 44 D1
Kunming 38 C6
Kunsan 38 H3
Kunszetmarton 10 K11
Kununurra 62 E3
Künzelsau 12 E7
Kuolayarvi 8 Q3
Kuopio 30 E2
Kupang 62 B2
Kupino 34 P7
Kup"yans'k 30 G5
Kuqa 34 Q9
Kura 46 E2
Kuragino 36 E6
Kurasia 44 D4
Kurchum 34 Q8
Kurduvadi 44 C5
Kure Island 60 J3
Kuressaare 8 M7
Kureyka 36 D3
Kureyka 36 E3
Kurgal'dzhinskiy 34 N7
Kurgan 30 N3
Kurikka 8 M5
Kuril Islands = Kuril'skiye Ostrova 36 S7
Kuril'sk 36 R7
Kuril'skiye Ostrova 36 S7
Kuril Trench 32 V5
Kuripapango 64 F4
Kurmuk 50 F5
Kurnool 44 C5
Kurow 64 C7
Kuršėnai 10 M1
Kursk 30 G4
Kuršumlija 26 J6
Kurşunlu 28 R4
Kuruman 58 C5
Kurume 38 J4
Kurumkan 36 J6
Kurunegala 44 D7
Kushir 36 H6
Kushiro 38 L2
Kushmurun 30 M4
Kushum 30 K4
Kütahya 28 M5
K'ut'aisi 46 D1
Kutina 26 D4
Kutno 10 J5
Kutu 54 H5
Kutum 50 D5
Kuujjua 68 J2
Kuujjuaq 68 T5
Kuujjuarapik 68 R5
Kuusamo 30 E1
Kuvango 58 B2
Kuwait 46 E4
Kuwait = Al Kuwayt 46 E4
Kuya 30 H1
Kuybyshev 34 P6
Kuygan 34 N8
Kuytun 34 R9
Kuyumba 36 F4
Kuznetsk 30 J4
Kuzomen' 30 G1
Kvaløya, *Norway* 8 M1
Kvaløya, *Norway* 8 J2
Kvalynsk 34 H7
Kwale 56 F4
Kwangju 38 H3
Kwango 56 B5
Kwazulu Natal 58 E5
Kwekwe 58 D3
Kwidzyn 8 K10
Kwilu 54 H5
Kyakhta 36 H6
Kyancutta 62 G6
Kyaukpyu 40 A3
Kyaukse 44 G4
Kyeburn 64 C7
Kyeintali 44 F5
Kyjov 22 N2
Kyklades 28 G7
Kyle of Lochalsh 16 G4
Kyll 14 J4
Kyllini 28 D7
Kymi 28 G6
Kyōto 38 K3
Kyparissia 28 D7
Kyperissiakos Kolpos 28 C7
Kyra Panagia 28 G5
Kyren 36 G6
Kyrgyzstan 34 N9
Kyritz 12 H4
Kyrta 30 L2
Kyshtovka 34 P6
Kystatyam 36 L3
Kytalyktakh 36 N3
Kythira 28 E8
Kythira 28 F8
Kythnos 28 G7
Kyushe 34 K8
Kyūshū 38 J4
Kyusyur 36 M2
Kyyiv 30 F4
Kyzyl 34 S7
Kyzyl-Adyr 34 N9

Kyzylorda 30 N6
Kzyl-Dzhar 30 N5
Kzyltu 34 N7

L

Laascaanood 56 H2
Laatzen 12 E4
Laâyoune 52 C3
Laba 54 F2
La Banda 78 J4
La Bañeza 20 E2
La Baule 18 C6
La Bazoge 18 F5
Labbezenga 52 F5
Labe 10 E7
Labé 54 B2
Labin 22 K5
Labinsk 30 H6
Laboulaye 78 J5
Labrador 68 U6
Labrador City 68 T6
Labrador Sea 68 V4
Lábrea 76 E5
Labuha 43 C3
Labuhan 42 D4
Labuhanbajo 43 A4
Labutta 40 A3
Labytnangi 34 M4
Laç 26 G8
Lac à l'Eau Claire 68 R5
Lacanau 18 D8
La Carlota 20 F7
La Carolina 20 G6
Lac Bienville 68 S5
Lac Brochet 68 L5
Laccadive Islands 44 B6
Lac d'Annecy 22 B5
Lac de Bizerte 24 D11
Lac Débo 52 E5
Lac de Kossou 54 C3
Lac de Lagdo 54 G3
Lac de Manantali 54 C2
Lac de Mbakaou 54 G3
Lac de Neuchâtel 22 B4
Lac de Retenue de la Lufira 56 D6
Lac de St-Croix 22 B7
Lac des Bois 68 G3
Lac de Sélingue 54 C2
Lac Do 52 E5
Lac du Bourget 22 A5
Lacedonia 24 K7
Lacepede Bay 62 G7
Lac Evans 68 R6
Lac Faguibine 52 E5
Lac Fitri 50 C5
La Charité-sur-Loire 18 J6
La Chaux-de-Fonds 22 B3
La Chorrera 76 C4
Lac Ichkeul 24 D11
La Ciotat 18 L10
Lac La Biche 68 J6
Lac La Martre 68 H4
Lac Léman = Lake Geneva 22 B4
Lac Mai-Ndombe 56 B4
Lac Minto 68 R5
Lac Mistassini 68 S6
Lac Nzilo 56 D6
Lac Onangué 54 F5
Laconi 24 D9
Lac Payne 68 S5
La Crosse 70 H3
La Cruz 70 E7
Lac St-Jean 70 M2
Lac St. Joseph 68 N6
Lac Seul 68 N6
Lac Tumba 56 B4
Lacul Brateş 26 Q4
Lacul Razim 26 R5
Lacul Sinoie 26 R5
Lac Upemba 56 D5
La Dorada 76 C2
Ladozhskoye Ozero 30 F2
Ladysmith 58 D5
Ladyzhenka 30 N4
La Esmeralda, *Bolivia* 78 J3
La Esmeralda, *Venezuela* 76 D3
Læsø 8 F8
Lafayette, *Ind., U.S.* 70 J3
Lafayette, *La., U.S.* 70 H5
La Ferté-St-Aubin 18 G6
Lafia 54 F3
Lafiagi 54 F3
La Flèche 18 E6
Lafnitz 22 M3
Lagan 8 G8
Lagan' 30 J5
Lage 14 L3
Lågen 8 E6
Laghouat 52 F2
Lagkadas 28 F4
Lagoa dos Patos 78 L5
Lagoa Mirim 78 L5
Lago Argentino 78 G9
Lago de Cahora Bassa 58 E3
Lago del Coghinas 24 C8
Lago del Flumendosa 24 D9
Lago de Maracaibo 76 C2
Lago de Nicaragua 72 G6
Lago de Poopó 76 D7
Lago di Bolsena 24 F6
Lago di Bracciano 24 G6
Lago di Caine 22 D5
Lago di Como 22 E4
Lago di Garda 22 F5
Lago di Lecco 22 E5
Lago di Lugano 22 E5
Lago d'Iseo 22 E5
Lago di Varano 24 K7
Lago Maggiore 22 D5
Lago Omodeo 24 C8
Lago Rogaguado 76 D6
Lagos, *Nigeria* 54 E3
Lagos, *Portugal* 20 B7
Lago Titicaca 76 D7
Lago Trasimeno 24 G5
La Goulette 24 E12
La Grand-Combe 18 K9
La Grande 70 C2
La Grange 70 J5
Lagrange 62 D3
La Gran Sabana 76 E2
Laguna 78 M4
Laguna de Caratasca 72 H5
Laguna Madre 72 E3
Laguna Mar Chiquita 74 E7
Lagunillas 76 E7
La Habana 72 H4
Lahad Datu 40 F5
Lahat 42 C3
La Haye-du-Puits 14 A5
Lāhījān 46 F2
Lahn 14 L4
Lahnstein 14 K4
Laholmsbukten 10 B1
Lahore 44 B2
Lahr 22 C2
Lahti 8 N6
Laï 56 B2
Laiagam 43 F4
Lai Chau 40 C2
L'Aigle 14 C6
Laihia 8 M5
Laingsburg 58 C6
Laiwu 38 F3
Laiyuan 38 E3
Lajes 78 L4
Lajosmizse 10 J10
La Junta 70 F4
Lake Abbe 56 G1
Lake Abitibi 70 L2
Lake Albert 56 D3
Lake Amadeus 62 F4
Lake Argyle 62 E3
Lake Athabasca 68 K5
Lake Austin 62 C5
Lake Balkhash = Ozero Balkhash 32 L5
Lake Bangweulu 58 E2
Lake Barlee 62 C5
Lake Benmore 64 C7
Lake Blanche 62 H5
Lake Callabonna 62 H5
Lake Carey 62 D5
Lake Carnegie 62 D5
Lake Chad 50 B5
Lake Chilwa 58 F3
Lake City 70 K5
Lake Claire 68 J5
Lake Coleridge 64 C6
Lake Constance 22 E3
Lake Diefenbaker 68 K6
Lake Disappointment 62 D4
Lake District 16 J7
Lake Dojran 28 E3
Lake Dora 62 D4
Lake Dundas 62 B6
Lake Edward 56 D4
Lake Erie 70 K3
Lake Eyasi 56 E4
Lake Eyre 60 D8
Lake Eyre Basin 62 G5
Lake Eyre North 62 G5
Lake Eyre South 62 G5
Lake Francis Case 70 G3
Lake Frome 62 H6
Lake Gairdner 62 G6
Lake Geneva 22 B4
Lake Gordon 62 H8
Lake Grace 62 C6
Lake Harbour 68 T4
Lake Hauroko 64 A7
Lake Hopkins 62 E4
Lake Huron 70 K3
Lake Kariba 58 D3
Lake Kerkinitis 28 L8
Lake Kivu 56 D4
Lake Kyoga 56 E3
Lake Ladoga = Ladozhskoye Ozero 30 F2
Lake Lefroy 62 D6
Lake Louis 68 H6
Lake Macdonald 62 E4
Lake Mackay 62 E4
Lake Macleod 62 B4
Lake Manapouri 64 A7
Lake Manitoba 68 M6
Lake Manyara 56 F4
Lake Maurice 62 F5
Lake Melville 68 U6
Lake Michigan 70 J3
Lake Moore 62 C5
Lake Murray 43 F4
Lake Mweru 56 D5
Lake Mweru Wantipa 56 E5
Lake Nash 62 G4
Lake Nasser 50 F3
Lake Natron 56 F4
Lake Neale 62 E4
Lake Nipigon 68 P6/7
Lake Nyasa 58 E2
Lake Oahe 70 F3
Lake of the Woods 70 H2
Lake Ohau 64 B7
Lake Ohrid 28 C4
Lake Onega = Onezhskoye Ozero 6 H1
Lake Ontario 70 L3
Lake Paringa 64 B6
Lake Peipus 8 P7
Lake Poteriteri 64 A8
Lake Powell 70 D4
Lake Prespa 28 D4
Lake Pskov 8 P7
Lake Pukaki 64 C7
Lake Rotorua 64 F4
Lake Rukwa 56 E5
Lake St. Lucia 58 E5
Lake Sakakawea 70 F2
Lake Scutari 26 G7
Lake Superior 70 J2
Lake Tahoe 70 C4
Lake Tanganyika 56 D5
Lake Taupo 64 E4
Lake Te Anau 64 A7
Lake Tekapo 64 C6
Lake Tekapo 64 C6
Lake Torrens 62 G6
Lake Turkana 56 F3
Lake Victoria 56 E4
Lakeview 70 B3
Lake Volta 54 D3
Lake Waikare 64 E3
Lake Waikaremoana 64 F4
Lake Wakatipu 64 B7
Lake Wanaka 64 B7
Lake White 62 E4
Lake Wills 62 E4
Lake Winnipeg 68 M6
Lake Winnipegosis 68 L6
Lake Woods 62 F3
Lake Xau 58 C4
Lake Yamma Yamma 62 H5
Lakhdaria 20 P8
Lakhimpur 44 D3
Lakhnadon 44 C4
Lakhpat 44 A4
Lakki 44 B2
Lakonikos Kolpos 28 E8
Lakota 70 G2
Lakselv 8 N1
Lalín 20 B2
La Línea 20 E8
Lalitpur 44 C4
Lal-Lo 40 G3
La Loche 68 K5
La Louvière 14 G4
La Maddalena 24 D7
Lamar 70 F4
La Marsa 24 E12
Lamballe 18 C5
Lambaréné 54 G5
Lambay Island 16 G8
Lambert's Bay 58 B6
Lam Chi 40 C3
Lamesa 70 F5
Lamia 28 E6
Lamone 22 G6
Lampang 40 B3
Lampedusa 52 H1
Lamu 56 G4
Lancang 40 B2
Lancaster 16 K7
Lancaster Sound 68 Q2
Lanciano 24 J6
Landau, *Germany* 14 L5
Landau, *Germany* 22 H2
Landeck 22 F3
Landerneau 18 A5
Landor 62 C5
Landsberg 22 F2
Land's End 16 F11
Landshut 22 H2
Landskrona 10 B2
Landstuhl 14 K5
Land Wursten 12 D3
La'nga Co 44 D2
Langebæk 12 H1
Langeland 12 F2
Langen, *Germany* 12 D3
Langen, *Germany* 14 L5
Langenau 22 F2
Langenhagen 12 E4
Langeoog 12 C3
Langeoog 12 C3
Langfang 38 F3
Langjökull 8 (1)C2
Langkawi 40 B5
Langkon 40 F5
Langogne 18 J9
Langon 18 E9
Langøya 8 H2
Langreo 20 E1
Langres 22 A3
Langsa 40 B6
Langvatnet 8 G3
Länkäran 46 E2
Lannion 18 B5
Lansing 70 K3
Lanxi 38 H1
Lanya 56 E2
Lanzarote 52 C3
Lanzhou 38 C3
Laoag 40 G3
Lao Cai 40 C2
Laohekou 38 E4
Laon 14 F5
La Oroya 76 B6
Laos 40 C3
Lapa 78 M4
La Palma 52 B3
La Palma 72 J7
La Paragua 76 E2
La Paz, *Arg.* 78 K5
La Paz, *Bolivia* 76 D7
La Paz, *Mexico* 72 B4
La Pedrera 76 D4
La Pérouse Strait 38 L1
Lapland 8 M2
La Plata 78 K5
Lappajärvi 8 M5
Lappeenranta 8 Q6
Laptev Sea = More Laptevykh 36 L1
Lapua 8 M5
Łapy 10 M5
La Quiaca 78 H3
L'Aquila 24 H6
Lār 46 F4
Larache 52 D1
Laramie 70 E3
Larantuka 43 B4
Larat 43 D4
Larba 20 P8
Laredo, *Spain* 20 G1
Laredo, *U.S.* 70 G6
L'Ariana 24 E12
Lariang 43 A3
La Rioja 78 H4
Larisa 28 E5
Larkana 46 J4
Larnaka 28 R10
Larne 16 G7
La Rochelle 18 D7
La Roche-sur-Yon 18 D7
La Roda 20 H5
La Romana 72 L5
La Ronge 68 K5
Larrimah 62 F3
Lar'yak 34 Q5
Las Cabezas de San Juan 20 E7
Las Cruces 70 E5
La Serena 78 G4
La Seu d'Urgell 20 M2
La Seyne-sur-Mer 18 L10
Lashio 40 B2
Lashkar Gāh 46 H3
Las Horquetas 78 G8
Łask 10 J6
Las Lomitas 78 J3
La Solana 20 G6
Las Palmas 52 B3
Las Petas 76 F7
La Spezia 22 E6
Las Plumas 78 H7
Las Taques 76 C1
Lastoursville 54 G5
Lastovo 26 D7
Las Varas 70 E7
Las Varillas 78 J5
Las Vegas, *Nev., U.S.* 70 C4
Las Vegas, *N. Mex., U.S.* 70 E4
La Teste 18 D9
Latina 24 G7
Latisana 22 J5
La Toma 78 H5
La Tuque 70 M2
Latur 44 C5
Latvia 8 M8
Lauchhammer 12 J5
Lauenburg 12 F3
Lauf 12 G7
Lau Group 60 J7
Launceston, *Aus.* 62 J8
Launceston, *U.K.* 16 H11
La Union 20 K7
Laupheim 22 E2
Laura 62 H3
Laurel 70 J5
Lauria 24 K8
Lausanne 22 B4
Laut, *Indonesia* 42 F3
Laut, *Malaysia* 42 D2
Lauter 14 K5
Lauterbach 12 E6
Lava 10 L3
Laval 18 E5
La Vall d'Uixo 20 K5
La Vega 72 K5
Laviana 20 E1
La Vila Joiosa 20 K6
Lavras 78 N3
Lavrentiya 36 Z3
Lavrio 28 G7
Lawdar 50 J5
Lawra 54 D2
Lawrence 64 B7
Lawton 70 G5
Laya 30 L1
Laylā 50 J3
Laysan Island 60 J3
Lazarev 36 Q6
Lázaro Cárdenas 72 D5
Lazdijai 10 N3
Lazo 36 P3
Lebach 14 J5
Lebanon 46 C3
Lębork 10 G3
Lebrija 20 D8
Lebu 78 G6
Lecce 24 N8
Lecco 22 E5
Lech 22 F3
Leck 12 D2
Le Creusot 18 K7
Le Crotoy 14 D4
Łęczna 10 M6
Łęczyca 10 J5
Ledmozero 8 R4
Lee 16 D10
Leeds 16 L8
Leek, *Netherlands* 14 J1
Leek, *U.K.* 14 A1
Leer 14 K1
Leesburg 70 K6
Leeston 64 D6
Leeuwarden 14 H1
Leeward Islands 72 M5
Lefkada 28 C6
Lefkada 28 C6
Lefkimmi 28 C5
Lefkosia 28 R9
Legaspi 40 G4
Legionowo 10 K5
Legnago 22 G5
Legnica 10 F6
Leh 44 C2
Le Havre 14 C5
Lehre 12 F4
Lehrte 12 F4
Leiah 44 B2
Leibnitz 22 L4
Leicester 14 A2
Leiden 14 G2
Leie 14 F4
Leigh Creek 62 G6
Leighton Buzzard 14 B3
Leine 12 E4
Leinster 62 D5
Leipzig 12 H5
Leiria 20 B5
Leiyang 38 E5
Lek 14 G3
Lelystad 14 H2
Le Mans 18 F6
Lemberg 12 D8
Lemesos 28 Q10
Lemgo 14 L2
Lemieux Islands 68 U4
Lemmer 14 H2
Lemmon 70 F2
Le Muret 18 E9
Lena 20 E1
Lena 36 L4
Lendava 22 M4
Lendinare 22 G5
Lengerich 14 K2
Lengshuijiang 38 E5
Lengshuitan 38 E5
Lenininsk-Kuznetskiy 34 R7
Leninskoye 30 J3
Lenmalu 43 D3
Lenne 14 K3
Lennestadt 14 L3
Lens 14 E4
Lensk 36 K4
Lenti 22 M4
Lentini 24 J11
Léo 54 D2
Leoben 22 L3
León, *Mexico* 72 D4
León, *Nicaragua* 72 G6
León, *Spain* 20 E2
Leonardville 58 B4
Leonberg 22 E2
Leonforte 24 J11
Leonidi 28 E7
Leonora 62 D5
Leova 26 R3
Le Palais 18 B6
Lepe 20 C7
Le Perthus 18 H11
Lepoura 28 G6
Lepsy 34 P8
Le Puy 18 J8
Léré 54 G3
Lerici 22 E6
Lerma 20 G2
Leros 28 J7
Lerwick 16 L1
Lešak 26 H6
Les Andelys 14 D5
Lesatima 56 F4
Lesbos = Lesvos 28 H5
Les Escaldes 20 G11
Les Escoumins 68 T7
Leshan 38 C5
Les Herbiers 18 D7
Leshukonskoye 30 J2
Leskovac 26 J7
Lesosibirsk 34 S6
Lesotho 58 D5
Lesozavodsk 38 J1
Lesparre-Médoc 18 E8
Les Sables-d'Olonne 18 D7
Les Sept Îles 18 B5
Lesser Antilles 72 L6
Lesser Slave Lake 68 J5
Lesvos 28 H5
Leszno 10 F6
Letaba 58 E4
Letchworth 14 B3
Letenye 22 M4
Lethbridge 68 J7
Lethem 76 F3
Leticia 76 D4
Letpadan 40 B3
Le Tréport 14 D4
Letterkenny 16 E7
Leutkirch 22 F3
Leuven 14 G4
Leuze 14 F4
Levadeia 28 E6
Levanzo 24 G10
Levashi 46 E1
Levaya Khetta 30 P2
Leverano 24 N8
Leverkusen 14 J3
Levice 10 H9
Levico Terme 22 G4
Levin 64 E5
Lévis 70 M2
Levitha 28 J7
Levoča 10 K9
Levski 26 N6
Lewes 14 C4
Lewis 16 F3
Lewis Range 68 J7
Lewiston, *Id., U.S.* 70 C2
Lewiston, *Me., U.S.* 70 M3
Lexington 70 K4
Leyte 40 G4
Lezhë 26 G8
Lhari 44 F2
Lhasa 44 F3
Lhazê 44 E3
Lhokseumawe 40 B5
Lian Xian 40 E2
Lianyuan 40 E1
Lianyungang 38 F4
Liaocheng 38 F3
Liaoyang 38 G2
Liaoyuan 38 H2
Liard 68 F5
Liard River 68 F5
Libenge 56 B3
Liberal 70 F4
Liberec 10 E7
Liberia 54 B3
Liberia 72 G6
Libjo 40 H4
Libourne 18 E9
Libreville 54 F4
Libya 50 C2
Libyan Desert 50 D2
Libyan Plateau 50 E1
Licata 24 H11
Lich 12 D6
Lichinga 58 F2
Lichtenfels 12 G6
Lida 8 N10
Lidköping 8 G7
Lidodi Jesolo 22 H5
Lido di Ostia 24 G7
Lidzbark Warmiński 10 K3
Liebenwalde 12 J4
Liechtenstein 22 E3
Liège 14 H4
Lieksa 8 R5
Lienz 22 H4
Liepāja 10 L1
Lier 14 G3
Liezen 22 K3
Lifford 16 E7
Lignières 18 H7
Ligueil 18 F6
Ligurian Sea 22 D7
Lijiang 40 C1
Likasi 56 D6
Lilienfeld 22 L2
Lille 14 F4
Lillebonne 14 C5
Lillehammer 8 F6
Lillerto 22 G3
Lilongwe 58 E2
Liloy 40 G5
Lima, *Peru* 76 B6
Lima, *Mont., U.S.* 70 D3
Lima, *Oh., U.S.* 70 K3
Limanowa 10 K8
Limassol = Lemesos 28 Q10
Limbaži 8 N8
Limburg 14 L4
Limeira 78 M3
Limerick 16 D9
Limingen 8 G4
Limni Kastorias 28 C4
Limni Kerkinitis 28 E3
Limni Koronia 28 F4
Limni Trichonida 28 D6
Limni Vegoritis 28 D4
Limni Volvi 28 F4
Limnos 28 H5
Limoges 18 G8
Limón 72 H7
Limoux 18 H10
Limpopo 58 D4
Linares, *Chile* 78 G6
Linares, *Mexico* 70 G7
Linares, *Spain* 20 G6
Linaria 28 G6
Lincang 40 C2
Linchuan 38 F5
Lincoln, *U.K.* 14 B1
Lincoln, *U.S.* 70 G3
Lindenow Fjord = Kangerlussuatsiaq 68 Y4
Lindesnes 8 D8
Lindi 56 D3
Lindi 56 F6
Lindos 28 L8
Line Islands 60 L5
Linfen 38 E3
Lingayen 40 G3
Lingen 14 K2
Lingga 42 C3
Lingshui 40 D3
Linguère 54 A1
Lingyuan 38 F2
Linhai 38 G5
Linhares 76 J7
Linhe 38 D2
Linköping 8 H7
Linosa 24 G13
Lins 78 M3
Linxi 38 F2
Linxia 38 C3
Lin Xian 38 E3
Linyi 38 F3
Linz 22 K2
Liobomil' 10 P6
Lipari 24 J10
Lipari 24 J10
Lipcani 26 P1
Lipetsk 30 G4
Lipin Bor 30 G2
Lipno 10 J5
Lipova 26 J3
Lippe 14 L3
Lippstadt 14 L3
Lipsoi 28 J7
Liptovský-Mikuláš 10 J8
Lipu 40 E2
Liqeni i Fierzës 26 H7
Liqeni Komanit 26 G7
Lira 56 E3
Liri 24 H7
Lisala 56 C3
Lisboa 20 A6
Lisbon = Lisboa 20 A6
Lisburn 16 G7
Liscannor Bay 16 C9
Lishi 38 E3
Lishui 38 F5
Lisieux 14 C5
Liski 30 G4
L'Isle-sur-la-Sorgue 18 L10
Lisse 14 G2
Lištica 24 M5
Listowel 16 C9
Listvyanka 36 H6
Litang 38 C5
Litani 76 G3
Litava 10 F8
Lithgow 62 K6
Lithuania 8 L9
Litke 36 Q6
Litomerice 12 K6
Litomyši 10 F8
Litovel 10 G8
Litovko 36 P7
Little Abaco 72 J3
Little Andaman 44 F6
Little Barrier Island 64 E3
Little Desert 62 H7

Mariy El 30 J3
Marka 56 G3
Markam 38 B5
Markaryd 10 C1
Marken 14 H2
Markermeer 14 H2
Market Harborough 14 B2
Marki 10 L5
Markit 34 P10
Markkleeberg 12 H5
Markovo 36 W4
Marktoberdorf 22 F3
Marktredwitz 12 H7
Marla 62 F5
Marle 14 F5
Marmande 18 F9
Marmara Adası 28 K4
Marmara Denizi 28 L4
Marmaris 28 L8
Marmolada 22 G4
Marne 14 F5
Marne-la-Vallée 14 E6
Maro 54 H3
Maroansetra 58 H3
Marolambo 58 H4
Maroni 76 G3
Maros 43 A3
Marotiri 60 M8
Maroua 54 G2
Marquesas Islands 60 M6
Marquette 70 J2
Marradi 22 G6
Marrakech 52 D2
Marra Plateau 50 D5
Marree 62 G5
Marrupa 58 F2
Marsa Alam 50 F2
Marsabit 56 F3
Marsala 24 G11
Marsberg 14 L3
Marsden 62 J6
Marseille 18 L10
Marseille-en-Beauvaisis 14 D5
Marshall Islands 60 G4
Marsh Island 70 H6
Martapura, *Indonesia* 42 C3
Martapura, *Indonesia* 42 E3
Martigny 22 C4
Martigues 18 L10
Martin 10 H8
Martina Franca 24 M8
Martinborough 64 E5
Martinique 72 M6
Marton 64 E5
Martos 20 G7
Maruchak 46 H2
Mårvatn 8 E6
Mary 46 H2
Maryborough 62 K5
Maryland 70 L4
Maryville 70 G3
Masai Steppe 56 F4
Masaka 56 E4
Masalembu Besar 42 E4
Masallı 46 E2
Masamba 43 B3
Masasi 56 F6
Masbate 40 G4
Masbate 40 G4
Mascara 52 F1
Maseru 58 D5
Mashhad 46 G2
Masi-Manimba 56 B4
Masindi 56 E3
Maşīrah 46 G5
Masjed Soleymān 46 E3
Mason Bay 64 A8
Mason City 70 H3
Masqaţ 46 G5
Massa 22 F6
Massachusetts 70 M3
Massachusetts Bay 66 H5
Massafra 24 M8
Massa Marittimo 24 E5
Massawa 50 G4
Masset 68 E6
Massif Central 18 H8
Massif de Guéra 50 C5
Massif de l'Aïr 52 G5
Massif des Écrins 22 B5
Massif du Chaillu 54 G5
Massif du Tsaratanana 58 H2
Massif Ennedi 50 D4
Massinga 58 F4
Masteksay 30 K5
Masterton 64 E5
Mastung 46 J4
Masty 8 N10
Masuguru 58 F2
Masvingo 58 E4
Matadi 56 A5
Matagorda Island 70 G6
Matakana Island 64 F3
Matakawau 64 E3
Matale 44 D7
Matam 54 B1
Matamoros 70 G6
Matane 68 T7
Matanzas 70 K7
Matara 44 D7
Mataram 42 F4
Mataranka 62 F3
Mataró 20 N3
Mataura 64 B8
Matawai 64 F4
Matera 24 L8
Mátészalka 26 K2
Mateur 24 D11
Mathraki 28 B5
Mathura 44 C3
Mati 40 H5
Matlock 14 A1
Matmata 52 G2
Mato Grosso 76 F6
Mato Grosso 76 F6
Mato Grosso do Sul 76 F7
Matosinhos 20 B3
Matrel 22 H4
Matrûh 50 E1
Matsiatra 58 H4
Matsu 38 G5
Matsumae 38 L2
Matsumoto 38 K3
Matsusaka 38 K4
Matsuyama 38 J4
Matterhorn 22 C5
Matthews Ridge 76 E2
Mattighofen 12 J8
Maturín 76 E2
Maubeuge 14 F4
Mauganj 44 D4
Maui 60 L3
Maullín 78 G7
Maun 22 K6
Maun 58 C3
Mauritania 52 C5
Mauritius 58 (1)B2
Mauron 18 C5
Mauthen 22 H4
Mavinga 58 C3
Mawlaik 40 A2
Maya 36 P5
Maya 42 D3
Mayaguana 72 K4
Mayagüez 72 L5
Mayamba 56 B4
Maych'ew 50 G5
Maydh 56 H1
Mayenne 18 E5
Mayenne 18 E5
Maykamys 34 P8
Maykop 30 G6
Maymecha 36 G3
Mayn 36 W4
Mayo 68 D4
Mayor Island 64 F3
Mayotte 58 H2
Mayrhofen 22 G3
Mayskiy 36 M6
Mayumba 54 G5
Mayya 36 N4
Mazagão 76 G4
Mazagran 18 K4
Mazamet 18 H10
Mazar 34 P10
Mazara del Vallo 24 G11
Mazār-e Sharīf 46 J2
Mazatlán 72 C4
Mažeikiai 10 M1
Mazomora 56 F5
Mazyr 30 E4
Mazzarino 24 J11
Mbabane 58 E5
Mbāiki 54 H4
Mbala 56 E5
Mbale 56 E3
Mbalmayo 54 G4
Mbamba Bay 58 E2
Mbandaka 56 B3
Mbanga 54 F4
M'banza Congo 56 A5
Mbarara 56 E4
Mbeya 56 E5
Mbomou 56 C3
Mbour 54 A2
Mbout 52 C5
Mbuji-Mayi 56 C5
Mbuyuni 56 F5
McBride 68 G6
McClintock 68 N5
McClintock Channel 68 L2
McComb 70 H5
McCook 70 F3
Mchinga 56 F5
McKinlay 62 H4
McLennan 68 H5
Meadow Lake 68 K6
Meadville 70 K3
Meander River 68 H5
Meaux 14 E6
Mecca = Makkah 50 G3
Mechelen 14 G3
Mechernich 14 J4
Mecidiye 28 J4
Mecklenburger Bucht 12 G2
Mecula 58 F2
Meda 20 C4
Medak 44 C5
Medan 42 B2
Médéa 20 N8
Medellín 76 B2
Medenine 52 H2
Mederdra 52 B5
Medford 70 B3
Medgidia 26 R5
Mediaş 26 M3
Medicine Hat 68 J7
Medina = Al Madīnah 50 G3
Medinaceli 20 H3
Medina de Campo 20 F3
Medina Sidonia 20 E8
Mediterranean Sea 6 E4
Medjerda 24 D12
Mednogorsk 30 L4
Medveditsa 30 H4
Medvezh'yegorsk 30 F2
Meekatharra 62 C5
Meerane 12 H6
Meerut 44 C3
Mēga 56 F3
Mega 43 D3
Megalopoli 28 E7
Meganisi 28 C6
Megara 28 F6
Megisti 28 M8
Mehrān 46 E3
Mehriz 46 F3
Meiktila 40 B2
Meiningen 12 F6
Meiringen 22 D4
Meißen 12 J5
Meizhou 40 F2
Mejez El Bab 24 D12
Mékambo 54 G4
Mek'elē 50 G5
Meknès 52 D2
Mekong 40 D4
Melaka 42 C2
Melanesia 60 F5
Melbourne, *Aus.* 62 H7
Melbourne, *U.S.* 70 K6
Melchor de Mencos 72 G5
Meldorf 12 D2
Meleuz 30 L4
Mélfi 50 C5
Melfi 24 K8
Melfort 68 L6
Melide 20 B2
Melilla 20 H9
Melitopol' 30 G5
Melk 22 L2
Melkosopochnik 34 N8
Mělník 12 K6
Melo 78 L5
Melton Mowbray 14 B2
Melun 18 H5
Melut 50 F5
Melville 68 L6
Melville Island, *Aus.* 62 F2
Melville Island, *Can.* 66 N2
Melville Peninsula 68 P3
Memba 58 G2
Memberamo 43 E3
Memboro 43 A4
Memmert 14 J1
Memmingen 22 F3
Mempawah 42 D2
Memphis 70 H4
Menai Strait 16 H8
Ménaka 52 F5
Mendawai 42 E3
Mende 18 J9
Menden 14 K3
Mendī 56 F2
Mendoza 78 H5
Menemen 28 K6
Menen 14 F4
Menfi 24 G11
Menggala 42 D3
Meniet 52 F4
Menindee 62 H6
Menkere 36 L3
Menongue 58 B2
Menorca 20 Q4
Mentok 42 D3
Menunu 43 B2
Menyuan 38 C3
Menzel Bourguiba 24 D11
Menzel Bouzelfa 24 E12
Menzel Temime 24 E12
Menzies 62 D5
Meppel 14 J2
Meppen 14 K2
Merano 22 G4
Merauke 43 F4
Mercato Saraceno 22 H7
Mercedes, *Arg.* 78 H5
Mercedes, *Arg.* 78 K4
Mercedes, *Uruguay* 78 K5
Mercury Islands 64 E3
Mere 14 F4
Mergenevo 30 K5
Mergui 40 B4
Mergui Archipelago 40 B4
Meriç 28 J4
Merichas 28 G7
Mérida, *Mexico* 72 G4
Mérida, *Spain* 20 D6
Mérida, *Venezuela* 72 K7
Meridian 70 J5
Mérignac 18 E9
Merinha Grande 20 B5
Meriruma 76 G3
Merke 34 N9
Merkys 8 N9
Merowe 50 F4
Merredin 62 C6
Merritt 68 G6
Mersch 14 J5
Merseburg 12 H5
Mers el Kébir 20 K9
Mersey 16 J8
Mersin = İcel 28 S8
Mersing 42 C2
Mērsrags 8 M8
Merthyr Tydfil 16 J10
Meru 56 F3
Méru 14 E5
Merzig 14 J5
Mesa 70 D5
Mesa de Yambi 76 C3
Mesagne 24 M8
Meschede 14 L3
Mesolongi 28 D6
Messaad 52 F2
Messina, *It.* 24 K10
Messina, *S.A.* 58 D4
Messini 28 E7
Messiniakos Kolpos 28 D8
Mestre 22 H5
Meta 76 C2
Metán 78 J4
Metangula 58 E2
Metema 50 G5
Meteor Depth 74 J9
Metković 26 E6
Metlika 22 L5
Metro 42 D4
Metsovo 28 D5
Mettet 14 G4
Mettlach 14 J5
Metz 14 J5
Metzingen 22 E2
Meulaboh 40 B6
Meuse 14 G4
Mexicali 70 C5
Mexico 72 D4
Meymaneh 46 H2
Meynypil'gyno 36 X4
Mezdra 26 L6
Mezen' 30 H1
Mezenskaya Guba 30 H1
Mezhdurechensk 34 R7
Mezőberény 26 J3
Mezőkövesd 26 H2
Mezőtúr 26 H2
Mfuwe 58 E2
Miajadas 20 E5
Miami 70 K6
Miandrivazo 58 H3
Mīāneh 46 E2
Miangyang 38 E4
Mianning 38 C5
Mianwali 44 B2
Mianyang 38 C4
Miaodao Qundao 38 G3
Miao'ergou 34 Q8
Miass 30 M4
Miastko 10 G4
Michalovce 10 L9
Michigan 70 J2
Michurinsk 30 H4
Micronesia 60 F4
Mičurin 26 Q7
Mid-Atlantic Ridge 74 G1
Middelburg, *Netherlands* 14 F3
Middelburg, *S.A.* 58 D6
Middelfart 12 E1
Middelkerke 14 E3
Middle America Trench 66 L8
Middle Andaman 40 A4
Middlesbrough 16 L7
Mīdī 50 H4
Midland 70 F5
Midway Islands 60 J3
Midzor 26 K6
Miechów 10 K7
Międzyrzec Podlaski 10 M5
Miedzyrzecz 10 E5
Mielan 18 F10
Mielec 10 L7
Miembwe 56 F5
Mien 10 D1
Miercurea-Ciuc 26 N3
Mieres 20 E1
Miesbach 22 G3
Mī'ēso 56 G2
Miging 44 F3
Mikhaylovka 30 H4
Mikhaylovskiy 34 P7
Mikino 36 U4
Mikkeli 8 P6
Mikulov 22 M2
Mikun' 30 K2
Mila 52 G1
Miladhunmadulu Atoll 44 B7
Milan = Milano 22 E5
Milano 22 E5
Milas 28 K7
Milazzo 24 K10
Miles 62 K5
Miles City 70 E2
Milford Haven 16 G10
Milford Sound 64 A7
Milford Sound 64 A7
Miliana 20 N8
Milicz 10 G6
Milk 68 J7
Mil'kovo 36 T6
Millau 18 J9
Millbank 70 G2
Millerovo 30 H5
Miloro 56 E5
Milos 28 G8
Milton 64 B8
Milton Keynes 14 B2
Miluo 38 E5
Milwaukee 70 J3
Mily 34 L8
Mimizan-Plage 18 D9
Mīnāb 46 G4
Minas, *Indonesia* 42 C3
Minas, *Uruguay* 78 K5
Minas Gerais 76 H7
Minas Novas 76 J7
Minatitlán 72 F5
Minbu 40 A2
Minchinmávida 78 G7
Mindanao 40 G5
Mindelheim 22 F2
Mindelo 54 (1)B1
Minden 14 L2
Mindoro 40 G4
Mindoro Strait 40 G4
Minehead 16 J10
Minerva Reefs 60 J8
Minfeng 34 Q10
Minga 56 D6
Mingäçevir 46 E1
Mingulay 16 D5
Minhe 38 C3
Minicoy 44 B7
Minilya Roadhouse 62 B4
Minna 54 F3
Minneapolis 70 H2
Minnesota 70 G2
Miño 20 C2
Minot 70 F2
Minsk 30 E4
Minusinsk 34 S7
Min Xian 38 C4
Min'yar 30 L3
Miquelon 70 L2
Miraflores 76 C3
Miramas 18 K10
Mirambeau 18 E8
Miranda 76 F8
Miranda de Ebro 20 H2
Miranda do Douro 20 D3
Mirandela 20 C3
Mirbāt 46 F6
Mīrjāveh 46 H4
Mirnyy 36 J4
Mirow 12 H3
Mirpur Khas 44 A3
Mirtoō Pelagos 28 F7
Mirzapur 44 D3
Miskolc 26 H1
Misoöl 43 D3
Mişrātah 50 C1
Missinaibi 68 Q6
Missinipe 68 L5
Mississippi 66 L6
Mississippi 70 H5
Mississippi River Delta 70 J6
Missoula 70 D2
Missouri 70 G3
Missouri 70 H4
Mistelbach 22 M2
Mitchell 70 G3
Mithankot 46 K4
Mithaylov 30 G4
Mithymna 28 J5
Mito 38 L3
Mitsamiouli 58 G2
Mitsinjo 58 H3
Mittellandkanal 14 K2
Mittersill 22 H3
Mittweida 12 H6
Mitú 76 C3
Mitzic 54 G4
Miyake-jima 38 K4
Miyakonojō 38 J4
Miyazaki 38 J4
Mīzan Teferī 56 F2
Mizdah 52 H2
Mizen Head 16 B10
Mizhhir"ya 26 L1
Mizil 26 P4
Mjölby 8 H7
Mjøsa 8 F6
Mkuze 58 E5
Mladá Boleslav 10 D7
Mladenovac 26 H5
Mława 10 K4
Mljet 26 E7
Mmabatho 58 D5
Moa 62 H2
Moanda 54 G5
Moba 56 D5
Mobaye 56 C3
Mobayi-Mbongo 56 C3
Mobile 70 J5
Moçambique 58 G3
Môc Châu 40 C2
Mochudi 58 D4
Mocímboa da Praia 58 G2
Mocuba 58 F3
Modane 22 B5
Modena 22 F6
Modica 24 J12
Mödling 22 M2
Modowi 43 D3
Modriča 26 F5
Moers 14 J3
Moffat 16 J6
Moffat Peak 64 B7
Mogadishu = Muqdisho 56 H3
Mogaung 40 B1
Mogilno 10 G5
Mogocha 36 K6
Mogochin 34 Q6
Mogok 40 B2
Mohács 26 F4
Mohammadia 20 L9
Mohe 36 L6
Mohembo 58 C3
Mohoro 56 F5
Mohyliv-Podil's'kyy 26 Q1
Moi 8 D7
Moincêr 44 D2
Moinești 26 P3
Mo i Rana 8 H3
Moissac 18 G9
Mojave Desert 66 N6
Mokau 64 E4
Mokohinau Island 64 E2
Mokolo 54 G2
Mokoreta 64 B8
Mokp'o 38 H4
Mol 14 H3
Mola di Bari 24 M7
Molat 22 K6
Molde 8 D5
Moldova 26 P2
Moldova 26 R2
Moldova Nouă 26 J5
Molepolole 58 C4
Molfetta 24 L7
Molina de Aragón 20 J4
Molina de Segura 20 J6
Möll 22 J4
Mollendo 76 C7
Molopo 58 C5
Molsheim 22 C2
Molucca Sea 43 C2
Moma 58 F3
Mombasa 56 G4
Momčilgrad 26 N8
Møn 12 H2
Monach Islands 16 E4
Monaco 22 C7
Monaco 22 C7
Mona Passage 72 L5
Monbetsu 38 L2
Moncalieri 22 C5
Monchegorsk 8 S3
Mönchengladbach 14 J3
Monchique 20 B7
Monclova 70 F6
Moncton 68 U7
Mondovi 22 C6
Mondragone 24 H7
Mondy 36 G6
Monemvasia 28 F8
Monfalcone 22 J5
Monforte 20 C5
Monforte de Lemos 20 C2
Monfredónia 24 K7
Monga 56 C3
Mongkung 40 B2
Mongo 50 C5
Mongolia 38 B2
Mongonu 54 G2
Mongora 44 B2
Mongu 58 C3
Mong Yai 40 B2
Mong Yu 40 B2
Monkoto 56 C4
Mono 54 E3
Monopoli 24 M8
Monor 10 J10
Monowai 64 A7
Monreal del Campo 20 J4
Monreale 24 H10
Monroe 70 H5
Monrovia 54 B3
Mons 14 F4
Monschau 14 J4
Monselice 22 G5
Montabaur 14 K4
Montague Island 74 J9
Montalbán 20 K4
Montalto Uffugo 24 L9
Montana 26 L6
Montana 70 D2
Montargis 18 H6
Montauban 18 G10
Mont aux Sources 58 D5
Montbard 18 K6
Montbéliard 22 B3
Mont Blanc 22 B5
Montblanc 20 M3
Montbrison 18 K8
Mont Cameroun 54 F4
Montceau-les-Mines 18 K7
Mont-de-Marsan 18 E10
Montdidier 14 E5
Monte Alegre 76 G4
Monte Azul 76 J7
Monte Bello Islands 62 B4
Montebelluna 22 H5
Monte Calvo 24 K7
Monte Cinto 24 C6
Montecristo 24 E6
Monte Etna 24 J11
Montefiascone 24 G6
Montego Bay 72 J5
Montélimar 18 K9
Monte Limbara 24 D8
Monte Lindo 78 K4
Monte Namuli 58 F3
Montenegro = Crna Gora 26 F7
Monte Perdino 20 L2
Monte Pollino 24 L9
Montepuez 58 F2
Montepulciano 24 F5
Monte Quemado 78 J4
Montereau-faut-Yonne 18 H5
Montería 76 B2
Montero 76 E7
Monte Rosa 22 C5
Monterotondo 24 G6
Monterrey 70 F6
Monte Sant'Angelo 24 K7
Montes Claros 76 J7
Montesilvano 24 J6
Montevarchi 22 G7
Montevideo 78 K5
Monte Viso 22 C6
Montgomery 70 J5
Monthey 22 B4
Montijo 20 D6
Montilla 20 F7
Mont-Laurier 70 L2
Montluçon 18 H7
Montmedy 14 H5
Mont Mézenc 18 K9
Montone 22 G6
Montoro 20 F6
Mont Pelat 18 M9
Montpelier 70 M3
Montpellier 18 J10
Montréal 70 M2
Montreul 14 D4
Montreux 22 B4
Montrose, *U.K.* 16 K5
Montrose, *U.S.* 70 E4
Monts Bagzane 52 G5
Mont Serkout 52 G4
Montserrat 72 M5
Monts Nimba 54 C3
Monts Otish 68 S6
Mont Tahat 52 G4
Monywa 40 A2
Monza 22 E5
Monzón 20 L3
Moonie 62 K5
Moorhead 70 G2
Moosburg 22 G1
Moose Jaw 68 K6
Moose Lake 68 M6
Moosomin 68 L6
Moosonee 68 Q6
Mopeia 58 F3
Mopti 52 E6
Moqor 46 J3
Mór 26 F2
Mora 8 H6
Móra 20 B6
Moradabad 44 C3
Morafenobe 58 G3
Morag 10 J4
Moramanga 58 H3
Morane 60 N8
Moratuwa 44 D7
Morava 10 G8
Moravské Budějovice 22 L1
Morawhanna 76 F2
Moray Firth 16 J4
Morbach 14 K5
Morbegno 22 E4
Morbi 44 B4

Morcenx 18 E9
Mordaga 36 L6
Mordoviya 30 H4
Morecambe 16 K7
Moree 62 J5
Morehead 43 F4
More Laptevykh 36 L1
Morelia 72 D5
Morella 20 K4
Moreton Island 62 K5
Morez 18 M7
Morfou 28 Q9
Morgan 62 G6
Morges 22 B4
Mori 38 L2
Morioka 38 L3
Morkoka 36 J4
Morlaix 18 B5
Mornington Island 62 G3
Morocco 48 C2
Morogoro 56 F5
Moro Gulf 40 G5
Morombe 58 G4
Mörön 36 G7
Morondava 58 G4
Morón de la Frontera 20 E7
Moroni 58 G2
Moron Us He 44 F2
Morotai 43 C2
Moroto 56 E3
Morpeth 16 L6
Morris 70 G2
Morristown 70 K4
Mors 8 E8
Morshansk 30 H4
Mortain 14 B6
Morteros 78 J5
Morvern 16 G5
Morwell 62 J7
Mosbach 12 E7
Moscow = Moskva 30 G3
Mosel 14 K4
Moselle 14 G6
Moses Lake 70 C2
Mosgiel 64 C7
Moshi 56 F4
Mosjøen 8 G4
Moskenesøy 8 F3
Moskva 30 G3
Mosonmagyaróvár 22 N3
Moss 8 F7
Mossburn 64 B7
Mosselbaai 58 C6
Mossoró 76 K5
Most 12 J6
Mostaganem 20 L9
Mostar 26 E6
Mostoles 20 G4
Møsvatn 8 E7
Mot'a 50 G5
Motala 8 H7
Motherwell 16 J6
Motihari 44 D3
Motilla del Palancar 20 J5
Motiti Island 64 F3
Motril 20 G8
Motru 26 K5
Motu One 60 L7
Motygino 34 S6
Mouchard 22 A4
Moudjéria 52 C5
Moudros 28 H5
Mouila 54 G5
Moulins 18 J7
Moulmein 40 B3
Moundou 50 C6
Mount Adam 78 J9
Mount Adams 70 B2
Mountain Nile =
Bahr el Jebel 56 E2
Mount Alba 64 B7
Mount Aloysius 62 E5
Mount Anglem 64 A8
Mount Apo 40 H5
Mount Ararat 46 D2
Mount Arrowsmith 64 C6
Mount Aspiring 64 B7
Mount Assiniboine 68 H6
Mount Augustus 62 C4
Mount Baco 40 G3
Mount Baker 70 B2
Mount Bartle Frere 62 J3
Mount Bogong 62 J7
Mount Brewster 64 B7
Mount Bruce 62 C4
Mount Cameroun 48 D5
Mount Columbia 68 H6
Mount Cook 64 C6
Mount Cook 64 C6
Mount Donald 64 A7
Mount Egmont 64 E4
Mount Elbert 70 E4
Mount Elgon 56 E3
Mount Essendon 62 D4
Mount Evelyn 62 F2
Mount Everest 44 E3
Mount Fairweather 68 D5
Mount Gambier 62 H7
Mount Garnet 62 J3
Mount Hood 70 B2
Mount Hutt 64 C6
Mount Huxley 64 B7
Mount Isa 62 G4
Mount Jackson 80 (2)MM2
Mount Karisimbi 56 D4
Mount Kendall 64 D5
Mount Kenya =
Kirinyaga 56 F4
Mount Kilimanjaro 56 F4
Mount Kirkpatrick 80 (2)AA1
Mount Kosciuszko 62 J7
Mount Liebig 62 F4
Mount Lloyd George 68 G5
Mount Logan 68 C4
Mount Magnet 62 C5
Mount Maunganui 64 F3
Mount McKinley 66 S3
Mount Meharry 62 C4
Mount Menzies 80 (2)L2
Mount Minto 80 (2)Y2
Mount Mulanje 58 F3
Mount Murchison 64 C6
Mount Nyiru 56 F3
Mount Olympus 70 B2
Mount Ord 62 E3
Mount Ossa 62 J8
Mount Owen 64 D5
Mount Paget 78 P9
Mount Pleasant 70 K3
Mount Pulog 40 G3
Mount Rainier 70 B2
Mount Ratz 68 E5
Mount Richmond 64 D5
Mount Roberts 62 K5
Mount Robson 68 H6
Mount Roosevelt 68 F5
Mount Roraima 76 E2
Mount Ross 64 E5
Mount Shasta 70 B3
Mount Somers 64 C6
Mount Stanley 56 D3
Mount Tahat 48 D3
Mount Travers 64 D6
Mount Usborne 78 K9
Mount Vernon 70 J4
Mount Victoria,
Myanmar 40 A2
Mount Victoria, *P.N.G.* 60 E6
Mount Waddington 68 F6
Mount Washington 68 S8
Mount Whitney 70 C4
Mount Woodroffe 62 F5
Mount Ziel 62 F4
Moura 20 C6
Mousa 16 L2
Moussoro 50 C5
Moutamba 54 G5
Mouth of the
Shannon 16 B9
Mouths of the
Amazon 74 G3
Mouths of the
Danube 26 S4
Mouths of the
Ganges 44 E4
Mouths of the Indus 46 J5
Mouths of the
Irrawaddy 40 A3
Mouths of the
Krishna 44 D5
Mouths of the
Mekong 40 D5
Mouths of the Niger 54 F4
Moûtiers 22 B5
Moutong 43 B2
Mouzarak 54 H2
Moyale 56 F3
Moyen Atlas 52 D2
Moyenvic 14 J6
Moyero 34 U4
Moyynty 34 N8
Mozambique 58 E3
Mozambique
Channel 58 F4
Mozhga 30 K3
Mozirje 22 K4
Mpanda 56 E5
Mpika 58 E2
Mporokoso 56 E5
Mpumalanga 58 D5
Mrągowo 10 L4
Mrkonjić-Grad 22 N6
M'Sila 52 F1
Mtsensk 30 G4
Mtwara 56 G6
Muang Khammouan 40 C3
Muang Không 40 D4
Muang Khôngxédôn 40 D3
Muang Khoua 40 C2
Muang Pakxan 40 C3
Muang Phin 40 D3
Muang Sing 40 C2
Muang Xai 40 C2
Muar 42 C2
Muarabungo 42 C3
Muaradua 42 C3
Muarasiberut 42 B3
Muaratewen 42 E3
Muarawahau 42 F2
Mubarek 34 M10
Mubende 56 E3
Mubrani 43 D3
Muck 16 F5
Muckadilla 62 J5
Muconda 56 C6
Mucur 28 S5
Mudanjiang 38 H2
Mudanya 28 L4
Mudurnu 28 P4
Mufulira 58 D2
Mughshin 46 F6
Muğla 28 L7
Mugodzhary 30 L5
Muhammad Qol 50 G3
Mühldorf 22 H2
Mühlhausen 12 F5
Muhos 8 N4
Muhu 8 M7
Muhulu 56 D4
Mukacheve 10 M9
Mukdahan 40 C3
Mukomuko 42 C3
Mukry 46 J2
Mukuku 58 D2
Mulaku Atoll 44 B8
Mulde 12 H5
Mulgrave Island 62 H2
Mulhacén 20 G7
Mülheim 14 J3
Mulhouse 22 C3
Muling 38 J1
Mull 16 G5
Mullaittivu 44 D7
Mullewa 62 C5
Müllheim 22 C3
Mullingar 16 E8
Mulobezi 58 D3
Multan 46 K3
Mumbai 44 B5
Mumbwa 58 D2
Muna 43 B4
Munaðarnes 8 (1)C1
Münchberg 12 G6
München 22 G2
Münden 12 E5
Mundo Novo 76 J6
Mundrabilla 62 E6
Munera 20 H5
Mungbere 56 D3
Munger 44 E3
Munich = München 22 G2
Munster, *France* 22 C2
Munster, *Germany* 12 F4
Münster, *Germany* 14 K3
Munte 43 A2
Muojärvi 8 Q4
Muonio 8 M3
Muqdisho 56 H3
Mur 22 L4
Murang'a 56 F4
Murashi 30 J3
Murat 46 D2
Muratlı 28 K3
Murchison 64 D5
Murcia 20 J7
Murdo 70 F3
Mureș 26 J3
Muret 18 G10
Murghob 46 K2
Muriaé 76 J8
Müritz 12 H3
Muriwai 64 F4
Murmansk 8 S2
Murnau 22 G3
Murom 30 H3
Muroran 38 L2
Muros 20 A2
Murray 62 H6
Murray Bridge 62 G7
Murray River Basin 62 H6
Murska Sobota 22 M4
Murter 22 L7
Murtosa 20 B4
Murud 44 B5
Murupara 64 F4
Mururoa 60 M8
Murwara 44 D4
Murzūq 52 H3
Mürzzuschlag 22 L3
Muş 46 D2
Mūša 10 N1
Musala 28 F2
Muscat = Masqaţ 46 G5
Musgrave Ranges 62 E5
Mushin 54 E3
Muskegon 70 J3
Musmar 50 G4
Musoma 56 E4
Mussende 56 B6
Mustafakemalpaşa 28 L4
Mut, *Egypt* 50 E2
Mut, *Turkey* 28 R8
Mutare 58 E3
Mutarnee 62 J3
Mutnyy Materik 30 L1
Mutoray 34 U5
Mutsamudu 58 G2
Mutsu 38 L2
Muttaburra 62 H4
Mutur 44 D7
Muyezerskiy 8 R5
Muyinga 56 E4
Muynak 34 K9
Muzaffarnagar 44 C3
Muzaffarpur 44 E3
Muzillac 18 C6
Muztagata 34 N10
Mwali 58 G2
Mwanza 56 E4
Mweka 56 C4
Mwenda 56 D6
Mwene-Ditu 56 C5
Mwenezi 58 E4
Mwenezi 58 E4
Mwinilunga 58 C2
Myanmar 40 B2
Myaungmya 40 A3
Myingyan 40 B2
Myitkyina 40 B1
Myjava 22 N2
Myjava 22 N2
Mykolayiv 10 N8
Mykonos 28 H7
Mymensingh 44 F4
Mynbulak 34 L9
Myndagayy 36 N4
Myōjin 38 K4
Myonggan 38 H2
Mýrdalsjökull 8 (1)D3
Myrina 28 H5
Myrtle Beach 70 L5
Mys Alevina 36 S5
Mys Aniva 38 L1
Mys Buorkhaya 36 N2
Mys Dezhneva 36 Z3
Mys Elizavety 36 Q6
Mys Enkan 36 P5
Mys Govena 36 V5
Mys Kanin Nos 30 H1
Mys Kril'on 38 L1
Myślenice 10 J8
Myślibórz 10 D5
Mys Lopatka, *Russia* 36 T6
Mys Lopatka, *Russia* 36 S2
Mys Navarin 36 X4
Mys Nemetskiy 8 S2
Mys Olyutorskiy 36 W5
Mysore 44 C6
Mys Peschanyy 34 J9
Mys Povorotnyy 38 J2
Mys Prubiynyy 30 F5
Mys Shelagskiy 36 V2
Mys Sivuchiy 36 U5
Mys Terpeniya 36 Q7
Mys Tolstoy 36 T5
Mys Yuzhnyy 36 T5
Mys Zhelaniya 34 M2
Myszksw 10 J7
My Tho 40 D4
Mytilini 28 J5
Mývatn 8 (1)E2
Mže 12 H7
Mzimba 58 E2
Mzuzu 58 E2

N

Naas 16 F8
Nabas 40 G4
Naberezhnyye Chelny 30 K3
Nabeul 24 E12
Nabire 43 E3
Nacala 58 G2
Nacaroa 58 F2
Náchod 10 F7
Nadiad 44 B4
Nador 52 E2
Nadvirna 26 M1
Nadym 30 P1
Nadym 30 P2
Næstved 12 G1
Nafpaktos 28 D6
Nafplio 28 E7
Naga 40 G4
Nagano 38 K3
Nagaon 44 F3
Nagarzê 44 F3
Nagasaki 38 J4
Nagaur 44 B3
Nagercoil 44 C7
Nago 38 H5
Nagold 12 D8
Nagorsk 30 K3
Nagoya 38 K4
Nagpur 44 C4
Nagqu 44 F2
Nagyatád 22 N4
Nagykálló 26 J2
Nagykanizsa 22 N4
Nagykáta 10 J10
Nagykőrös 26 G2
Naha 38 H5
Nahanni 68 G4
Nahanni Butte 68 G4
Nahr en Nile = Nile 50 F2
Naiman Qi 38 G2
Nain 68 U5
Nairn 16 J4
Nairobi 56 F4
Naivasha 56 F4
Naizishan 38 H2
Najafābād 46 F3
Nájera 20 H2
Najibabad 44 C3
Najin 38 J2
Najrān 50 H4
Nakamura 38 J4
Nakhodka, *Russia* 34 P4
Nakhodka, *Russia* 38 J2
Nakhon Ratchasima 40 C3
Nakhon Sawan 40 B3
Nakhon Si
Thammarat 40 B5
Nakina 68 P6
Nakło nad Notecią 10 G4
Nakonde 56 E5
Nakskov 12 G2
Nakten 8 H5
Nakuru 56 F4
Nal'chik 46 D1
Nallihan 28 P4
Nālūt 52 H2
Namanga 56 F4
Namangan 34 N9
Namapa 58 F2
Namasagali 56 E3
Nam Can 40 C5
Nam Co 44 F2
Namdalen 8 G4
Nam Dinh 40 D2
Namib Desert 58 A4
Namibe 58 A3
Namibia 58 B4
Namidobe 58 F3
Namlea 43 C3
Namo 43 A3
Nampa 46 C3
Nampala 54 C1
Nam Ping 40 B3
Namp'o 38 H3
Nampula 58 F3
Namsos 8 F4
Namtsy 36 M4
Namur 14 G4
Namwala 58 D3
Nan 40 C3
Nanaimo 70 B2
Nanao 38 K3
Nanchang 38 F5
Nanchong 38 D4
Nancy 22 B2
Nanda Devi 44 C2
Nānded 44 C5
Nandurbar 44 B4
Nandyal 44 C5
Nanfeng 38 F5
Nangalala 62 G2
Nangapinoh 42 E3
Nangatayap 42 E3
Nangis 18 J5
Nangong 38 F3
Nang Xian 44 F3
Nanjing 38 F4
Nannine 62 C5
Nanning 40 D2
Nanortalik 68 X4
Nanpan 40 D2
Nanping 38 F5
Nansei-shotō 38 H5
Nantes 18 D6
Nanton 70 D1
Nantong 38 G4
Nanumea 60 H6
Nanuque 76 J7
Nanutarra
Roadhouse 62 C4
Nanyang 38 E4
Napalkovo 34 N3
Napas 36 C4
Napasoq 68 W3
Napier 64 F4
Naples = Napoli, *It.* 24 J8
Naples, *U.S.* 70 K6
Napo 76 C4
Napoli 24 J8
Nara 52 D5
Narathiwat 40 C5
Narbonne 18 H10
Nardò 24 N8
Nares Strait 66 J2
Narew 10 N5
Narew 10 L5
Narib 58 B4
Narmada 44 C4
Narnaul 44 C3
Narni 24 G6
Narok 56 F4
Närpes 8 L5
Narrabi 62 J6
Narrandera 62 J6
Narsimhapur 44 C4
Nart 38 F2
Narva 8 P7
Narva 8 Q7
Narva Bay 8 P7
Narvik 8 J2
Nar'yan Mar 30 K1
Naryn 36 F6
Năsăud 26 M2
Nashua 70 M3
Nashville 70 J4
Našice 26 F4
Nasik 44 B4
Nasir 56 E2
Nassarawa 54 F3
Nassau 72 J3
Nässjö 8 H8
Nastapoka Islands 68 R5
Nasugbu 40 G4
Naswá 46 G5
Nata 58 D4
Natal 76 K5
Natara 36 L3
Natashquan 68 U6
Natchez 70 H5
Natchitoches 70 H5
National Park 64 E4
Natitingou 54 E2
Natuna Besar 42 D2
Naucelle 18 H9
Nauchas 58 B4
Nauders 22 F4
Naujoji Akmenė 10 M1
Naumburg 12 G5
Nauru 60 G6
Nauta 76 C4
Nautonwa 44 D3
Navahermosa 20 F5
Navahrudak 8 N10
Navalero 20 H3
Navalmoral de la
Mata 20 E5
Navalvillar de Pela 20 E5
Navapolatsk 30 E3
Navlya 30 F4
Navoi 34 M9
Navojoa 70 E6
Navrongo 54 D2
Navsari 44 B4
Nawabshah 46 J4
Nāwah 46 J3
Naxçıvan 46 E2
Naxos 28 H7
Naxos 28 H7
Nayakhan 36 T4
Nāy Band 46 G3
Nayoro 38 L2
Nazaré 20 A5
Nazarovo 34 S6
Nazca 76 C6
Nazca Ridge 78 E3
Naze 38 H5
Nazilli 28 L7
Nazino 34 P6
Nazrēt 56 F2
Nazwá 46 G5
Nazyvayevsk 30 P3
Ncojane 58 C4
Ndélé 56 C2
Ndjamena 50 B5
Ndjolé 54 G5
Ndola 58 D2
Nea Ionia 28 E5
Neapoli 28 F8
Nea Roda 28 F4
Nea Zichni 28 F3
Nebbi 56 E3
Nebitdag 46 F2
Nebo 62 J4
Nebraska 70 F3
Neckar 12 D7
Neckar 12 D8
Neckarsulm 12 E7
Necker Island 60 K3
Necochea 78 K6
Nédély 50 C4
Nedre Soppero 8 L3
Needles 70 D5
Nefedovo 30 P3
Nefta 52 G2
Neftçala 46 E2
Neftekamsk 30 K3
Neftekumsk 30 H6
Nefteyugansk 30 P2
Nefza 24 D12
Negage 56 B5
Negēlē 56 F2
Negele 56 F2
Negev 50 F1
Negomane 58 F2
Negombo 44 C7
Negotin 26 K5
Negotino 28 E3
Négrine 52 G2
Negro, *Arg.* 78 J7
Negro, *Brazil* 76 E4
Negros 40 G5
Negru Vodă 26 R6
Nehbandān 46 G3
Nehe 36 M7
Nehoiu 26 P4
Neijiang 38 C5
Nei Monggol 38 E2
Neiva 76 B3
Neixiang 38 E4
Nejanilini Lake 68 M5
Nek'emtē 56 F2
Nelidovo 30 F3
Nellore 44 C6
Nel'ma 36 P7
Nelson 68 N5
Nelson, *Can.* 70 C2
Nelson, *N.Z.* 64 D5
Nelspruit 58 E5
Nëma 52 D5
Neman 10 M2
Nëman 8 N10
Nemours 18 H5
Nemperola 43 B5
Nemunas 10 P3
Nemuro 38 M2
Nen 36 L7
Nenagh 16 D9
Nene 14 B2
Nenjiang 36 M7
Nepa 36 H5
Nepal 44 D3
Nepalganj 44 D3
Nepomuk 12 J7
Ner 10 H5
Nera 24 G6
Neratovice 12 K6
Neris 10 P2
Nerja 20 G8
Neryungri 36 L5
Nesebăr 26 Q7
Netherlands 14 H2
Netherlands Antilles 72 L6
Nettilling Lake 68 S3
Neubrandenburg 12 J3
Neuburg 12 G8
Neuchâtel 22 B3
Neuenhagen 12 J4
Neufchâteau,
Belgium 14 H5
Neufchâteau, *France* 18 L5
Neufchâtel-en-Bray 14 D5
Neuhof 12 E6
Neukirchen 12 D2
Neumarkt 12 G7
Neumünster 12 F2
Neunkirchen, *Austria* 22 M3
Neunkirchen,
Germany 12 C7
Neuquén 78 H6
Neuruppin 12 H4
Neusiedler 10 F10
Neusiedler See 22 M3
Neuss 14 J3
Neustadt, *Germany* 12 F2
Neustadt, *Germany* 12 F7
Neustadt, *Germany* 12 G6
Neustadt, *Germany* 12 G8
Neustadt, *Germany* 12 H7
Neustadt, *Germany* 14 L5
Neustrelitz 12 J3
Neu-Ulm 12 F8
Neuwerk 12 D3
Neuwied 14 K4
Nevada 70 C4
Nevada 70 H4
Nevado Auzangate 76 C6
Nevado de Colima 72 D5
Nevado de Cumbal 76 B3
Nevado de
Huascaran 76 B5
Nevado de Illampu 76 D7
Nevado Sajama 76 D7
Nevados de Cachi 78 H4
Never 36 L6
Nevers 18 J7
Nevesinje 26 F6
Nevėžis 8 M9
Nevinnomyssk 30 H6
Nevşehir 28 S6
Newala 56 F6
New Amsterdam 76 F2
Newark 70 M3
Newark-on-Trent 14 B1
New Bedford 70 M3
New Britain 60 F6
New Brunswick 68 T7
Newbury 14 A3
New Bussa 54 E3
Newcastle 62 K6
Newcastle-under-
Lyme 16 K8
Newcastle upon Tyne 16 L6
Newcastle Waters 62 F3
New Delhi 44 C3
Newfoundland 68 V7
Newfoundland 68 V7
New Georgia Islands 60 F6
New Glasgow 68 U7
New Guinea 32 S10
New Hampshire 70 M3
New Hanover 60 F6
New Haven 70 M3
Newhaven 14 C4
New Iberia 72 F2

New Ireland 60 F6
New Jersey 70 M3
Newman 62 C4
Newmarket 14 C2
New Mexico 70 E5
New Orleans 70 H6
New Plymouth 64 E4
Newport, *Eng., U.K.* 14 A4
Newport, *Wales, U.K.* 16 K10
Newport, *U.S.* 70 B3
New Providence 72 J3
Newquay 16 G11
Newry 16 F7
New Siberia Islands = Novosibirskiye Ostrova 36 P1
New South Wales 62 H6
Newton 70 G4
Newtownards 16 G7
New Ulm 70 G3
New York 70 L3
New York 70 M3
New Zealand 64 B5
Neya 30 H3
Neyrīz 46 F4
Neyshābūr 46 G2
Ngabang 42 D2
Ngalu 43 B5
Ngamring 44 E3
Ngaoundéré 54 G3
Ngara 56 E4
Ngawihi 64 E5
Ngo 54 H5
Ngoura 50 C5
Ngozi 56 D4
Nguigmi 54 G2
Nguru 54 G2
Nhachengue 58 F4
Nha Trang 40 D4
Nhulunbuy 62 G2
Niafounké 52 E5
Niakaramandougou 54 C3
Niamey 54 E2
Niangara 56 D3
Nia-Nia 56 D3
Nias 42 B2
Nicaragua 72 G6
Nicastro 24 L10
Nice 22 C7
Nicobar Islands 40 A5
Nicosia = Lefkosia 28 R9
Nida 10 K7
Nidym 36 F4
Nidzica 10 K4
Niebüll 12 D2
Niedere Tauern 22 J3
Niefang 54 G4
Niemegk 12 H4
Nienburg 12 E4
Niesky 12 K5
Nieuw Amsterdam 76 F2
Nieuw Nickerie 76 F2
Nieuwpoort 14 E3
Niğde 28 S7
Niger 52 G5
Niger 54 E2
Nigeria 54 F2
Nigoring Hu 38 B3
Niigata 38 K3
Nijar 20 H8
Nijmegen 14 H3
Nikel' 8 R2
Nikolayevsk-na-Amure 36 Q6
Nikol'sk 30 J3
Nikol'skoye 36 V5
Nikopol' 30 F5
Nikšić 26 F7
Nilande Atoll 44 B8
Nile 50 F3
Nimach 44 B4
Nîmes 18 K10
Nimule 56 E3
Nin 22 L6
Nine Degree Channel 44 B7
9 de Julio 78 J6
Ning'an 38 H2
Ningbo 38 G5
Ningde 38 F5
Ninghai 38 G5
Ninh Binh 40 D2
Ninh Hoa 40 D4
Niobrara 70 G3
Nioro 52 D5
Nioro du Sahel 54 C1
Niort 18 E7
Nipigon 70 J2
Niquelândia 76 H6
Nirmal 44 C5
Niš 26 J6
Nisa 20 C5
Niscemi 24 J11
Nisporeni 26 R2
Nisyros 28 K8
Niterói 78 N3
Nitra 10 H9
Nitra 10 H9
Nitsa 30 M3
Niue 60 K7
Nivelles 14 G4
Nizamabad 44 C5
Nizhnekamsk 30 K3
Nizhnekamskoye Vodokhranilishche 30 K3
Nizhneudinsk 36 F5
Nizhnevartovsk 30 Q2
Nizhneyansk 36 P2
Nizhniy Lomov 30 H4
Nizhniy Novgorod 30 H3
Nizhniy Tagil 30 M3
Nizhnyaya Tunguska 36 H4
Nizhyn 30 F4
Nizip 46 C2
Nizza Monferrato 22 D6
Njazidja 58 G2
Njombe 56 E5
Njombe 56 E5
Nkambe 54 G3
Nkhotakota 58 E2
Nkongsamba 54 F4
Nkurenkuru 58 B3
Nobeoka 38 J4
Noci 24 M8
Nogales 70 D5
Nogat 10 J3
Nogent-le-Rotrou 18 F5
Noginsk 30 G3
Noginskiy 34 S5
Nogliki 36 Q6
Noia 20 B2
Noire 40 C2
Noirmoutier-en-l'Île 18 C6
Nok Kundi 46 H4
Nokou 52 H6
Nola, *C.A.R.* 56 B3
Nola, *It.* 24 J8
Nolinsk 30 J3
Nomoi Islands 60 F5
Nong Khai 40 C3
Noord-beveland 14 F3
Noord-Oost-Polder 14 H2
Noordwijk aan Zee 14 G2
Norak 46 J2
Nordaustlandet 80 (1)L1
Nordborg 12 E1
Norden 12 C3
Nordenham 12 D3
Norderney 12 C3
Norderney 12 C3
Norderstedt 12 F3
Nordfjordeid 8 D6
Nordfriesische Inseln 12 D2
Nordhausen 12 F5
Nordhorn 14 K2
Nordkapp 8 N1
Nordkinn 8 P1
Nordkinnhalvøya 8 P1
Nordkvaløya 8 J1
Nordli 8 G4
Nördlingen 12 F8
Nord-Ostsee-Kanal 12 E2
Nordstrand 12 D2
Nordvik 34 W3
Nore 16 E9
Norfolk 70 L4
Norfolk Island 60 G8
Noril'sk 34 R4
Norman 70 G4
Normandia 76 F3
Normanton 62 H3
Norman Wells 68 F3
Nørre Åby 12 E1
Nørre Alslev 12 G2
Norrköping 8 J7
Norrtälje 8 K7
Norseman 62 D6
Norsk 36 N6
Northallerton 16 L7
Northam 62 C6
North America 66 L5
Northampton, *Aus.* 62 B5
Northampton, *U.K.* 14 B2
North Andaman 40 A4
North Battleford 68 K6
North Bay 70 L2
North Cape 64 D2
North Carolina 70 K4
North Channel 16 G6
North Dakota 70 F2
Northeim 12 F5
Northern Cape 58 C5
Northern Ireland 16 E7
Northern Mariana Islands 60 E4
Northern Province 58 D4
Northern Territory 62 F4
North Foreland 14 D3
North Horr 56 F3
North Island 64 D3
North Korea 38 H3
North Platte 70 F3
North Platte 70 F3
North Ronaldsay 16 K2
North Sea 16 N4
North Stradbroke Island 62 K5
North Taranaki Bight 64 D4
North Uist 16 E4
Northumberland Strait 68 U7
North West 58 C5
North West Basin 62 C4
North West Cape 62 B4
North West Christmas Island Ridge 60 K4
North West Highlands 16 G4
Northwest Territories 68 G4
Norton Sound 66 T3
Nortorf 12 E2
Norway 8 F5
Norwegian Sea 8 B4
Norwich 14 D2
Nos 30 H1
Nos Emine 26 Q7
Nosevaya 30 K1
Noshiro 38 K2
Nos Kaliakra 26 R6
Nosratābād 46 G4
Nos Šabla 26 R6
Nossen 12 J5
Nosy Barren 58 G3
Nosy Bé 58 H2
Nosy Boraha 58 J3
Nosy Mitsio 58 H2
Nosy Radama 58 H2
Nosy-Varika 58 H4
Notec 10 G4
Notios Evvoïkos Kolpos 28 F6
Notre Dame Bay 68 V7
Notsé 54 E3
Nottingham 14 A2
Nottingham Island 68 R4
Nouâdhibou 52 B4
Nouakchott 52 B5
Nouâmghar 52 B5
Nouméa 60 G8
Nouvelle Calédonie 60 G8
Nova Gorica 22 J5
Nova Gradiška 26 E4
Nova Iguaçu 78 N3
Nova Mambone 58 F4
Nova Pazova 26 H5
Novara 22 D5
Nova Scotia 68 T8
Nova Xavantina 76 G6
Novaya Igirma 36 G5
Novaya Karymkary 30 N2
Novaya Kasanka 30 J5
Novaya Lyalya 30 M3
Novaya Zemlya 34 J3
Nova Zagora 26 P7
Novelda 20 K6
Nové Město 10 F8
Nové Mesto 10 G9
Nové Zámky 10 H10
Novgorod 30 F3
Novi Bečej 26 H4
Novigrad 24 H3
Novi Iskăr 26 L7
Novi Ligure 22 D6
Novi Marof 22 M4
Novi Pazar, *Bulgaria* 26 Q6
Novi Pazar, *Yugoslavia* 26 H6
Novi Sad 26 G4
Novi Vinodolski 22 K5
Novoaleksandrovsk 30 H5
Novoalekseyevka 30 L4
Novoanninskiy 30 H4
Novocheboksarsk 30 J3
Novocherkassk 30 H5
Novodvinsk 30 H2
Novo Hamburgo 78 L4
Novohrad-Volyns'kyy 30 E4
Novokazalinsk 30 M5
Novokuybyshevsk 30 J4
Novokuznetsk 34 R7
Novoletov'ye 34 U3
Novo Mesto 22 L5
Novomoskovsk 30 G4
Novonazimovo 36 E5
Novorossiysk 30 G6
Novorybnoye 36 H2
Novoselivka 26 S2
Novosergiyevka 30 K4
Novosibirsk 34 Q6
Novosibirskiye Ostrova 36 P1
Novosil' 30 G4
Novotroitsk 30 L4
Novouzensk 30 J4
Novozybkov 30 F4
Novyy 34 V3
Nový Bor 12 K6
Nový Jičín 10 H8
Novyy Port 34 N4
Novyy Uoyan 36 J5
Novyy Urengoy 34 P4
Novyy Urgal 36 N6
Novyy Uzen' 34 J9
Nowa Dęba 10 L7
Nowa Ruda 10 F7
Nowogard 10 E4
Nowo Warpno 12 K3
Nowra 62 K6
Now Shahr 46 F2
Nowy Dwór Mazowiecki 10 K5
Nowy Sącz 10 K8
Nowy Targ 10 K8
Nowy Tomyśl 10 F5
Noyabr'sk 34 P5
Noyon 14 E5
Nsombo 58 D2
Ntem 54 G4
Ntwetwe Pan 58 C4
Nu 44 G2
Nuasjärvi 8 Q4
Nubian Desert 50 F3
Nudo Coropuna 76 C7
Nueltin Lake 68 M4
Nueva Lubecka 78 G7
Nueva Rosita 70 F6
Nueva San Salvador 72 G6
Nuevo Casas Grandes 70 E5
Nuevo Laredo 70 G6
Nugget Point 64 B8
Nuhaka 64 F4
Nuku'alofa 60 J8
Nuku Hiva 60 M6
Nukumanu Islands 60 F6
Nukunonu 60 J6
Nukus 34 K9
Nullagine 62 D4
Nullarbor Plain 62 E6
Numan 54 G3
Numbulwar 62 G2
Numfor 43 E3
Numto 30 P2
Nunap Isua 68 Y5
Nunarsuit 68 X4
Nunavik 68 W2
Nunavut 68 M3
Nuneaton 14 A2
Nungnain Sum 38 F1
Nunivak Island 66 T4
Nunligram 36 Y3
Nuoro 24 D8
Nuquí 76 B2
Nura 30 P4
Nurābād 46 F3
Nurata 46 J1
Nurmes 8 Q5
Nürnberg 12 G7
Nürtingen 22 E2
Nurzec 10 M5
Nushki 46 J4
Nutak 68 U5
Nuuk 68 W4
Nuussuaq 68 W2
Nyagan' 30 N2
Nyahururu 56 F3
Nyala 50 D5
Nyalam 44 E3
Nyamlell 56 D2
Nyamtumbo 56 F6
Nyandoma 30 H2
Nyantakara 56 E4
Nyborg 12 F1
Nybro 8 H8
Nyda 34 N4
Nyima 44 E2
Nyingchi 44 F3
Nyírbátor 26 K2
Nyíregyháza 10 L10
Nykarleby 8 M5
Nykøbing 12 G2
Nyköping 8 J7
Nylstroom 58 D4
Nymburk 10 E7
Nynäshamn 8 J7
Nyngan 62 J6
Nyon 22 B4
Nysa 10 D6
Nysa 10 G7
Nysted 12 G2
Nyukhcha 30 J2
Nyunzu 56 D5
Nyurba 36 K4
Nyuya 36 K4
Nzega 56 E4
Nzérékoré 54 C3
N'zeto 56 A5
Nzwami 58 G2

O

Oahu 60 L3
Oakham 14 B2
Oakland 70 B4
Oakley 70 F4
Oak Ridge 70 K4
Oamaru 64 C7
Oaxaca 72 E5
Ob' 30 N2
Oban 16 G5
O Barco 20 D2
Oberdrauburg 22 H4
Oberhausen 14 J3
Oberkirch 12 D8
Oberndorf 22 H3
Oberstdorf 22 F3
Oberursel 12 D6
Obervellach 10 C11
Oberwart 22 M3
Obi 43 C3
Obidos 76 F4
Obigarm 46 K2
Obihiro 38 L2
Obluch'ye 36 N7
Obninsk 30 G3
Obo, *C.A.R.* 56 D2
Obo, *China* 38 C3
Oborniki 10 F5
Obouya 54 H5
Oboyan' 30 G4
Obskaya Guba 34 N4
Obuasi 54 D3
Ob'yachevo 30 J2
Ocala 70 K6
Ocaña, *Col.* 76 C2
Ocaña, *Spain* 20 G5
Ocean Falls 68 F6
Oceania 60 G7
Oceanside 70 C5
Och'amch'ire 46 D1
Ochsenfurt 12 E7
Oda 54 D3
Ōdate 38 L2
Odda 8 D6
Odemira 20 B7
Ödemiş 28 L6
Odense 12 F1
Oder = Odra 10 F6
Oderzo 22 H5
Odesa 30 F5
Odessa = Odesa, *Ukraine* 30 F5
Odessa, *U.S.* 70 F5
Odienné 54 C3
Odorheiu Secuiesc 26 N3
Odra 10 F6
Odžaci 26 G4
Oeh 38 C2
Oeiras 76 J5
Oelsnitz 12 H6
Oeno 60 N8
Oestev 78 H7
Offenbach 12 D6
Offenburg 22 C2
Ogasawara-shotō 32 T7
Ogbomosho 54 E3
Ogden 70 D3
Ogdensburg 68 R8
Ogilvie Mountains 68 C4
Oglio 22 E5
Ogosta 26 L6
Ogre 8 N8
Ogre 8 N8
O Grove 20 B2
Ogulin 22 L5
Ohai 64 A7
Ohanet 52 G3
Ohio 70 J4
Ohio 70 K3
Ohre 12 J6
Ohrid 28 C3
Ohura 64 E4
Oia 28 H8
Oiapoque 76 G3
Oise 14 E5
Ōita 38 J4
Ojinaga 70 F6
Ojos del Salado 78 H4
Oka 36 G6
Okaba 43 E4
Okahandja 58 B4
Okanagan Lake 70 C2
Okano 54 G4
Okara 44 B2
Okarem 46 F2
Okato 64 D4
Okavango Delta 58 C3
Okayama 38 J4
Okene 54 F3
Oker 12 F4
Okha, *India* 46 J5
Okha, *Russia* 36 Q6
Okhansk 30 L3
Okhotsk 36 Q5
Okhtyrka 30 F4
Okinawa 38 H5
Okinawa 38 H5
Oki-shotō 38 J3
Okitipupa 54 E3
Oklahoma 70 G5
Oklahoma City 70 G4
Okoyo 54 H5
Okranger 8 E5
Oksino 30 K1
Oktinden 8 H4
Oktyabr'sk 30 L5
Oktyabr'skiy 30 K4
Okurchan 36 S5
Okushiri-tō 38 K2
Ólafsvík 8 (1)B2
Öland 8 J8
Olanga 8 Q3
Olava 12 J7
Olavarría 78 J6
Oława 10 G7
Olbia 24 D8
Olching 22 G2
Old Crow 68 D3
Oldenburg, *Germany* 12 D3
Oldenburg, *Germany* 12 F2
Oldenzaal 14 J2
Oldham 16 L8
Old Head of Kinsale 16 D10
Olecko 10 M3
Olekma 36 L5
Olekminsk 36 L4
Oleksandriya 30 F5
Olenegorsk 8 S2
Olenek 36 J3
Olenëk 36 L2
Olenëkskiy Zaliv 36 L2
Oleśnica 10 G6
Olesno 10 H7
Olhão 20 C7
Olib 22 K6
Olinda 76 L5
Oliva 20 K6
Olivet 18 G6
Olmos 76 B5
Olochi 36 K6
Olonets 30 F2
Olongapo 40 G4
Oloron-Ste-Marie 18 E10
Olot 20 N2
Olovyannaya 36 K6
Olpe 14 K3
Olsztyn 10 K4
Olt 26 M4
Olten 22 C3
Oltenița 26 P5
Oltu 46 D1
Oluanpi 40 G2
Olvera 20 E8
Olympia 70 B2
Olympos 28 E4
Olympus 28 Q10
Olyutorskiy 36 W4
Olyutorskiy Zaliv 36 V4
Om' 34 N6
Oma 44 D2
Omagh 16 E7
Omaha 70 G3
Omakau 64 B7
Oman 46 G5
Omapere 64 D2
Omarama 64 B7
Omaruru 58 B4
Omba, *China* 44 E2
Omba, *Russia* 34 E4
Omboué 54 F5
Ombrone 24 F6
Omdurman = Umm Durman 50 F4
Omegna 22 D5
Omeo 62 J7
Om Hajer 50 G5
Omis 22 M7
Ommen 14 J2
Omolon 36 T3
Omoloy 36 N3
Omo Wenz 56 F2
Omsk 34 N6
Omsukchan 36 S4
Omulew 10 L4
Ōmuta 38 H4
Onang 43 A3
Onda 20 K5
Ondangwa 58 B3
Ondjiva 58 B3
Ondo 54 E3
Ondörhaan 38 E1
One and a Half Degree Channel 44 B8
Onega 30 G2
O'Neill 70 G3
Onești 26 P3
Onezhskoye Ozero 30 F2
Ongole 44 D5
Onguday 34 R7
Onilahy 58 G4
Onitsha 54 F3
Onon 36 J7
Onon 36 J7
Onslow Bay 72 J2
Ontario 68 N6
Ontinyent 20 K6
Oodnadatta 62 G5
Oostburg 14 F3
Oostelijk-Flevoland 14 H2
Oostende 14 E3
Oosterhout 14 G3
Oosterschelde 14 F3
Oost-Vlieland 14 H1
Ootsa Lake 68 F6
Opala 56 C4
Oparino 30 J3
Opava 10 G8
Opochka 30 E3
Opoczno 10 K6
Opole 10 G7
Opornyy 34 J8
Opotiki 64 F4
Opunake 64 D4
Opuwo 58 A3
Oradea 26 J2
Orahovac 26 H7
Orai 44 C3
Oran 20 K9
Orán 78 J3
Orange 58 C5
Orange, *Aus.* 62 J6
Orange, *France* 18 K9
Orangemund 58 B5
Orango 54 A2
Oranienburg 12 J4
Orapa 58 D4
Orăștie 26 L4
Oravița 26 J4
Orbec 18 F4
Orbetello 24 F6
Orco 22 C5
Ordes 20 B1
Ordes Santa Comba 20 B1
Ordu 46 C1
Öreälven 8 K4
Örebro 8 H7
Oregon 70 B3
Orekhovo-Zuyevo 30 G3
Orel 30 G4
Ören 28 K7
Orenburg 30 L4
Orestiada 28 J3
Orewa 64 E3
Orford Ness 14 D2
Orhei 26 R2
Orihuela 20 K6
Orillia 70 L3
Orinoco 76 D2
Orinoco Delta = Delta del Orinoco 76 E2
Orissaare 8 M7
Oristano 24 C9
Orivesi 8 Q5
Orkla 8 F5
Orkney Islands 16 K3
Orlando 70 K6
Orléans 18 G6
Orlik 36 F6
Orly 14 E6
Ormara 46 H4
Ormoc 40 G4
Ormos Almyrou 28 G9
Ormos Mesara 28 G9
Ornans 18 M6
Ornö 8 K7
Örnsköldsvik 8 K5
Orocué 76 C3
Orona 60 J6
Oronoque 76 F3
Oroqen Zizhiqi 36 L6
Orosei 24 D8
Orosháza 26 H3
Oroszlany 10 H10
Orotukan 36 S4
Orroroo 62 G6
Orsa 8 H6
Orsay 18 H5
Orsha 30 F4
Orsk 30 L4
Orșova 26 K5
Ørsta 8 D5
Ortaklar 28 K7
Orthez 18 E10
Ortigueira 20 C1
Ortisei 22 G4
Ortles 22 F4
Ortona 24 J6
Orūmīyeh 46 E2
Oruro 76 D7
Orvieto 24 G6
Orville 18 L6
Ōsaka 38 K4
Osăm 26 M6
Oschatz 12 J5
Oschersleben 12 G4
O Seixo 20 B3
Osh 34 N9
Oshawa 70 L3
Oshkosh 70 J3
Oshogbo 54 E3
Osijek 26 F4
Osimo 22 J7
Oskarshamn 8 J8
Oslo 8 F7
Oslofjorden 8 F7
Osmancık 46 B1
Osmaniye 46 C2
Osnabrück 14 L2
Osor 22 K6
Osorno 78 G7
Osprey Reef 62 J2
Oss 14 H3
Ossa de Montiel 20 H6
Ossora 36 U5
Ostashkov 30 F3
Oste 12 E3
Osterburg 12 G4
Østerdalen 8 F6
Osterholz-Scharmbeck 12 D3
Osterode 12 F5
Östersund 8 H5

Ostfriesische Inseln 12 C3
Ostiglia 22 G5
Ostrava 10 H8
Ostróda 10 K4
Ostrołęka 10 L4
Ostrov, *Czech Rep.* 12 H6
Ostrov, *Russia* 30 E3
Ostrova Arkticheskogo
Instituta 34 P2
Ostrova Medvezh'I 36 T2
Ostrov Atlasova 36 S6
Ostrova Vrangelya 66 V4
Ostrov Ayon 36 V2
Ostrov Belyy 34 N3
Ostrov Beringa 36 V6
Ostrov Bol'shevik 34 V2
Ostrov Bol'shoy
Begichev 36 J2
Ostrov Bol'shoy
Lyakhovskiy 36 Q2
Ostrov Bol'shoy
Shantar 36 P6
Ostrov Iturup 36 R8
Ostrov Karaginskiy 36 U5
Ostrov Kil'din 8 T2
Ostrov Kolguyev 34 H4
Ostrov Komsomolets 34 T1
Ostrov Kotel'nyy 36 P1
Ostrov Kunashir 36 R8
Ostrov Mednyy 36 V6
Ostrov
Mezhdusharskiy 34 H3
Ostrov Morzhovets 30 H1
Ostrov Novaya Sibir' 36 S2
Ostrov Ogurchinskiy 46 F2
Ostrov Oktyabr'skoy 34 S2
Ostrov Onekotan 36 S7
Ostrov Paramushir 36 T6
Ostrov Rasshua 36 S7
Ostrov Shiashkotan 36 S7
Ostrov Shumshu 36 T6
Ostrov Simushir 36 S7
Ostrov Urup 36 S7
Ostrov Ushakova 34 Q1
Ostrov Vaygach 34 K3
Ostrov Vise 34 P2
Ostrov
Vosrozhdeniya 34 K9
Ostrov Vrangelya 36 W2
Ostrowiec
Świętokrzyski 10 L7
Ostrów Mazowiecka 10 L5
Ostrów Wielkopolski 10 G6
Ostuni 24 M8
Osum 28 C4
Ōsumi-shotō 38 H4
Osuna 20 E7
Oświęcim 10 J7
Otago Peninsula 64 C7
Otaki 64 E5
Otaru 38 L2
Oțelu Roșu 26 K4
Othonoi 28 B5
Oti 54 E3
Otira 64 C6
Otjiwarongo 58 B4
Otočac 22 L6
Otog Qi 38 D3
Otorohanga 64 E4
Otranto 24 N8
Otrøy 8 D5
Otrozhnyy 36 W3
Otta 8 E6
Ottawa 70 L2
Ottawa, *Can.* 70 L2
Ottawa, *U.S.* 70 G4
Ottawa Islands 68 Q5
Otterøy 8 F4
Ottobrunn 22 G2
Ottumwa 70 H3
Otukpo 54 F3
Ouadâne 52 C4
Ouadda 56 C2
Ouagadougou 54 D2
Oualâta 52 D5
Ouallam 54 E2
Ouanda-Djallé 56 C2
Ouargla 52 G2
Ouarzazate 52 D2
Oudenaarde 14 F4
Oudenbosch 14 G3
Oudtshoorn 58 C6
Oued Laou 20 E9
Oued Tiélat 20 K9
Oued Zem 52 D2
Ouéléssébougou 54 C2
Ouésso 54 H4
Ouezzane 52 D2
Oujda 52 E2
Oujeft 52 C4
Oulainen 8 N4
Ould Yenjé 52 C5
Oulu 8 N4
Oulujärvi 8 P4
Oulujoki 8 P4
Oulx 22 B5
Oum-Chalouba 50 D4
Oum-Hadjer 50 C5
Ounarjoki 8 N3
Our 14 J4
Ourense 20 C2
Ouricurí 76 J5
Ourthe 14 H4
Oustreham 14 B5
Outer Hebrides 16 D4
Outjo 58 B4
Outokumpu 8 Q5
Out Skerries 16 M1
Ouyen 62 H7
Ovacık 28 R8
Ovada 22 D6
Ovalle 78 G5
Overflakkee 14 G3
Overlander
Roadhouse 62 B5
Övertorneå 8 M3
Ovidiopol' 26 T3
Oviedo 20 E1
Owaka 64 B8
Owando 54 H5
Owen River 64 D5
Owensboro 70 J4
Owen Sound 70 K3
Owerri 54 F3
Owo 54 F3
Owyhee 46 C3
Oxford, *N.Z.* 64 D6
Oxford, *U.K.* 14 A3
Oxnard 70 C5
Oyapock 76 G3
Oyem 54 G4
Oyen 70 D1
Oyonnax 22 A4
Özd 10 K9
Ozernovskiy 36 T6
Ozero Alakol' 34 Q8
Ozero Aralsor 30 J5
Ozero Aydarkul' 34 M9
Ozero Balkhash 34 N8
Ozero Baykal 36 H6
Ozero Beloye 30 G2
Ozero Chany 34 P7
Ozero Chernoye 30 N3
Ozero Il'men' 30 F3
Ozero-Imandra 8 R2
Ozero Inder 34 J8
Ozero Janis'jarvi 8 R5
Ozero Kamennoje 8 R4
Ozero Kanozero 8 T3
Ozero Khanka 38 J2
Ozero Kolvitskoye 8 S3
Ozero Kovdozero 8 S3
Ozero Kulundinskoye 34 P7
Ozero Kushmurun 30 N4
Ozero Lama 36 D2
Ozero Leksozero 8 R5
Ozero Lovozero 8 T2
Ozero Nyuk 8 R4
Ozero Ozhogino 36 R3
Ozero Pirenga 8 R3
Ozero Pyaozero 8 R3
Ozero Saltaim 30 P3
Ozero Sarpa 30 J5
Ozero
Segozeroskoye 30 F2
Ozero Seletyteniz 34 N7
Ozero Srednee
Kuyto 8 R4
Ozero Taymyr 34 U3
Ozero Teletskoye 34 R7
Ozero Tengiz 30 N4
Ozero Topozero 8 R4
Ozero Umbozero 8 T3
Ozero Vygozero 30 G2
Ozero Yalpug 26 R4
Ozero Zaysan 34 Q8
Ozero Zhaltyr 30 K5
Ozero Zhamanakkol' 30 M5
Ozersk 10 M3
Ozhogina 36 R3
Ozhogino 36 R3
Ozieri 24 C8
Ozinki 30 J4

P

Paamiut 68 X4
Paar 12 G8
Paarl 58 B6
Pabbay 16 E4
Pabianice 10 J6
Pabna 44 E4
Pacasmayo 76 B5
Pachino 24 K12
Pachuca 72 E4
Pacific Ocean 60 M3
Pacitan 42 E4
Padalere 43 B3
Padang 42 C3
Padangpanjang 42 C3
Padangsidempuan 42 B2
Padborg 12 E2
Paderborn 12 D5
Padova 22 G5
Padre Island 70 G6
Padrón 20 B2
Paducah 70 J4
Padum 44 C2
Paeroa 64 E3
Pafos 28 Q10
Pag 22 K6
Pag 22 L6
Paga Conta 76 G4
Pagadian 40 G5
Pagai Selatan 42 B3
Pagai Utara 42 B3
Pagalu = Annobón 54 F5
Pagan 60 E4
Pagatan 42 F3
Pagri 44 E3
Pahiatua 64 E5
Paide 8 N7
Päijänne 8 N6
Painan 42 C3
Paisley 16 H6
Paita 76 A5
Pakaraima
Mountains 76 E2
Pakch'ŏn 38 H3
Pakhachi 36 V4
Paki 54 F2
Pakistan 46 J4
Pakokku 40 A2
Pakotai 64 D2
Pakrac 22 N5
Paks 26 F3
Pakxé 40 D3
Pala 50 B6
Palafrugell 20 P3
Palagonia 24 J11
Palagruža 24 L6
Palaiochora 28 F9
Palamós 20 P3
Palana 36 U5
Palanan 40 G3
Palanga 10 L2
Palangkaraya 42 E3
Palanpur 44 B4
Palantak 46 H4
Palapye 58 D4
Palatka 36 S4
Palau 24 D7
Palau 60 D5
Palau 60 D5
Palaw 40 B4
Palawan 40 F5
Palazzolo Arceide 24 J11
Palembang 42 C3
Palencia 20 F2
Paleokastritsa 28 B5
Palermo 24 H10
Palestine 70 G5
Palestrina 24 G7
Paletwa 40 A2
Palghat 44 C6
Pali 44 B3
Palikir 60 F5
Palimbang 40 G5
Pälkohda 44 D5
Palk Strait 44 C7
Palma del Rio 20 E7
Palma de Mallorca 20 N5
Palma di
Montechiaro 24 H11
Palmanova 22 J5
Palmares 76 K5
Palmarola 24 G8
Palmas 76 H6
Palmas 78 L4
Palmerston 64 C7
Palmerston Island 60 K7
Palmerston North 64 E5
Palmi 24 K10
Palmira 76 B3
Palmyra Island 60 K5
Palojärvi 8 M2
Palopo 43 B3
Palu 43 A3
Palyavaam 36 W3
Pama 54 E2
Pamekasan 42 E4
Pamhagen 22 M3
Pamiers 18 G10
Pamlico Sound 70 L4
Pampa 70 F4
Pampas 78 J6
Pamplona, *Col.* 72 K7
Pamplona, *Spain* 20 J2
Panagjurište 26 M7
Panaji 44 B5
Panama 72 H7
Panamá 76 B2
Panama Canal =
Canal de Panamá 72 J7
Panama City 70 J5
Panarea 24 K10
Panarik 42 D2
Panaro 22 G6
Panay 40 G4
Pančevo 26 H5
Panciu 26 Q4
Pandan 40 G4
Pandharpur 44 C5
Panevėžys 10 P2
Pangani 56 F5
Pangin 44 F3
Pangkajene 43 A3
Pangkalanbuun 42 E3
Pangkalpinang 42 D3
Pangnirtung 68 T3
Pangutaran Group 40 G5
Panipat 44 C3
Panjāb 46 J3
Panjgur 46 H4
Pankshin 54 F3
Pantanal 76 F7
Pantar 43 B4
Pantelleria 52 H1
Pantemakassar 43 B4
Paola 24 L9
Paoua 56 B2
Pápa 26 E2
Papakura 64 E3
Papantla 72 E4
Paparoa 64 E3
Papa Stour 16 L1
Papatowi 64 B8
Papa Westray 16 K2
Papenburg 12 C3
Papey 8 (1)F2
Papua New Guinea 60 E6
Papun 40 B3
Para 76 H4
Pará 76 G5
Parabel' 34 Q6
Paracatu 76 H7
Paracel Islands 40 E3
Paraćin 26 J6
Pará de Minas 76 J7
Paragua, *Bolivia* 76 E6
Paragua, *Venezuela* 76 E2
Paraguay 74 F6
Paraguay 78 J3
Paraíba 76 K5
Parakou 54 E3
Paralia 28 E8
Paramaribo 76 F2
Paraná 78 J5
Paraná 78 K4
Paraná 78 L3
Paranã 76 H6
Paranã 76 H6
Paranaguá 78 M4
Paranaíba 76 G7
Paranaíba 76 G7
Paranavaí 78 L3
Paranestio 28 G3
Paraparaumu 64 E5
Paray-le Monial 18 K7
Parbhani 44 C5
Parchim 12 G3
Pardo 76 J7
Pardubice 10 E7
Parepare 43 A3
Parga 28 C5
Parigi 43 B3
Parika 76 F2
Parintins 76 F4
Paris 18 H5
Parkersburg 70 K4
Parla 20 G4
Parma 22 F6
Parma 22 F6
Parnaíba 76 J4
Parnaíba 76 J4
Parnassus 64 D6
Pärnu 8 N7
Pärnu 8 N7
Paros 28 H7
Paros 28 H7
Parry Bay 68 Q3
Parry Islands 68 L1
Parry Sound 70 L2
Parthenay 18 E7
Partinico 24 H10
Partizansk 38 J2
Paru 76 G4
Parvatipuram 44 D5
Paryang 44 D2
Pasadena 70 C5
Paşalimani Adası 28 K4
Pasawng 40 B3
Paşcani 26 P2
Pascual 40 G4
Pasewalk 12 K3
Pasig 40 G4
Pasłęk 10 J3
Pasłek 10 J3
Pasleka 8 L9
Pašman 22 L7
Pasni 46 H4
Paso de Hachado 78 G6
Paso de Indios 78 H7
Paso de la Cumbre 78 H5
Paso de San
Francisco 78 H4
Paso Río Mayo 78 G8
Passau 12 J8
Passo Fundo 78 L4
Passos 76 H8
Pastavy 8 P9
Pasto 76 B3
Pastos Bons 76 J5
Pasvalys 10 P1
Pásztó 26 G2
Patagonia 78 G8
Patan, *India* 44 B4
Patan, *Nepal* 44 E3
Patea 64 E4
Pate Island 56 G4
Paterna 20 K5
Paternò 24 J11
Paterson 70 M3
Pathankot 44 C2
Patia 76 B3
Patiala 44 C2
Patmos 28 J7
Patna 44 E3
Patnos 46 D2
Patos de Minas 76 H7
Patra 28 D6
Patraikis Kolpos 28 D6
Patreksfjörður 8 (1)B2
Pattani 40 C5
Pattaya 40 C4
Patti 24 J10
Paturau River 64 D5
Pau 20 K1
Pauini 76 D5
Pauini 76 D5
Paulatuk 68 G3
Paulo Afonso 76 K5
Päveh 46 E2
Pavia 22 E5
Pävilosta 8 L8
Pavlikeni 26 N6
Pavlodar 34 P7
Pavlohrad 30 G5
Pavlovsk 30 H4
Pavlovskaya 30 G5
Pavullo nel Frignano 22 F6
Paxoi 28 C5
Paxson 68 B4
Payerne 22 B4
Payne's Find 62 C5
Paysandú 78 K5
Payturma 34 S3
Pazardžik 26 M7
Pazin 22 J5
Peace 68 H5
Peace River 68 H5
Pebane 58 F3
Pebas 76 C5
Peć 26 H7
Pechora 30 K1
Pechora 30 L1
Pechorskoye More 34 J4
Pechory 8 P8
Pecos 72 D2
Pécs 26 F3
Pedja 8 P7
Pedra Azul 76 J7
Pedra Lume 54 (1)B1
Pedreiras 76 J4
Pedro Afonso 76 H5
Pedro Juan Caballero 78 K3
Pedro Luro 78 J6
Peel Sound 68 M2
Peene 12 J3
Peenemünde 12 J2
Pegasus Bay 64 D6
Pegnitz 12 G7
Pegu 40 B3
Pegunungan Barisan 42 B2
Pegunungan Iran 42 F2
Pegunungan Maoke 43 E3
Pegunungan Meratus 42 F3
Pegunungan
Schwaner 42 E3
Pegunungan Van
Rees 43 E3
Pehuajó 78 J6
Peine 12 F4
Peiraias 28 F7
Peißenberg 22 G3
Peixe 76 H6
Pekalongan 42 D4
Pekanbaru 42 C2
Peking = Beijing 38 F3
Pelaihari 42 E3
Peleduy 36 J5
Peleng 43 B3
Pelhřimov 10 E8
Pelješac 24 M6
Pello 8 N3
Pellworm 12 D2
Pelly Bay 68 P3
Peloponnisos 28 D7
Pelotas 78 L5
Pelym 30 M2
Pemangkat 42 D2
Pematangsiantar 42 B2
Pemba 58 G2
Pemba Island 56 F5
Pembroke, *Can.* 70 L2
Pembroke, *U.K.* 16 H10
Peñafiel 20 F3
Peñaranda de
Bracamonte 20 E4
Peñarroya-
Pueblonuevo 20 E6
Pendik 28 M4
Pendleton 70 C2
Pendolo 42 G3
Peniche 20 A5
Península de Azuero 72 H7
Peninsula de Guajira 72 K6
Península Valdés 78 J7
Péninsule de Gaspé 68 T7
Péninsule d'Ungava 68 R4
Penmarch 18 A6
Penne 24 H6
Pennines 16 K7
Pennsylvania 70 L3
Penrith 16 K7
Pensacola 72 G2
Penticton 70 B2
Penza 30 J4
Penzance 16 G11
Penzhina 36 V4
Penzhinskaya Guba 36 U4
Penzhinskiy Khrebet 36 V4
Peoria 70 J3
Percival Lakes 62 D4
Peregrebnoye 30 N2
Pereira 76 B3
Pergamino 78 J5
Périers 18 D4
Périgueux 18 F8
Peristera 28 G5
Perito Moreno 78 G8
Perleberg 12 G3
Perm' 30 L3
Përmet 28 C4
Pernambuco 76 K5
Pernik 26 L7
Péronne 14 E5
Perpignan 18 H11
Perth, *Aus.* 62 C6
Perth, *U.K.* 16 J5
Pertuis Breton 18 D7
Peru 76 C6
Peru-Chile Trench 74 D5
Perugia 24 G5
Pervomays'k 30 F5
Pervoural'sk 30 L3
Pesaro 22 H7
Pescara 24 J6
Pescia 22 F7
Peshawar 44 B2
Peshkopi 28 C3
Peski Karakumy 46 G2
Peski Kyzylkum 34 L9
Peski Priaral'skiye
Karakumy 34 L8
Pesnica 22 L4
Pessac 18 E9
Peštera 28 G2
Petalioi 28 G7
Pétange 14 H5
Petare 72 L6
Petauke 58 E2
Peterborough, *Can.* 70 L3
Peterborough, *U.K.* 16 M9
Peterhead 16 L4
Peter I Øy 80 (2)JJ3
Petersburg 70 L4
Petersfield 14 B3
Petershagen 12 D4
Petit Mécatina 68 U6
Peto 72 G4
Petre Bay 64 (1)B1
Petrič 28 F3
Petrila 26 L4
Petrinja 22 M5
Petrolina 76 J5
Petropavlovka 36 H6
Petropavlovsk 30 N4
Petropavlovsk-
Kamchatskiy 36 T6
Petrópolis 78 N3
Petroșani 26 L4
Petrovac 26 J5
Petrovsk-
Zabaykal'skiy 36 H6
Petrozavodsk 30 F2
Petrun 30 M1
Petukhovo 30 N3
Pevek 36 W3
Pezinok 10 G9
Pfaffenhofen 12 G8
Pfarrkirchen 12 H8
Pflach 22 F3
Pforzheim 12 D8
Pfunds 22 F4
Pfungstadt 12 D7
Phalaborwa 58 E4
Phalodi 44 B3
Phan Rang 40 D4
Phan Thiêt 40 D4
Phatthalung 40 C5
Phet Buri 40 B4
Phichit 40 C3
Philadelphia 70 L4
Philippeville 14 G4
Philippines 40 G5
Philippine Trench 32 R8
Philips 68 K7
Phitsanulok 40 C3
Phnum Penh 40 C4
Phoenix 58 (1)B2
Phoenix 70 D5
Phoenix Islands 60 J6
Phôngsali 40 C2
Phuket 40 B5
Phumĭ Sâmraông 40 C4
Piacenza 22 E5
Piadena 22 F5
Pianoro 22 G6
Pianosa 24 E6
Piatra-Neamț 26 P3
Piauí 76 J5
Piazza Armerina 24 J11
Pibor Post 56 E2
Pichilemu 78 G5
Pico 52 (1)B2
Pico Almanzor 20 E4
Pico Cristóbal Colón 72 K6
Pico da Bandeira 78 N3
Pico da Neblina 76 D3
Pico de Itambé 78 N2
Pico de Teide 52 B3
Pico Duarte 72 K5
Picos 76 J5
Picton 64 D5
Pic Toussidé 50 C3
Piedras Negras 70 F6
Pieksämäki 8 P5
Pielinen 8 Q5
Pierre 70 F3
Pierrelatte 18 K9
Piers do Rio 76 H7
Piešťany 10 G9
Pietermaritzburg 58 E5
Pietersburg 58 D4
Pietrasanta 22 F6
Piet Retief 58 E5
Pieve di Cadore 22 H4
Pihlájavesi 8 P6
Pik Aborigen 36 R4
Piketberg 58 B6
Pik Kommunizma 46 K2
Pik Pobedy 34 P9
Piła 10 F4
Pilaya 78 H3
Pilcomayo 78 J4
Pilibhit 44 C3
Pilica 10 J7
Pimba 62 G6
Pimenta Bueno 76 E6
Pinamalayan 40 G4
Pinamar 78 K6
Pinang 40 B5
Pinar del Río 72 H4
Pinarhisar 28 K3
Pińczów 10 K7
Pindaré Mirim 76 H4
Pindos 28 D5
Pine Bluff 70 H5
Pine Creek 62 F2
Pinega 30 H2
Pineios 28 E5
Pine Island Bay 80 (2)GG3
Pinerolo 22 C6
Pingdingshan 38 E4
Pingguo 40 D2
Pingle 40 E2
Pingliang 38 D3
Pingshi 38 E5
P'ingtung 40 G2
Pingxiang, *China* 40 D2
Pingxiang, *China* 40 E1
Pinhel 20 C4
Pini 42 B2
Pinka 22 M3
Pink Mountain 68 G5
Pinneberg 12 E3
Pinsk 30 E4
Piombino 24 E6
Pionerskiy, *Russia* 10 K3
Pionerskiy, *Russia* 30 M2
Piopio 64 E4
Piotrków Trybunalski 10 J6
Piove di Sacco 22 H5
Piperi 28 G5
Pipiriki 64 E4
Piracicaba 78 M3
Pirin 28 F3
Piripiri 76 J4
Pirmasens 12 C7
Pirna 12 J6
Pirot 26 K6
Piru 43 C3
Pisa 10 L4
Pisa 22 F7
Pisco 76 B6
Písek 10 D8
Pishīn 46 H3
Pishin 46 J3
Piska 10 L4
Pisticci 24 L8
Pistoia 22 F7
Pisz 10 L4
Pitcairn Islands 60 P8
Piteå 8 L4
Piteälven 30 C1
Pitești 26 M5
Pithara 62 C6
Pithiviers 18 H5
Pitkyaranta 30 F2

Pitlochry 16 J5
Pitlyar 30 N1
Pitt Island 64 (1)B2
Pittsburgh 70 L3
Pitt Strait 64 (1)B2
Piura 76 A5
Pivka 22 K5
Placer 40 G4
Plaiamonas 28 E5
Plainview 70 F5
Plampang 42 F4
Planalto Central 76 H6
Planalto da Borborema 76 K5
Planalto do Mato Grosso 76 G6
Plasencia 20 D5
Plast 30 M4
Plateau du Djado 52 H4
Plateau du Limousin 18 F8
Plateau du Tademaït 52 F3
Plateau of Tibet = Xizang Gaoyuan 44 D2
Plateaux Batéké 54 G5
Plato 72 K7
Plato Ustyurt 34 J9
Plattling 12 H8
Plattsburgh 70 M3
Plau 12 H3
Plauen 12 H6
Plavnik 22 K6
Plavsk 30 G4
Playa de Castilla 20 D7
Playas 76 A4
Plây Cu 40 D4
Pleiße 12 H5
Plesetsk 30 H2
Pleven 26 M6
Pljevlja 26 G6
Płock 10 J5
Pločno 26 E6
Ploërmel 18 C6
Ploiești 26 P5
Plomari 28 J6
Plön 12 F2
Płońsk 10 K5
Plovdiv 26 M7
Plumtree 58 D4
Plungė 10 L2
Plymouth 16 H11
Plyussa 8 Q7
Plyussa 30 E3
Plzeň 10 C8
Po 22 E5
Pocahontas 72 F1
Pocatello 70 D3
Pochet 36 F5
Pochinok 30 F4
Pocking 22 J2
Podgorica 26 G7
Podkamennaya Tunguska 36 F4
Podol'sk 30 G3
Podravska Slatina 26 E4
Poel 12 G2
Pofadder 58 B5
Pogradec 28 C4
P'ohang 38 H3
Pohnpei 60 F5
Pohokura 64 F4
Pohořelice 22 M2
Point Arena 70 B4
Point Barrow 66 S2
Point Conception 70 B5
Point Culver 62 D6
Point d'Entrecasteaux 62 B6
Pointe-Noire 54 G5
Point Hope 66 T3
Point Pedro 44 D7
Poitiers 18 F7
Pokaran 44 B3
Pokhara 44 D3
Poko 56 D3
Pokrovsk 36 M4
Pola de Siero 20 E1
Poland 10 G6
Polar Bluff 72 F1
Polatlı 28 Q5
Polatsk 30 E3
Police 12 K3
Polichnitos 28 J5
Policoro 24 L8
Poligny 18 L7
Poligus 34 S5
Polillo Islands 40 G4
Poliocastro 24 L9
Polis 28 Q9
Polistena 24 L10
Pollachi 44 C6
Pollença 20 P5
Polohy 30 G5
Polomoloc 40 H5
Polonnaruwa 44 D7
Poltava 30 F5
Põltsamaa 8 N7
Poluostrov Shmidta 36 Q6
Poluostrov Taymyr 34 R3
Poluostrov Yamal 34 M3
Poluy 34 M4
Põlva 8 P7
Polyaigos 28 G8
Polyarnye Zori 8 S3
Polyarnyy 36 X3
Polykastro 28 E4
Polynesia 60 J6
Pombal 20 B5
Pomeranian Bay 10 D3
Pomorie 26 Q7
Pompei 24 J8
Ponce 72 L5
Pondicherry 44 C6
Pond Inlet 68 R2
Ponferrada 20 D2
Poniatowa 10 M6
Ponoy 30 H1
Pons 18 E8
Ponta Delgada 52 (1)B2
Ponta do Podrão 54 G6
Ponta do Sol 54 (1)B1
Ponta Grossa 78 L4
Ponta Khehuene 58 F5
Pont-à-Mousson 18 M5
Ponta Porã 78 K3
Pontarlier 18 M7
Pontassieve 22 G7
Ponta Zavora 58 F4
Pont-d'Alin 18 L7
Ponteareas 20 B2
Ponte da Barca 20 B3
Pontedera 22 F7
Ponte de Sor 20 C5
Pontevedra 20 B2
Pontianak 42 D3
Pontivy 18 C5
Pontoise 14 E5
Pontorson 18 D5
Pontremoli 22 E6
Ponza 24 G8
Poogau 22 J3
Poole 16 L11
Poole Bay 16 L11
Pooncarie 62 H6
Poopó 76 D7
Poopó Challapata 78 H2
Poor Knights Islands 64 E2
Popayán 72 J8
Poperinge 14 E4
Popigay 34 W3
Poplar Bluff 70 H4
Popocatépetl 72 E5
Popoh 42 E4
Popokabaka 54 H6
Popovača 22 M5
Popovo 26 P6
Poprad 10 K8
Poprad 10 K8
Porangatu 76 H6
Porbandar 46 J5
Porcupine 68 D3
Pordenone 22 H5
Poreč 22 J5
Porechye 24 H3
Pori 8 L6
Porirua 64 E5
Porlamar 72 M6
Poronaysk 36 Q7
Poros 28 F7
Porosozero 30 F2
Porozina 22 K5
Porpoise Bay 80 (2)T3
Porriño 20 B2
Porsangen 8 N1
Porsgrunn 8 E7
Portadown 16 F7
Portage 70 J3
Portage la Prairie 70 G1
Port Alberni 70 B2
Port Albert 62 J7
Portalegre 20 C5
Port Arthur, *Aus.* 62 J8
Port Arthur, *U.S.* 70 H6
Port Augusta 62 G6
Port-au-Prince 72 K5
Port Blair 40 A4
Port Burwell 68 U4
Port Charlotte 70 K6
Port Douglas 62 J3
Portel, *Brazil* 76 G4
Portel, *Portugal* 20 C6
Port Elizabeth 58 D6
Port Ellen 16 F6
Port Fitzroy 64 E3
Port-Gentil 54 F5
Port Harcourt 54 F4
Port Hardy 68 F6
Port Hawkesbury 68 U7
Port Hedland 62 C4
Port Hope Simpson 68 V6
Portimão 20 B7
Portland, *Aus.* 62 H7
Portland, *N.Z.* 64 E2
Portland, *Me., U.S.* 70 M3
Portland, *Oreg., U.S.* 70 B2
Portland Island 64 F4
Port Laoise 16 E8
Port Lavaca 70 G6
Port Lincoln 62 G6
Port Loko 54 B3
Port Louis 58 (1)B2
Port Macquarie 62 K6
Port-Menier 68 U7
Port Moresby 62 J1
Port Nolloth 58 B5
Porto, *Corsica* 24 C6
Porto, *Portugal* 20 B3
Porto Alegre, *R.G.S., Brazil* 78 L5
Porto Alegre, *Pará, Brazil* 76 G4
Porto Amboim 58 A2
Portocheli 28 F7
Porto do Son 20 A2
Porto Esperidião 76 F7
Portoferraio 24 E6
Porto Franco 76 H5
Port of Spain 76 E1
Pôrto Grande 76 G3
Portogruaro 22 H5
Porto Inglês 54 (1)B1
Portomaggiore 22 G6
Porto Murtinho 78 K3
Porto Nacional 76 H6
Porto-Novo 54 E3
Porto San Giorgio 24 H5
Pôrto Santana 76 G3
Porto Santo 52 B2
Pôrto Seguro 76 K7
Porto Tolle 22 H6
Porto Torres 24 C8
Porto-Vecchio 24 D7
Pôrto Velho 76 E5
Portoviejo 76 A4
Port Pire 62 G6
Portree 16 F4
Port Said = Bûr Sa'îd 50 F1
Port St. Johns 58 D6
Port Shepstone 58 E6
Portsmouth, *U.K.* 14 A4
Portsmouth, *U.S.* 70 K4
Port Sudan = Bur Sudan 50 G4
Port Talbot 16 J10
Portugal 20 B5
Portugalete 20 G1
Port-Vendres 18 J11
Port-Vila 60 G7
Port Warrender 62 E2
Posadas 78 K4
Poschiavo 22 F4
Poshekhon'ye 30 G3
Poso 43 B3
Posse 76 H6
Pößneck 12 G6
Postmasburg 58 C5
Postojna 22 K5
Post Weygand 52 F4
Posušje 26 E6
Pota 42 G4
Potapovo 34 R4
Potenza 22 J7
Potenza 24 K8
Potgietersrus 58 D4
Potiskum 54 G2
Potosí 76 D7
Potsdam 12 J4
Pottuvil 44 D7
Pourerere 64 F5
Pouto 64 E3
Póvoa de Varzim 20 B3
Povorino 30 H4
Powder 70 E2
Powell River 68 G7
Poyang Hu 38 F5
Požarevac 26 J5
Poza Rica 72 E4
Požega 26 H6
Poznań 10 F5
Pozoblanco 20 F6
Pozzuoli 24 J8
Prabumulih 42 C3
Prachatice 10 D8
Prachuap Khiri Khan 40 B4
Prado 76 K7
Præstø 12 H1
Prague = Praha 10 D7
Praha 10 D7
Praia 54 (1)B2
Prainha 76 G4
Prapat 42 B2
Praslin Island 58 (2)B1
Pratas = Dongsha Qundao 40 F2
Prato 22 G7
Pratt 70 G4
Praya 42 F4
Preetz 12 F2
Preganziòl 22 H5
Preiļi 8 P8
Premnitz 12 H4
Premuda 22 K6
Prenzlau 10 C4
Preobrazhenka 36 H4
Preparis Island 40 A4
Preparis North Channel 40 A3
Preparis South Channel 40 A4
Přerov 10 G8
Preševo 26 J7
Presidencia Roque Sáenz Peña 78 J4
Presidente Prudente 78 L3
Presidio 70 F6
Preslav 26 P6
Presnogorkovka 30 N4
Prešov 10 L9
Presque Isle 68 T7
Přeštice 12 J7
Preston 16 K8
Pretoria 58 D5
Preveza 28 C6
Priargunsk 36 K6
Pribilof Islands 66 U4
Priboj 26 G6
Příbram 10 D8
Price 70 D4
Priego de Córdoba 20 F7
Priekule 8 L8
Prienai 10 N3
Prieska 58 C5
Prievidza 10 H9
Prijedor 26 D5
Prijepolje 26 G6
Prikaspiyskaya Nizmennost' 30 K5
Prilep 28 D3
Primolano 22 G5
Primorsk 8 Q6
Primorsko Akhtarsk 30 G5
Prince Albert 68 K6
Prince Albert Peninsula 68 H2
Prince Albert Sound 68 H2
Prince Charles Island 68 R3
Prince Edward Island 48 G10
Prince Edward Island 68 U7
Prince George 68 G6
Prince of Wales Island, *Aus.* 62 H2
Prince of Wales Island, *Can.* 68 L2
Prince of Wales Island, *U.S.* 68 E5
Prince of Wales Strait 68 H2
Prince Patrick Island 66 Q2
Prince Regent Inlet 68 N2
Prince Rupert 68 E6
Princess Charlotte Bay 62 H2
Prince William Sound 68 B4
Príncipe 54 F4
Prineville 70 B3
Priozersk 8 R6
Priština 26 J7
Pritzwalk 12 H3
Privas 18 K9
Privolzhskaya Vozvyshennost' 30 H4
Prizren 26 H7
Probolinggo 42 E4
Proddatur 44 C6
Progreso 72 G4
Prokop'yevsk 34 R7
Prokuplje 26 J6
Proletarsk 30 H5
Proliv Longa 36 X2
Proliv Matochkin Shar 34 K3
Proliv Vil'kitskogo 34 U2
Prophet 68 G5
Propriano 24 C7
Prorer Wiek 12 J2
Proserpine 62 J4
Prosna 10 G6
Prosperidad 40 H5
Prostojov 10 G8
Proti 28 D7
Provadija 26 Q6
Prøven = Kangersuatsiaq 68 W2
Providence 70 M3
Providence Island 58 (2)B2
Provideniya 36 Z4
Provins 18 J5
Provost 68 J6
Prudnik 10 G7
Prüm 14 J4
Pruszków 10 K5
Prut 26 R4
Prużany 10 P5
Prvić 22 K6
Pryluky 30 F4
Prypyats' 6 G2
Przasnysz 10 K4
Przemyśl 10 M8
Przeworsk 10 M7
Psara 28 H6
Psebay 30 H6
Pskov 30 E3
Ptolemaïda 28 D4
Ptuj 22 L4
Pucallpa 76 C5
Pucheng 38 F5
Púchov 10 H8
Pucioasa 26 N4
Puck 10 H3
Pudasjärvi 8 P4
Pudozh 30 G2
Puebla 72 E5
Puebla de Don Rodrigo 20 F5
Pueblo 70 F4
Puelches 78 H6
Puelén 78 H6
Puente-Genil 20 F7
Puerto Acosta 76 D7
Puerto Aisén 78 G8
Puerto Alegre 76 E6
Puerto Angel 72 E5
Puerto Ayacucho 72 L7
Puerto Barrios 72 G5
Puerto Berrío 76 C2
Puerto Cabezas 72 H6
Puerto Carreño 72 L7
Puerto del Rosario 52 C3
Puerto de Navacerrada 20 G4
Puerto Guarini 76 F8
Puerto Heath 76 D6
Puerto Inírida 76 D3
Puerto Leguizamo 76 C4
Puerto Limón 76 B3
Puertollano 20 F6
Puerto Madryn 78 J7
Puerto Maldonado 76 D6
Puerto Montt 78 G7
Puerto Natáles 78 G9
Puerto Nuevo 72 K7
Puerto Páez 76 D2
Puerto Princesa 40 F5
Puerto Real 20 D8
Puerto Rico 72 L5
Puerto Rico 76 D6
Puerto Rico Trench 74 E1
Puerto Santa Cruz 78 H9
Puerto Suárez 76 F7
Pukapuka 60 N7
Pukatawagen 68 L5
Pukch'ŏng 38 H2
Pukë 26 G7
Pukeuri Junction 64 C7
Pula 22 J6
Puławy 10 M6
Pułtusk 8 L10
Pultusk 10 L5
Pulu 34 Q10
Puncak Jaya 43 E3
Puncak Mandala 43 F3
Pune 44 B5
Punia 56 D4
Puno 76 C7
Punta Albina 58 A3
Punta Alice 24 M9
Punta Angamos 78 G3
Punta Arena 70 B4
Punta Arenas 78 G9
Punta Ballena 78 G4
Punta da Estaca de Bares 20 C1
Punta Dungeness 78 H9
Punta Eugenia 72 A3
Punta Galera 78 G6
Punta Gallinas 72 K6
Punta La Marmora 24 D8
Punta Lavapié 78 G6
Punta Lengua de Vaca 78 G5
Punta Mala 76 B2
Punta Mariato 72 H7
Punta Medanosa 78 H8
Punta Negra 76 A5
Punta Norte, *Arg.* 78 J7
Punta Norte, *Arg.* 78 K6
Punta Pariñas 76 A5
Punta Rasa 78 J7
Puntarenas 72 H6
Punta San Telmo 72 D5
Punta Sarga 52 B4
Puponga 64 D5
Puqi 38 E5
Pur 34 P4
Puri 44 E5
Purmerend 14 G2
Purpe 36 B4
Purukcahu 42 E3
Purus 76 E5
Puruvesi 8 Q6
Pusan 38 H3
Pushkin 30 F3
Püspökladany 10 L10
Putao 40 B1
Putaruru 64 E3
Putian 38 F5
Putna 26 P4
Puttalami 44 C7
Putten 14 G3
Puttgarden 12 G2
Putumayo 76 C4
Putusibau 42 E2
Puvurnituq 68 R5
Puy de Dôme 18 H8
Puy de Sancy 18 H8
Puysegur Point 64 A8
Pweto 56 D5
Pwllheli 16 H9
Pyal'ma 30 G2
Pyasina 34 R3
Pyatigorsk 46 D1
Pyè 40 B3
Pyhäjärvi 8 M6
Pyinmana 40 B3
Pylos 28 D8
P'yŏngyang 38 H3
Pyramid Island 64 (1)B2
Pyramid Lake 46 C3
Pyrenees 18 E11
Pyrgos 28 D7
Pyrzyce 10 D4
Pyshchug 30 J3
Pytalovo 8 P8

Q

Qadīmah 46 C5
Qādub 46 F7
Qagan Nur 38 F2
Qal'aikhum 46 K2
Qalamat Nadqān 46 F5
Qalāt 46 J3
Qal'at Bīshah 46 D5
Qal'eh-ye Now 46 H3
Qamdo 38 B4
Qamīnīs 50 C1
Qandala 56 H1
Qardho 56 H2
Qasr Farafra 50 E2
Qatar 46 F4
Qattâra Depression 50 E2
Qāyen 46 G3
Qazax 46 E1
Qazımämmäd 46 E1
Qazvīn 46 E2
Qena 50 F2
Qeqertarsuaq 68 V2
Qeqertarsuatsiaat 68 W4
Qeqertarsuup Tunua 68 V3
Qeshm 46 G4
Qianshanlaoba 34 Q8
Qiaowan 38 B2
Qidukou 44 G2
Qiemo 34 R10
Qijiang 38 D5
Qijiaojing 34 S9
Qila Saifullah 46 J3
Qilian 38 C3
Qilian Shan 38 B3
Qingdao 38 G3
Qinghai Hu 38 B3
Qinghai Nanshan 38 B3
Qingjiang 38 F4
Qingshuihe 38 E3
Qingyang 38 D3
Qingyuan, *China* 38 E6
Qingyuan, *China* 38 G2
Qinhuangdao 38 F3
Qinzhou 40 D2
Qionghai 40 E3
Qiqian 36 L6
Qiqihar 36 L7
Qira 34 Q10
Qishn 46 F6
Qolleh-ye Damāvand 46 F2
Qom 46 F3
Qomishēh 46 F3
Qotūr 46 D2
Quang Ngai 40 D3
Quangolodougou 54 C3
Quang Tri 40 D3
Quanzhou 40 F2
Quaqtaq 68 T4
Quarto Sant'Elena 24 D9
Quba 46 E1
Quchan 46 G2
Québec 68 S6
Québec 70 M2
Quedlinburg 12 G5
Queen Charlotte 68 E6
Queen Charlotte Islands 68 E6
Queen Charlotte Sound 68 E6
Queen Charlotte Strait 68 F6
Queen Elizabeth Islands 66 M2
Queen Maud Gulf 68 L3
Queen Maud Land 80 (2)F2
Queensland 62 G4
Queenstown, *Aus.* 62 J8
Queenstown, *N.Z.* 64 B7
Queenstown, *S.A.* 58 D6
Quelimane 58 F3
Querétaro 72 D4
Quesnel 68 G6
Quetta 46 J3
Quezaltenango 72 F6
Quezon 40 F5
Quezon City 40 G4
Qufu 38 F3
Quibala 58 A2
Quibdó 72 J7
Quiberon 18 B6
Quillagua 78 H3
Quilmes 78 K5
Quilpie 62 H5
Quimbele 56 B5
Quimilí 78 J4
Quimper 18 A5
Quimperlé 18 B6
Qui Nhon 40 D4
Quionga 56 G6
Quirindi 62 K6
Quito 76 B4
Qujing 40 C1
Qumar He 44 F1
Qumaryan 44 F1
Qurayyāt 46 G5
Qŭrghonteppa 46 J2
Qurlurtuuq 68 H3
Qus 50 F2
Quseir 50 F2
Quzhou 38 F5

R

Raab 22 L3
Raahe 8 N4
Raalte 14 J2
Raasay 16 G4
Raas Caseyr 46 F7
Rab 22 K6
Rab 22 K6
Raba 43 A4
Rába 26 E2
Răbăgani 26 K3
Rabak 50 F5
Rabat, *Malta* 24 J13
Rabat, *Morocco* 52 D2
Rabca 22 N3
Rābigh 46 C5
Rabka 10 K8
Rach Gia 40 D5
Racine 70 J3
Ráckeve 26 F2
Rădăuți 26 N2
Radbuza 12 H7
Radeberg 12 J5
Radebeul 12 J5
Radhanpur 44 B4
Radnevo 26 N7
Radom 10 L6
Radomir 26 K7
Radomsko 10 J6
Radoviš 28 E3
Radstadt 10 C10
Raduznny 34 P5
Radviliškis 10 N2
Radzyń Podlaski 10 M6
Rae-Edzo 68 H4
Raetihi 64 E4
Raevavae 60 M8
Rafaela 78 J4
Rafaï 56 C3
Rafḥā 46 D4
Raglan 64 E3
Ragusa 24 J12
Raha 43 B3
Rahad el Berdi 50 D5
Rahimyar Khan 46 K4
Raichur 44 C5
Raiganj 44 E3
Raigarh 44 D4
Rainach 22 L4
Rainbow Lake 68 H5
Raipur 44 D4
Rai Valley 64 D5
Rajahmundry 44 D5
Raja-Jooseppi 8 Q2
Rajapalaiyam 44 C7
Rajgarh 44 C3
Rajkot 46 K5
Raj Nangaon 44 D4
Rajsamand 44 B3
Rajshahi 44 E4
Rakhiv 26 M1
Rakovica 22 L6
Rakovník 10 C7
Rakovski 26 M7
Rakvere 8 P7
Raleigh 70 L4
Ralik Chain 60 G5
Rama 72 H6
Rambouillet 18 G5
Rameswaram 44 C7
Ramlat Rabyānah 50 C3
Râmnicu Sărat 26 Q4
Râmnicu Vâlcea 26 M4
Ramonville-St-Agne 18 G10
Rampur, *India* 44 C2
Rampur, *India* 44 C3
Ramree Island 40 A3
Ramsgate 16 P10
Ranau 42 F1
Rancagua 78 G5
Ranchi 44 E4
Randazzo 24 J11
Randers 8 F8
Randijaure 8 K3

Salinas, *Brazil* 76 J7
Salinas, *Ecuador* 76 A4
Salinas, *U.S.* 70 B4
Salinas Grandes 78 J4
Salinópolis 76 H4
Salisbury, *U.K.* 14 A3
Salisbury, *U.S.* 70 L4
Salisbury Island 68 R4
Salla 8 Q3
Salluit 68 R4
Salmon 70 C2
Salmon Arm 68 H6
Salo 8 M6
Salò 22 F5
Salon-de-Provence 18 L10
Salonta 26 J3
Sal'sk 30 H5
Salsomaggiore Terme 22 E6
Salta 78 H3
Saltee Islands 16 F9
Saltillo 70 F6
Salt Lake City 70 D3
Salto 78 K5
Salto del Guairá 78 K3
Salûm 50 E1
Saluzzo 22 C6
Salvador 76 K6
Salvadore 74 H5
Salween 40 B2
Salyan 46 E2
Salym 30 P3
Salzach 22 H2
Salzburg 22 J3
Salzgitter 12 F4
Salzwedel 12 G4
Samaipata 76 E7
Samar 40 H4
Samara 30 K4
Samarinda 42 F3
Samarkand 46 J2
Sambalpur 44 D4
Sambas 42 D2
Sambava 58 J2
Sambhal 44 C3
Sambir 10 N8
Sambo 43 A3
Samboja 42 F3
Sambre 14 F4
Same 56 F4
Sami 28 C6
Samoa 60 J7
Samobor 22 L5
Samoded 30 H2
Samokov 26 L7
Šamorín 10 G9
Samos 28 J7
Samos 28 J7
Samothraki 28 H4
Samothraki 28 H4
Sampit 42 E3
Samsang 44 D2
Samsø 8 F9
Samsun 46 C1
Samtredia 46 D1
Samut Songkhram 40 B4
San 10 L7
San 54 D2
Şan'ā 50 H4
Sanaga 54 G4
San Ambrosio 78 F4
Sanana 43 C3
Sanana 43 C3
Sanandaj 46 E2
San Antonia Abad 20 M6
San Antonio, *Chile* 78 G5
San Antonio, *U.S.* 72 E3
San Antonio de los Cobres 78 H3
San Antonio-Oeste 78 H7
Sanāw 46 F6
San Benedetto del Tronto 24 H6
San Bernardino 70 C5
San Bernardo 78 H5
San Borja 76 D6
San Carlos, *Chile* 78 G6
San Carlos, *Phil.* 40 G3
San Carlos, *Venezuela* 76 D3
San Carlos de Bariloche 78 G7
San Carlos de Bolívar 78 J6
San Carlos del Zulia 76 C2
San Cataldo 24 H11
Sanchahe 38 H1
Sanchakou 34 P10
Sanchor 44 B4
Sanchursk 30 J3
San Clemente Island 70 C5
San Cristobal 60 G7
San Cristóbal, *Arg.* 78 J5
San Cristóbal, *Venezuela* 76 C2
San Cristóbal de las Casas 72 F5
Sancti Spíritus 72 J4
Sandakan 42 F1
Sandane 8 D6
Sandanski 28 F3
Sanday 16 K2
Sandby 12 G2
Sandefjord 8 F7
Sanderson 70 F5
Sandfire Flat Roadhouse 62 D3
San Diego 70 C5
Sandıklı 28 N6
Sandnes 8 C7
Sandnessjøen 8 G4
Sandoa 56 C5
Sandomierz 10 L7
San Donà di Piave 22 H5
Sandoway 44 F5
Sandpoint 70 C2
Sandray 16 E5
Sandviken 8 J6
Sandy Cape 62 K4
Sandy Island 62 D2
Sandy Lake 68 N6
Sandy Lake 68 N6
San Felipe 70 D5
San Félix 78 E4
San Fernando, *Chile* 78 G5
San Fernando, *Phil.* 40 G3
San Fernando, *Spain* 20 D8
San Fernando de Apure 76 D2
San Fernando de Atabapo 76 D3
San Francisco, *Arg.* 78 J5
San Francisco, *U.S.* 70 B4
Sangamner 44 B5
Sangān 46 H3
Sangar 36 M4
Sangāreddi 44 C5
Sangasanga 42 F3
Sângeorz-Băi 26 M2
Sangerhausen 12 G5
Sanggau 42 E2
Sangha 54 H4
Sanghar 46 J4
San Gimignano 22 G7
San Giovanni in Fiore 24 L9
San Giovanni Valdarno 22 G7
Sangir 43 C2
Sangkhla Buri 40 B3
Sangkulirang 42 F2
Sangli 44 B5
Sangmélima 54 G4
Sangsang 44 E3
Sangue 76 F6
Sangüesa 20 J2
San Jose 70 B4
San José 72 H7
San Jose de Buenavista 40 G4
San José de Chiquitos 76 E7
San Jose de Jáchal 78 H5
San José del Cabo 72 C4
San José de Ocuné 76 C3
San Juan 72 H4
San Juan, *Arg.* 78 H5
San Juan, *Costa Rica* 72 H6
San Juan, *Puerto Rico* 72 L5
San Juan, *Venezuela* 76 D2
San Juan Bautista, *Paraguay* 78 K4
San Juan Bautista, *Spain* 20 M5
San Juan de los Cayos 76 D1
San Juan de los Morros 76 D2
San Juan Mountains 70 E4
San Julián 78 H8
Sankt-Peterburg 30 F3
Sankuru 56 C4
Sanlıurfa 46 C2
Sanlúcar de Barrameda 20 D8
San Lucas 72 C4
San Luis 78 H5
San Luis Obispo 70 B4
San Luis Potosí 70 F7
San Marino 22 H7
San Marino 22 H7
San Martín 76 E6
Sanmenxia 38 E4
San Miguel 72 G6
San Miguel 76 E7
San Miguel de Tucumán 78 H4
San Miniato 22 F7
San Nicolas de los Arroyos 78 J5
Sânnicolau Mare 26 H3
Sanok 10 M8
San Pablo 40 G4
San-Pédro 54 C4
San Pedro, *Arg.* 78 J3
San Pedro, *Bolivia* 76 E7
San Pedro, *Paraguay* 78 K3
San Pedro, *Phil.* 40 G4
San Pedro Sula 72 G5
San Pellegrino Terme 22 E5
San Pietro 24 C9
San Rafael 78 H5
San Remo 22 C7
San Roque 20 E8
Sansalé 54 B2
San Salvador 72 G6
San Salvador 72 K4
San Salvador de Jujuy 78 H3
Sansar 44 C4
San Sebastián = Donostia 20 J1
San Sebastian de los Reyes 20 G4
Sansepolcro 22 H7
San Severo 24 K7
Sanski Most 22 M6
Santa Ana, *Bolivia* 76 D7
Santa Ana, *El Salvador* 72 G6
Santa Bárbara 70 E6
Santa Catalina 78 H4
Santa Catarina 78 L4
Santa Clara, *Columbia* 76 D4
Santa Clara, *Cuba* 70 K7
Santa Comba Dão 20 B4
Santa Cruz 78 G9
Santa Cruz, *Bolivia* 76 E7
Santa Cruz, *Phil.* 40 G3
Santa Cruz, *U.S.* 70 B4
Santa Cruz de Tenerife 52 B3
Santa Cruz Islands 60 G7
Santa Elena 76 E3
Santa Eugenia 20 A2
Santa Fe 70 E4
Santa Fé 78 J5
Sant'Agata di Militello 24 J10
Santa Isabel 60 F6
Santa Isabel 78 H6
Santa la Grande 70 K7
Santa Margarita 70 D7
Santa Margherita Ligure 22 E6
Santa Maria 52 (1)B2
Santa Maria, *Brazil* 78 L4
Santa Maria, *U.S.* 70 B5
Santa Maria das Barreiras 76 H5
Santa Marinella 24 F6
Santa Marta, *Col.* 72 K6
Santa Marta, *Spain* 20 D6
Santana do Livramento 78 K5
Santander 20 G1
Sant'Antioco 24 C9
Sant'Antioco 24 C9
Santanyí 20 P5
Santa Pola 20 K6
Santarém, *Brazil* 76 G4
Santarém, *Spain* 20 B5
Santa Rosa, *Arg.* 78 J6
Santa Rosa, *Acre, Brazil* 76 C5
Santa Rosa, *R.G.S., Brazil* 78 L4
Santa Rosa, *U.S.* 70 B4
Santa Vitória do Palmar 78 L5
Sant Boi 20 N3
Sant Carlos de la Ràpita 20 L4
Sant Celoni 20 N3
Sant Feliu de Guixols 20 P3
Santiago 78 G5
Santiago, *Brazil* 78 L4
Santiago, *Dominican Republic* 72 K5
Santiago, *Phil.* 40 G3
Santiago, *Spain* 20 B2
Santiago de Cuba 72 J5
Santiago del Estero 78 J4
Santo André 78 M3
Santo Antão 54 (1)A1
Santo Antônio de Jesus 76 K6
Santo Antônio do Içá 76 D4
Santo Domingo 72 L5
Santo Domingo de los Colorados 76 B4
Santoña 20 G1
Santos 78 M3
San Vicente 40 G3
San Vincenzo 24 E5
Sanya 40 D3
Sao Bernardo do Campo 76 E4
São Borja 78 K4
São Carlos 78 M3
São Félix, *M.G., Brazil* 76 G6
São Félix, *Pará, Brazil* 76 G5
São Filipe 54 (1)B2
São Francisco 76 J6
São João de Madeira 20 B4
São Jorge 52 (1)B2
São José do Rio Prêto 78 L3
São Luís 76 J4
São Miguel 52 (1)B2
Saône 18 K7
São Nicolau 54 (1)B1
São Paulo 78 L3
São Paulo 78 M3
São Paulo de Olivença 76 D4
São Raimundo Nonato 76 J5
São Tiago 54 (1)B1
São Tomé 54 F4
São Tomé 54 F4
São Tomé and Príncipe 54 F4
São Vicente 54 (1)A1
São Vicente 78 M3
Sapanca 28 M4
Saparua 43 C3
Sapele 54 F3
Sapes 28 H4
Sapientza 28 D8
Sa Pobla 20 P5
Sapporo 38 L2
Sapri 24 K8
Sapudi 42 E4
Saqqez 46 E2
Sara Buri 40 C4
Sarajevo 26 F6
Sarakhs 46 H2
Saraktash 30 L4
Saramati 44 G3
Saran 34 N8
Sarandë 28 C5
Sarangani Islands 43 C1
Saranpul 30 M2
Saransk 30 J4
Sarapul 30 K3
Sarapul'skoye 36 P7
Sarata 26 S3
Saratov 30 J4
Saravan 46 H4
Sarawak 42 E2
Saray 28 K3
Sarayköy 28 L7
Sarayönü 28 Q6
Sarbāz 46 H4
Sarbīsheh 46 G3
Sárbogárd 26 F3
Sardegna 24 E8
Sardinia = Sardegna 24 E8
Sar-e Pol 46 J2
Sargodha 46 K3
Sarh 54 H3
Sārī 46 F2
Saria 28 K9
Sarikei 42 E2
Sarina 62 J4
Sariñena 20 K3
Sarīr Tibesti 50 C3
Sariwŏn 38 H3
Sarıyer 28 M3
Sark 18 C4
Sarkad 26 J3
Sarkand 34 P8
Şarkikaraağaç 28 P6
Şarkişla 46 C2
Şarköy 28 K4
Sarmi 43 E3
Särna 8 G6
Sarnia 70 K3
Sarny 30 E4
Sarolangun 42 C3
Saronno 22 E5
Saros Körfezi 28 J4
Sárospatak 10 L9
Sarre 18 M5
Sarrebourg 18 N5
Sarreguemines 18 N4
Sarria 20 C2
Sartène 24 C7
Sartyn'ya 30 M2
Saruhanli 28 K6
Sárvár 22 M3
Sarviz 26 F2
Sarykamyshkoye Ozero 34 K9
Saryozek 34 P9
Saryshagan 34 N8
Sarysu 34 M8
Sary-Tash 46 K2
Sarzana 22 E6
Sasaram 44 D4
Sasebo 38 H4
Saskatchewan 68 K6
Saskatchewan 68 L6
Saskatoon 68 K6
Saskylakh 34 W3
Sassandra 54 C4
Sassari 24 C8
Sassnitz 12 J2
Sasso Marconi 22 G6
Sassuolo 22 F6
Satadougou 54 B2
Satara 44 B5
Satna 44 D4
Sátoraljaújhely 10 L9
Satti 44 C2
Sättna 8 J5
Satu Mare 26 K2
Satun 42 B1
Sauce 78 K5
Saudi Arabia 46 D4
Saulgau 22 E2
Saulieu 18 K6
Sault Ste. Marie, *Can.* 70 K2
Sault Ste. Marie, *U.S.* 70 K2
Saumlakki 43 D4
Saumur 18 E6
Saunders Island 74 J9
Saura 34 J9
Saurimo 56 C5
Sauðárkrókur 8 (1)D2
Sava 22 L5
Savaii 60 J7
Savalou 54 E3
Savannah 66 K6
Savannah 70 K5
Savannakhet 40 C3
Savaştepe 28 K5
Save 58 E4
Savè 54 E3
Sāveh 46 F2
Saverne 12 C8
Savigliano 22 C6
Savona 22 D6
Savonlinna 8 Q6
Savu 43 B5
Sawahlunto 42 C3
Sawai Madhopur 44 C3
Sawqirah 46 G6
Sawu Sea 43 B4
Sayanogorsk 34 S7
Sayansk 36 G6
Sayhūt 46 F6
Säylac 50 H5
Saynshand 38 E2
Sayram Hu 34 Q9
Say'ūn 46 E6
Say-Utes 34 J9
Sazan 28 B4
Sazin 46 K2
Sbaa 52 E3
Scafell Pike 16 J7
Scalea 24 K9
Scarborough 16 M7
Scargill 64 D6
Scarp 16 E3
Schaalsee 12 F3
Schaffhausen 22 D3
Schagen 14 G2
Scharbeutz 12 F2
Schärding 22 J2
Scharhörn 12 D3
Scheeßel 12 E3
Schefferville 68 T6
Scheibbs 22 L3
Schelde 14 F3
Scheveningen 14 G2
Schiedam 14 G3
Schiermonnikoog 14 H1
Schiermonnikoog 14 J1
Schio 22 G5
Schiza 28 D8
Schkeuditz 12 H5
Schlei 12 E2
Schleiden 14 J4
Schleswig 12 E2
Schlieben 12 J5
Schlüchtern 12 E6
Schneeberg 12 G6
Schneeberg 12 H6
Schönebeck 12 G4
Schongau 22 F3
Schöningen 12 F4
Schouwen 14 F3
Schramberg 22 D2
Schrems 22 L2
Schull 16 C10
Schwabach 12 G7
Schwäbische Alb 22 E2
Schwäbisch-Gmünd 22 E2
Schwäbisch-Hall 12 E7
Schwalmstadt 12 E6
Schwandorf 12 H7
Schwarzenbek 12 F3
Schwarzenberg 12 H6
Schwarzwald 22 D3
Schwaz 22 G3
Schwechat 10 F9
Schwedt 10 D4
Schweich 14 J5
Schweinfurt 12 F6
Schwenningen 22 D2
Schwerin 12 G3
Schweriner See 12 G3
Schwetzingen 12 D7
Schwyz 22 D3
Sciacca 24 H11
Scicli 24 J12
Scotia Ridge 78 K9
Scotia Sea 80 (2)A4
Scotland 16 H5
Scott Inlet 68 T2
Scott Island 80 (2)Z3
Scott Reef 62 D2
Scottsbluff 70 F3
Scranton 70 L3
Scunthorpe 16 M8
Seal 68 M5
Sea of Azov 30 G5
Sea of Japan 38 J2
Sea of Marmara = Marmara Denizi 28 L4
Sea of Okhotsk 36 Q5
Sea of the Hebrides 16 E4
Searcy 70 H4
Seattle 70 B2
Sebeş 26 L4
Sebkha Azzel Matti 52 F3
Sebkha de Timimoun 52 E3
Sebkha de Tindouf 52 D3
Sebkha Mekerrhane 52 F3
Sebkha Oum el Drouss Telli 52 C4
Sebkhet de Chemchâm 52 C4
Sebnitz 12 K6
Secchia 22 F6
Sechura 76 A5
Secretary Island 64 A7
Secunderabad 44 C5
Sécure 76 D7
Sedan 14 G5
Sedano 20 G2
Seddon 64 D5
Seddonville 64 C5
Sedeh 46 G3
Sedico 22 H4
Seeheim 58 B5
Seelow 12 K4
Sées 18 F5
Seesen 12 F5
Seevetal 12 E3
Séez 22 B5
Seferihisar 28 J6
Segamat 42 C2
Segezha 30 F2
Seghnān 46 K2
Ségou 54 C2
Segovia 20 F4
Segré 18 E6
Séguédine 52 H4
Segura 20 H6
Sehithwa 58 C4
Sehnde 12 E4
Seiland 8 M1
Seinäjoki 8 M5
Seine 18 F4
Sekayu 42 C3
Sekondi 54 D3
Selassi 43 D3
Selat Bangka 42 D3
Selat Berhala 42 C3
Selat Dampir 43 D3
Selat Karimata 42 D3
Selat Makassar 42 F3
Selat Mentawai 42 B3
Selat Sunda 42 D4
Selb 12 H6
Selby 70 F2
Selçuk 28 K7
Selebi-Phikwe 58 D4
Sélestat 22 C2
Selfoss 8 (1)C3
Sélibabi 52 C5
Seljord 8 E7
Selkirk 70 G1
Selkirk Mountains 68 H6
Selm 14 K3
Selpele 43 D3
Selvas 76 C5
Selwyn Lake 68 L5
Selwyn Mountains 68 E4
Semanit 28 B4
Semarang 42 E4
Sematan 42 D2
Sembé 54 G4
Semiozernoye 34 L7
Semipalatinsk 34 Q7
Semiyarka 34 P7
Semois 14 H5
Semporna 42 F2
Sena Madureira 76 D5
Senanga 58 C3
Sendai 38 L3
Senec 22 N2
Senegal 54 A2
Sénégal 54 B1
Senftenberg 12 J5
Sengerema 56 E4
Senhor do Bonfim 76 J6
Senica 10 G9
Senigallia 22 J7
Senj 22 K6
Senja 8 J2
Senlis 14 E5
Sennar 46 B7
Senneterre 70 L2
Sens 18 J5
Senta 26 H4
Seoni 44 C4
Seoul = Sŏul 38 H3
Separation Point 64 D5
Sepinang 42 F2
Sept-Îles 68 T6
Seraing 14 H4
Serakhs 46 H2
Seram 43 D3
Seram Sea 43 C3
Serang 42 D4
Serbia = Srbija 26 H6
Serdobsk 30 H4
Serebryansk 34 Q8
Sered' 26 E1
Şereflikoçhisar 28 R6
Seregno 22 E5
Serein 18 J6
Seremban 42 C2
Serenje 58 E2
Sergelen 38 E1
Sergeyevka 30 N4
Sergipe 76 K6
Sergiyev Posad 30 G3
Seria 42 E2
Serifos 28 G7
Serifos 28 G7
Serik 28 P8
Seringapatam Reef 62 D2
Sermata 43 C4
Seronga 58 C3
Serov 30 M3
Serowe 58 D4
Serpa 20 C7
Serpneve 26 S3
Serpukhov 30 G4
Serra Acari 76 F3
Serra Curupira 76 E3
Serra da Chela 58 A3
Serra da Espinhaço 76 J7
Serra da Ibiapaba 76 J4
Serra da Mantiqueira 78 M3
Serra de Maracaju 78 K3
Serra do Cachimbo 76 F5
Serra do Caiapó 76 G7
Serra do Dois Irmãos 76 J5
Serra do Roncador 76 G6
Serra dos Carajás 76 G5
Serra dos Parecis 76 E6
Serra do Tiracambu 76 H4
Serra Estrondo 76 H5
Serra Formosa 76 F6
Serra Geral de Goiás 76 H6
Serra Geral do Paranã 76 H7
Serra Lombarda 76 G3
Serra Pacaraima 76 E3
Serra Parima 76 E3
Serra Tumucumaque 76 F3
Serra da Estrela 20 C4
Serres, *France* 18 L9
Serres, *Greece* 28 F3
Serrinha 76 K6
Sertã 20 B5
Serui 43 E3
Servia 28 D4
Sêrxü 38 B4
Sese Islands 56 E4
Sesfontein 58 A3
Sesheke 58 C3
Sessa Aurunca 24 H7
Sestri Levante 22 E6
Sestroretsk 8 Q6
Sestrunj 22 K6
Sestu 24 D9
Sesvete 22 M5
Sète 18 J10
Sete Lagoas 76 J7
Setesdal 8 D7
Sétif 52 G1
Settat 52 D2
Setúbal 20 B6
Sŏul 60 C2
Seurre 18 L7
Sevastopol' 6 H3
Sevenoaks 14 C3
Sévérac-le-Château 18 J9
Severn, *Can.* 68 P5
Severn, *U.K.* 16 K10
Severnaya Dvina 30 H2
Severnaya Zemlya 34 U1
Severn Estuary 16 J10
Severnoye 30 K4
Severnyy 34 L4
Severobaykal'sk 36 H5
Severodvinsk 30 G2
Severo-Kuril'sk 36 T6
Severomorsk 8 S2
Severoural'sk 30 M2
Severo-Yeniseyskiy 34 S5
Sevier Lake 70 D4
Sevilla 20 E7
Sevlievo 26 N7
Seyakha 34 N3
Seychelles 58 (2)B2
Seychelles Islands 48 J6
Seydişehir 28 P7
Seymchan 36 S4
Seymour, *Aus.* 62 J7
Seymour, *U.S.* 70 G5
Seyðisfjörður 8 (1)G2
Sézanne 18 J5

Sezze 24 H7
Sfakia 28 G9
Sfântu Gheorghe, *Romania* 26 N4
Sfântu Gheorghe, *Romania* 26 S5
Sfax 52 H2
's-Gravenhage 14 G2
Shabunda 56 D4
Shabwah 46 E6
Shache 34 P10
Shagamu 54 E3
Shagonar 34 S7
Shag Rocks 78 N9
Shahdol 44 D4
Shah Fuladi 46 J3
Shahjahanpur 44 C3
Shahrak 46 H3
Shahr-e Bābāk 46 G3
Shahrtuz 46 J2
Shakhrisabz 46 J2
Shakhtërsk 36 Q7
Shakhty 30 H5
Shakhun'ya 30 J3
Shaki 54 E3
Shama 56 E5
Shamattawa 68 N5
Shand 46 H3
Shandan 38 C3
Shandong Bandao 38 G3
Shangani 58 D3
Shangdu 38 E2
Shanghai 38 G4
Shanghang 38 F6
Shangqui 38 F4
Shangrao 38 F5
Shangzhi 38 H1
Shangzhou 38 D4
Shantarskiye Ostrova 36 P5
Shantou 38 F6
Shanwei 40 F2
Shanyin 38 E3
Shaoguan 38 E6
Shaoxing 38 G5
Shaoyang 38 E5
Shapkina 30 K1
Sharga 34 T8
Sharjah = Ash Shāriqah 46 G4
Shark Bay 60 B8
Shark Reef 62 J2
Sharmah 50 G2
Sharm el Sheikh 50 F2
Sharūrah 46 E6
Shashe 58 D4
Shashi 38 E4
Shats'k 10 N6
Shatsk 30 H4
Shcherbakove 36 U3
Shchigry 30 G4
Shchuch'ye 34 L6
Shchuchyn 8 N10
Sheberghān 46 J2
Sheboygan 70 J3
Sheffield, *N.Z.* 64 D6
Sheffield, *U.K.* 16 L8
Shegmas 30 J2
Shelburne 68 T8
Shelby 70 D2
Shendam 54 F3
Shendi 50 F4
Shenkursk 30 H2
Shenyang 38 G2
Shenzhen 38 E6
Shepetivka 30 E4
Shepparton 62 J7
Sherbro Island 54 B3
Sherbrooke 70 M2
Sherkaly 30 N2
Sherlovaya Gora 36 K6
Sherman 70 G5
's-Hertogenbosch 14 H3
Shetland Islands 16 M1
Shetpe 34 J9
Shiant Islands 16 F4
Shibetsu 38 L2
Shiderty 34 N7
Shihezi 34 R9
Shijiazhuang 38 E3
Shikarpur 46 J4
Shikoku 38 J4
Shikotan-tō 36 R8
Shiliguri 44 E3
Shilka 36 K6
Shilka 36 K6
Shillong 44 F3
Shilovo 30 H4
Shimla 44 C2
Shimoda 38 K4
Shimoga 44 C6
Shimoni 56 F4
Shimonoseki 38 J4
Shindan 46 H3
Shinjō 38 L3
Shinyanga 56 E4
Shiono-misaki 38 K4
Shiquan 38 D4
Shīrāz 46 F4
Shire 58 E3
Shiretoko-misaki 38 M2
Shir Kūh 46 F3
Shiv 44 B3
Shivpuri 44 C3
Shiyan 38 E4
Shizuishan 38 D3
Shizuoka 38 K3
Shkodër 26 G7
Shomishko 34 K8
Shorap 46 J4
Shoreham 14 B4
Shostka 30 F4
Shoyna 30 H1
Shreveport 70 H5
Shrewsbury 16 K9
Shuangliao 38 G2
Shuangyashan 36 N7
Shubarkuduk 34 K8
Shulan 38 H2
Shumikha 30 M3
Shuqrah 46 E7
Shurchi 46 J2
Shurinda 36 J5
Shuryshkary 30 N1
Shuya 30 H3
Shuyang 38 F4
Shwebo 40 B2
Shymkent 34 M9
Sia 43 D4
Sialkot 46 K3
Siatista 28 D4
Šiauliai 10 N2
Sibay 30 L4
Šibenik 26 C6
Siberia = Sibir 32 N3
Siberut 42 B3
Sibi 46 J4
Sibigo 42 B2
Sibir 32 N3
Sibiu 26 M4
Sibolga 42 B2
Sibu 42 E2
Sibuco 40 G5
Sibut 56 B2
Sicilia 24 G11
Sicilian Channel 24 F11
Sicily = Sicilia 24 G11
Šid 26 G4
Siddipet 44 C5
Siderno 24 L10
Sidi Barrani 50 E1
Sidi Bel Abbès 52 E1
Sidi Kacem 52 D2
Sidirokastro 28 F3
Sidoan 43 B2
Sidorovsk 34 Q4
Sieburg 14 K4
Siedlce 10 M5
Sieg 14 K4
Siegen 14 L4
Siemiatycze 10 M5
Siĕmréab 40 C4
Siena 22 G7
Sieradz 10 H6
Sierpc 10 J5
Sierra Colorada 78 H7
Sierra de Calalasteo 78 H4
Sierra de Córdoba 78 H5
Sierra de Gata 20 D4
Sierra de Gúdar 20 K4
Sierra del Nevado 78 H6
Sierra de Perija 72 K7
Sierra Grande 78 H7
Sierra Leone 54 B3
Sierra Madre 72 F5
Sierra Madre del Sur 72 E5
Sierra Madre Occidental 70 E6
Sierra Morena 20 E6
Sierra Nevada, *Spain* 20 G7
Sierra Nevada, *U.S.* 70 B4
Sierra Vizcaino 70 D6
Sierre 22 C4
Sifnos 28 G8
Sig 20 K9
Sigean 18 H10
Sighetu Marmaţiei 26 L2
Sighişoara 26 M3
Siglufjörður 8 (1)D1
Sigmaringen 22 E2
Siguiri 54 C2
Sihanoukville 40 C4
Siilinjärvi 8 P5
Siirt 46 D2
Sikar 44 C3
Sikasso 54 C2
Sikea 28 F4
Sikeston 70 H4
Sikhote Alin 38 J2
Sikinos 28 G8
Siklós 26 F4
Siktyakh 36 L3
Sil 20 C2
Šilalė 10 M2
Silandro 22 F4
Silba 22 K6
Silchar 44 F4
Şile 28 M3
Silhouette Island 58 (2)B1
Siliana 24 D12
Silifke 28 R8
Siling Co 44 E2
Silistra 26 Q5
Silivri 28 L3
Siljan 8 H6
Sillamäe 8 P7
Siluas 42 D2
Šilutė 10 L2
Silver Bay 70 H2
Silver City 70 E5
Silver Plains 62 H2
Simanggang 42 E2
Simao 38 C6
Simav 28 L5
Simeonovgrad 26 N7
Simeria 10 N12
Simeulue 42 A2
Simferopol' 30 F6
Şimleu Silvaniei 26 K2
Simmerath 14 J4
Simojärvi 8 P3
Simpang 42 C3
Simpson Desert 62 G4
Sinabang 42 B2
Sinai 50 F2
Sinaia 26 N4
Sinalunga 24 F5
Sinbaungwe 40 B3
Sincelejo 76 B2
Sinclair's Bay 16 J3
Sindangbarang 42 D4
Sindelfingen 12 E8
Sines 20 B7
Singa 50 F5
Singapore 42 C2
Singapore 42 C2
Singaraja 42 E4
Singen 22 D3
Sîngerei 26 R2
Singida 56 E4
Singkawang 42 D2
Singkep 42 C3
Singkilbaru 42 B2
Singleton 62 K6
Siniscola 24 D8
Sinj 26 D6
Sinjai 43 B4
Sinjār 46 D2
Sinkat 50 G4
Sinni 24 L8
Sinop 46 C1
Sinsheim 12 D7
Sintang 42 E2
Sinŭiju 38 G2
Sinyaya 36 L4
Sió 26 F3
Siófok 26 F3
Sion 22 C4
Sioux City 70 G3
Sioux Falls 70 G3
Sioux Lookout 70 H2
Siping 38 G2
Sipiwesk 68 M5
Sipura 42 B3
Sira 8 D7
Siracusa 24 K11
Sir Edward Pellew Group 62 G3
Siret 26 P2
Siret 26 Q4
Sirgān 46 H4
Şiria 10 L11
Siri Kit Dam 40 B3
Sirk 46 G4
Sirohi 44 B4
Sirsa 44 C3
Sirsi 44 B6
Sisak 26 D4
Sisian 46 E2
Sisimiut 68 W3
Sisŏphŏn 40 C4
Sisseton 70 G2
Sistema Central 20 E4
Sistema Iberico 20 H3
Sisteron 22 A6
Sitapur 44 D3
Sitasjaure 8 J3
Siteia 28 J9
Sitges 20 M3
Sithonia 28 F4
Sitka 68 D5
Sittard 14 H4
Sittwe 44 F4
Sivas 46 C2
Sivrihisar 28 P5
Siwa 50 E1
Siyäzän 46 E1
Sjælland 8 F9
Sjenica 26 H6
Sjenica Jezero 26 G6
Sjöbo 10 C2
Skädlderviken 10 B1
Skærbæk 12 D1
Skagen 8 F8
Skagerrak 8 D8
Skala 28 E8
Skantzoura 28 G5
Skardu 46 L2
Skarżysko-Kamienna 10 K6
Skaulo 8 L3
Skawina 10 J8
Skaymat 52 B4
Skegness 14 C1
Skellefteå 8 L4
Ski 8 F7
Skiathos 28 F5
Skibotn 8 L2
Skidal' 10 P4
Skien 8 E7
Skikda 52 G1
Skipton 16 L8
Skjern 8 E9
Škofja Loka 22 K4
Skopelos 28 F5
Skopje 26 J7
Skövde 8 G7
Skovorodino 36 L6
Skuodas 8 L8
Skye 16 F4
Skyros 28 G6
Skyros 28 G6
Slagelse 12 G1
Slagnäs 8 K4
Slaney 16 F9
Slano 26 E7
Slantsy 8 Q7
Slaný 12 K6
Slatina 26 M5
Slave 66 N3
Slave Lake 68 J5
Slavonska Požega 26 E4
Slavonski Brod 26 F4
Sławno 10 F3
Sleaford 14 B1
Sleeper Islands 68 Q5
Sligo 16 D7
Sligo Bay 16 D7
Slite 8 K8
Sliven 26 P7
Slobozia, *Moldova* 26 S3
Slobozia, *Romania* 26 Q5
Slonim 8 N10
Slough 14 B3
Slovak Republic 10 H9
Slovenia 22 K4
Slovenj Gradec 22 L4
Slovenska Bistrica 22 L4
Slov"yans'k 30 G5
Słubice 10 D5
Slunj 22 L5
Słupca 10 G5
Słupsk 10 G3
Slussfors 8 J4
Slutsk 30 E4
Slyudyanka 36 G6
Smålandsfarvandet 12 G1
Smallwood Reservoir 68 U6
Smargon' 8 P9
Smederevo 26 H5
Smila 30 F5
Smirnykh 36 Q7
Smiths Falls 70 L3
Smoky 68 H6
Smoky Hills 70 G4
Smøla 8 D5
Smolensk 30 F4
Smoljan 28 G3
Snæfell 8 (1)F2
Snake 70 C3
Snake River Plain 70 D3
Snåsavatnet 8 F4
Sneek 14 H1
Sneem 16 C10
Sneznhogorsk 34 R4
Snežnik 22 K5
Snina 10 M9
Snøhetta 8 E5
Snøtinden 8 G3
Snowdon 16 H8
Snowdrift 68 J4
Snyder 70 F5
Soalala 58 H3
Soanierana-Ivongo 58 H3
Soa-Siu 43 C2
Sobral 76 J4
Sochaczew 10 K5
Sochaux 22 B3
Sochi 46 C1
Socotra = Suquţrā 46 F7
Socuéllamos 20 H5
Sodankylä 8 P3
Söderhamn 8 J6
Södertälje 8 J7
Sodo 56 F2
Soe 43 B4
Soest 14 L3
Sofia = Sofija 26 L7
Sofija 26 L7
Sofiysk, *Russia* 36 N6
Sofiysk, *Russia* 36 P6
Sofporog 8 R4
Sōfu-gan 38 L5
Sogamoso 76 C2
Sognefjorden 8 C6
Sogod 40 G4
Sog Xian 44 F2
Sohâg 50 F2
Soignies 14 G4
Soissons 14 F5
Sokch'o 38 H3
Söke 28 K7
Sokhumi 46 D1
Sokode 54 E3
Sokol 30 H3
Sokółka 8 M10
Sokolo 54 C2
Sokolov 12 H6
Sokołów Podlaski 10 M5
Sokoto 54 F2
Sokoto 54 F2
Sokyryany 26 Q1
Solander Island 64 A8
Solapur 44 C5
Sölden 22 F4
Solenzara 24 D7
Solikamsk 30 L3
Sol'-Iletsk 30 L4
Soliman 24 E12
Solingen 14 K3
Sollefteå 8 J5
Soller 20 N5
Solna 8 J7
Solomon Islands 60 F6
Solothurn 22 C3
Solov'yevsk 36 K6
Šolta 26 D6
Soltau 12 E4
Sol'tsy 30 F3
Solway Firth 16 J7
Solwezi 58 D2
Soma 28 K5
Somalia 56 H2
Sombor 26 G4
Somerset 62 H2
Somerset Island 68 N2
Someş 26 K2
Somme 14 E4
Sommen 8 H8
Sömmerda 12 G5
Sømna 8 F4
Sondags 58 D6
Sønderborg Ærø 12 E2
Sondershausen 12 F5
Sondrio 22 E4
Songavatn 8 D7
Songea 56 F6
Song Hông 40 C2
Songhua 38 H1
Songhua Hu 38 H2
Songkan 38 D5
Songkhla 40 C5
Songnim 38 H3
Songo 58 E3
Songololo 54 G6
Songpan 38 C4
Sonid Yuoqi 38 E2
Sonid Zuoqi 38 E2
Son La 40 C2
Sonneberg 12 G6
Sono 76 H6
Sonsorol Islands 43 D1
Sonthofen 22 F3
Sopot 8 K9
Sopron 22 M3
Sora 24 H7
Soracaba 78 M3
Sorgun 46 C2
Soria 20 H3
Sorø 12 G1
Soroca 26 R1
Sorochinsk 30 K4
Sorong 43 D3
Soroti 56 E3
Sørøya 8 L1
Sorrento 24 J8
Sorsele 8 J4
Sorso 24 C8
Sorsogon 40 G4
Sort 20 M2
Sortavala 8 R6
Sørvagen 8 G3
Sosnogorsk 34 J5
Sosnovka 34 G4
Sosnovo 8 R6
Sosnowiec 10 J7
Sos'va 30 M3
Sos'vinskaya 30 M2
Soto la Marina 70 G7
Soubré 54 C3
Soufli 28 J3
Souilly 14 H5
Souk Ahras 24 B12
Sŏul 38 H3
Soulac-sur-Mer 18 D8
Soumussalmi 8 Q4
Soûr 50 G1
Soure 20 B5
Sour el Ghozlane 20 P8
Souris 70 F2
Souris 70 G2
Sousa 76 K5
Sousse 52 H1
South Africa 58 C6
South America 74 F5
Southampton 14 A4
Southampton Island 68 Q4
South Andaman 44 F6
South Atlantic Ocean 78 P6
South Australia 62 F5
South Bend 70 J3
South Carolina 70 K5
South China Sea 40 E4
South Dakota 70 F3
South Downs 14 B4
South East Cape 62 J8
South East Point 62 J7
Southend-on-Sea 14 C3
Southern Alps 64 B6
Southern Cross 62 C6
Southern Indian Lake 68 M5
Southern Uplands 16 H6
South Georgia 78 P9
South Harris 16 F4
South Island 64 B6
South Korea 38 H3
South Orkney Islands 80 (2)A3
South Pacific Ocean 78 P6
South Platte 70 F3
Southport 16 J8
South Ronaldsay 16 K3
South Sandwich Islands 80 (2)C4
South Sandwich Trench 74 H9
South Saskatchewan 70 D1
South Shetland Islands 80 (2)MM4
South Shields 16 L7
South Taranaki Bight 64 D4
South Uist 16 E4
South West Cape, *Auckland Island* 64 (2)A1
South West Cape, *Aus.* 62 H8
Southwest Cape 64 A8
South West Pacific Basin 60 L9
Southwold 14 D2
Sovata 26 N3
Soverato 24 L10
Sovetsk, *Russia* 8 L9
Sovetsk, *Russia* 30 J3
Soweto 58 D5
Sozopol 26 Q7
Spa 14 H4
Spain 20 F5
Spalding 14 B2
Spartanburg 70 K5
Sparti 28 E7
Spassk-Dal'niy 38 J2
Spencer Gulf 62 G6
Spetses 28 F7
Spey 16 J4
Speyer 14 L5
Spiekeroog 12 C3
Spiez 22 C4
Spilimbergo 22 H4
Spišska Nová Ves 10 K9
Spitsbergen 80 (1)P2
Spittal 22 J4
Split 26 D6
Spokane 70 C2
Spoleto 24 G6
Spratly Islands 40 E4
Spree 12 K4
Spremberg 12 K5
Sprimont 14 H4
Springbok 58 B5
Springe 12 E4
Springfield, *Ill., U.S.* 70 J4
Springfield, *Mass., U.S.* 70 M3
Springfield, *Mo., U.S.* 70 H4
Springs 58 D5
Springs Junction 64 D6
Springsure 62 J4
Spulico 24 L9
Squinzano 24 N8
Srbija 26 H6
Srbobran 26 G4
Srebrenica 26 G5
Sredenekolymsk 36 S3
Sredinnyy Khrebet 36 T6
Srednesibirskoye Ploskogor'ye 36 G3
Srednogorie 28 G2
Srem 10 G5
Sretensk 36 K6
Sri Jayawardenapura-Kotte 44 D7
Srikakulam 44 D5
Sri Lanka 44 D7
Srinagar 44 B2
Stack Skerry 16 H2
Stade 8 E10
Stadlandet 8 C5
Stadskanaal 14 J2
Stadtallendorf 12 E6
Stadthagen 12 E4
Staffa 16 F5
Staffelstien 12 F6
Stafford 16 K9
Staines 14 B3
Stainz 22 L4
Stakhanov 30 G5
Stalowa Wola 10 M7
Stamford 14 B2
Stanley, *Aus.* 62 J8
Stanley, *Falkland Islands* 78 K9
Stanovaya 36 T3
Stanovoye Nagor'ye 36 J5
Stanovoy Khrebet 36 L5
Staphorst 14 J2
Starachowice 10 L6
Stara L'ubovňa 10 K8
Stara Pazova 26 H5
Stara Planina 28 F1
Staraya Russa 30 F3
Stara Zagora 26 N7
Starbuck Island 60 L6
Stargard Szczeciński 8 H10
Starnberg 22 G2
Starnberger See 22 G3
Starogard Gdański 10 H4
Staro Orjahovo 26 Q7
Start Point 18 B3
Staryy Oskol 30 G4
Staszów 10 L7
Stavanger 8 C7
Stavoron 14 H2
Stavropol' 30 H5
Stavropol'skaya Vovyshennost' 30 H5
Steens Mountains 46 C3
Steenwijk 14 J2
Stefansson Island 68 L2
Stege 12 H1
Ştei 26 K3
Stein 12 G7
Steinach am Brenner 22 G3
Steinfurt 14 K2
Steinhausen 58 B4
Steinkjer 8 F4
Stenay 14 H5
Stendal 12 G4
Steno Antikythiro 28 F9
Sterling 70 F3
Sterlitamak 30 L4
Sternberk 10 G8
Stettiner Haff 8 G10
Stevenage 14 B3
Stevens Village 68 B3
Stewart 68 D4
Stewart 68 F5
Stewart Island 64 A8
Steyr 22 K2
Stillwater 70 G4
Štip 28 E3
Stirling 16 J5
Stjørdal 8 F5
Stockach 22 E3
Stockerau 22 M2
Stockholm 8 K7
Stockport 16 K8
Stockton 70 B4
Stockton-on-Tees 16 L7
Stœng Trêng 40 D4
Stoke-on-Trent 16 K8
Stokksnes 8 (1)F2
Stolac 26 F6
Stolberg 14 J4
Stolin 30 E4
Stollberg 12 H6
Stomio 28 E5
Stonehaven 16 K5
Stony Rapids 68 K5
Stör 12 E2
Stora Lulevatten 8 K3
Storavan 8 J4
Stord 8 C7
Store Bælt 12 F1
Støren 8 F5
Store Sotra 8 B6
Storjord 8 H3
Storlien 8 G5
Storm Bay 62 J8
Stornoway 16 F3
Storozhevsk 30 K2
Storozhynets' 26 N1
Storsjøen 8 F6
Storsjön, *Sweden* 8 G5
Storsjön, *Sweden* 8 J6
Storuman 8 J4
Storuman 8 J4
Stour 14 C2
Stowmarket 14 D2
Strabane 16 E7
Stradella 22 E5
Strait of Belle Isle 68 V6
Strait of Bonifacio 24 D7
Strait of Dover 14 D4
Strait of Gibraltar 20 E9
Strait of Hormuz 46 G4
Strait of Juan de Fuca 70 B2
Strait of Malacca 42 C2
Straits of Florida 70 K7

Strakonice 12 J7
Stralsund 8 G9
Strand 58 B6
Stranda 8 D5
Strandavatn 8 D6
Stranraer 16 H7
Strasbourg 22 C2
Străşeni 26 R2
Stratford 64 E4
Stratford-upon-Avon 14 A2
Stratoni 28 F4
Straubing 22 H2
Straumnes 8 (1)B1
Strausberg 12 J4
Streaky Bay 62 F6
Strehaia 26 L5
Strelka, *Russia* 36 E5
Strelka, *Russia* 36 S4
Strezhevoy 30 Q2
Strimonas 28 F4
Strjama 26 M7
Strofades 28 C7
Stromboli 24 K10
Strömsund 8 H5
Stronsay 16 K2
Stroud 16 K10
Struga 28 C3
Strugi-Krasnyye 8 Q7
Strumica 28 E3
Stryy 10 N8
Stryy 10 N8
Strzegom 10 F7
Strzelce Opolskie 10 H7
Strzelin 10 G7
Strzelno 10 H5
Studholme Junction 64 C7
Šturkö 10 E1
Štúrova 10 H10
Sturt Stony Desert 62 G5
Stuttgart 22 E2
Stykkishólmur 8 (1)B2
Suai 43 C4
Suakin 50 G4
Subcule 50 H5
Subi Besar 42 D2
Subotica 26 G3
Suceava 26 P2
Suck 16 D8
Suckow 12 G3
Sucre 76 D7
Sudak 30 F6
Sudan 50 E5
Sudan 54 D2
Suday 30 H3
Sudbury, *Can.* 70 K2
Sudbury, *U.K.* 14 C2
Sudd 56 E2
Sudová Vyshnya 10 N8
Suez = El Suweis 50 F2
Suez Canal 50 F1
Sugun 46 L2
Suḩār 46 G5
Suhl 12 F6
Suide 38 E3
Suigam 44 B4
Suihua 36 M7
Suippes 14 G5
Suir 16 E9
Suixi 38 E6
Suizhong 38 G2
Suizhou 38 E4
Sukabumi 42 D4
Sukadana 42 D3
Sukhinichi 30 G4
Sukhona 30 H3
Sukkertoppen = Maniitsoq 68 W3
Sukkur 46 J4
Sula 30 K1
Sula 30 K1
Sula Sgeir 16 F2
Sulawesi 43 A3
Sulejówek 10 L5
Sule Skerry 16 H2
Sulgachi 36 N4
Sulina 26 S4
Sulingen 14 L2
Sullana 76 A4
Sulmona 24 H6
Sulphur Springs 70 G5
Sultan 50 D1
Sultanhanı 28 R6
Sultanpur 44 D3
Sulu Archipelago 40 G5
Sulu Sea 40 F5
Sulzbach 14 K5
Sulzbach-Rosenberg 12 G7
Sulzberger Bay 80 (2)CC2
Sumatera 42 C2
Sumatra = Sumatera 42 C2
Sumba 43 A5
Sumbawa 43 A4
Sumbawabesar 43 A4
Sumbawanga 56 E5
Sumbe 58 A2
Sumeih 56 D2
Šumen 26 P6
Sumenep 42 E4
Sumisu-jima 38 L4
Sumkino 30 N3
Summerville 70 K5
Summit 68 B4
Šumperk 10 G8
Sumqayıt 46 E1
Sumy 30 F4
Sunch'ŏn 38 H4
Sun City 58 D5
Sundarbans 44 E4
Sunday Strait 62 D3
Sunderland 16 L7
Sundsvall 8 J5
Sundsvallsbukten 8 J5
Sungaipenuh 42 C3
Sungei Petani 40 C5
Suntar 36 K4
Suntsar 46 H4
Sunwu 36 M7
Sunyani 54 D3
Suomussalmi 30 E2
Suonenjoki 8 P5
Suordakh 36 P3
Suoyarvi 30 F2
Superior 70 H2
Supetar 26 D6
Süphan Daği 46 D2
Suqian 38 F4
Suquṭrā 46 F7
Sūr 46 G5
Sura 30 J4
Surab 46 J4
Surabaya 42 E4
Surakarta 42 E4
Šurany 26 F1
Surat 44 B4
Surat Thani 40 B5
Surdulica 26 K7
Sûre 14 H5
Surfers Paradise 62 K5
Surgut 34 N5
Surgutikha 34 R5
Surigao 40 H5
Surin 40 C4
Suriname 76 F3
Surkhet 44 D3
Surovikino 30 H5
Surskoye 30 J4
Surt 52 J2
Surtsey 8 (1)C3
Susa 22 C5
Sušac 26 D7
Susak 22 K6
Susanville 70 B3
Sušice 12 J7
Susitma 68 A4
Susuman 36 R4
Susurluk 28 L5
Sutak 44 C2
Sutherland 58 C6
Sutlej 44 B3
Suusamyr 34 N9
Suva 60 H7
Suvorov Island 60 K7
Suwałki 10 M3
Suwannaphum 40 C3
Suwŏn 38 H3
Suzak 30 N6
Suzhou, *China* 38 F4
Suzhou, *China* 38 G4
Suzuka 38 K4
Suzu-misaki 38 K3
Svalbard 80 (1)Q2
Svalyava 26 L1
Svappavaara 8 L3
Svatove 30 G5
Sveg 8 H5
Svendborg 8 F9
Šventoji 8 N9
Sverdrup Islands 80 (1)DD2
Svetac 26 C6
Sveti Nikole 28 D3
Svetlaya 36 P7
Svetlogorsk 10 K3
Svetlograd 30 H5
Svetlyy, *Russia* 10 K3
Svetlyy, *Russia* 34 L7
Svidník 10 L8
Svilengrad 28 J3
Svištov 26 N6
Svitava 10 F8
Svitavy 10 F8
Svobodnyy 36 M6
Svratka 10 F8
Svyetlahorsk 30 E4
Swain Reefs 62 K4
Swains Island 60 J7
Swakopmund 58 A4
Swale 16 K7
Swan 74 C2
Swan Hill 62 H7
Swan Islands 72 H5
Swan River 68 L6
Swansea, *Aus.* 62 J8
Swansea, *U.K.* 16 J10
Swaziland 58 E5
Sweden 8 H6
Sweetwater 70 F5
Swider 10 L5
Świdnica 10 F7
Świdnik 10 M6
Świdwin 10 E4
Świebodzin 10 E5
Świecie 10 H4
Swift Current 70 E1
Swindon 14 A3
Świnoujście 8 H10
Switzerland 22 C4
Syalakh 36 L3
Syamzha 30 H2
Syców 10 G6
Sydney, *Aus.* 62 K6
Sydney, *Can.* 68 U7
Syke 14 L2
Syktyvkar 30 K2
Sylhet 44 F4
Sylt 8 E9
Sym 34 R5
Sym 34 R5
Symi 28 K8
Synya 30 L1
Syracuse 70 L3
Syrdar'ya 34 L8
Syrdar'ya 46 J1
Syria 46 C3
Syrian Desert = Bādiyat ash Shām 46 C3
Syrna 28 J8
Syros 28 G7
Sytomino 30 P2
Syzran' 30 J4
Szamos 26 K1
Szamotuły 10 F5
Szarvas 10 K11
Szczecin 10 D4
Szczecinek 10 F4
Szczytno 10 K4
Szeged 26 H3
Szeghalom 26 J2
Székesfehérvár 26 F2
Szekszárd 26 F3
Szentendre 26 G2
Szentes 26 H3
Szerencs 10 L9
Szigetvár 26 E3
Szolnok 26 H2
Szombathely 26 D2
Szprotawa 10 E6
Sztum 10 J4
Szydlowiec 10 K6

T

Tab 26 F3
Tabarka 24 C12
Tabas 46 G3
Table Cape 64 G4
Tabong 44 G3
Tabor 36 R2
Tábor 10 D8
Tabora 56 E5
Tabou 54 C4
Tabrīz 46 E2
Tabuaeran 60 K5
Tabūk 46 C4
Tacheng 34 Q8
Tachov 12 H7
Tacloban 40 H4
Tacna 76 C7
Tacoma 70 B2
Tacuarembó 78 K5
Tacurong 43 B1
Tadjoura 50 H5
Tadmur 46 C3
Taegu 38 H3
Taejŏn 38 H3
Tafahi 60 J7
Tafalla 20 J2
Tafi Viejo 78 H4
Tagab 50 F4
Taganrog 30 G5
Taganrogskiy Zaliv 30 G5
Tagbilaran 40 G5
Tagul 36 F6
Tagum 40 H5
Tagus 20 B5
Taharoa 64 E4
Taheke 64 D2
Tahiti 60 M7
Tahoe Lake 68 K2
Tahoua 54 F2
Tahuna 40 H6
Tai'an 38 F3
T'aichung 38 G6
Taihape 64 E4
Taihe 38 E5
Taikeng 38 E4
Tailem Bend 62 G7
Tain 16 H4
T'ainan 38 G6
T'aipei 38 G6
Taiping 42 C1
Taipingchuan 38 G2
T'aitung 40 G2
Taivalkoski 8 Q4
Taiwan 40 G2
Taiwan Strait 40 F2
Taiyuan 38 E3
Taizhou 38 F4
Ta'izz 46 D7
Tajikistan 46 J2
Tajo 6 D3
Tak 40 B3
Takaka 64 D5
Takamatsu 38 J4
Takapuna 64 E3
Takengon 42 B2
Takestān 46 E2
Ta Khmau 40 D4
Takht 36 P6
Takhta-Bazar 46 H2
Takhtabrod 34 M7
Takhtakupyr 34 L9
Takijuq Lake 68 J3
Takikawa 38 L2
Takoradi 54 D4
Taksimo 36 J5
Takua Pa 40 B5
Takum 54 G3
Talak 52 F5
Talara 76 A4
Talas 34 N9
Talavera de la Reina 20 F5
Talaya 36 S4
Talca 78 G6
Talcahuano 78 G6
Taldykorgan 34 P9
Tālesh 46 E2
Taliabu 43 B3
Talibon 40 G4
Talitsa 30 M3
Tall 'Afar 46 D2
Tallahassee 70 K5
Tallaimannar 44 C7
Tallinn 8 N7
Tallulah 70 H5
Tălmaciu 26 M4
Tal'menka 34 Q7
Talon 36 R5
Tāloqān 34 N10
Taloyoak 68 N3
Talsi 8 M8
Taltal 78 G4
Tamale 54 D3
Tamanrasset 52 G4
Tamanthi 44 G3
Tamási 26 F3
Tamazunchale 70 G7
Tambacounda 54 B2
Tambey 34 N3
Tambo 62 J4
Tambov 30 H4
Tambu 43 A3
Tambura 56 D2
Tampa 70 K6
Tampere 8 M6
Tampico 72 E4
Tamsagbulag 38 F1
Tamsweg 22 J3
Tamworth, *Aus.* 62 K6
Tamworth, *U.K.* 14 A2
Tana, *Kenya* 56 G4
Tana, *Norway* 8 P2
Tana bru 8 P1
Tanacross 68 C4
Tanafjorden 8 Q1
T'ana Hāyk' 50 G5
Tanahgrogot 42 F3
Tanahjampea 43 A4
Tanahmerah 43 F4
Tanami 62 E4
Tanami Desert 62 F3
Tanaro 22 C6
Tanda 54 D3
Tandag 40 H5
Ţăndărei 26 Q5
Tandil 78 K6
Tanega-shima 38 J4
Tanew 10 M7
Tanezrouft 52 E4
Tanga, *Russia* 36 J6
Tanga, *Tanzania* 56 F5
Tanger 52 D1
Tangermünde 12 G4
Tanggu 38 F3
Tangmai 44 G2
Tangra Yumco 44 E2
Tangshan 38 F3
Tanimbar 60 D6
Tanjona Ankaboa 58 G4
Tanjona Bobaomby 58 H2
Tanjona Masoala 58 J3
Tanjona Vilanandro 58 G3
Tanjona Vohimena 58 H5
Tanjung 42 F3
Tanjungbalai 42 B2
Tanjung Cangkuang 42 C4
Tanjung Datu 42 D2
Tanjung d'Urville 43 E3
Tanjungkarang Telukbetung 42 D4
Tanjung Libobo 43 C3
Tanjung Lumut 42 D3
Tanjung Mengkalihat 42 F2
Tanjungpandan 42 D3
Tanjung Puting 42 E3
Tanjungredeb 42 F2
Tanjung Selatan 42 E3
Tanjungselor 42 F2
Tanjung Vals 43 E4
Tankovo 34 R5
Tankse 44 C2
Tanlovo 30 P1
Tanney 14 G5
Tanout 54 F2
Tanta 50 F1
Tan-Tan 52 C3
Tanzania 56 E5
Tao'an 38 G1
Taongi 60 J4
Taormina 24 K11
Taoudenni 52 E5
Taourirt 52 E2
T'aoyüan 40 G2
Tapa 8 N7
Tapachula 72 F6
Tapajós 76 F4
Tapauá 76 E5
Tapolca 26 E3
Tapsuy 30 M2
Tapuaenuku 64 D6
Taquarí 76 F7
Tara 30 Q3
Tara 34 N6
Tarābulus 52 H2
Taraclia 26 R4
Taracua 76 D3
Tarāghin 52 H3
Tarakan 40 F6
Taran 34 N3
Taranaki = Mount Egmont 64 E4
Tarancón 20 H5
Taranto 24 M8
Tarapoto 76 B5
Tarare 18 K8
Tarascon 18 K10
Tarauacá 76 C5
Tarauacá 76 C5
Tarawa 60 H5
Tarawera Lake 64 F4
Taraz 34 N9
Tarazona 20 J3
Tarbert, *Scot., U.K.* 16 F4
Tarbert, *Scot., U.K.* 16 G6
Tarbes 18 F10
Tarcoola 62 F6
Taree 62 K6
Tareya 34 S3
Tarfaya 52 C3
Târgovište 26 P6
Târgovişte 26 N5
Târgu Frumos 26 Q2
Târgu Jiu 26 L4
Târgu Lăpuş 26 L2
Târgu Mureş 26 M3
Târgu-Neamţ 26 P2
Târgu Ocna 26 P3
Târgu Secuiesc 26 P3
Tarhunah 52 H2
Tarifa 20 E8
Tarija 78 J3
Tarīm 46 E6
Tarim 34 Q9
Tarim Pendi 34 Q10
Tarīn Kowt 46 J3
Tariskay Shan 34 Q9
Taritatu 43 E3
Tarko Sale 34 P5
Tarlac 40 G3
Tarn 18 H10
Tarna 10 K10
Tärnaby 8 H4
Târnăveni 26 M3
Tarnogskiy Gorodok 30 H2
Târnovo 28 K2
Tarnów 10 K7
Tarnowskie Góry 10 H7
Taro 22 E6
Taroom 62 J5
Taroudannt 52 D2
Tarquinia 24 F6
Tarragona 20 M3
Tarras 64 B7
Tàrrega 20 M3
Tarso Emissi 50 C3
Tarsus 46 B2
Tartagal 78 J3
Tartu 8 P7
Tarutyne 26 S3
Tarvisio 22 J4
Tasbuget 34 M9
Tashigang 44 F3
Tashkent 34 M9
Tash-Kumyr 34 N9
Tashtagol 34 R7
Tasikmalaya 42 D4
Taskesken 34 Q8
Taşkopru 28 S3
Tasman Bay 64 D5
Tasmania 60 E10
Tasmania 62 H8
Tasman Mountains 64 D5
Tasman Sea 64 B3
Tăşnad 26 K2
Tassili du Hoggar 52 F4
Tassili-n'-Ajjer 52 G3
Tasty 34 M9
Tata, *Hungary* 26 F2
Tata, *Morocco* 52 D3
Tataba 43 B3
Tatabánya 26 F2
Tataouine 52 H2
Tatarbunary 26 S4
Tatariya 30 J3
Tatarsk 34 P6
Tatarskiy Proliv 36 P7
Tathlina Lake 68 H4
Tatta 46 J5
Tatvan 46 D2
Tauá 76 J5
Tauberbischofsheim 12 E7
Tauern 22 J4
Taumarunui 64 E4
Taungdwingyi 40 B2
Taung-gyi 44 G4
Taungup 44 F5
Taunsa 44 B2
Taunton 16 J10
Taunus 14 L4
Taunusstein 14 L4
Taupo 64 F4
Tauragė 10 M2
Tauranga 64 F3
Tauroa Point 64 D2
Tavda 30 N3
Tavda 30 N3
Tavira 20 C7
Tavoy 40 B4
Tavşanli 28 M5
Taw 16 J11
Tawau 42 F2
Tawitawi 42 F1
Taxkorgan 34 P10
Tay 16 J5
Tayga 34 R6
Taym 46 C4
Taymā' 50 G2
Taymura 36 F4
Taymylyr 36 L2
Tay Ninh 40 D4
Tayshet 36 F5
Tayuan 36 L6
Tayyebād 46 H3
Taza 52 E2
Tazenakht 52 D2
Tāzirbū 50 D2
Tazovskaya Guba 34 N4
Tazovskiy 34 P4
Tazovskiy Poluostrov 34 N4
Tazungdam 40 B1
T'bilisi 46 D1
Tchamba 54 G3
Tchibanga 54 G5
Tchin Tabaradene 52 G5
Tczew 10 H3
Te Anau 64 A7
Te Araroa 64 G3
Te Aroha 64 E3
Te Awamutu 64 E4
Tébessa 52 G1
Tebingtinggi 42 B2
Téboursouk 24 D12
Techa 30 M3
Techiman 54 D3
Tecuci 26 Q4
Tedzhen 46 H2
Tees 16 L7
Tegal 42 D4
Tegernsee 22 G3
Tegina 54 F2
Teglio 22 F4
Tegucigalpa 72 G6
Tegul'det 34 R6
Te Hapua 64 D2
Te Haroto 64 F4
Tehek Lake 68 M3
Teheran = Tehrān 46 F2
Tehrān 46 F2
Teignmouth 16 J11
Tejo = Tagus 20 B5
Te Kaha 64 F3
Te Kao 64 D2
Tekirdağ 28 K4
Teknaf 44 F4
Teku 43 B3
Te Kuiti 64 E4
Tel Aviv-Yafo 46 B3
Telegraph Creek 68 E5
Telén 78 H6
Teles Pires 76 F5
Telford 16 K9
Telfs 22 G3
Telsen 78 H7
Telšiai 10 M2
Teltow 12 J4
Teluk Berau 43 D3
Teluk Bone 43 B3
Teluk Cenderawasih 43 E3
Telukdalem 42 B2
Teluk Kumai 42 E3
Telukpakedai 42 D3
Teluk Sampit 42 E3
Teluk Sukadana 42 D3
Teluk Tomini 43 B2
Tema 54 D3
Tembenchi 34 T4
Temerin 26 G4
Temerloh 40 C6
Teminabuan 43 D3
Temirtau 34 N7
Tempio Pausaria 24 D8
Temple 70 G5
Temryuk 30 G5
Temuco 78 G6
Temuka 64 C7
Tenali 44 D5
Tendaho 50 H5
Ten Degree Channel 44 F7
Tendrara 52 E2
Ténéré 52 G5
Ténéré du Tafassasset 52 G4
Tenerife 52 B3
Ténès 52 F1
Tenggarong 42 F3
Tenke 58 D2
Tenkodogo 54 D2
Tennant Creek 62 F3
Tennessee 66 K6
Tennessee 70 J4
Tenojoki 8 P2
Tenteno 43 B3
Tenterfield 62 K5
Teo 20 B2
Teófilo Otoni 76 J7
Tepa 43 C4
Tepehuanes 70 E6
Tepic 70 F7
Teplice 10 C7
Ter 20 N2
Terceira 52 (1)B2
Teresina 76 J5
Tergnier 14 F5
Termez 46 J2
Termini Imerese 24 H11
Termoli 26 C8
Ternate 43 C2
Terneuzen 14 F3
Terni 24 G6
Ternitz 22 M3
Ternopil' 30 E5
Terracina 24 H7
Terrassa 20 N3
Terre Haute 70 J4
Tersa 30 H4
Terschelling 14 H1
Teruel 20 J4
Tervel 26 Q6
Tervola 8 N3
Teseney 50 G4
Teslin 68 E4
Teslin 68 E4
Tessalit 52 F4
Têt 18 H11
Tete 58 E3
Teterow 12 H3
Teteven 28 G2
Tétouan 52 D1
Tetovo 26 H8
Teuco 78 J3
Teulada 24 C10
Tevere 24 G6
Tevriz 30 P3
Te Waewae Bay 64 A8
Texarkana 70 H5
Texas 70 F5
Texel 14 G1
Teya 34 S5
Teykovo 30 H3
Tfarity 52 C3
Thaba Putsoa 58 D5
Thabazimbi 58 D4
Thailand 40 C4
Thai Nguyên 40 D2
Thal 44 B2
Thale Luang 40 C5
Thamarīt 46 F6
Thames 16 L10
Thamūd 46 E6
Thane 44 B5
Thanh Hoa 40 D3
Thanjavur 44 C6
Thann 22 C3
Tharad 44 B4
Thar Desert 44 B3
Thargomindah 62 H5
Thasos 28 G4
Thasos 28 G4
Thaton 40 B3
Thaya 10 E9
The Bahamas 72 K4
The Dalles 70 B2
The Fens 14 B2
The Gambia 54 A2
The Gulf 46 F4
The Hague = 's-Gravenhage 14 G2
Thelon 68 L4
The Minch 16 F3
The Naze 14 D3
Thenia 20 P8

Ust'-Ishim 34 N6
Ustka 10 F3
Ust'-Kamchatsk 36 U5
Ust'-Kamenogorsk 34 Q8
Ust'-Kamo 34 T5
Ust'-Karenga 36 K6
Ust'-Khayryuzovo 36 T5
Ust'-Kulom 30 K2
Ust'-Kut 36 G5
Ust'-Kuyga 36 P3
Ust'-Maya 36 N4
Ust'-Mukduyka 34 R4
Ust'-Muya 36 K5
Ust' Nem 30 K2
Ust'-Nera 36 Q4
Ust'-Nyukzha 36 L5
Ust'-Olenek 36 K2
Ust'-Omchug 36 R4
Ust' Ozernoye 36 D5
Ust' Penzhino 36 V4
Ust'-Pit 36 E5
Ustrem 30 N2
Ust'-Sopochnoye 36 T5
Ust' Tapsuy 30 M2
Ust'-Tarka 34 P6
Ust'-Tatta 36 N4
Ust'-Tsil'ma 34 J4
Ust' Un'ya 30 L2
Ust'-Urkima 36 L5
Ust'-Usa 30 L1
Ust'-Uyskoye 34 L7
Usu 34 Q9
Utah 70 D4
Utata 36 G6
Utena 8 N9
Uthal 46 J4
Utica 70 M3
Utiel 20 J5
Utrecht 14 H2
Utrera 20 E7
Utsjoki 8 P2
Utsunomiya 38 K3
Uttaradit 40 C3
Utva 30 K4
Uummannaq 68 W2
Uusikaupunki 8 L6
Uvalde 72 E3
Uvargin 36 X3
Uvat 30 N3
Uvinza 56 E5
Uvira 56 D4
Uvs Nuur 34 S7
Uy 30 M4
Uyar 34 S6
Uyuk 34 N9
Uyuni 78 H3
Uzbekistan 34 L9
Uzgen 34 N9
Uzhhorod 26 K1
Užice 26 G6
Uzunköprü 26 P8

V

Vaal 58 D5
Vaasa 8 L5
Vác 26 G2
Vacaria 78 M4
Vachi 46 E1
Vadodara 44 B4
Vado Ligure 22 D6
Vadsø 8 Q1
Vaduz 22 E3
Værøy 8 G3
Vaganski Vhr 22 L6
Vagay 30 N3
Váh 10 H8
Vakh 30 Q2
Valbonnais 22 A6
Valcheta 78 H7
Valdagno 22 G5
Valday 30 F3
Val-de-Meuse 22 A2
Valdemoro 20 G4
Valdepeñas 20 G6
Valdez 68 B4
Valdivia 78 G6
Val-d'Or 70 L2
Valdosta 70 K5
Valdres 8 E6
Valea lui Mihai 26 K2
Valence 18 K9
Valencia, *Spain* 20 K5
Valencia, *Venezuela* 76 D1
Valencia de Alcántara 20 C5
Valenciennes 14 F4
Vălenii de Munte 26 P4
Valentia Island 16 B10
Valentine 70 F3
Valenza 22 D5
Valera 76 C2
Valga 30 E3
Val Horn 70 F5
Valjevo 26 G5
Valka 8 N8
Val'karay 36 X3
Valkeakoski 8 N6
Valkenswaard 14 H3
Valladolid, *Mexico* 72 G4
Valladolid, *Spain* 20 F3
Valle 8 D7
Valledupar 76 C1
Vallée de Azaouagh 52 F5
Vallée du Tîlemsi 52 F5
Vallentuna 8 K7
Valletta 24 J13
Valley of the Kings 50 F2
Valli di Comacchio 22 H6
Vallorbe 22 B4
Valls 20 M3
Valmiera 8 N8
Valognes 14 A5
Valparai 44 C6
Valparaíso 78 G5
Valsad 44 B4
Val'tevo 30 H2
Valuyki 30 G4
Valverde del Camino 20 D7
Vammala 8 M6
Van 46 D2
Vanadzor 46 E1
Vanavara 36 G4
Vancouver, *Can.* 66 P5
Vancouver, *U.S.* 70 B2
Vancouver Island 68 F7
Vanderbijlpark 58 D5
Vanderhoof 68 G6
Van Diemen Gulf 62 F2
Vänern 8 G7
Vangaindrano 58 H4
Van Horn 70 F5
Vanimo 43 F3
Vanino 36 Q7
Vankarem 36 Y3
Vanna 8 K1
Vännäs 8 K5
Vannes 18 C6
Vanrhynsdorp 58 B6
Vantaa 8 N6
Vanua Levu 60 H7
Vanuatu 60 G7
Vanzevat 30 N2
Vanzhil'kynak 36 C4
Varāmīn 46 F2
Varanasi 44 D3
Varangerfjorden 8 R2
Varaždin 26 D3
Varazze 22 D6
Varberg 8 G8
Varda 28 D6
Vardar 28 E3
Varde 8 E9
Vardø 8 R1
Varel 12 D3
Varėna 10 P3
Varese 22 D5
Vârful Moldoveanu 26 M4
Vârfurile 26 K3
Varginha 78 M3
Varkaus 8 P5
Varna 26 Q6
Värnamo 8 H8
Varnsdorf 12 K6
Várpalota 26 F2
Varzi 22 E6
Varzy 18 J6
Vásárosnamény 26 K1
Vaslui 26 Q3
Västerås 8 J7
Västervik 8 J8
Vasto 24 J6
Vasvár 22 M3
Vatan 18 G6
Vathia 28 E8
Vatican City 24 F7
Vatnajökull 8 (1)E2
Vatomandry 58 H3
Vatra Dornei 26 N2
Vättern 8 H7
Vawkavysk 10 P4
Växjö 8 H8
Vayuniya 44 D7
Vazhgort 30 J2
Vecht 14 J2
Vechta 14 L2
Vecsés 26 G2
Vedaranniyam 44 C6
Vedea 26 N6
Veendam 14 J1
Veenendaal 14 H2
Vega 8 F4
Vegreville 68 J6
Vejen 12 E1
Vejer de la Frontera 20 E8
Vejle 8 E9
Vel' 34 G5
Vela Luka 26 D7
Velenje 22 L4
Veles 28 D3
Vélez-Málaga 20 F8
Velika Gorica 22 M5
Velika Plana 26 J5
Velikaya 36 W4
Velikiye Luki 30 F3
Velikiy Ustyug 30 J2
Veliko Tărnovo 26 N6
Vélingara 54 B2
Velingrad 26 L7
Velita Kladuša 22 L5
Velké Meziříčí 10 F8
Velký Krtíš 10 J9
Velletri 24 G7
Vellinge 10 C2
Vellore 44 C6
Velopoula 28 F8
Vel'sk 30 H2
Velten 12 J4
Venaria 22 C5
Vence 22 C7
Venda Nova 20 C3
Vendôme 18 G6
Venev 30 G4
Venezia 22 H5
Venezuela 76 D2
Vengurla 44 B5
Venice = Venezia, *It.* 22 H5
Venice, *U.S.* 70 J6
Venlo 14 J3
Venray 14 H3
Venta 30 D3
Venta de Baños 20 F3
Ventimiglia 22 C7
Ventotene 24 H8
Ventspils 8 L8
Vera, *Arg.* 78 J4
Vera, *Spain* 20 J7
Veracruz 72 E5
Veraval 44 B4
Verbania 22 D5
Vercelli 22 D5
Verdalsøra 8 F5
Verde 76 G8
Verden 12 E4
Verdun 14 H5
Vereeniging 58 D5
Vereshchagino 36 D4
Verín 20 C3
Verkhneimbatsk 36 D4
Verkhne-Imbatskoye 34 R5
Verkhnetulomskoe Vodokhranilishche 8 R2
Verkhneural'sk 30 L4
Verkhniy Baskunchak 30 J5
Verkhnyaya Amga 36 M5
Verkhnyaya Toyma 30 J2
Verkhnyaya Tura 30 L3
Verkhovyna 26 M1
Verkhoyansk 36 N3
Verkhoyanskiy Khrebet 36 M3
Vermillion 70 G3
Vermont 70 M3
Verneuil 14 C6
Vernon, *France* 14 D5
Vernon, *U.S.* 70 G5
Veroia 28 E4
Verona 22 F5
Versailles 14 E6
Verviers 14 H4
Veselí 22 N2
Vesijarvi 8 N6
Vesoul 12 B9
Vesterålen 8 G2
Vestfjorden 8 G3
Vestmannaeyjar 8 (1)C3
Vestvagøy 8 G2
Vesuvio 24 J8
Veszprém 26 E2
Vet 58 D5
Vetluga 30 J3
Vetluga 30 J3
Veurne 14 E3
Vevey 22 B4
Viana do Castelo 20 B3
Vianden 14 J5
Viangchan 40 C3
Viareggio 22 F7
Viborg 8 E8
Vibo Valentia 24 L10
Vibraye 18 F5
Vic 20 N3
Vicenza 22 G5
Vichuga 30 H3
Vichy 18 J7
Victor Harbor 62 G7
Victoria 62 H7
Victoria, *Arg.* 78 J5
Victoria, *Can.* 68 G7
Victoria, *Chile* 78 G6
Victoria, *Malta* 24 J12
Victoria, *Romania* 26 M4
Victoria, *Seychelles* 58 (2)C1
Victoria, *U.S.* 70 G6
Victoria de las Tunas 72 J4
Victoria Falls 58 D3
Victoria Island 68 J2
Victoria Land 80 (2)W2
Victoria River 62 F3
Victoria Strait 68 M3
Victoria West 58 C6
Vidalia 70 K5
Vidamlja 10 N5
Videle 26 N5
Vidin 26 K6
Viedma 78 J7
Vienenburg 12 F5
Vienna = Wien 22 M2
Vienne 18 F7
Vienne 18 K8
Vientiane = Viangchan 40 C3
Vierzon 18 H6
Vieste 24 L7
Vietnam 40 D3
Viêt Tri 40 D2
Vigan 40 G3
Vigevano 22 D5
Vigia 76 H4
Vigo 20 B2
Vigo di Cadore 22 H4
Viho Valentia 24 L10
Vijayawada 44 D5
Vík 8 (1)D3
Vikna 8 E4
Vila de Conde 20 B3
Vilafranca del Penedès 20 M3
Vila Franca de Xira 20 A6
Vila Nova de Gaia 20 B3
Vilanova y la Geltru 20 M3
Vila Real 20 C3
Vila-real 20 K5
Vilar Formoso 20 D4
Vila Velha 76 G3
Vilhelmina 8 J4
Vilhena 76 E6
Vilija 8 N9
Viljandi 8 N7
Vilkaviškis 10 N3
Villa Ahumada 72 C2
Villablino 20 D2
Villacarrillo 20 G6
Villach 22 J4
Villacidro 24 C9
Villa Constitución 70 D7
Villa de Cos 72 D4
Villafranca de los Barros 20 D6
Villafranca di Verona 22 F5
Villagarcia 20 B2
Villahermosa 72 F5
Villa Huidobro 78 J5
Villalba 20 C1
Villalpando 20 E3
Villamartin 20 E8
Villa Montes 78 J3
Villanueva de Cordoba 20 F6
Villaputzu 24 D9
Villarrobledo 20 H5
Villa San Giovanni 24 K10
Villavelayo 20 H2
Villavicencio 76 C3
Villaviciosa 20 E1
Villazon 78 H3
Villedieu-les-Poêles 14 A6
Villefranche-de-Rouergue 18 H9
Villefranche-sur-Saône 18 K8
Villena 20 K6
Villeneuve-sur-Lot 18 F9
Villers-Bocage 14 B5
Villers-Cotterêts 14 F5
Villerupt 14 H5
Villeurbanne 18 K8
Villingen 22 D2
Vilnius 8 N9
Vilsbiburg 22 H2
Vilshofen 22 J2
Vilvoorde 14 G4
Vilyuy 36 L4
Vilyuysk 36 L4
Vilyuyskoye Vodokhranilishche 36 J4
Vimoutiers 14 C6
Vimperk 22 J1
Viña del Mar 78 G5
Vinaròs 20 L4
Vincennes 70 J4
Vinh 40 D3
Vinkovci 26 F4
Vinnytsya 30 E5
Vinson Massif 80 (2)JJ2
Vinstri 8 E6
Vinzili 30 N3
Viöl 12 E2
Vioolsdrift 58 B5
Vipava 22 J5
Vipiteno 22 G4
Vir 22 L6
Virac 40 G4
Virawah 44 B4
Vire 14 B6
Virginia 70 H2
Virginia 70 L4
Virginia Beach 70 L4
Virgin Islands, *U.K.* 74 E2
Virgin Islands, *U.S.* 74 E2
Virihaure 8 J3
Virôchey 40 D4
Virovitica 26 E4
Virton 14 H5
Virtsu 8 M7
Virudunagar 44 C7
Vis 26 D6
Visby 8 K8
Viscount Melville Sound 68 J2
Viseu, *Brazil* 76 H4
Viseu, *Portugal* 20 C4
Vişeu de Sus 26 M2
Vishakhapatnam 44 D5
Vishera 34 K5
Vishnevka 34 N7
Visoko 26 F6
Visp 22 C4
Visšegrad 26 G6
Visselhövede 12 E4
Vistula = Wisła 6 F2
Viterbo 24 G6
Vitez 26 E5
Viti Levu 60 H7
Vitim 36 J5
Vitolište 28 D3
Vitória 78 N3
Vitória da Conquista 76 J6
Vitoria-Gasteiz 20 H2
Vitré 18 D5
Vitry-le-François 14 G6
Vitsyebsk 30 F3
Vitteaux 18 K6
Vittel 22 A2
Vittoria 24 J12
Vittorio Veneto 22 H5
Viveiro 20 C1
Vivi 34 T4
Vivonne 18 F7
Vize 28 K3
Vizhas 30 J1
Vizianagaram 44 D5
Vizinga 34 H5
Vizzini 24 J11
Vjosë 28 C4
Vladikavkaz 46 D1
Vladimir 30 H3
Vladivostok 38 J2
Vlasotince 26 K7
Vlasovo 36 N2
Vlieland 14 G1
Vlissingen 14 F3
Vlorë 28 B4
Vltava 10 D8
Vöcklabruck 22 J2
Vodice 22 L7
Vodnjan 22 J6
Vogelsberg 12 E6
Voghera 22 D6
Vohipeno 58 H4
Vöhringen 22 F2
Voi 56 F4
Voinjama 54 C3
Voiron 18 L8
Voitsberg 22 L3
Vojens 12 E1
Vojmsjön 8 J4
Vojvodina 26 G4
Volary 12 J8
Volcán Antofalla 78 H4
Volcán Barú 72 H7
Volcán Cayambe 76 B3
Volcán Citlaltépetl 66 L7
Volcán Corcovado 78 G7
Volcán Cotopaxi 76 B4
Volcán Domuyo 78 G6
Volcán Lanin 78 G6
Volcán Llullaillaco 78 H3
Volcán San Pedro 78 H3
Volcán Tajumulco 72 F5
Volga 30 J5
Volgodonsk 30 H5
Volgograd 30 H5
Völkermarkt 22 K4
Volkhov 30 F3
Völklingen 14 J5
Volksrust 58 D5
Volochanka 34 S3
Volodarskoye 30 N4
Vologda 30 H3
Volonga 30 J1
Volos 28 E5
Volosovo 8 Q7
Volta Redonda 76 J8
Volterra 22 F7
Voltri 22 D6
Volzhskiy 30 H5
Voorne 14 F3
Voranava 8 N9
Vorderrhein 22 E4
Vordingborg 12 G1
Voreios Evvoïkos Kolpos 28 E6
Voreria Pindos 28 C4
Vorkuta 30 M1
Vormsi 8 M7
Vorona 30 H4
Voronezh 30 G4
Vorstershoop 58 C5
Võru 8 P8
Vosges 22 C2
Voss 8 D6
Vostochno-Sibirskoye More 36 U2
Vostochnyy Sayan 34 T7
Vostok Island 60 L6
Votkinsk 34 J6
Vozhgora 30 J2
Vraca 26 L6
Vranje 26 J7
Vranov 10 L9
Vranov nad Toplau 26 J1
Vrbas 26 E5
Vrbas 26 G4
Vrbovsko 22 L5
Vrendenburg 58 B6
Vriddhachalam 44 C6
Vršac 26 J4
Vryburg 58 C5
Vryheid 58 E5
Vsetín 10 G8
Vstrechnyy 36 V3
Vučitrn 26 J7
Vukovar 26 G4
Vuktyl' 30 L2
Vulcăneşti 26 R4
Vulcano 24 J10
Vung Tau 40 D4
Vuollerim 8 L3
Vuotso 8 P2
Vyatka 30 K3
Vyazemskiy 36 N7
Vyaz'ma 30 F3
Vyborg 8 Q6
Vychegda 30 K2
Vyksa 30 H3
Vylkove 26 S4
Vynohradiv 10 N9
Vyshniy Volochek 30 F3
Vyškov 10 G8
Vytegra 30 G2

W

Wa 54 D3
Waal 14 H3
Waalwijk 14 H3
Wabē Shebelē Wenz 56 G2
Wabush 68 T6
Waco 70 G5
Wad Banda 50 E5
Waddān 50 C2
Waddeneilanden 14 G1
Waddenzee 14 H1
Wādī al Fārigh 50 C1
Wādī al Hamīm 50 D1
Wadi Halfa 50 F3
Wad Medani 50 F5
Wafangdian 38 G3
Wager Bay 68 P3
Wagga Wagga 62 J7
Wahai 43 C3
Waiau 64 D6
Waiblingen 22 E2
Waidhofen 22 K3
Waidhofen an der Ybbs 26 B2
Waigeo 43 D3
Waiheke Island 64 E3
Waihi 64 E3
Waikabubak 43 A4
Waikaia 64 B7
Waikaremoana 64 F4
Waikato 64 E4
Waikawa 64 B8
Waimana 64 F4
Waimate 64 C7
Waingapu 62 B1
Waiouru 64 E4
Waipara 64 D6
Waipawa 64 F4
Waipiro 64 G4
Waipu 64 E2
Waipukurau 64 F5
Wairoa 64 F4
Waitakaruru 64 E3
Waitaki 64 C7
Waitangi 64 (1)B1
Waitara 64 E4
Waitotara 64 E4
Waiuku 64 E3
Wajir 56 G3
Wakayama 38 K4
Wakefield 16 L8
Wake Island 60 G4
Wakkanai 38 L1
Waku-Kungo 58 B2
Wałbrzych 10 F7
Walcheren 14 F3
Wałcz 10 F4
Waldmünchen 12 H7
Waldshut-Tiengen 22 D3
Walen See 22 E3
Wales 16 J9
Wales Island 68 P3
Walgett 62 J6
Walkerville 62 J7
Wallis et Futuna 60 J7
Walpole 62 C6
Walsall 16 L9
Walsrode 12 E4
Waltershausen 12 F6
Walvis Bay 58 A4
Wamba 56 D3
Wana 46 J3
Wanaaring 62 H5
Wanaka 64 B7
Wandel Sea 66 A1
Wandingzhen 40 B2
Wanganui 64 E4
Wanganui 64 E4
Wangen 22 E3
Wangerooge 12 C3
Wangiwangi 43 B4
Wan Hsa-la 40 B2
Wanxian 38 D4
Wanyuan 38 D4
Warangal 44 C5
Warburg 12 D5
Ward 64 E5
Wardha 44 C4
Waregem 14 F4
Waremme 14 H4
Waren 12 H3
Warendorf 14 K3
Warka 10 L6
Warmandi 43 D3
Warminster 16 K10
Warrenton 58 C5
Warri 54 F3
Warrington 16 K8
Warrnambool 62 H7
Warsaw = Warszawa 10 K5
Warstein 12 D5
Warszawa 10 K5
Warta 10 F5
Warwick 16 L9
Washap 46 H4
Washburn Lake 68 K2
Washington 70 B2
Washington D.C. 66 J6
Wassenaar 14 G2
Wasserburg 22 H2
Watampone 43 B3
Watansoppeng 43 A3
Waterford 16 E9
Waterloo, *Belgium* 14 G4
Waterloo, *U.S.* 70 H3
Watertown 70 L3
Watford 14 B3
Watmuri 43 D4
Watrous 68 K6
Watsa 56 D3
Watson Lake 68 F4
Wau 56 D2
Waukegan 70 J3
Wausau 70 J3
Waverley 64 E4
Wavre 14 G4
Wawa 70 K2
Wāw al Kabīr 50 C2
Waxxari 34 R10
Waycross 70 K5
Weber 64 F5
Webi Shaabeelle 56 G3
Weddell Island 78 J9
Weddell Sea 80 (2)A2
Wedel 12 E3
Weert 14 H3
Węgorzewo 10 L3
Wei 38 D4
Weichang 38 F2
Weida 12 H6
Weiden 12 H7
Weifang 38 F3
Weihai 38 G3
Weilburg 12 D6
Weilheim 22 G3
Weimar 12 G6
Weinan 38 D4
Weinheim 12 D7
Weining 38 C5
Weipa 62 H2
Weiser 46 C3
Weißenburg 12 F7
Weißenfels 12 G5
Weißwasser 12 K5
Weixi 40 B1
Wejherowo 10 H3
Welkom 58 D5
Welland 14 B2
Wellawaya 44 D7
Wellesley Islands 62 G3
Wellingborough 18 E1
Wellington, *N.Z.* 64 E5
Wellington, *U.S.* 70 G4
Wells 46 D3
Wellsford 64 E3
Wels 22 K2
Welshpool 16 J9
Welwyn Garden City 14 B3
Wenatchee 70 B2
Wenchang 40 E3
Wenga 56 B3
Wenman 76 (1)A1
Wentworth 62 H6
Wen Xian 38 C4
Wenzhou 38 G5
Werdēr 56 H2